# READING CONFEDERUMENTS

# READING CONFEDERATE
# MONUMENTS

Edited by **Maria Seger**

Afterword by **Joanna Davis-McElligatt**

University Press of Mississippi / Jackson

The University Press of Mississippi is the scholarly publishing agency of
the Mississippi Institutions of Higher Learning: Alcorn State University,
Delta State University, Jackson State University, Mississippi State University,
Mississippi University for Women, Mississippi Valley State University,
University of Mississippi, and University of Southern Mississippi.

www.upress.state.ms.us
The University Press of Mississippi is a member
of the Association of University Presses.

First printing 2022
∞

Library of Congress Cataloging-in-Publication Data

Names: Seger, Maria C., editor. | Davis-McElligatt, Joanna, author of
afterword.
Title: Reading Confederate monuments / edited by Maria Seger, afterword by
Joanna Davis-McElligatt.
Description: Jackson : University Press of Mississippi, 2022. | Includes
bibliographical references and index.
Identifiers: LCCN 2022019451 (print) | LCCN 2022019452 (ebook) | ISBN
9781496841636 (hardback) | ISBN 9781496841643 (trade paperback) | ISBN
9781496841650 (epub) | ISBN 9781496841667 (epub) | ISBN 9781496841681
(pdf) | ISBN 9781496841674 (pdf)
Subjects: LCSH: Soldiers' monuments—Southern States—History and
criticism. | Lost Cause mythology. | Collective memory in art. |
Collective memory in literature. | United States—History—Civil War,
1861–1865—Monuments. | LCGFT: Essays. | Literary criticism.
Classification: LCC PS228.R32 R43 2022 (print) | LCC PS228.R32 (ebook) |
DDC 810.9/3587376—dc23/eng/20220607
LC record available at https://lccn.loc.gov/2022019451
LC ebook record available at https://lccn.loc.gov/2022019452

British Library Cataloging-in-Publication Data available

# CONTENTS

vii    Acknowledgments

3    Introduction: How and Why to Read Confederate Monuments
       —Maria Seger

## READING
Reading Confederate Monuments as Texts and in Textual Contexts

21    Chapter 1: Complicating Today's Myth of the Myth of the Lost Cause: The Calhoun Monument, Reconstruction, and Reconciliation
       —Brook Thomas

43    Chapter 2: Print Culture and the Enduring Legacy of Confederate War Monuments
       —Michael C. Weisenburg

72    Chapter 3: South by Southwest: Confederate and Conquistador Memorials Crossing/Closing Borders
       —Spencer R. Herrera

## CULTURAL PRODUCTION
Reading Literary and Cultural Texts as Confederate Monuments and Counter-Monuments

99    Chapter 4: Weaponizing Silent Sam: Heritage Politics and *The Third Revolution*
       —Danielle Christmas

118    Chapter 5: "Wasting the Past": Albion Tourgée, Confederate Memory, and the Politics of Context
       —Garrett Bridger Gilmore

142    Chapter 6: Redeeming White Women in/through Lost Cause Films
       —Maria Seger

166    Chapter 7: Performing Counter-Monumentality of the Civil War in Natasha Trethewey's *Native Guard* and Suzan-Lori Parks's *Father Comes Home from the Wars: Parts 1, 2, and 3*
       —Stacie McCormick

## PEDAGOGY
Reading Confederate Monuments and Counter-Monuments for How They Teach
Belonging and Social Justice

191    Chapter 8: Rewriting the Landscape: Black Communities and the Confederate Monuments
       They Inherited
       —Cassandra Jackson
213    Chapter 9: Battle of the Billboards: White Supremacy and Memorial Culture
       in #Charlottesville
       —Lisa Woolfork
230    Chapter 10: Teaching Confederate Monuments as American Literature
       —Randi Lynn Tanglen

251    Conclusion: Challenging Monumentality, Channeling Counter-Monumentality
       —Maria Seger
255    Afterword
       —Joanna Davis-McElligatt

261    Suggestions for Further Reading
265    About the Contributors
269    Index

# ACKNOWLEDGMENTS

Much as I tried to resist it, this project in many ways chose me, and I have lots of people to thank for that. First and foremost, working on this collection amidst the George Floyd uprisings in summer 2020, I drew renewed energy and purpose from activists on the ground in my community, across the nation, and indeed around the globe. Their imagination of a different world and their dedication to building it was—and continues to be—truly inspiring. Randi Tanglen is, for all intents and purposes, the coeditor of this volume, and it's always been Travis Foster's brainchild. Travis's standing-room-only "Reading Confederate Monuments" panels at the American Literature Association's Annual Conference in 2018 rightly convinced him that this inquiry needed a more sustained and permanent home. He drafted an initial proposal, and panelists Randi, Brook Thomas, Michael Weisenburg, and I signed on. When other projects demanded his attention, Randi picked up the project and, in a thoughtful and caring conversation, convinced me to become her coeditor. While other professional demands required her to eventually step back from coeditorship, the collection's cohesiveness and organization continue to bear her mark, and the volume is so much the better for it. Thank you, Randi, for being a wonderful friend and collaborator. I cannot imagine having undertaken this work without you. Anna Mae Duane encouraged my pursuit of this project as I began on the tenure track, when conventional wisdom was that junior scholars shouldn't edit collections before publishing a monograph. One of the things I admire most about her work is how it collaborates, connects, and builds collectives; I hope that this project, in that way, follows her example. Additionally, I'm thankful to Jarvis McInnis for organizing a panel on Confederate memory for the Modern Language Association's Annual Convention in 2020. On that panel, I met Spencer Herrera, whose contribution brought much-needed complexity to the volume. Danielle Christmas, Cassandra Jackson, Stacie McCormick, and Lisa Woolfork, all of whose work I've long taught and admired, graciously signed onto the collection before it had a publisher. I'm so grateful for the opportunity to think with them here and to learn from their stunning contributions to the project. Garrett Bridger Gilmore provided the perfect piece to round out the volume, and

Jo Davis-McElligatt penned a breathtaking afterword. I'm incredibly fortunate to have once been her colleague and continue to value her friendship.

I'm thrilled that this project found a home at the University Press of Mississippi, a press that takes seriously the intersection of Black Studies and southern studies and believes in public audiences for academic books. At the press, Katie Keene has been so much more than anyone could ask for from an editor working amidst a global pandemic. She treats authors and their work with special attention and care, and this volume illustrates that. I'm grateful to Lynn Page Whittaker for carefully copyediting the collection, to Todd Lape for designing an engaging cover, to Joey Brown for helping the book find its readers, and to Laura Strong for delivering everything ahead of schedule. Thanks, too, to Cynthia Foster, Mary Heath, and Caroline O'Connor. I'm also deeply indebted to the anonymous peer reviewers, whose feedback was thoughtful, generous, and clarifying. The collection's reach and impact no doubt owe much to your reading and your support. Thank you.

I developed this project across two institutional homes. The seeds of my thinking on this topic germinated in my time at the United States Military Academy at West Point. An assignment I developed for cadets about that campus's Confederate monument, called Reconciliation Plaza (a Lost Cause name if there ever was one), benefitted from discussion with Trivius Caldwell, Colleen Eils, and Tony McGowan. At the University of Louisiana at Lafayette (UL), I'm grateful to the Department of English, the College of Liberal Arts, and the Division of Academic Affairs for conference funding to present early thoughts on this subject. An invitation from Pearson Cross to participate on a public panel on Confederate monuments with Ian Beamish and D'Weston Haywood when I first arrived in Lafayette in 2017 also developed my ideas. Serving on the college's Task Force on Building Names and presenting our work at Louisiana Historical Association and American Historical Association conferences have directly informed the collection; for that, I'm thankful to have collaborated with Tre Ambroise, Theo Foster, Phebe Hayes, Laura Hughes, Jordan Kellman, Michael Martin, and Marissa Petrou. To the members of my writing group, who are the very best readers I know, many, many thanks for reading early drafts of this work: Ian, Jackie Beatty, Dine Faucheux, Manuel Morales Fontanilla, Liz Skilton, and David Squires. I'd never get anything done without y'all. I'm also grateful for department colleagues and friends who have supported and encouraged my work more generally: Jessica Alexander, Felicia Brown, Jo, Jack Ferstel, Michael Kightley, Shelley Ingram, Clancy Ratliff, Kerry Reaux, Henk Rossouw, Laurel Ryan, David, and Yung-Hsing Wu, especially. And learning from and collaborating with Theo on Black Studies initiatives has been a true highlight of my time at UL. In my community, the work of Move the Mindset and the Equal Justice Initiative coalition, led by Fred Prejean, has been so important and instructive.

May we honor Fred's memory by continuing his vital work. And, of course, my graduate and undergraduate students and Context Learning students teach me every day. Thank you, always, for contributing to our collective inquiries and for showing up to do the work.

Finally, to my friends and family who buoyed me enough to press forward with the project when the world was on fire, I'm so grateful for you. Text messages, phone and video chats, and all-too-infrequent visits with longtime friends were vital and spirit lifting; thank you to Kim Armstrong, Jackie, Shannon Deep, Julie Ficarra, and Megan Sloan in particular. Academic and non-academic conversations with Elwin Cotman, Dan Graham, Rachel Nolan, and Nate Windon were a breath of fresh air. In Lafayette, I'm so fortunate to have colleagues across the university who have become true friends: Jess, Ian, Kelly Robinson, Liz, Beth Stauffer, and David. Thanks for your company and your solidarity. My "little sister" Olivia brings so much wonder and joy into my life and encourages me to see the world through a different lens. (She'll think it's pretty awesome that her name is in a book.) And Courtney Larson, Marybeth LeJeune, Angel DeClouet, and Alexa Thibodeaux have made Lafayette feel like home. I appreciate y'all more than you know. I spent much of the period that I was working on this project in Pittsburgh. For the support that I received there, I'm ever so grateful to my family: Lucy, my mom, and Mark Cichon and Mariah, Mathew, and Jonathan; and Donn, my dad, and Shirley Seger. My sister, Monica Seger, has always been the best listener and ally, and I'm so very lucky to call her my best friend. I'm forever grateful to my partner Stephen Hebert for seeing me and for believing in the value of my work. And finally, to my dog, Luna, who has been by my side for all of the ups and downs of our life in Lafayette, who has taught me that I'm both stronger and gentler than I give myself credit for, and who fittingly attended my first Confederate monument protest with me in 2017: thank you, sweet girl.

# READING CONFEDERATE MONUMENTS

# INTRODUCTION

## How and Why to Read Confederate Monuments

## —Maria Seger

My own small city in south Louisiana has been grappling with how to read its Confederate monument. Located prominently at the intersection providing entrance to downtown Lafayette, the 1922 statue erected by the United Daughters of the Confederacy (UDC) honors Alfred Mouton, an enslaver and former Confederate general. Directly south of the city building that houses organizations for economic revitalization and development, adjacent to the city court and marshal's office, and just southeast of the parish court, jail, and sheriff's office, the statue's placement seems hardly a coincidence. For nearly a century now, to do business, to engage with the criminal legal system of the city or parish, to attend a community festival, one must be confronted by this Confederate symbol surrounded by some of the only green space downtown. In 1980, Lafayette wanted to move the statue to its new city hall, but the UDC obtained a permanent injunction to prevent its removal for any reason but necessary roadwork. A local activist group called Move the Mindset, led by Fred Prejean, has been pushing back against this injunction in court and in the streets for years.[1] Fittingly, as I concluded writing this introduction on July 17, 2021, the city government removed the statue, having come to a legal agreement with the UDC the day prior that the city would pay to have it moved, insured, and put on a new base in a location of the UDC's choosing.[2]

The beginning of the end occurred amidst the George Floyd uprisings in summer 2020, as protestors toppling Confederate statues gained momentum nationwide. Lafayette Mayor-President Josh Guillory, a conservative Republican, released a videotaped address calling for the Mouton statue's relocation. He opened that address with seeming fear of its forcible removal: "The violence and destruction we have seen across our nation seem to be rooted in promoting racial division. . . . We have successfully avoided this kind of mayhem in our city and parish. . . . Despite threats, we've had several spirited protests and demonstrations without major incident so far."[3] Phrases like "despite threats" and "so far" revealed Guillory's concern that, if he didn't remove the statue voluntarily, it'd be taken down against his will and without his oversight. Indeed, he went so far as to say that he'd met with the local chapter of the UDC to discuss "how best to protect this monument from illegal destruction or defacement." Guillory suggested that the 1980 injunction might be circumvented because the court "has discretion to alter the agreement . . . to protect public safety and the statue from destruction." Thus, Guillory harnessed the threat of forcible removal to motivate the UDC and the court to approve relocation for the safety of the statue and its defenders, entirely neglecting the past and present safety of Lafayette's Black community.

But even in calling for its relocation, Guillory didn't quite make meaning of the Mouton statue, didn't quite *read* it for his constituents, because to do so would be to disrupt the mythologies and ideologies that the statue embodied for many white Cajun people. Instead, in closing his address, Guillory explained that, at the gateway to downtown, the statue doesn't welcome visitors: "We want visitors to experience the vibrant optimism and determination of our people when they come here. We should honestly ask ourselves whether this statue is the best symbol for that."[4] In other words, the statue (and the possibility of its forcible removal by protestors) inhibits tourism and potentially economic development. Affirming military veterans and law enforcement and blaming "incendiary [race] rhetoric" for dividing the community, Guillory concluded, "We will work to ensure the statue of General Mouton finally rests at its most appropriate place, offering proper historical context for his life and legacy." But because Guillory didn't actually reveal and analyze the nuanced connotations of the Mouton statue—interpreting and making meaning of its presence on the Lafayette landscape with attention to context, form, or reception, for example— we can't be entirely sure what he makes of Mouton's "life and legacy." The mixed messaging of affirming the Confederacy then the US military and law enforce- ment, which uprisings nationwide had been directly condemning, before calling for the statue's relocation probably left his constituents scratching their heads.

The colorblindness of Guillory's address necessitated leaving the Mouton statue unread, even in calling for its relocation. Indeed, Guillory went out of his way to avoid analyzing the statue's impact on the local Black community and repeatedly neglected to acknowledge the structural racisms of his own moment, as well as how they had undergirded his administration. In twice emphasizing that everyone should be "treated fairly no matter where [they] live in Lafay- ette Parish," Guillory avoided speaking directly about race, instead implicitly referring to race through segregation—the Black community residing in north Lafayette, and the white community elsewhere—without denouncing segrega- tion itself.[5] Weeks following his statement, Guillory's proposed budget closed four city recreation centers, all conveniently located on the northside.[6] Mean- while, the city continued to spend in excess of $10,000 per week to "protect" the statue.[7] Through these decisions, Guillory made clear what he meant by fair treatment, crystallizing his vision of who and what the state is meant to protect and affirming the not-so-anti-racist reasons why the statue should be relocated. In the end, taking down the Mouton statue without actually *reading it* leaves white supremacy in the community untouched and firmly in place.

Lafayette, Louisiana, is not alone in grappling with how to read—and whether to remove—its Confederate monument in this cultural moment. Since the 2015 Charleston, South Carolina, Mother Emanuel church massacre, more than eighty Confederate monuments have been removed from public lands in the United States—some toppled by protestors, many relocated to museums, and others put into storage.[8] Meanwhile, the Southern Poverty Law Center, which continues to track public symbols of the Confederacy in real time, reports that more than seven hundred monuments remain,[9] and at least twenty, mostly installed on private lands and funded by the Sons of Confederate Veterans, have been newly unveiled.[10] Yet none can any longer lay claim to apolitical neutrality or the noncontroversial commemoration of history, especially in light of the 2017 Unite the Right rally in Charlottesville, Virginia. Waves of removal, beginning in the wake of the Charleston church massacre, continuing after the Unite the Right rally, and most recently, following the 2020 George Floyd uprisings, have revealed that the physical visibility and presence of Confederate monuments activate agonistic public discussion and action surrounding Civil War memory, so-called white southern heritage, the legacies of slavery, and the persistence of anti-Blackness. From courts and legislatures to town squares and city parks, in not only the South but the North and the West, the public is now actively engaged with how to read Confederate monuments—interpreting the meanings of their existence and their persistence or removal.[11]

Given local contexts like these around the nation, this collection of essays written by literary and cultural studies scholars addresses the urgent and vital need for scholars, educators, and the general public to be able to read literal and cultural Confederate monuments pervading life in the contemporary United States. In using the verb *read*, this volume means to gesture to the necessary act of interpretation, of making meaning of Confederate monuments and memory as complex cultural objects and movements whose connotations and implications are neither singular nor obvious. Put simply, Confederate monuments exceed their literal denotations. Employing the tools of literary and cultural studies—contextualization, close reading, and reception, to name a few—*produces* meaning, enriching our breadth and depth of understanding of the patterns of erasure, narration, and performance that surround Confederate monuments, memorialization, and memory. This is because although *monuments* (in the way we use the term herein) try to "shut a lid on history," emphasizing "its permanence [and] eternity," in reality, "history" and making meaning of texts that claim to be or represent history "is about change, contingency, [and] fallibility," in the words of Kirk Savage.[12] Thus, *Reading Confederate Monuments* demonstrates what critics of US literature and culture can offer to ongoing scholarly and public discussions about Confederate monuments. The varied and layered approaches and methods used in literary and cultural studies scholarship— including those from literary history, reception studies, material culture studies, new historicism, performance studies, race and ethnic studies, feminist studies, and pedagogical theory—uniquely position thinkers in this collection to enhance and expand upon the terms, analyses, and ethical frameworks through which we understand Confederate memory and memorialization.

Engaging many different archives and methods, the essays in this collection instruct us in not only how to read literal Confederate monuments as texts and in the context of the assortment of texts that produced and celebrated them, but also how to read the literary texts advancing and contesting Confederate ideology in the US cultural imaginary—then and now—as monuments in and of themselves. On top of that, the essays published here lay bare the cultural and pedagogical work of Confederate monuments and counter-monuments— how and what they teach their readers as communal and yet contested narratives—showing why the persistence of Confederate monuments matters greatly to local and national notions of belonging and social justice. Because even as we remove, relocate, and recontextualize the physical symbols of the Confederacy dotting the US landscape, the complicated histories, cultural products, and pedagogies of Confederate ideology remain embedded in the national consciousness. To disrupt and potentially dismantle these enduring narratives alongside the statues themselves, we must be able to recognize, analyze, and resist them in US life. The pieces in this collection position us to think deeply about how and why we should continue that work.

For the most part, historians have rightly provided the scholarly voice in public debates about Confederate monuments.[13] In response to events in Charleston and Charlottesville, they've developed crowdsourced resources such as the #CharlestonSyllabus and the Confederate Monuments Syllabus that curate myriad primary and secondary sources contextualizing the monuments' construction and white supremacist legacies.[14] Historians such as David W. Blight, Karen L. Cox, and Eric Foner remind us that Confederate monuments' construction largely occurred not in the immediate aftermath of the Civil War but instead as part of the rise of Jim Crow and, later, as part of an early backlash against the civil rights movement.[15] Other historians, like Alice Fahs, Joan Waugh, Caroline E. Janney, and Nina Silber, teach us that Civil War memory performed important cultural work, from ushering children into white supremacy to facilitating the reunion of North and South.[16] Further, some historians, such as Adam H. Domby, Gary W. Gallagher, and Alan T. Nolan, expose the pernicious myth of the Lost Cause—put simply, the notion of a just and heroic

Confederacy—showing how its origins, exaggerations, and outright lies have not only shaped Civil War history but also propagated white supremacy.[17] On the whole, the field of US history has fittingly positioned debates over Confederate memory as vital in negotiating the United States' racist future even more than in settling its racist past.

Within the academy, US art and architectural historians have interpreted the visuality of existing Confederate monuments in a nation especially disposed to memorialization. Beginning with Kirk Savage and continuing with Cynthia Mills, Pamela H. Simpson, and Dell Upton, this body of work suggests that prolific Civil War (and, later, civil rights) monument building serves as an important site for social and political struggles over race, gender, and collective memory but, in the end, often functions to reinforce white supremacist nationalism.[18] Their attention to how Confederate monuments occupy and police space, demand public attention, and aesthetically render a static sense of the Civil War has been instructive in thinking through the implications of such monuments' persistent visibility on public landscapes across the United States.

Building on this foundation, literary and cultural studies methods employed in this collection make possible fresh interpretations and reflections on how Confederate monuments conveyed and continue to convey meaning in their own time and in ours. Southern studies scholars working with historical and media studies methods, such as Cox, Gallagher, and Tara McPherson, have begun the examination of Confederate popular cultural texts—from literature to music to film—to understand how notions of Dixie, the Lost Cause, and the Civil War were formed in and through the US cultural imaginary.[19] In literary studies, scholars like Brook Thomas—a contributor to this volume—and those whose work appears in Gordon Hutner's special issue of *American Literary History* titled "Reenvisioning Reconstruction" have recently refocused our attention on the literature of the Reconstruction era.[20] This scholarship has laid the groundwork for a more sustained conversation about the literary and cultural legacies of and responses to Confederate memory and Jim Crow, not only in nineteenth-century US but also in Black literary and cultural studies. While literal Confederate monuments have received sustained attention, literary and cultural monuments have thus far been underexamined, perhaps because their racism is so abhorrent (as I suggest elsewhere in this collection) or because we assume they lack complexity. But, if we want to understand and resist the power of Confederate (and neo-Confederate) white supremacy, we have to recognize and analyze its literary and cultural forms, patterns, and discourses, as well as those of counter-monuments, which provide strategies for mounting opposition. By *counter-monuments*, we mean to denote texts that "adopt anti-monumental strategies" that counter how traditional monuments understand history and/or texts that "are designed to counter a specific existing monument and the values it represents."[21]

Thus, *Reading Confederate Monuments* aims to jumpstart the discipline's inquiries and entrance into this discussion by mapping the possibilities of three interrelated literary and cultural studies themes: reading, cultural production, and pedagogy. The first section of the collection, titled "Reading," contains essays that highlight approaches, texts, and contexts for reading and interpreting physical Confederate monuments. These essays demonstrate that methods of literary and cultural studies criticism provide invaluable means to interpret Confederate monuments as, after all, precisely what they were designed to be: texts conveying meaning to audiences in the public sphere. Through close analysis of Confederate monuments' inscriptions, materials, and sites, alongside speeches from their dedications, literary historical biographies of the figures memorialized, and print cultural materials like advertisements and postcards, the essays in this section help us better understand how Confederate monuments synthesize form and content in their arguments about the national future, from their inceptions to their dedications to their current existence in public space. In line with recent literary and cultural studies scholarship, these essays advance a robust set of theoretical arguments about history, memory, loss, war, and memorialization in close reading the text(s) of and surrounding their chosen Confederate monuments. Foregrounding these monuments' reception histories, the literary historical work of the nineteenth-century US, Black, and Latinx literature experts featured in this section demonstrates how reception impacts meaning then and now and positions monuments within larger historical, political, and social patterns, including not only Reconstruction and Jim Crow but also settler colonialism and the Mexican-American War.

Leading this section is Brook Thomas's essay "Complicating Today's Myth of the Myth of the Lost Cause: The Calhoun Monument, Reconstruction, and Reconciliation," in which Thomas argues that the current debates over Confederate monuments are not so much about the Civil War and the southern defense of slavery, as is commonly publicly understood, as they are about the United States' retreat from Reconstruction. Confederate monuments, such as the 1887 John C. Calhoun monument in Charleston, South Carolina, that Thomas close reads, often represent white intersectional reconciliation facilitated by Reconstruction's end. Indeed, this era of monument building reflected and furthered the healing developed through establishing a white consensus about the myth of the Lost Cause, not only in the South but in the North as well. In the end, Thomas highlights the irony that such misguided attempts at healing have impeded racial justice in the present, as Confederate monuments like Calhoun's have, until recently, persisted through time and in space. Thomas closes his essay with a provocative question that turns current thinking about Confederate memory upside down: "Is hope of reconciliation as a way of completing, not defeating, Radical Reconstruction, the new Lost Cause of the nation?"[22]

While Thomas reads dedication speeches and literary biographies sur-rounding Calhoun and his monument, Michael C. Weisenburg's essay "Print Culture and the Enduring Legacy of Confederate War Monuments" turns its attention to monuments' ephemeral print materials published locally and dis-tributed regionally. Reading several accompanying figures from the University of South Carolina's archives, Weisenburg analyzes how different print media—from promotional broadsides to newspaper advertisements to commemorative postcards—rhetorically encouraged and celebrated Confederate monument building. By attending to these highly local artifacts, Weisenburg reveals how communities "adapted residual and emergent communication networks and technologies" to imagine, fundraise for, and publicize the erection of their own Confederate monuments.[23] Importantly, small publishers' print pieces show how communities appropriated existing cultural discourses, narratives, and myths from classical, historical, and religious traditions to inaugurate a new phase of white supremacy. Such work provides insight into how and why the Confederate values expressed in these fleeting ephemera nonetheless remain entrenched in US culture today.

While Thomas and Weisenburg read texts of Confederate monument build-ing in the US South, Spencer R. Herrera's essay "South by Southwest: Confed-erate and Conquistador Memorials Crossing/Closing Borders" interprets a Confederate monument in the Southwest, specifically in El Paso, Texas. Located next to the border fence separating the US from Mexico, a fascinating and truly puzzling series of four historical markers stand together: one dedicated to local Confederates, another to a historic migration route, a third to a settler colonial agent, and the fourth completely blank—whether by intentional defacement, weather erasure, or abandoned plans. This odd ensemble of memorials in this far west Texas border town raises important questions about the interdepen-dent histories and legacies of slavery and settler colonialism across the United States, not just in the South. Read together, the series of markers unwittingly makes the case that white supremacist dispossession and disavowal form the foundation of the US nation-state. To conclude, Herrera meditates on monu-ments' temporality, with the absent history of the blank marker emblematizing futurity, beckoning for (and yet resisting) our attempts to read it. Herrera's work proves that we may assign meaning to such texts only through a literary and cultural studies lens that accounts for the complexity of multiple competing interpretations existing simultaneously.

While the section on "Reading" shows us how to read Confederate monu-ments as texts and in textual contexts, the following section, titled "Cultural Production," interprets literary and cultural texts that reflect, advance, or disrupt Confederate memory, working in tandem with or countering the monuments explored in the previous section. Using the methods of literary and cultural studies, the essays presented in this section analyze the various narrative and discursive modes of Confederate memory and counter-memory as articulated, disseminated, and received in and through cultural production. Literary and cultural studies provide the necessary critical methods for thinkers in this section to apply close reading to narrative texts that monumentalize and recast the Confederacy, from early blockbuster films to contemporary neo-Confederate novels. Like physical Confederate monuments, these cultural texts work to shift historical memory in the service of white supremacist futurity. Close and comparative analysis of such texts alongside monuments themselves therefore opens up new ways of thinking about how the monumentalization process works and why it was—and remains—so culturally and politically influential, not only in the wake of Reconstruction but also today. Yet, essays in this section are not just concerned with how white supremacist power has been channeled in and advanced through literary and cultural Confederate monuments. Indeed, they are also committed to reading and interpreting textual counter-monuments, from Reconstruction novels to contemporary Black poetry and theatrical productions, which anticipate and push back against the discursive influence of the Lost Cause. As the essays appearing here attest, methods from new historicism, Black studies, and performance theory unsettle some of our existing assumptions about the inevitability, temporality, and permanence of Confederate monuments on the whole.

Leading the section on "Cultural Production" is Danielle Christmas's essay "Weaponizing Silent Sam: Heritage Politics and *The Third Revolution*," which deconstructs contemporary press coverage of the Confederate monument debates that is often framed in binary terms as a dispute of proud southerners versus judgmental elites by examining how the white nationalist press and associated literary texts reveal that something much deeper is at stake. Indeed, through an analysis of the stories that literary and cultural neo-Confederate monuments tell, Christmas shows that the fight to preserve Confederate monuments like Silent Sam—a monument on her University of North Carolina at Chapel Hill campus—is actually driven by what she calls *heritage politics*. Heritage politics, Christmas suggests, is "a strategy that frames the removal of Confederate monuments and the ethnic cleansing of white Americans as two sides of the same coin."[24] In close reading articles from the white nationalist newspaper the *Daily Stormer* and Gregory Kay's novel *The Third Revolution* (2004), Christmas ultimately reveals how neo-Confederate cultural production narratively links Confederate heritage with white survival in order to engender violence for the white nationalist cause. We must, Christmas urges, be able to read these texts to stave off the so-called third revolution.

Where Christmas analyzes contemporary neo-Confederate cultural production in the context of Silent Sam's 1913 dedication, Garrett Bridger Gilmore's essay "'Wasting the Past': Albion Tourgée, Confederate Memory, and the Politics of Context" analyzes Tourgée's Reconstruction novel *A Fool's Errand* (1879) as anticipating that statue's legacies. In close reading this canonical novel as a preemptive counter-monument to prolific Confederate memorialization during the Jim Crow era, Gilmore makes the case that institutions small and large—from the university to the federal government—further white supremacy through seemingly innocuous inactions, compromises, and equivocations. Complimenting Thomas's analysis of the unwieldy intersection of healing and justice earlier in the collection, Gilmore unpacks the political debates of Tourgée's novel to show how fabricated historical memory normalized white supremacy even in Reconstruction-era political institutions. Gilmore's work proves that one of the most important and perhaps least acknowledged legacies of Lost Cause storytelling is how it, in tandem with extralegal violence, built institutions whose white supremacy defined the "very structures and logics" of "institutional action and inaction."[25] In the end, Gilmore daringly asks, in the vein of *A Fool's Errand*: what good would contextualizing Confederate statues like Silent Sam do if "such knowledge only serves as a fig leaf for inaction in the face of ongoing inequity"?

While Christmas and Gilmore examine the position of white men in Confederate memorialization, my own essay "Redeeming White Women in/through Lost Cause Films" elucidates white women's role in Confederate ideology by reading two of the biggest blockbusters in US film history: D. W. Griffith's *The Birth of a Nation* (1915) and Victor Fleming's *Gone with the Wind* (1939). Attending to these two films reveals how and why Hollywood studios have, from their founding obsession with Lost Cause narratives, reflected and promoted white supremacy and anti-Blackness in developing the form and content of their offerings. Through close analysis of the films' adherence to and divergence from the generic patterning of lynching and romance narratives, this essay argues that Lost Cause popular cultural products imagined white women eagerly embracing their status as property in order to facilitate the South's so-called redemption. Specifically, in these Lost Cause films, white women threatened by Blackness become the literal and figurative property of white men through acts of elimination, containment, and sexual violence. Thus, the white masculine victimization inherent in Lost Cause ideology actually depends upon constructing and then displacing white women's victimization. The repetition and endurance of such plots reveal the extent to which they successfully garner white women's complicity—their willingness to use their agency to further their constraint—all in the service of remasculinizing white men and advancing white supremacy.

While Christmas, Gilmore, and I focus on unpacking Confederate and neo-Confederate meaning-making, Stacie McCormick's essay "Performing Counter-Monumentality of the Civil War in Natasha Trethewey's *Native Guard* and Suzan-Lori Parks's *Father Comes Home from the Wars: Parts 1, 2, and 3*" turns our attention to contemporary Black theatrical and poetic counter-monuments. Focusing on works first performed in 2014, McCormick argues that Trethewey's adaptation and Parks's play write a history of the Black present while simultaneously counter-narrativizing the Civil War. In other words, these works are forms of counter-monumentality, direct responses to Confederate monuments and memory, that make "visible Black subjectivity and the consequences of this history on Black subjects living in the ongoing present."[26] The ephemerality of performance—unlike the ephemerality of the print cultural materials Weisenburg examines—and the fluid temporal space of the stage allow these theatrical productions to "make history," in Parks's words. But the histories these plays write/right, to use McCormick's phrasing, are not akin to that of physical Confederate monuments. Rather, these plays serve as living counter-monuments, dynamically manifesting repressed voices and erased stories, collapsing time, and spurring communal participation and action. In the end, McCormick suggests, Trethewey and Parks pierce and confront the wound that Confederate monuments represent, "facilitat[ing] a reckoning long overdue in US society."[27]

If "Reading" shows us how to read Confederate monuments as texts and "Cultural Production" demonstrates how to read texts as Confederate monuments and counter-monuments, the final section of the collection, titled "Pedagogy," instructs us to read all types of Confederate monuments for how they teach their communities belonging and social justice and for what they teach us about our identities and ourselves. While many of the essays earlier in the collection critique institutional sites of learning—archives, universities, and academic disciplines, to name a few—for advancing white supremacy, the essays in this section more closely examine how such pedagogies develop, operate, and can be disrupted, both in public space and in the carefully cultivated classroom. Indeed, in these essays, critics use the methods of literary and cultural analysis to examine the pedagogical function of Confederate monuments in their own day and in ours, thinking through the cultural rhetorics about and communal responses to their persistence. As English professors hailing from and teaching in the South, the literary and cultural studies critics featured here are uniquely positioned to use Confederate monuments themselves, problematic and repugnant as they are, as teaching tools for a new generation of students, scholars, and activists looking for meaningful and ethical ways to discuss Confederate memory and its legacies. Through this lens, these essays investigate local communities' multiple, often conflicting, readings of the literal and psychic presence of Confederate monuments in their towns, from major cities like Birmingham, Alabama, and New Orleans, Louisiana, to college towns like Charlottesville, Virginia, and Sherman, Texas.

Cassandra Jackson's "Rewriting the Landscape: Black Communities and the Confederate Monuments They Inherited" opens this section by examining urban Black communities' efforts to disrupt the power of Confederate monuments passed down to them in the wake of white flight. Framed by her own past and recent engagements with the Confederate monument in her hometown of Florence, Alabama, Jackson argues that, in majority-Black cities like Baltimore, New Orleans, and Birmingham, Confederate monuments reminded Black people of "their powerlessness to control space in their own communities" due to state laws that previously prohibited their removal.[28] To counteract the pedagogical work of those Confederate statues that told urban Black communities that they "are not and can never be the proprietors of the land," these communities employed creative strategies that signaled monuments' temporality and, by extension, their mutability. By establishing contexts that exposed the white supremacy of Confederate memory and interrupted monuments' static presence, urban Black communities altered the pedagogical work of the monuments that they inherited. Examining successful and less effective responses to Confederate statues in Memphis, Tennessee, Atlanta, Georgia, and Birmingham, as well as Kehinde Wiley's counter-monument *Rumors of War* (2019), Jackson ultimately concludes that some monuments with new contextualizations compelled interaction, disrupting our vision and inviting us into interpretation, that was vital to contesting white supremacy.

While Jackson reveals how the pedagogies of Confederate monuments in public space might be revised with visual alterations and interferences, Lisa Woolfork's essay "Battle of the Billboards: White Supremacy and Memorial Culture in #Charlottesville" analyzes the pedagogical work of activists' competing texts about Confederate monuments, examining materials published for and against the removal of the Robert E. Lee statue installed near the University of Virginia campus. Both a professor and a founding member of Black Lives Matter Charlottesville, Woolfork speaks to the gap between #Charlottesville, the hashtag of solidarity that arose in the wake of the Unite the Right rally, and Charlottesville, the city plagued by structural and violent white supremacy. The distance between these two concepts, Woolfork suggests, "is the difference between neutralizing white supremacy and taking action to eradicate it."[29] Analyzing a local struggle over Confederate memory between opposing activist groups in Charlottesville, Woolfork applies close reading to a set of billboards: an anti-statue billboard erected by the Make It Right Project and a subsequent pro-statue parody of that billboard erected by the Charlottesville Free Press. Using reception theory and rhetorical and visual analysis, Woolfork unpacks why the Make It Right Project failed to convey its intended meaning and untangles the bizarre, layered meanings of the racist parody billboard, which contains many allusions. Only literary and cultural studies methods could unearth the teaching these groups receive from the statue as well as that which they, in turn, aim to teach their viewers. Ultimately, for Woolfork, this battle of the billboards reveals the extent to which Charlottesville has thus far chosen to defuse rather than dismantle white supremacy.

While Jackson and Woolfork focus on the pedagogical work of Confederate monuments and their supporting texts in the public sphere, Randi Lynn Tanglen turns to their educational value in the university classroom in her essay "Teaching Confederate Monuments as American Literature." Outlining a close reading assignment in which her students researched the history and reception of the Confederate monument located less than a mile from the small, residential liberal arts college where she taught, Tanglen describes how that monument in her Texas community provided a means of critically examining the role of US literature and literary history in establishing and maintaining a national culture of white supremacy. The assignment set up the Confederate monument as a lens for identifying and critically engaging the subtext of white supremacy in the US literature many of her students would one day teach in their own classrooms, such as Harper Lee's *To Kill a Mockingbird* (1960). In another class, her assignment highlighted the present-day urgency of the critique of Confederate ideology in Charles W. Chesnutt's *The Marrow of Tradition* (1901). Employing the assumptions of critical pedagogy, Tanglen acknowledges that the classroom replicates unequal power relations, and she grapples with the implications of teaching Confederate monuments on a majority minority campus as a white professor. But, she concludes, critical pedagogy also assumes that the educational experience can transform individuals, so that they can, in turn, transform the world, as many of her students aimed to do after completing the assignment.

Taken together, the essays in *Reading Confederate Monuments* light the way to developing our collective ability to read Confederate monuments and counter-monuments of all kinds. This literary and cultural literacy, they prove, is vital not only to advancing ongoing discussions about Confederate monuments in public space and Confederate memory in US culture but also to fighting neo-Confederate and white nationalist ideologies rapidly increasing their foothold nationwide. If we neglect *reading* Confederate monuments, then toppling them becomes merely another racist liberal project. As the opening to this introduction demonstrates, if the removal of the Mouton statue in my own city of Lafayette has taught me anything, it's this: whether we destroy, remove, contain, relocate, or recontextualize the physical and literary Confederate monuments currently saturating US culture, we must continually disassemble the white supremacist ideologies and legacies that support those monuments as much as stone or word.

# NOTES

Thank you to Ian Beamish, Dine Faucheux, Manuel Morales Fontanilla, Liz Skilton, and David Squires for their feedback on early drafts of this essay.

1. Claire Taylor, "Guillory Wants Confederate Mouton Statue Removed from Downtown Lafayette," *Acadiana Advocate*, July 2, 2020, https://www.theadvocate.com/acadiana/news/article_5eb10f3a-bbf4-11ea-860d-035a5d993cb7.html.

2. Claire Taylor, "'The Confederacy Has Surrendered': Mouton Statue Will Be Removed from Downtown Lafayette," *Acadiana Advocate*, July 16, 2021, https://www.theadvocate.com/acadiana/news/article_0198b56a-e636-11eb-9d07-fb6304fba994.html.

3. "Lafayette Mayor-President Requests Removal of Confederate Monument," KLFY.com, last modified July 1, 2020, https://www.klfy.com/local/breaking-lcg-announces-the-removal-of-confederate-monument/.

4. "Lafayette Mayor-President."

5. "Lafayette Mayor-President."

6. William Taylor Potter, "Mayor-President Josh Guillory Defends Closing Northside Lafayette Centers Serving Minorities," *Lafayette Daily Advertiser*, July 21, 2020, https://www.theadvertiser.com/story/news/local/2020/07/21/lafayette-recreation-centers-minority-neighborhoods-closing-mayor-josh-guillory/5474877002/.

7. Chris Welty, "Getting Answers: What's Next for the Mouton Statue," KATC, July 2, 2020, https://www.katc.com/news/getting-answers/getting-answers-whats-next-for-the-mouton-statue.

8. Bonnie Berkowitz and Adrian Blanco, "Confederate Monuments Are Falling, But Hundreds Still Stand. Here's Where," *Washington Post*, July 2, 2020, https://www.washingtonpost.com/graphics/2020/national/confederate-monuments/.

9. "Whose Heritage? Public Symbols of the Confederacy," Southern Poverty Law Center, last modified August 4, 2020, https://www.splcenter.org/data-projects/whose-heritage.

10. Marc Fisher, "As Confederate Monuments Tumble, Die-Hards Are Erecting Replacements," *Washington Post*, July 25, 2020, https://www.washingtonpost.com/national/as-confederate-monuments-tumble-die-hards-are-erecting-replacements/2020/07/25/44f537ee-cd04-11ea-b0e3-d55bda07d66a_story.html.

11. Indeed, in 2017, based on data from the Southern Poverty Law Center, the *Washington Post* calculated that roughly 8 percent of Confederate memorials are located in the North. Philip Bump, "About 1 in 12 Confederate Memorials in the US Is in a Union State," *Washington Post*, August 15, 2017, https://www.washingtonpost.com/news/politics/wp/2017/08/15/about-one-out-of-every-12-confederate-memorials-in-the-u-s-is-in-a-union-state/.

12. Kirk Savage, *Monument Wars: Washington, D.C., the National Mall, and the Transformation of the Memorial Landscape* (Berkeley: University of California Press, 2009), 10.

13. For a list of historians' op-eds, interviews, and media engagement in the wake of the Charlottesville tragedy, see "Historians on the Confederate Monument Debate," American Historical Association, accessed August 11, 2020, https://www.historians.org/news-and-advocacy/everything-has-a-history/historians-on-the-confederate-monument-debate.

14. See "#CharlestonSyllabus," African American Intellectual History Society, accessed August 11, 2020, https://www.aaihs.org/resources/charlestonsyllabus/; and "Confederate Monuments Syllabus," Confederate Memory, accessed August 11, 2020, http://cwmemory.com/civilwarmemorysyllabus/.

15. See David W. Blight, *Race and Reunion: The Civil War in American Memory* (Cambridge, MA: Belknap Press, 2001); Karen L. Cox, *Dixie's Daughters: The United Daughters of the*

*Confederacy and the Preservation of Confederate Culture* (Gainesville: University Press of Florida, 2003); Karen L. Cox, *No Common Ground: Confederate Monuments and the Ongoing Fight for Racial Justice* (Chapel Hill: University of North Carolina Press, 2021); and Eric Foner, *The Second Founding: How the Civil War and Reconstruction Remade the Constitution* (New York: Norton, 2019).

16. See Alice Fahs and Joan Waugh, eds., *The Memory of the Civil War in American Culture* (Chapel Hill: University of North Carolina Press, 2004); Caroline E. Janney, *Remembering the Civil War: Reunion and the Limits of Reconciliation* (Chapel Hill: University of North Carolina Press, 2013); and Nina Silber, *The Romance of Reunion: Northerners and the South, 1865–1900* (Chapel Hill: University of North Carolina Press, 1993).

17. See Adam H. Domby, *The False Cause: Fraud, Fabrication, and White Supremacy in Confederate Memory* (Charlottesville: University of Virginia Press, 2020); and Gary W. Gallagher and Alan T. Nolan, eds., *The Myth of the Lost Cause and Civil War History* (Bloomington: Indiana University Press, 2000).

18. See Kirk Savage, *Standing Soldiers, Kneeling Slaves: Race, War, and Monument in Nineteenth-Century America* (Princeton, NJ: Princeton University Press, 1997); Cynthia Mills and Pamela H. Simpson, eds., *Monuments to the Lost Cause: Women, Art, and the Landscapes of Southern Memory* (Knoxville: University of Tennessee Press, 2003); and Dell Upton, *What Can and Can't Be Said: Race, Uplift, and Monument Building in the Contemporary South* (New Haven, CT: Yale University Press, 2015).

19. See Karen L. Cox, *Dreaming of Dixie: How the South Was Created in American Popular Culture* (Chapel Hill: University of North Carolina Press, 2011); Gary W. Gallagher, *Causes Won, Lost, and Forgotten: How Hollywood and Popular Art Shape What We Know about the Civil War* (Chapel Hill: University of North Carolina Press, 2008); and Tara McPherson, *Reconstructing Dixie: Race, Gender, and Nostalgia in the Imagined South* (Durham, NC: Duke University Press, 2003).

20. See Brook Thomas, *The Literature of Reconstruction: Not in Plain Black and White* (Baltimore: Johns Hopkins University Press, 2017); and Gordon Hutner, ed., "Reenvisioning Reconstruction," *American Literary History* 30, no. 3 (Fall 2018).

21. Quentin Stevens, Karen A. Franck, and Ruth Fazakerley, "Counter-Monuments: The Anti-Monumental and the Dialogic," *Journal of Architecture* 23, no. 5 (2018): 718–39.

22. See, in this volume, Brook Thomas, "Complicating Today's Myth of the Myth of the Lost Cause: The Calhoun Monument, Reconstruction, and Reconciliation," in *Reading Confederate Monuments*, ed. Maria Seger (Jackson: University Press of Mississippi, 2022), 21–42.

23. See, in this volume, Michael C. Weisenburg, "Print Culture and the Enduring Legacy of Confederate War Monuments," in Seger, *Reading Confederate Monuments*, 43–71.

24. See, in this volume, Danielle Christmas, "Weaponizing Silent Sam: Heritage Politics and *The Third Revolution*," in Seger, *Reading Confederate Monuments*, 99–117.

25. See, in this volume, Garrett Bridger Gilmore, "'Wasting the Past': Albion Tourgée, Confederate Memory, and the Politics of Context," in Seger, *Reading Confederate Monuments*, 118–41.

26. See, in this volume, Stacie McCormick, "Performing Counter-Monumentality of the Civil War in Natasha Trethewey's *Native Guard* and Suzan-Lori Parks's *Father Comes Home from the Wars: Parts 1, 2, and 3*," in Seger, *Reading Confederate Monuments*, 166–87.

27. McCormick, "Performing Counter-Monumentality of the Civil War in Natasha Trethewey's *Native Guard* and Suzan-Lori Parks's *Father Comes Home from the Wars: Parts 1, 2, and 3*," in *Reading Confederate Monuments*, in Seger. 166–87.

28. See, in this volume, Cassandra Jackson, "Rewriting the Landscape: Black Communities and the Confederate Monuments They Inherited," in Seger, *Reading Confederate Monuments*, 191–212.

29. See, in this volume, Lisa Woolfork, "Battle of the Billboards: White Supremacy and Memorial Culture in #Charlottesville," in Seger, *Reading Confederate Monuments*, 213–29.

# Bibliography

African American Intellectual History Society. "#CharlestonSyllabus." Accessed August 11, 2020. https://www.aaihs.org/resources/charlestonsyllabus/.

American Historical Association. "Historians on the Confederate Monument Debate." Accessed August 11, 2020. https://www.historians.org/news-and-advocacy/everything-has-a-history/historians-on-the-confederate-monument-debate.

Berkowitz, Bonnie, and Adrian Blanco. "Confederate Monuments Are Falling, But Hundreds Still Stand. Here's Where." *Washington Post*, July 2, 2020. https://www.washingtonpost.com/graphics/2020/national/confederate-monuments/.

Blight, David W. *Race and Reunion: The Civil War in American Memory*. Cambridge, MA: Belknap Press, 2001.

Bump, Philip. "About 1 in 12 Confederate Memorials in the US Is in a Union State." *Washington Post*, August 15, 2017. https://www.washingtonpost.com/news/politics/wp/2017/08/15/about-one-out-of-every-12-confederate-memorials-in-the-u-s-is-in-a-union-state/.

Confederate Memory. "Confederate Monuments Syllabus." Accessed August 11, 2020. http://cwmemory.com/civilwarmemorysyllabus/.

Cox, Karen L. *Dixie's Daughters: The United Daughters of the Confederacy and the Preservation of Confederate Culture*. Gainesville: University Press of Florida, 2003.

Cox, Karen L. *Dreaming of Dixie: How the South Was Created in American Popular Culture*. Chapel Hill: University of North Carolina Press, 2011.

Cox, Karen L. *No Common Ground: Confederate Monuments and the Ongoing Fight for Racial Justice*. Chapel Hill: University of North Carolina Press, 2021.

Domby, Adam H. *The False Cause: Fraud, Fabrication, and White Supremacy in Confederate Memory*. Charlottesville: University of Virginia Press, 2020.

Fahs, Alice, and Joan Waugh, eds. *The Memory of the Civil War in American Culture*. Chapel Hill: University of North Carolina Press, 2004.

Fisher, Marc. "As Confederate Monuments Tumble, Die-Hards Are Erecting Replacements." *Washington Post*, July 25, 2020. https://www.washingtonpost.com/national/as-confederate-monuments-tumble-die-hards-are-erecting-replacements/2020/07/25/44f537ee-cd04-11ea-b0e3-d55bda07d66a_story.html.

Foner, Eric. *The Second Founding: How the Civil War and Reconstruction Remade the Constitution*. New York: Norton, 2019.

Gallagher, Gary W. *Causes Won, Lost, and Forgotten: How Hollywood and Popular Art Shape What We Know about the Civil War*. Chapel Hill: University of North Carolina Press, 2008.

Gallagher, Gary W., and Alan T. Nolan, eds. *The Myth of the Lost Cause and Civil War History*. Bloomington: Indiana University Press, 2000.

Hutner, Gordon, ed. "Reenvisioning Reconstruction." *American Literary History* 30, no. 3 (Fall 2018).

Janney, Caroline E. *Remembering the Civil War: Reunion and the Limits of Reconciliation*. Chapel Hill: University of North Carolina Press, 2013.

KLFY.com. "Lafayette Mayor-President Requests Removal of Confederate Monument." Last modified July 1, 2020. https://www.klfy.com/local/breaking-lcg-announces-the-removal-of-confederate-monument/.

McPherson, Tara. *Reconstructing Dixie: Race, Gender, and Nostalgia in the Imagined South.* Durham, NC: Duke University Press, 2003.

Mills, Cynthia, and Pamela H. Simpson, eds. *Monuments to the Lost Cause: Women, Art, and the Landscapes of Southern Memory.* Knoxville: University of Tennessee Press, 2003.

Potter, William Taylor. "Mayor-President Josh Guillory Defends Closing Northside Lafayette Centers Serving Minorities." *Lafayette Daily Advertiser*, July 21, 2020. https://www .theadvertiser.com/story/news/local/2020/07/21/lafayette-recreation-centers-minority -neighborhoods-closing-mayor-josh-guillory/5474877002/.

Savage, Kirk. *Monument Wars: Washington, D.C., the National Mall, and the Transformation of the Memorial Landscape.* Berkeley: University of California Press, 2009.

Savage, Kirk. *Standing Soldiers, Kneeling Slaves: Race, War, and Monument in Nineteenth-Century America.* Princeton, NJ: Princeton University Press, 1997.

Silber, Nina. *The Romance of Reunion: Northerners and the South, 1865–1900.* Chapel Hill: University of North Carolina Press, 1993.

Southern Poverty Law Center. "Whose Heritage? Public Symbols of the Confederacy." Last modified August 4, 2020. https://www.splcenter.org/data-projects/whose-heritage.

Stevens, Quentin, Karen A. Franck, and Ruth Fazakerley. "Counter-Monuments: The Anti-Monumental and the Dialogic." *Journal of Architecture* 23, no. 5 (2018): 718–39.

Taylor, Claire. "'The Confederacy Has Surrendered': Mouton Statue Will Be Removed from Downtown Lafayette." *Acadiana Advocate*, July 16, 2021. https://www.theadvocate.com/ acadiana/news/article_0198b56a-e636-11eb-9d07-fb6304fba994.html.

Taylor, Claire. "Guillory Wants Confederate Mouton Statue Removed from Downtown Lafayette." *Acadiana Advocate*, July 2, 2020. https://www.theadvocate.com/acadiana/news/ article_5eb10f3a-bbf4-11ea-860d-035a5d993cb7.html.

Thomas, Brook. *The Literature of Reconstruction: Not in Plain Black and White.* Baltimore: Johns Hopkins University Press, 2017.

Upton, Dell. *What Can and Can't Be Said: Race, Uplift, and Monument Building in the Contemporary South.* New Haven, CT: Yale University Press, 2015.

Welty, Chris. "Getting Answers: What's Next for the Mouton Statue." KATC, July 2, 2020. https:// www.katc.com/news/getting-answers/getting-answers-whats-next-for-the-mouton-statue.

# READING

## Reading Confederate Monuments as Texts and in Textual Contexts

# CHAPTER 1

# COMPLICATING TODAY'S MYTH OF THE MYTH OF THE LOST CAUSE

## The Calhoun Monument, Reconstruction, and Reconciliation

### —Brook Thomas

This essay is about a monument in limbo. A statue of John C. Calhoun once occupied a prominent public space in Charleston, South Carolina. In June 2020, it was removed with the intention of placing it in a museum. At the time of writing, no museum has taken it, a sign that the Confederate monument controversy is still unresolved. Given this controversy, it is helpful to start with some agreement. There is general consensus that Confederate monuments honor the Lost Cause of the South in the Civil War. Gary W. Gallagher describes the myth as nurturing "a public memory of the Confederacy that placed [southerners'] wartime sacrifice and shattering defeat in the best possible light."[1] According to the myth, Confederate soldiers defended the ideal of local self-government through states' rights and lost the war only because of the commercial and material resources of the North. Today's controversy is not about the gallantry of Confederate soldiers but their defense of slavery, which motivated the doctrine of states' rights. Thus, the controversy is portrayed as a country still fighting the Civil War.[2]

With white supremacists donning Confederate uniforms and waving the Stars and Bars while violently protesting the removal of monuments and others demanding their destruction, that characterization seems accurate. But it is misleading. There are calls to remove statues of Abraham Lincoln and Ulysses S. Grant as well. At the same time, the majority who question removal do not advocate the Lost Cause. They worry about an Orwellian rewriting of history. Condemning the Confederacy's defense of slavery, they feel, nonetheless, that history, including its unseemly aspects, should not be erased. The monuments should be used instead to educate the public about the past. Agreeing on the importance of education, more moderate advocates for removal respond that the issue is not about erasing the past but the location of the monuments. They belong in museums, not public spaces.

A newspaper's response to a 1971 proposal to remove a rock commemorating the Confederacy from the University of Missouri campus helps to highlight the stakes of the controversy: "You can't change history by removing a rock."[3] True, keeping the rock in its place would have been a reminder of past celebrations of the Confederacy. But moving it did not change the fact of those celebrations. The issue is not whether the Confederacy was celebrated in the past; it is the use of public spaces to continue that celebration. Only a limited number of monuments can occupy prominent public spaces. What they commemorate matters. Nonetheless, the debate is complicated because public monuments are themselves part of a place's history.

We cannot understand the difficulties of achieving racial justice in the present, I argue, without doing justice to the complicated past that generated the monument controversy. Employing a cultural approach that relies on the literary technique of close reading to explore the complicated history of the myth of the Lost Cause, I show that the past being erased in today's debates is not the Civil War and the South's defense of slavery. On the contrary, descriptions of a country still fighting the war highlight that history. What is too often forgotten is the role played by the country's retreat from Reconstruction. A comparison with Germany reinforces that point. Germany no longer has public monuments to Nazis. Built under Hitler, they were destroyed or removed with his defeat. In contrast, the controversial monuments in the United States were not built during the reign of the Confederacy. Most were built when sectional reconciliation triumphed over Radical Reconstruction. Historically, then, the controversy over the monuments is somewhat different from the one over the display of the Confederate battle flag. The Stars and Bars is a relic of the Confederacy. The monuments are the product of an era remembering the Civil War past. To be sure, not all have the same relation to that past. In honoring the Confederate dead, some perpetuated tensions between the North and South. But many celebrated sectional reconciliation as southerners admitted defeat in the war and northerners honored at least parts of the myth of the Lost Cause while condoning—even praising—monuments in the South as they constructed their own in the North.

The second part of this essay returns to that moment in history by analyzing the 1887 dedication of the Calhoun monument. That dedication confirms David W. Blight's influential argument in *Race and Reunion: The Civil War in American Memory* (2001) that commemorative events celebrating the Civil War legitimated the era of Jim Crow segregation by stressing the desire for sectional reconciliation over a program promoting civil and political equality for African Americans. Ironically, then celebrations intended to heal the nation's wounds have contributed to the racial divisions that in part generate today's monument controversy. Nonetheless, Blight's indispensable thesis needs to be supplemented because of the difference between commemorations and monuments. Commemorative events are in the past. A dedication can be reinterpreted, but it remains a historical event. In contrast, a monument exists in the present. The significance of a public monument that people see every day is not confined to the moment of its dedication. In the final section, I pose a challenge to those intent on racial justice today by drawing on what literary critics call a history of reception in order to trace the changing significance of the Calhoun monument over time.[4]

## THE LOST CAUSE AND RECONSTRUCTION

The first step in getting to that point is to revisit the myth of the Lost Cause. Associated with a romantic nostalgia for a past that never was, it has many versions that change over time and serve multiple purposes. What is too often forgotten is that the myth originated as a strategy of reconciliation to defeat radical plans for Reconstruction. The first person to give the myth a name was Richmond journalist Edward A. Pollard. In 1866, Pollard drew on histories of the war he published while it was underway to produce *The Lost Cause: A New Southern History of the War of the Confederates*, which is frequently mentioned but rarely closely read.[5] *The Lost Cause* contains many staples of the myth as characterized today. For instance, Pollard insists that "slavery" is the wrong word for "that system of servitude in the South which was really the mildest in the world which did not rest on acts of debasement and disenfranchisement, but elevated the African, and was in the interest of human improvement."[6] The war was not over slavery. It was about liberty, which could be preserved only by states, not a concentrated central government distant from the people. Secession was forced upon the South by northerners meddling in a way of life that was superior to their commercialism. Pollard was also one of the first to turn Robert E. Lee into the hero of the war. His next book was *Lee and His Lieutenants* (1867).[7]

Championing the way of life Lee allegedly embodied, *The Lost Cause* nonetheless contains elements that don't fit the myth as understood today. Not putting the southern effort to repel northern invaders in the best light, Pollard describes deserters who were "eating into the vital parts of our resources. . . . All the stories of Confederate decay are traced at last to one source: the misgovernment that had made makeshifts in every stage of the war, at last to the point of utter deprivation, and had finally broken down the spirit of the armies and the patience of its people."[8] Incompetent political leadership, not overwhelming northern resources, was the cause of defeat: "The great and melancholy fact remains that the Confederates, with an abler government and more resolute spirit, might have accomplished their independence."[9]

Most of *The Lost Cause*'s almost eight hundred pages are devoted to descriptions of battles and the workings of the Confederate government that Pollard wrote during the war. Only in the last chapter does Pollard mention a Lost Cause. In a striking account of Lee's surrender, he writes: "The public mind of the South was fully represented in that surrender. The people had become convinced that the Confederate cause was lost; they saw that the exertions of four years, misdirected and abused, had not availed, and they submitted to what they conceived now to be the determined fortune of the war."[10] For Pollard, although the Confederate cause was lost, the South's was not. The leadership did not represent the people. In an 1869 book on Jefferson Davis, Pollard insisted that the Confederate president misrepresented and degraded the people's cause through his personal ambition, his commitment to slavery, and his devotion to a decaying and arrogant aristocracy.[11] With the Confederacy's demise, Pollard saw a chance for the South. In the final pages, he rallies the cause: "The war has not swallowed up everything. There are great interests which stand out of the pale of the contest, which it is for the South still to cultivate and maintain. She must submit fairly and truthfully to *what the war has properly decided*. But the war properly decided only what was put in issue; the restoration of the Union and the excision of slavery; and to those two conditions the South submits. But the war did not decide negro equality; it did not decide negro suffrage, it did not decide State Rights, although it might have exploded their abuse."[12]

*The Lost Cause* concludes, in other words, by looking forward to a fight for what could be won, not looking nostalgically at a war that was lost. That meant siding with President Andrew Johnson in his battle with radicals in Congress and controlling the terms of reunion. The president, Pollard insists, stands for the Constitution and the liberties it guarantees against "a rebellion" that would undermine "all the written and traditional authority of American statesmanship; a war quite as distinct as that of bayonets and more comprehensive in its results than the armed contest that has just closed."[13] If the radicals prevail, he warns, the North will soon learn that "the South has abandoned the contest of the last four years, merely to resume it in a wider arena, and on a larger issue, and in a change of circumstances wherein may be asserted the profit of experience, and raised a new standard of Hope!"[14] In a wider arena on a larger issue, the battle of Reconstruction is, for Pollard, more significant than the recent war.

The last chapter of Pollard's most cited work is the only one completely written after surrender. It anticipates a transformation in his appeal to the Lost Cause. He does not make that appeal in the book on Lee, whom he continued to revere. But writing for the 1868 election, he articulates it in *The Lost Cause Regained*. Neglected today, with its Miltonic allusion, that book advised southerners to stop looking backward and wishing for a return to slavery. Instead, Pollard urged southern whites to embrace the Union and join forces with northern Democrats to take political control of the country by defeating radical Republicans. No longer fighting the Civil War, Pollard was fighting Radical Reconstruction. In this shift, Pollard found Johnson a better representative of the Lost Cause than former Confederates. In his book on Davis, Pollard evokes the dramatic scene in the Senate when the senior senator from Mississippi led others in walking out, leaving Johnson the lone loyal southerner. Praising "this brave knight" as "a champion of the Union," Pollard writes, "A simple man arose as if almost providentially qualified to supply the occasion."[15]

Johnson defended three fundamental principles for Pollard: limited government as established in the Constitution by the founders, white supremacy, and loyalty to the Union. "The Union may be more effectively destroyed by consolidation," he proclaims, "than by secession."[16] Complicating his defense of slavery in *The Lost Cause* as a mild and benevolent system of servitude, he now emphasized its role in maintaining white supremacy. Johnson's wisdom was showing that slavery was not needed to keep whites in control. The Lost Cause will be won not through secession and war, but by the South's finding new allies and working within the US political system. The book's epigraph is Jesus's decision in John Milton's *Paradise Regained* (1671) to forsake the methods of war. The last lines read:

More humane, more heavenly first
By winning words to conquer willing hearts,
And make persuasion do the work of fear
At least to try and teach the erring soul
Not willfully misdoing, but unaware
Misled, the stubborn only to subdue.[17]

Championing political persuasion, the passage stresses the need to address both southerners misled in the recent war and northerners misled by radical Republicans. Because neither are guilty of "willfully misdoing," Pollard is optimistic. He ends predicting a glorious future for the Union restored to what it was.

During the Civil War, the slogan of pro-Union Democrats was "the Union as it was; the Constitution as it is." Although Pollard sought an alliance with those northerners, he did not use the second half of the slogan because the Constitution had been amended. Like Johnson, he had no problem with the Thirteenth Amendment that abolished slavery. But he was wary of the Fourteenth Amendment, ratified in 1868, that granted African Americans citizenship and equal protection under the law. In 1868, he also opposed Black suffrage. When Ulysses S. Grant won the 1868 election, the new president lent his support to the

Fifteenth Amendment. Ratified in 1870, the compromise measure did not posi-
tively grant African Americans suffrage. But it did forbid states from using race
to disqualify someone from voting. Undeterred, Pollard continued to modify
his views, increasing his commitment to the Union in subsequent years while
maintaining his opposition to radicals.

Writing no new books after the one on Davis, Pollard published numerous
pamphlets and articles. Notably, he began to write for the *Galaxy* magazine.
Located in New York, the *Galaxy* was edited by the Church brothers, who also
edited the *Army & Navy Journal* that kept Union soldiers informed during the
war. Other contributors included Walt Whitman, Mark Twain, Henry James, and
Rebecca Harding Davis. Pollard's first contribution was "The Story of a Hero"
(1868), not about a Confederate but about Henry H. Bell, a naval officer from
North Carolina who chose the Union over his home state.[18] Pollard also published "The Romance of the Negro" (1871), which demystifies a "Lost Theory as
well as a 'Lost Cause.'"[19] Although Pollard and other southerners once believed
that African Americans were so dependent on slavery that they would die out
with emancipation, he remarks on their progress and ends extolling their oratorical talent: "Who knows, indeed but that 'the forest born Demosthenes' may
yet prove to be a black man?"[20]

"The Romance of the Negro" expressed Pollard's evolving views on race. Still
believing in the superiority of whites, he opposed "social equality." Nonetheless,
he acknowledged that educated Black people needed to vote to protect their
interests. For the 1869 election in Virginia, he wrote a pamphlet addressed to
Black voters, urging them to vote Democratic. He encouraged education for
freed people while advocating for segregated schools. He explicitly condemned
the black codes southern states imposed in 1865. In 1868, Pollard prophetically
warned that, although the South was not capable of "the *grand duello* of the
past," it was capable of "a war of vengeance. She may repeat on a much larger
scale the Fenianism of Ireland, and may even take a lesson from the few Indian
tribes which have sufficed to hold a year's campaign against the military power
of the United States. Such vengeful rebellions . . . have sometimes . . . been more
difficult to quell than regular wars."[21] Later, he published a pamphlet denouncing the Ku Klux Klan "as one of the vilest demonstrations of lynch law"; its
members, he said, should be "ruthlessly hunted down, and exterminated, without compunction and without mercy."[22]

Pollard's commitment to the Union did not diminish his identification with
the South. The last essay he wrote was "Anti-Slavery Men of the South" (1873).
Proud that the North was not alone in criticizing slavery, he praised southern
antislavery men as "purer and honester than those of the North" because they
spoke against their economic interests.[23] Nonetheless, whereas he now acknowledged cruelty and exploitation under slavery, he retained his view that it had a

civilizing effect. Indeed, freed people's advances after emancipation showed how well slavery had prepared them for citizenship. For northerners to admit this would create "an opportunity for the broadest reconciliation."[24]

When Pollard died on December 17, 1872, his frequently revised vision of the Lost Cause had not triumphed. In the 1872 election, Pollard had thrown his support behind Horace Greeley, the former abolitionist who opposed Grant by advocating a return to home rule in the South. Once again, Grant prevailed. But by the end of Grant's second term, federal troops were supporting Republican governments in only three states in the South. With the redemption of all southern states after the disputed election of 1876, sectional reconciliation fulfilled many of Pollard's hopes. His vision came closer to realization in 1883 when the Supreme Court declared most of the Civil Rights Act of 1875 unconstitutional, undermining what opponents called radicals' attempt to impose "social equality." The court's decision made it possible for states to pass the separate but equal laws that Pollard had advocated. The next year Grover Cleveland was elected president. Cleveland was a northern Democrat of the sort with whom Pollard hoped to work. Cleveland appointed ex-Confederates to high positions. In 1886, Jefferson Davis had a triumphant tour celebrating the silver anniversary of assuming the presidency of the Confederacy. At Grant's funeral in 1885, two former Confederate generals were pallbearers. For the most part, the movement to build today's controversial monuments began with this retreat from Reconstruction. That included the erection of a monument to Calhoun in Charleston, South Carolina, in 1887.

## THE CALHOUN MONUMENT AND RECONCILIATION

Calhoun died in 1850 before secession, but in his authoritative history, Thomas J. Brown includes the Calhoun monument as a site of Confederate memory. He does so for good reason. Calhoun was considered the patron saint of the Confederacy. Confederate constitutional theory was indebted to him. Confederate military units were named after him, as was a naval vessel. Matthew Brady's daguerreotype of him appeared on Confederate currency and bonds. As Brown puts it, "when southern military fortunes crumbled, Calhoun offered an intersectional symbol of what the Confederacy had defended and lost."[25] Because Calhoun came to represent Confederate ideology, his monument, "more clearly than the statues of Confederate soldiers," has served "as a reminder of the ideas at stake in the sectional conflict."[26]

Calhoun was honored in his lifetime. As he prepared to run for president in 1844, bankers commissioned a portrait statue by Hiram Powers, famous for "The Greek Slave." Living in Europe, Powers was slow to finish the task. The statue arrived in 1850, soon after Calhoun died. With his death, the Ladies' Calhoun Monument Association pushed for a larger public monument. Plans were not realized before or during the war, but by 1876, with South Carolina's redemption in sight, the association held a national contest for a monument. Although not everyone had liked Powers's depiction of Calhoun in a toga, when his statue was destroyed during Sherman's march, it became associated with southern suffering. Contestants were instructed to include some of its elements in the new design. The sculptor chosen was thirty-six-year-old Albert E. Harnisch, a northerner living in Rome as part of the expatriate community associated with the sculptor William Wetmore Story, son of former Supreme Court justice Joseph Story, a close friend of Calhoun's rival Daniel Webster. The monument was ready for dedication on April 26, 1887, the anniversary of Calhoun's funeral. April 26 was also the date of the surrender of General Joseph Johnston to General William Sherman. In some states, it marked Confederate Memorial Day, but in South Carolina, that holiday was May 10, Stonewall Jackson's birthday.

According to Brown, "As a secessionist project that survived the death of the Confederacy, the Calhoun monument illustrates the postwar adjustments of white southern commemoration."[27] A major adjustment was the organizers' stress on sectional reconciliation. In this spirit, they chose Lucius Quintus Cincinnatus Lamar as dedication speaker. Lamar served Mississippi after the war in both the House and the Senate. Cleveland appointed him secretary of the interior and then the first former Confederate on the US Supreme Court. Once a firebrand secessionist, he had gained a national reputation in 1874 when he delivered a moving eulogy for radical Massachusetts senator Charles Sumner. John F. Kennedy honors Lamar with a chapter in *Profiles in Courage*, claiming that his eulogy "marked a turning point in relations between North and South."[28] Endorsing reunion, Joel Chandler Harris insisted that Lamar's views "have become the views of the southern people" and that Lamar's "liberal and progressive views" articulated the "highest ideal of American statesmanship, which means love for the whole country."[29]

Quoted by Frederick Jackson Turner in his speech on the frontier, Lamar's dedication warrants close reading. Lamar started with the intimate connection between Calhoun and South Carolina and his service to the state while working in the nation's capital. Calhoun's estate in Fort Hill epitomized plantation culture: an "alliance between man's intellect and nature's laws of production," imparting "habits of industry, firmness of purpose, fidelity to dependents, self-reliance, and the sentiment of justice" characteristic of the South's statesmen and military leaders, like George Washington, Thomas Jefferson, James Madison, James Monroe, John Marshall, and Andrew Jackson.[30] Belonging to that select group, Calhoun was distinguished by his statesmanship, scholarship on government, and moral purity. Expounding on all three, Lamar made Calhoun a unionist, not a secessionist. No easy task, this required a revisionist account of some of Calhoun's most famous beliefs.

Calhoun believed that sovereignty was indivisible and resided in individual states. Lamar insisted that at the founding this was true, but the country had changed, especially with the Louisiana Purchase that added vast territory and produced new states: "In 1789 the Federal Government had derived all the powers delegated to it by the Constitution from the States; in 1861 a majority of the States derived all their powers and attributes as States from Congress under the Constitution."[31] Calhoun would have understood this change. As proof, Lamar emphasized a career devoted to the Union. There was, for instance, his strong support for the War of 1812, which gave "independence abroad as the Revolution gave independence at home."[32] His service in Congress, in multiple cabinets, and as vice president exhibited "the strongest sentiments of devotion to the Union." For Calhoun, "the liberty and union of the country were inseparably united."[33] As Lamar knew, that phrase echoed Daniel Webster's stirring pronouncement in Abraham Lincoln's favorite speech: "Liberty and Union now and forever, one and inseparable."[34] In order to make the statesman from South Carolina as vital to the nation's history as the one from Massachusetts, Lamar had to confront Calhoun's doctrine of nullification: the belief that a state could refuse to follow a law passed by Congress by declaring it unconstitutional. The doctrine anticipated secession, causing Brown to refer to Calhoun as "the Nullifier." Lamar, however, insisted that the doctrine was "within the limits of the Constitution and conducive to the preservation of the Union."[35] Calhoun was a sincere patriot with no intention of "tearing the Union asunder."[36] Lamar continued, "Whatever may be objections to this doctrine, it must be admitted that it had not in it an element of disunion."[37]

Lamar addressed the issue of slavery without condoning Calhoun's views: "Fellow-citizens: The institution of slavery! That question has been settled. Slavery is dead—buried in a grave that never gives up its dead. Why reopen it today? Let it rest. Yet, if I remain silent upon the subject it will be taken as an admission that there is one part of Mr. Calhoun's life of which it is prudent for his friends to say nothing to the present generation."[38] Adamant about the death of slavery, Lamar nonetheless portrayed it in a way that did honor to the South. Benevolent planters had taken "a race of untamed savages, with habits that could only inspire disgust, with no arts, no single tradition of civilization" and created "the finest body of agricultural and domestic laborers the world has ever seen," elevating "them in the scale of rational existence to such a height as to cause them to be deemed fit for admission into the charmed circle of American freedom, and to be clothed with the rights and duties of American citizenship."[39] Slavery's "elevating agencies" led to the "inevitable destruction of the system"; the mistake defenders of slavery made was to regard it as permanent "instead of a process of emergence and a transition from barbarism to freedom."[40] As condescending and racist as this account was, it acknowledged African Americans' right to citizenship. Lamar's Calhoun would have accepted this new world for South Carolina and sought "the happiness of her people, their greatness and glory, in the greatness and glory of the American Republic." Lamar continued, "He would say that a heroic and liberty-loving state, like South Carolina, should cherish for the great Republic, of which she is part, that ardent, genuine patriotism which is the life and soul and light of all heroism and liberty."[41]

To transform Calhoun into a Unionist, Lamar promoted a view of US history in which conflict was essential to the affirmation of unity. Describing the famous debates between Calhoun, Webster, Henry Clay, and Jackson that generated important compromises, Lamar remarked: "The eloquence and wisdom and services of our greatest statemen are exhibited, not in united efforts and harmonious co-operation, but in conflict among themselves, and victories of one party over another. But when a supreme moment comes the fact is revealed that what seems to be fierce combat among themselves is but the ardent striving of each for the honor, perpetuity, and glory of a common country."[42] Even the Civil War turned out to be, as Dudley H. Miles would later call it, a "unifier."[43] The South would accept the results of the war, and the North would treat the South fairly and embrace a view of federalism that continued to promote liberty by giving states substantial control over their own affairs.

Radical Reconstruction delayed reconciliation by creating new conflicts. But it too ended in unity. As Lamar wrote:

> Its unmistakable purpose was the reversal of every rational, social and political relation on which, I will not say, the civilization of the South, but of the world and the whole Union, rested. But in process of time a large portion of the dominant section saw not only the odious injustice of the system fastened upon the South, but the danger to the whole country which its maintenance threatened. Then followed a course of magnanimity on the part of the Northern people, unexampled in the annals of civil war and accepted by the South in a spirit not less magnanimous and great-hearted. The result was the full and equal restoration of the Southern States with all their rights under the Constitution, upon the one condition that they would recognize, as elements of their new political life, the validity of the Thirteenth, Fourteenth and Fifteenth Amendments to the Constitution, guaranteeing and establishing the indissolubility of the American Union and the universality of American freedom.[44]

Lamar's conflictual view of history allowed him to place the myth of the Lost Cause into the service of progressive nationalism. According to Brown, "Unlike the Union tributes, remembrance of the Confederacy could not justify sacrifices on its behalf by pointing to the permanence of the nation. White Southerners who had maintained that their cause implemented God's plan for humanity were compelled to explain the apparent evidence of divine disfavor."[45] As versed in Milton's notion of a happy fall as Pollard, Lamar could manage that dilemma. If *Paradise Lost* (1667) addresses the apparent evidence of divine disfavor through portrayal of the fall, *Paradise Regained* affirms hope. Southerners might not be able to justify their sacrifices by pointing to the permanence of the nation, but those intent on reconciliation came up with a more complicated narrative. Prior to the Civil War, they argued, the country was a union of states, not a nation. It was only through a challenge to its unity that a nation—embraced by all—was born. The bloody conflict of the Civil War turned out to be a *felix culpa* in which disobedience was redeemed and southern sacrifices were as essential as northern ones to the emerging national consciousness. This redemptive view of history was the foundation of President Woodrow Wilson's speech commemorating the fiftieth anniversary of the Battle of Gettysburg. Marveling at "how complete the Union has become and how dear to all of us," he turns to the sacrifices on both sides needed to give birth to a nation: "We are made by these tragic, epic things to know what it costs to make a nation—the blood and sacrifice of multitudes of unknown men lifted to a great stature in the view of all generations by knowing no limit in their manly willingness to serve."[46]

Calhoun did not experience the war, but Lamar turned his service to the Union into proof that he would have embraced the nation, given its full birth, only with the retreat from Reconstruction. That nation had many of the qualities Pollard felt necessary for the Lost Cause to be regained. Pollard, like Lamar, accepted African American citizenship, so long as Reconstruction's "unnatural" order of Black people ruling white people was reversed. Pollard's and Lamar's accounts of slavery's demise and its beneficial aspects are almost identical, as is their patriotic embrace of the Union. Pollard even anticipated Lamar's Calhoun. As early as *The Lost Cause*, he argued that branding Calhoun a "Disunionist" was "a curious instance of Northern misrepresentation in politics." In fact, nullification was "*directly addressed to saving the Union*." It was intended "to preserve and protect the Union."[47] In 1869, Pollard wrote a short account of Calhoun stressing even more his devotion to the Union.

In 1887, northerners joined southerners in celebrating this version of Calhoun. The dedication was attended by the secretaries of the treasury, war, and navy, as well as the postmaster general, all from the North. Northern governors and Clara Barton sent best wishes. Grant's secretary of state Hamilton Fish praised Calhoun's "lofty genius," which entitled him to have "his fame and his memory perpetuated to future eyes, by monuments and symbols."[48] President Cleveland noted the "universal pride in the greatness of this illustrious

American" and insisted that all "charged with public duty" should know "all his aspirations for the welfare and prosperity of our Republic."[49]

The Calhoun monument, like others so controversial today, was the responsibility of the nation, not just the South. As Henry M. Field, a New England minister, put it in 1898: "if there is nothing so terrible as Disunion, there has been nothing more glorious than Reunion.... Foreigners do not know what to make of it. We are raising monuments to those who fought and fell on both sides.... These heroic monuments are the proud possession of us all."[50] In 1902, Charles Francis Adams Jr. gave a speech called "Shall Cromwell Have a Statue?" published in *Lee at Appomattox and Other Papers*. It used the recent controversy in Great Britain over whether Oliver Cromwell should finally get a statue near Parliament to make a case for erecting a statue of Lee in Washington, DC. According to Adams, Lee deserved a statue, not only because he fought with bravery and honor but primarily because he had accepted defeat and re-embraced the Union: "Lee's monument will be educational.... It will symbolize and commemorate that loyal acceptance of the consequences of defeat" while also marking "the patient upbraiding" of a reunited people; thus, "The Confederate, as well as the Unionist, enters as an essential factor into the nation that now is, and, in future, is to be."[51] For both Field and Adams, the speed with which former enemies reunited demonstrated the uniqueness of the United States.

The cost of that speedy reconciliation is all too clear today. Reconstruction's promise of equal civil and political rights was either forgotten or denigrated. Despite guarantees by those like Lamar, African Americans were treated at best as second-class citizens, usually much worse. The record of Field's New England family confirms that cost. Field's brother Stephen was a Supreme Court justice who frequently undercut Reconstruction measures. His brother David Dudley defended white supremacists in the infamous Supreme Court case *US v. Cruikshank* (1876), which ruled unconstitutional most of the act designed to combat the Ku Klux Klan. There were no southerners on that court. In 1890, Henry defended the South by pointing out that there was a color line in New England as well. Justifying white people's desire not to share social space such as railroad cars with Black people, he anticipated the logic of the court in *Plessy v. Ferguson* (1896), writing that "Social intercourse cannot be regulated by law; it must be left to those natural attractions and affinities which the Almighty has planted in our breasts.... This is a matter of instinct, which is often wiser than reason. We cannot fight against instinct, nor legislate against it; if we do, we shall find it stronger than our resolutions and our laws." The just solution, he wrote, was separate but equal: "If there be on the part of whites an unwillingness to occupy the same cars and to sit in the same seats with blacks, let them be separate, only let equally good cars be provided for both, if both pay for them."[52]

When Field claimed that the period's monuments are the proud possession of us all, he clearly leaves out Black people. When Adams argued that a monument to Lee would be educational because of his acceptance of defeat, he does not acknowledge that Lee advocated restoration of the Union, not its reconstruction. When Lamar marveled at the "magnitude" of northerners and southerners uniting to overcome the "odious injustice" of Reconstruction, he distorted the consequences for African Americans. All three, in other words, confirm Blight's argument that celebrations of reconciliation too often promoted racial injustice, which is why the monument controversy needs to be understood in the context of the failure to fulfill the racially egalitarian ideals of Reconstruction. To portray the monument controversy as refighting the Civil War is to place responsibility for racial injustice solely on the South. To link it to the retreat from Reconstruction is to stress the responsibility of the nation.

Nonetheless, as important as it is to recall that many of today's controversial monuments were constructed in the spirit of reconciliation, history did not stand still. The monuments took on new significance as time moved forward. The process by which they transformed from objects dedicated to national reconciliation into objects fostering new divisions is also part of their history. The next—and final—section starts by examining that transformation. It ends by speculating on what the imperative to do justice to the past in the monument controversy tells us about the nation's continued failure to achieve racial justice.

## JUSTICE TO THE PAST AND RACIAL JUSTICE

How people viewed monuments changed as the myth of the Lost Cause changed. A component part of the myth is a self-righteous sense of loss. Pollard exploited that sense of loss to argue for reconciliation and regain what had been lost to Radical Reconstruction. Once that goal was achieved, however, Pollard's version lost much of its force, which is one reason it is so misunderstood today. Increasingly, monuments dedicated in celebration of intersectional unity began to be seen through the lens of versions of the myth that stressed an ongoing threat of loss. For those who still believe in the myth today, the call for removal powerfully confirms that threat. The Calhoun monument is ideally suited to trace this transformation, since the monument Lamar dedicated is not even the one recently removed.

Lamar's dedication, it turns out, did not match the symbolism of the monument unveiled. In choosing the northern sculptor Harnisch, the women of Charleston hoped to stress sectional reconciliation. But Harnisch did not get the message. From distant Italy, he assumed what white southerners would want and depicted Calhoun representing South Carolina in the Senate as a spokesman for the South. His model was a monument to Camillo di Cavour in Milan. According to Brown, Calhoun and Cavour were both "aristocrats, intellectuals, statesmen. As Cavour had expanded the small kingdom of Piedmont into a unified Italy, Calhoun's defense of South Carolina's sovereignty provided the foundation of the Confederacy."[53] Discontent with Harnisch's design increased because the statue he delivered was missing some parts. Another reason for dissatisfaction was the short column, which made the figure of Calhoun vulnerable to mockery and vandalism, especially by African Americans. To remedy these problems, a new monument was commissioned with explicit instructions to have a more imposing column. The designer was New York sculptor J. Massey Rhind, who was working on decorations for the Grant monument in his hometown, including a bas-relief surrounding Grant's "Let us have peace" as a symbol of intersectional harmony.[54] The new monument with Calhoun having a commanding view over the surroundings was unceremoniously put in place in June 1896. Its installation coincided with a major change in South Carolina politics, which altered the significance of the Calhoun monument while producing monuments that are also objects of controversy today.

Paying homage to the planter class in his dedication, Lamar heaped praise on Wade Hampton, one of the wealthiest plantation owners in the antebellum South. Lamar especially stressed Hampton's role in redeeming South Carolina. Running for governor in 1876 against the carpetbagger incumbent, Hampton won a disputed election, signaling a return to home rule. A decade later, however, Ben Tillman challenged the dominance of Hampton and his planter class in South Carolina politics. Representing poor white people, Tillman promoted a populist message stressing class division. He mobilized support through virulent racism that attacked the paternalistic elite for reconciling itself to the forms, if not substance, of Black citizenship. In his 1876 run for governor, Hampton had the support of a number of African Americans, including Martin Delany. In contrast, Tillman participated in the massacre of Black militiamen in revenge for their allegedly making white people get out of the way while parading in Hamburg, South Carolina, on the day of the national centennial. Proud of his role, later in life Tillman boasted, "[W]e had to shoot negroes to get relief from the galling tyranny to which we had been subjected."[55] It was "Pitchfork" Ben who brought about the disenfranchisement of freedmen. Although Tillman did not influence the design of the 1896 monument, its commanding view made it more suitable to his program of racial domination than Lamar's 1887 promotion of paternalistic protection.

Tillman's version of the Lost Cause was fabricated even more than most. He portrayed himself as the champion of poor white people. Having sacrificed the most during the war for a planter class that looked down on them, these hardworking laborers had to fend for themselves after the war while planters helped their formerly enslaved people. In fact, Tillman was from the planter class. His most enduring legacy has a direct link to Calhoun. Part of his campaign against Hampton was to establish an agricultural college to give laboring white people an opportunity for higher education in competition with the University of South Carolina, which was attended by the sons of planters and open to Black people during Reconstruction. The plan was realized when Thomas Green Clemson, Calhoun's son-in-law, died and willed his plantation and $60,000 to establish what is now Clemson University.[56] Tillman's role in establishing Clemson in 1889 has caused even some skeptics grudgingly to admit that he did some good. Stephen Kantorowitz, Tillman's most recent biographer, disagrees. Today's integrated Clemson is the opposite of what Tillman stood for. Rhondda Robinson Thomas writes: "People struggling to make a new world from the ashes of Confederate defeat needed a better friend than Ben Tillman. His 'love' for his 'common people' was mixed with disdain and always limited by his fear of offering Black Americans the opportunity to pursue their own visions."[57] Tillman used poor white people for political advancement. One of the long-term consequences of his success was to reinforce the stereotype of "rednecks" as the most extreme racists. Yet the image of him as the defender of disadvantaged white people persisted. His statue erected in 1940 on the grounds of the statehouse in Columbia, South Carolina, was inscribed, as Thomas notes, with "the friend and leader of the common people" who had "taught them their political power." Protests advocating removal of Tillman's statue intensify as I write.

Tillman's statue contrasts with Hampton's, erected in 1906. "Pitchfork" Ben is portrayed in plain clothes, a man of the people, while Hampton is portrayed in a classic equestrian pose. But although Hampton, unlike the younger Tillman, had fought in the war, he is not represented as the Confederate general he had been. Instead, he is depicted in his campaign for governor in 1876. As reported at the unveiling of his statue, he was honored for his role as the "chieftain of Carolinians when the prostrate South was given the spirit to arise and stand."[58] This account of Hampton as South Carolina's redeemer is more militant than Lamar's two decades earlier. Challenged by Tillman, Hampton's supporters felt the need to appropriate some of the populist's rhetoric. In the process, the spirit of sectional reconciliation was replaced by one of sectional defiance. At the 1896 Democratic convention that nominated William Jennings Bryan, Tillman shouted, "I come from the South, from the home of secession" and insisted that the issues of the election were sectional.[59] Republicans used Tillman to depict Democrats as threatening to divide the nation as they had in 1861—this time over class, not slavery.[60]

As Brown notes, "Confederate commemoration created a cultural infrastructure that in some ways became more rather than less strident."[61] With developments in the New Deal and the civil rights movement threatening the world of legalized segregation, a militant myth of the Lost Cause arose to combat perceived threats of federal interference. In 1938, Senator Ellison "Cotton Ed" Smith was challenged in the primary by Governor Olin D. Johnston, a supporter of the New Deal. Smith charged that Johnston was opening the door for too much federal control in the state. In his victory speech, Smith addressed a crowd wearing red shirts associated with Hampton's supporters in 1876, saying, "We conquered in '76 and we conquered in '38. . . . Boys the symbol you see tonight is the symbol we hurled to the world after the Confederate War between the States when negroes and carpetbaggers got control of the state government." Hampton "did not agree that our civilization should be threatened by federal bayonets"; condemning President Franklin D. Roosevelt's campaign for Johnston, he warned: "No man dares come into South Carolina and try to dictate to the sons of those men who held high the hands of Lee and Hampton."[62] In Smith's timeless, unified South Carolina, the class divisions between Hampton and Tillman disappear. Although Smith cites Hampton, his defiant tone comes closer to Tillman than to the redeeming governor who, at least on the surface, advocated harmonious sectional reconciliation. "Cotton Ed," however, identified with Hampton's planter class, and he wanted nothing to do with Tillman's use of the government to help the poor. Indeed, at the unveiling of Tillman's monument, a former protégé called him "the state's first 'New Dealer.'"[63]

If the white South was divided over the New Deal, it was united in opposing interference to promote civil rights. With President Harry S. Truman's integration of the military, Dixiecrats broke with the Democratic Party in the 1948 election. South Carolina's Strom Thurmond, representing the Dixiecrats, won thirty-nine electoral votes. In his campaign, he "cast himself as a modern-day Red-Shirt ready to defend the South against a repeat of Reconstruction."[64] Nonetheless, despite waving the Stars and Bars in his campaign, Thurmond was as patriotic as Lamar's imagined Calhoun. He served under the Stars and Stripes with honor in World War II, receiving numerous medals and decorations. Indeed, advocates of the Lost Cause frequently championed national unity. D. W. Griffith's *The Birth of a Nation* (1915) is called a cinematic monument to the Lost Cause. It is not, however, an endorsement of secession. The final image on the screen is the line from Webster that Lamar echoed in his praise of Calhoun's patriotism: "Liberty and Union now and forever, one and inseparable."[65] What most white southerners could not abide was federal interference to protect Black rights.

In almost all versions of the myth of the Lost Cause, Reconstruction plays a major role. The myth was born as a self-conscious strategy to turn acceptance of defeat into a victory over Radical Reconstruction. Once that victory was won, it was mobilized to warn against a return to what even Kennedy called the South's "black nightmare."[66] For white South Carolinians of Thurmond's generation and later, the Calhoun monument was a reminder of how northern meddling could destroy the harmony brought about by the abandonment of Reconstruction. At the centennial celebration of the firing on Fort Sumter, Thurmond proclaimed, "Calhoun believed that local problems required local solutions because local people knew how to handle local problems."[67]

Few have been more effective than Blight in linking the cause of racial justice with the need to do justice to the past by combatting the myth of the Lost Cause. He acknowledges that efforts to bring about sectional reconciliation stem from "a noble and essential human impulse."[68] But the negative consequences for African Americans undermined even the best intentions. "The tragedy of Reconstruction," he writes, "is rooted in this American paradox. The imperative of healing and the imperative of justice could not, ultimately, cohabit the same house."[69] Nonetheless, the eloquent balance of Blight's formulation does not do full justice to the past. There was not—and is not—only one sense of justice and one sense of healing. In his dedication, Lamar stressed Calhoun's love of justice. Poems written for the occasion did the same. The base of Harnisch's design had four allegorical figures: History, Truth, the Constitution, and Justice. At the same time, most advocates of Radical Reconstruction were not opposed to healing. Although some waving the bloody shirt were unforgiving, many did not object to reintegrating most former Confederates into the national community. Homer Plessy's attorney, Albion W. Tourgée, and Charles W. Chesnutt portray numerous ex-Confederate soldiers in their fiction. Tourgée's *Bricks without Straw* (1880) and Chesnutt's *The Colonel's Dream* (1905) both have them as protagonists. What matters is not their actions during the war, but their willingness to support Black people once it was over. In contrast, in *The Birth of a Nation*, Phil Stoneman fought for the North and Ben Cameron for the South, but both are heroes because they oppose Reconstruction.

Healing and justice need not be mutually exclusive. There can be justice in efforts to heal, and healing can arise from just outcomes. What matters is how justice is defined. Thomas Dixon Jr.'s sense of justice is easy to distinguish from Tourgée's and Chesnutt's. But most promoting reconciliation in the postbellum period had a sense of justice in between. To understand why the nation supported reconciliation, we need to assess how those like Pollard, Lamar, Field, and Adams weighed the imperatives of healing and justice. Feeling that other measures of justice were more important than racial equality, they sincerely believed that reconciliation was serving racial justice. Historical hindsight makes it clear how mistaken that view was. One reason to do justice to the past is to learn from such mistakes. Without understanding the past in all of its complexity, it is impossible to understand racial injustice today. Unfortunately, however, accurately reporting the past is no guarantee that racial justice will be achieved today. Wrongs, after all, are easier to identify than remedies. If it is clear what was unjust, it is still not clear how to bring about justice, which is why Walter Benjamin proposed a different way of doing justice to the past. It is tempting to judge the past according to present standards. Until we have realized full justice ourselves, however, Benjamin urged that we abandon the seat of judgment and use past injustices to pose challenges to the present. For instance, rather than feel superior to the past, we need to acknowledge that the conflict between competing notions of justice is still with us.[70]

As the monument controversy shows, the nation remains divided on what racial justice and its relation to the past entail. Indeed, the controversy has created new divisions between some who otherwise agree on racial injustice. I have stressed the irony that some of the monuments generating those new divisions were erected during a time intended to heal. Lamar depicts a Calhoun who would have been willing to accept the end of slavery and patriotically embrace the Union emerging from the Confederate defeat. Northerners were willing to keep that Calhoun in their pantheon of honored statesmen. That effort at healing, we can see today, was misguided and premature. There is no reason why anyone today should buy into the myth Lamar spun at the dedication, especially because it was not even for the monument recently removed. At the same time, it is hard to imagine racial justice being realized without the nation at some time healing its divisions. Those in the past who, in Milton's phrase, "not willfully misdoing" perpetuated injustice in the pursuit of healing pose this question to us in the present. Is hope of reconciliation as a way of completing, not defeating, Radical Reconstruction, the new Lost Cause of the nation?

## NOTES

1. Gary W. Gallagher, "Introduction," in *The Myth of the Lost Cause and Civil War History*, ed. Gary W. Gallagher and Alan T. Nolan (Bloomington: Indiana University Press, 2000), 1.

2. For one of many examples, see Vimal Patel, "Chapel Hill's New Civil War," *Chronicle of Higher Education*, December 18, 2017.

3. LeeAnn Whites, "You Can't Change History by Moving a Rock: Gender, Race, and the Cultural Politics of Confederate Memorialization," in *The Memory of the Civil War in American Culture*, ed. Alice Fahs and Joan Waugh (Chapel Hill: University of North Carolina Press, 2004), 230.

4. Hans Robert Jauss, *Toward an Aesthetic of Reception* (Minneapolis: University of Minnesota Press, 1982).

5. According to Jack P. Maddex Jr., "Pollard and his intellectual biography have remained curiously unknown to historians quite familiar with his name." Maddex suggests, "Most have supposed that he stood by a single set of ideas through his adult life." Maddex, *The Reconstruction of Edward A. Pollard: A Rebel's Conversion to Postbellum Unionism* (Chapel Hill: University of North Carolina Press, 1974), 1, 8.

6. Edward A. Pollard, *The Lost Cause: A New Southern History of the War of the Confederates* (New York: E. B. Treat, 1866), 48.

7. Denigration of Ulysses S. Grant went along with celebration of Robert E. Lee. According to Brooks D. Simpson, "Perhaps the first book that set forth the Confederate case against the generalship of Ulysses S. Grant was Edward A. Pollard's *The Lost Cause*." Simpson, "Continuous Hammering and Mere Attrition: Lost Cause Critics and the Military Reputation of Ulysses S. Grant," in Gallagher and Nolan, *Myth of the Lost Cause*, 148.

8. Pollard, *Lost Cause*, 652.

9. Pollard, *Lost Cause*, 729.

10. Pollard, *Lost Cause*, 742–43.

11. Edward A. Pollard, *Life of Jefferson Davis, with a Secret History of the Southern Confederacy Gathered "Behind the Scenes" at Richmond* (Philadelphia: National Publishing Company, 1869), 104.

12. Pollard, *Lost Cause*, 752.

13. Pollard, *Lost Cause*, 748.

14. Pollard, *Lost Cause*, 728.

15. Pollard, *Life of Jefferson Davis*, 70. David W. Blight acknowledges Pollard's strategy of reconciliation but fails to distinguish him from Jefferson Davis, who, Blight claims, "helped give the Lost Cause its lifeblood." Blight, *Race and Reunion: The Civil War in American Memory* (Cambridge, MA: Harvard University Press, 2001), 260.

16. Edward A. Pollard, *The Lost Cause Regained* (New York: G. W. Carleton, 1868), 211.

17. Pollard, *Lost Cause Regained*, 5.

18. Edward A. Pollard, "The Story of a Hero," *Galaxy* 6 (November 1868): 598–605.

19. Edward A. Pollard, "The Romance of the Negro," *Galaxy* 12 (October 1871): 470.

20. Pollard, "Romance of the Negro," 478.

21. Pollard, *Lost Cause Regained*, 152–53.

22. Edward A. Pollard quoted in Maddex, *Reconstruction of Edward A. Pollard*, 478.

23. Edward A. Pollard, "The Anti-Slavery Men of the South," *Galaxy* 16 (September 1873): 330.

24. Pollard, "Anti-Slavery Men," 341.

25. Thomas J. Brown, *Civil War Canon: Sites of Confederate Memory in South Carolina* (Chapel Hill: University of North Carolina Press, 2015), 63.

26. Thomas J. Brown, "The Monumental Legacy of Calhoun," in Fahs and Waugh, *Memory of the Civil War*, 149.

27. Brown, *Civil War Canon*, 38.

28. John F. Kennedy, *Profiles in Courage: Inaugural Edition* (New York: Harper and Brothers, 1961), 154.

29. Joel Chandler Harris, *Joel Chandler Harris: Editor and Essayist*, ed. Julia Collier Harris (Boston: Houghton Mifflin, 1918), 73.

30. L. Q. C. Lamar, "Oration of the Hon. L. Q. C. Lamar," in *A History of the Calhoun Monument at Charleston, S.C.* (Charleston: Lucas, Richardson, 1888), 64.

31. Lamar, "Oration," 70.

32. Lamar, "Oration," 79.

33. Lamar, "Oration," 84.

34. Daniel Webster, *The Papers of Daniel Webster: Speeches and Formal Writings, v. 1. 1800–1833*, ed. Charles M. Wiltse and Alan R. Berolzheimer (Dartmouth, NH: Dartmouth University Press, 1986), 348.

35. Lamar, "Oration," 86.

36. Lamar, "Oration," 88.

37. Lamar, "Oration," 92.

38. Lamar, "Oration," 102–3.

39. Lamar, "Oration," 64.

40. Lamar, "Oration," 104.

41. Lamar, "Oration," 72.

42. Lamar, "Oration," 94–95.

43. Dudley H. Miles, "The Civil War as Unifier," *Sewanee Review* 21 (1913): 188–97.

44. Lamar, "Oration," 71.

45. Thomas J. Brown, *The Public Art of Civil War Commemoration: A Brief History with Documents* (Boston: Bedford, 2004), 10.

46. Brown, *Public Art*, 21.

47. Pollard, *Lost Cause*, 43.

48. *A History of the Calhoun Monument at Charleston, S.C.* (Charleston: Lucas, Richardson, 1888), 153.

49. *History of the Calhoun Monument*, 128.

50. Henry M. Field, *The Life of David Dudley Field* (New York: Scribner's, 1898), 180.

51. Charles Francis Adams Jr., *Lee at Appomattox and Other Papers* (Boston: Houghton Mifflin, 1902), 429.

52. Henry M. Field, "Capacity of the Negro—His Position in the North, the Color Line in New England," in *Plessy v. Ferguson: A Brief History with Documents*, ed. Brook Thomas (Boston: Bedford, 1997), 118–19.

53. Brown, *Civil War Canon*, 81.

54. Joan Waugh, *U. S. Grant: American Hero, American Myth* (Chapel Hill: University of North Carolina Press, 2009), 297.

55. Stephen Kantorowitz, *Ben Tillman and the Reconstruction of White Supremacy* (Chapel Hill: University of North Carolina Press, 2009), 261.

56. On Clemson University as a site for Confederate memorials, see Rhondda Robinson Thomas, "Reconstruction, Public Memory, and the Making of Clemson University on John C. Calhoun's Fort Hill Plantation," *American Literary History* 30, no. 3 (Fall 2018): 584–607.

57. Thomas, "Reconstruction," 307.

58. Brown, *Civil War Canon*, 160.

59. Kantorowitz, *Ben Tillman*, 251.

60. On the 1896 election, see Patrick J. Kelly, "The Election of 1896 and the Restructuring of Civil War Memory," in Fahs and Waugh, *Memory of the Civil War*, 180–212.

61. Brown, *Public Art*, 11.

62. Ellison Smith quoted in Charles J. Holden, "'Is Our Love for Wade Hampton Foolishness?' South Carolina and the Lost Cause," in Gallagher and Nolan, *Myth of the Lost Cause*, 80.

63. Kantorowitz, *Ben Tillman*, 307.

64. Bruce E. Baker, *What Reconstruction Meant: Historical Memory in the American South* (Charlottesville: University of Virginia Press, 2007), 140. Baker provides the best account of South Carolina's response to the New Deal; see 89–109.

65. Webster, *Papers*, 348.

66. Kennedy, *Profiles in Courage*, 153.

67. Brown, *Civil War Canon*, 193.

68. Blight, *Race and Reunion*, 387.

69. Blight, *Race and Reunion*, 57.

70. Walter Benjamin, "Theses on the Philosophy of History," in *Illuminations* (New York: Schocken, 1969), 253–64.

# Bibliography

Adams, Charles Francis, Jr. *Lee at Appomattox and Other Papers*. Boston: Houghton Mifflin, 1902.

Benjamin, Walter. "Theses on the Philosophy of History." In *Illuminations*, 253–64. New York: Schocken, 1969.

Brown, Thomas J. *Civil War Canon: Sites of Confederate Memory in South Carolina*. Chapel Hill: University of North Carolina Press, 2015.

Brown, Thomas J. "The Monumental Legacy of Calhoun." In *The Memory of the Civil War in American Culture*, edited by Alice Fahs and Joan Waugh, 130–56. Chapel Hill: University of North Carolina Press, 2004.

Brown, Thomas J. *The Public Art of Civil War Commemoration: A Brief History with Documents*. Boston: Bedford, 2004.

Field, Henry M. "Capacity of the Negro—His Position in the North, the Color Line in New England." In *Plessy v. Ferguson: A Brief History with Documents*, edited by Brook Thomas, 101–19. Boston: Bedford, 1997.

Field, Henry M. *The Life of David Dudley Field*. New York: Scribner's, 1898.

Gallagher, Gary W. "Introduction." In *The Myth of the Lost Cause and Civil War History*, edited by Gary W. Gallagher and Alan T. Nolan, 1–10. Bloomington: Indiana University Press, 2000.

Harris, Joel Chandler. *Joel Chandler Harris: Editor and Essayist*, edited by Julia Collier Harris. Boston: Houghton Mifflin, 1918.

*A History of the Calhoun Monument at Charleston, S.C.* Charleston: Lucas, Richardson, 1888.

Holden, Charles J. "'Is Our Love for Wade Hampton Foolishness?': South Carolina and the Lost Cause." In *The Myth of the Lost Cause and Civil War History*, edited by Gary W. Gallagher and Alan T. Nolan, 60–88. Bloomington: Indiana University Press, 2000.

Jauss, Hans Robert. *Toward an Aesthetic of Reception*. Minneapolis: University of Minnesota Press, 1982.

Kantorowitz, Stephen. *Ben Tillman and the Reconstruction of White Supremacy*. Chapel Hill: University of North Carolina Press, 2009.

Kelly, Patrick J. "The Election of 1896 and the Restructuring of Civil War Memory." In *The Memory of the Civil War in American Culture*, edited by Alice Fahs and Joan Waugh, 180–212. Chapel Hill: University of North Carolina Press, 2004.

Kennedy, John F. *Profiles in Courage: Inaugural Edition*. New York: Harper and Brothers, 1961.

Lamar, L. Q. C. "Oration of the Hon. L. Q. C. Lamar." In *A History of the Calhoun Monument at Charleston, S.C.*, 63–107. Charleston: Lucas, Richardson, 1888.

Maddex, Jack P., Jr. *The Reconstruction of Edward A. Pollard: A Rebel's Conversion to Postbellum Unionism*. Chapel Hill: University of North Carolina Press, 1974.

Miles, Dudley H. "The Civil War as Unifier." *Sewanee Review* 21 (1913): 188–97.

Patel, Vimal. "Chapel Hill's New Civil War." *Chronicle of Higher Education*, December 18, 2017.

Pollard, Edward A. "The Anti-Slavery Men of the South." *Galaxy* 16 (September 1873): 329–41.

Pollard, Edward A. *Life of Jefferson Davis, with a Secret History of the Southern Confederacy Gathered "Behind the Scenes" at Richmond*. Philadelphia: National Publishing Company, 1869.

Pollard, Edward A. *The Lost Cause: A New Southern History of the War of the Confederates*. New York: E. B. Treat, 1866.

Pollard, Edward A. *The Lost Cause Regained*. New York: G. W. Carleton, 1868.

Pollard, Edward A. "The Romance of the Negro." *Galaxy* 12 (October 1871): 470–78.

Pollard, Edward A. "The Story of a Hero." *Galaxy* 6, no. 5 (November 1868): 598–605.

Simpson, Brooks D. "Continuous Hammering and Mere Attrition: Lost Cause Critics and the Military Reputation of Ulysses S. Grant." In *The Myth of the Lost Cause and Civil War History*, edited by Gary W. Gallagher and Alan T. Nolan, 147–69. Bloomington: Indiana University Press, 2000.

Thomas, Rhondda Robinson. "Reconstruction, Public Memory, and the Making of Clemson University on John C. Calhoun's Fort Hill Plantation." *American Literary History* 30, no. 3 (Fall 2018): 584–607.

Waugh, Joan. *U. S. Grant: American Hero, American Myth*. Chapel Hill: University of North Carolina Press, 2009.

Webster, Daniel. *The Papers of Daniel Webster: Speeches and Formal Writings, v. 1. 1800–1833*, edited by Charles M. Wiltse and Alan R. Berolzheimer. Dartmouth, NH: Dartmouth University Press, 1986.

Whites, LeeAnn. "You Can't Change History by Moving a Rock: Gender, Race, and the Cultural Politics of Confederate Memorialization." In *The Memory of the Civil War in American Culture*, edited by Alice Fahs and Joan Waugh, 213–36. Chapel Hill: University of North Carolina Press, 2004.

# CHAPTER 2

# PRINT CULTURE AND THE ENDURING LEGACY OF CONFEDERATE WAR MONUMENTS

—Michael C. Weisenburg

Debates surrounding the legitimacy of Confederate monuments and concerns that the South's Lost Cause ideology have come to dominate the national consciousness are by no means new or unique to our current historical-political moment. On December 11, 1912, Brevet Brigadier-General Thomas H. Hubbard addressed an assembly of the "Loyal Legion" at Delmonico's in New York in terms that can only be described as appalled and exasperated. The source of Hubbard's consternation was the advent of national sympathy for the Confederacy in the historical imagination. Hubbard, who served as a colonel for the Union during the Civil War, opens his remarks by remembering an occurrence in the late 1860s in which a speaker was yelled off stage for speculating that there would come a day when the nation shall "speak the praise of Lee and of Stonewall Jackson."[1] Hubbard next juxtaposes the public condemnation of a Confederate sympathizer during the early years of Reconstruction with two recent events of public memorialization. The first is on May 31, 1909, when Secretary of War Jacob M. Dickinson addressed the unveiling of the Gettysburg monument by saying, "At this day there are but few, if any, dispassionate thinkers in the North who question the patriotism of those of the South who on this stricken field gave an example of American valor that will forever fill the minds and hearts of mankind in all countries and in all ages." Dickinson's perverse echoing of Abraham Lincoln's Gettysburg Address, which undermines the Union's cause and raises traitors of the Confederacy to the level of patriots, is anathema to Hubbard. That Dickinson usurps the conscience of the Union, or rather "the North," and ventriloquizes that northerners accede to the fundamentally American, patriotic valor of the South, or rather "the Confederacy," labors to change the hearts and minds of a new generation of Americans, a generation that is capable of seeing the Confederate generals as heroes. Hubbard is further shocked and appalled to read in a "respected New York Magazine" that the "War Secretary has helped memorably to complete the work of reconciliation of the section that met in conflict on that battlefield." In the summer of 1909, reconciliation had come to mean concession to the memory of the Confederacy—the only way to maintain peace within the Union was to let the South have the final word. This peace, as a matter of course, was a peace among white men, and the political advantages of the North's cultural concession to and proliferation of a white supremacist agenda revealed the moral cost of closing the rift between the two regions.

Hubbard's second example occurred not quite a month before his own speech, when, in November 1912, President William Howard Taft addressed the United Daughters of the Confederacy as they laid the cornerstone for a monument to the Confederate dead at Arlington. That the president of the United States would encourage a hopeful memory of the Confederacy was utterly mind-boggling to Hubbard. It was no less than the total abandonment of the Union and the Constitution that he had fought to maintain and an affront to the nation's Black population that he had helped to free and whose rights he strove to defend. Hubbard then goes on for about ten pages of ironic, rhetorical questions that seem so increasingly absurd that they could not possibly admit credence. "Should the cause whose purpose was to destroy the nation be commemorated or honored by the nation?" he asks; and "Should the nation commemorate by monuments, or statues, or in any way indicating its approval, the attempt to perpetuate slavery?"[2] And yet, at the moment of his address, Confederate monuments were being erected at an unprecedented rate. Hubbard concluded by cautioning that "Monuments have a meaning and transmit a message," and that "if monuments are to perpetuate the memory of failure and deserved defeat some new device must be found to perpetuate the memory of honorable achievement."[3] While Hubbard recognized the threat that Confederate memory posed to the nation, his closing remarks betray a lack of understanding regarding the manner by which such subversive ideas and the monuments that represent them so successfully spread through the formerly rebellious states. Furthermore, recent history has revealed that, over the course of the twentieth century, no effective response was offered to rebuke the racist appeal of these monuments and their remediation of the nation's history of slavery, the Civil War, Reconstruction, and Jim Crow and to make the Union safe and equitable for all of its citizens.

Hubbard's remarks on Confederate memorialization and their entry into and circulation through the print public sphere remind us that shock and confusion over the ongoing role played by Confederate memory in US life have been a subject of debate for well over a century. Whereas Hubbard tacitly asked his audience the question "How did we get here?," we now, in the twenty-first century, seem to be asking ourselves "Why are we still here?" The answer appears to be a complicated one, involving a confluence of economic, political, and ideological forces that have been perpetuated and maintained by a retinue of genres and media. The ambiguity of national allegiance versus regional pride has its origins in an earlier filial-Confederate backlash that immediately succeeded Reconstruction, and then, as now, there was an equally confused and bewildered federalist reaction to the pervasive cultural strength of Confederate memory in the US cultural imagination.

This essay seeks to illustrate the rise and spread of Confederate monuments at the local level by focusing on how they were promoted and disseminated in print. It also works to show how the lasting effects of this cultural work influence our own historical moment and, as such, it makes a transhistorical argument for how the myths and values of the Confederacy have endured the twentieth century and have uncannily come to dominate the twenty-first. By attending to the production and circulation of ephemeral print, which was produced by small, local publishers and distributed regionally, we gain a more nuanced understanding of how the communities who produced these monuments adapted residual and emergent communication networks and technologies to engender enthusiasm for these monuments as well as how they appropriated pre-existing cultural norms and mythologies in order to normalize and perpetuate a revised system of white supremacy.

## REGIONAL PRINT CULTURE AND THE PROMOTION OF MONUMENTS

Perhaps the most readily available and yet least studied body of documents regarding Confederate monuments are the printed items that were intended to propose the construction of and disseminate information about the various statues, plaques, and museums that memorialize and venerate the Confederacy and the southern Lost Cause ideology. The printing of circulars, broadsides, newspaper reports, tourism and guidebooks, and artistic and architectural histories that blend historical fact with legend and hero worship constitutes a genre of writing that is ripe for literary analysis. These oft-overlooked printed objects contain the rhetoric and ideals of the people employed to generate support for their production, and they reveal metaphors and symbols the initial audience used to describe the monuments, thus affording us a more nuanced analysis of the historical context of their inception. These ephemeral print representations of Confederate memorialization are marked by a variety of rhetorical effects such as hyperbole and ekphrasis and are often remediated and selectively contextualized through the process of scrapbooking and amateur antiquarian history. Additionally, the advertisements and industry trade publications for the construction and dissemination of Confederate war monuments illustrate a concerted effort from the supply side to maintain interest in Confederate history and local tradition that aided in instigating later generations to continue the process of memorialization, which thereby unmoored the events of the Civil War from their temporal bounds and allowed emotional affiliation with the Confederacy to become a transhistorical phenomenon. Furthermore, the emergence of the new medium of the postcard was coincidental with the proliferation of Confederate monuments and allowed the monuments to be disseminated across space and, through the agency of the post office, to come to synecdochally represent the South in national iconography. In contextualizing newspaper reports on the dedications of some of the early monuments as exemplifying the emergence of Lost Cause ideology in the print public sphere, we are better able to consider how these print histories influence our own historical moment by comparing the South Carolina State House grounds and the institutionalization of Confederate statehood with the campus of the University of South Carolina and the mythology of the plantation idyll. Monuments that embody the ideology of the Confederacy in the modern era, such as the statue of former Senator Strom Thurmond, valorize the Lost Cause and make modern-day Confederate heroes of conservative ideologues. Additionally, more recent movements toward equality and recontextualization often work to give equal credence to both the legacy of Black suffering and the suffering scripted by Lost Cause ideology, which has effectively transformed the university's historic campus, known as the Horseshoe, into a space of antebellum nostalgia. Attending to the various elements that underwrite the monuments reveals the perpetual work involved in reinforcing the Lost Cause as a means of defending the monuments and perpetuating the racist ideology they represent.

Invoking Eric Foner's assessment of the United States' "unfinished revolution," Brook Thomas argues elsewhere in this collection that the monument controversy is not so much about the Civil War as it is about Reconstruction and the South's Lost Cause. Essential to understanding these monuments, the Lost Cause was and remains a central tenet of white culture in the South, and ignoring it, Thomas contends, divorces us from the national responsibility of retreating from the Civil War. A product of Reconstruction, the Lost Cause functions as a means to maintain white supremacy by vindicating a defeated people, valorizing their soldiers, and sanctifying a mythology of the home front. Charles Reagan Wilson has referred to the Lost Cause as the civil religion of the South, and C. Vann Woodward has described it as a cult founded in racism.[4] Gary W. Gallagher and Rollin G. Osterweis have each defined it as a myth,[5] whereas Gaines M. Foster has argued that the Lost Cause is the fundamental tradition of the South and "had not just a temporary cultural importance but served as a permanent basis of social identity."[6] For all of the attention paid to the South's reinterpretation of the Civil War and Reconstruction, recent scholars

such as Karen L. Cox have persuasively argued that, overall, "historians have
. . . underestimated the long-term significance of the Lost Cause for the South"
and that it functioned as a validation of the Confederacy and was "particularly
useful for sustaining white southerners during Reconstruction."[7] Products of
such a strong and pervasive ideological force, Confederate monuments have not
only shaped the landscape of the South but the hearts and minds of those who
dwell there. However, being material objects, they have clearly identifiable origins that can be located in the historical record, and these documents can shed
light on both the motivations of those who advocated for their erection as well
as contextualize the aesthetic and political milieu in which they were initially
received. Doing so allows us to recover the means by which these monuments
were produced as well as the methods by which they were publicized, thereby
further contextualizing both what the original producers had in mind and how
their message has evolved over time.

  While the Lost Cause permeated the culture and manifested itself across a
variety of genres and media, it was initially associated with southern monuments through the celebrations of Confederate Memorial Day, which included
the decoration of cemeteries in memory of the dead. This practice led to the
erection of monuments for fallen Confederate soldiers in cemeteries, a practice that steadily spread throughout Reconstruction. A promotional broadside
for Memorial Day celebrations hosted by the Ladies' Memorial Association
of Charleston, South Carolina, printed by the News and Courier Job Presses,
offers a glimpse into such proceedings (see Figure 2.1). In addition to the
decoration of graves, public prayers, addresses, and odes were delivered and
recited, mimicking the days of public worship in the colonial period and collegiate celebrations in the antebellum period. In situating these activities within
recognizable social constructs that have their own preestablished traditions,
celebrations of the Confederacy were grafted onto recognizable civic behavior.
That the local newspaper offices printed broadsides in advance of the event
registers both a desire to promote and commemorate the event of memorialization and ties these rituals to the regional print public sphere of the South
and its associate economies.

  These types of ephemeral print documents also had corollary material
printed in newspapers and magazines. Many newspaper editors, such as those
at the Charleston *News and Courier*, the Columbia *Phoenix*, the Manning *Herald*, and the *Yorkville Enquirer*, were closely aligned with local booster organizations such as the Ladies' Memorial Association and the United Daughters of the
Confederacy as well as local quarries and monument sculptors. Additionally,
many state and federal politicians actively helped to secure the funds necessary
to build the monuments. Editors' involvement with both politicians and local
quarries and monument dealers reveals how necessary print was in encouraging

# MEMORIAL DAY,

## MAY 10th, 1875,

## AT MAGNOLIA CEMETERY,

### UNDER THE AUSPICES OF THE

## Ladies Memorial Association,

### CHARLESTON, S. C.

## PRAYER, BY REV. W. T. CAPERS, D. D.

### MEMORIAL ODE,

*BY REV. C. S. VEDDER.*

Why wake the silent air
That canopies our Dead,
With mournful dirge and solemn prayer,
With tribute words, though sweet and rare,
And a whole city's tread?

Why, on their dreamless sleep,
Shall waking life intrude?
It's task is now to work, not weep;
It's Present, now; it's Future, reap—
Not o'er the Past to brood!

Of what avail the wreath
That circles grave and stone?
They reck it not, who sleep beneath;
Their work accomplished, they bequeath
The Lesson of our own!

They ask no sigh or tear,
Nor grateful praise, nor vow;
Our hymn falls voiceless on their ear,
Our prayer they need not God should hear,
For they are with Him now!

Why, then, with solemn rite,
Which cannot cheer their dust,
Bid Labor pause—in need's despite—
That hearts may keep their names more bright
Than storied urn or bust!

Oh, not that bitter days
May never lose their sting!
Ah, not that vengeful fires may blaze
Through all our years; o'er all our ways—
The martyred Dead we sing!

We feed no torch of Hate;
We stem no tide of Love;
We turn no stubborn heart to fate;
We bring no will unconsecrate
To Him who rules above!

We but our strength renew
For needful toil and care,
When thus, with flowers, these graves we strew,
And thus, with tears, this sod bedew,
And lift our hands in prayer.

Not for the Dead we come—
Theirs is the better part;
They need no laurels on their tomb,
But we—as they the beat of drum,
Must follow beat of Heart.

From out their voiceless rest—
With better words than speech—
They bid us meet the sorer test
Of patient Trust, at God's behest,
And ne'er our lot impeach!

They grandly fell to save;
We stand, when all is lost
But Honor! Where its signals wave,
Be we—as they were—strong and brave,
Each steadfast on his post!

Woe, woe the land betide
Where Virtue sleeps unblessed,
And where the life of those who died,
Its heroes—lives not, far and wide,
On other lives impressed.

## ADDRESS, - - - - - BY COL. B. H. RUTLEDGE.

### MEMORIAL ODE,

*BY "GRACE RAYMOND."*

Beyond the clamor of the town,
Where forests brush the city's gown,
With Heaven's sapphire calm o'erhead,
All dreamless sleep our soldier Dead.
No bugle call, no battle breath,
Profanes the holy truce of Death.

With snowy blooms and kingly grace,
The Laurel shades their resting place;
With drooping wreaths of ashen moss,
The Oak laments our nation's loss.
While Pine-born psalm, and wind-sung hymn
Whisper their only requiem.

Over each grave, in wild, sweet way,
The God-taught flowers and grasses stray;
The sunshine smiles with softer gleam,
Like one enwraps in holy dream.
While mellow stars, through midnight mild,
Keep watch above each Southern child.

To-day we throng the silent street,
With beating hearts and reverent feet;
As on some sacred shrine to lay
The glory and the wealth of May.
We deck with bloom each hero's bier,
And supplement sweet Nature's care.

Yes, twine the laurel and the bay,
The victor's palmy crown!—for they
Ye honor with this flowery rain
Have neither lived—nor died—in vain.
Does not, e'en now, their story shed
A glory round our State's bowed head?

High on the glowing page of Fame
Truth yet shall write each treasured name;
More constant yet—can aught efface
From Southern hearts that story's grace?
Hearts where the Hope for which they bled,
Lies sacred still, though crushed and dead!

Heroes of our lost cause! we may
No longer strive, in hapless way,
With our sad destiny—and God
To-day unfurls above this sod
No other flag within our view
But Heaven's glad banners of blue.

Ah, let us offer, with our tears,
At this blest shrine, the fruit of years;
Here, where all nature seems a prayer,
And Peace broods, dove-like, in the air,
Entomb our hate beside the dead,
And welcome Christly love instead.

## DECORATION OF GRAVES

### BY LADIES OF THE MEMORIAL ASSOCIATION.

The Trains will leave Magnolia, to return to the City, at half-past six, and a quarter to seven o'clock, P. M.

The News and Courier Job Presses.

Figure 2.1: "Memorial Day, May 10, 1875, at Memorial Cemetery, under the Auspices of the Ladies' Memorial Association, Charleston, S.C." Image courtesy of the South Caroliniana Library, University of South Carolina.

a protracted interest in monument production as well as disseminating news about the monuments and the celebrations that occasioned their unveiling. The steady flow of promotional material not only encouraged more monuments to be built, thereby extending the memorialization process, but the confluence between politics and economics also helped to underwrite the steady increase in monument production throughout the period, thereby ensuring that there would not only be an inflated demand for monuments but the financial means to produce them as well.

While local and regional periodical and job presses were the essential front-line of the Confederate monuments, there was also a steady growth in regional and national readerships. After 1877, associations and periodicals whose sole purpose was the promotion of Confederate Lost Cause ideology emerged, and certain regional periodicals gained a modest national status. Founded in Nashville in 1893 by Sumner A. Cunningham as a fundraising organ for the Jefferson Davis memorial, *Confederate Veteran* quickly became aligned with various organizations, such as the United Confederate Veterans and the United Daughters of the Confederacy, and steadily spread in geographic reach. Similarly, Louisville's *Lost Cause* began in 1898, and both monthlies published articles and editorials that strove to recontextualize the South's role in the Civil War and the Confederacy's place in US history. The periodicals often covered monument celebrations throughout the South and encouraged the establishment of more monuments through editorials and advertisements.

Though by no means as extensive or influential as the national print products of the Northeast, the South's print sphere was capable of focusing and solidifying its message and was able to attract the attention of regional businesses in both the North and South to generate advertisement revenue, thus entrenching a separate print community while engaging in the national economic network. At a time when staid standards like *Harper's* and *Scribner's* cost fifty cents and had circulations of around a hundred thousand and upstarts like *McClure's* and *Ladies' Home Journal* cost fifteen cents and had circulations of anywhere between forty thousand and eighty thousand, the *Confederate Veteran* cost ten cents and had a circulation of around twenty thousand.[8] While by no means a competitor with the big, bourgeois literary monthlies, the niche publication gained the attention of northern advertisers, including monument dealers (see Figure 2.2). Douglas J. Butler has pointed out that "Northern firms also sought Confederate commemorative commissions. The Monumental Bronze Company of Bridgeport, Connecticut, Manufacturers of 'Soldiers' monuments in white bronze' claimed to have erected 'over a hundred' such memorials in 'recent years, including Confederate monuments.'"[9] While the limited national scope of magazines such as the *Confederate Veteran* and the *Lost Cause* gave credence to a growing national tolerance of Lost Cause ideology and Confederate memory,

Coŋfederat̪e Ueteraŋ.      9⁹

Figure 2.2: *Confederate Veteran* 15, no. 3 (1907): 99. Image courtesy of the Thomas Cooper Library, University of South Carolina.

the communal influence of local papers ought not to be overlooked, especially when considering the fundraising activities and celebrations these statues and monuments needed.

Among the most readily available to analyze yet perhaps easiest to overlook historical items is the promotional literature produced by regional printing outfits for local quarries, masons, and monument builders. Often published in local and regional newspapers, and occasionally appearing in national magazines as well as stand-alone promotional pamphlets, these documents comprise a genre of literature that both encourages and memorializes Confederate memory while simultaneously preying upon fears of inadequacy and historical erasure. The language these companies use to drum up business often reads like a standard sales pitch that preys on fears of being left out or left behind. Most southern states have some version of a local quarry master or cemetery monument mason who sought to encourage the purchase of large-scale monuments of Confederate soldiers, and since every small town and hamlet in the South was likely to have lost some of its men during the war, these advertisements, broadsides, and pamphlets appealed to a community's feelings of loss, bereavement, and insufficiency, of being the only town or community that had yet to erect a monument to their dead and their veterans. Whereas major cities and state capitols often imported their monuments from France or Italy, smaller towns could not afford such luxury and often relied on regional artisans for their monuments. This difference highlights the regional anxieties and tensions of monument production while revealing the global scope that underwrote some of the more elaborate monuments. Two examples of the smaller regional order from South Carolina are the Southern Marble and Granite Company based in Spartanburg and L. D. Childs, a monument and headstone maker in the Piedmont region. However, it should be noted that this type of promotional literature was produced in most southern states.

The Southern Marble and Granite Company published promotional pamphlets that were distributed to regional chapters of the United Daughters of the Confederacy. Advertising that "No monument too small, none too large for us to handle," the Southern Marble and Granite Company worked closely with the United Daughters of the Confederacy, the Ladies' Memorial Association, and local schools and municipalities to raise funds for the construction of monuments. The company's pamphlet on "A Few Confederate Monuments" showcases its work for other towns in the region and acts as a "reminder to the U. D. C. chapters who have not purchased a monument to commemorate the valiant soldiers" that the company owns its own quarries and can "quote most attractive prices," and the pamphlet assures patrons that the company has a "system of raising funds without any obligation on your part to purchase from us." The pamphlet is essentially a brochure that highlights the company's best work and offers a litany of common tropes—generally obelisks and soldiers atop columns flanked by either the accoutrement of war or idealized symbols of the home front—that make up the genre of Confederate memorialization.[10]

The Southern Marble and Granite Company wasn't alone in this type of solicitous behavior. L. D. Childs, who was originally a gravestone maker, often colluded with local newspapers in the Piedmont and upcountry to bolster support for and interest in monuments. During the summer and autumn of 1891, Childs wrote a series of letters to local government officials and newspapers detailing the dimensions, materials, and estimated cost of a monument he was designing for Fort Mill, South Carolina. Communications among Childs, Spratt, Lewis M. Grist, editor of the *Yorkville Enquirer*, Senator Charles Vance, and Captain Samuel White reveal a well-planned promotional campaign in both the *Yorkville Enterprise* and the *Yorkville Enquirer*, two regional papers that were "anxious to give the unveiling of [the] monument a good notice . . . and to do it the day after it takes place."[11] Childs reports that the *Yorkville Enquirer* "wants a sketch of the monument in time to make a [wood] cut of it."[12] The correspondence among the monument builders, memorial associations, local and federal government officials, and newspapers in drumming up interest and support for the monuments and their proliferation reveals a mutually beneficial relationship among printers, architects, and politicians. The news reports printed in both papers are melodramatic puff pieces that rely on a swelling of regional pride to help increase regional sales of papers and statues alike and act as a salient reminder that, in many cases, the regional press and the local monument were mutually beneficial to local businessmen and politicians, each working to perpetuate a desire for more monuments for cultural and economic profit.

Broadsides also circulated encouraging the construction of monuments and often working to organize fundraising activities. Many of these advertised benefit shows, the proceeds of which would support local Ladies' Memorial Association and United Daughters of the Confederacy chapters, strove to make participants feel emotionally as well as financially invested in the work of erecting the monument. Often these benefits featured or functioned as minstrel shows that worked to codify power dynamics by coercing or attempting to entice a segregated Black audience to become performatively involved in the production of the monuments that would further symbolize their oppression and disenfranchisement. Some earlier broadsides even went so far as to try to include local African Americans in the fundraising activities, such as one advertisement that states "a portion of the hall reserved for colored people" (see Figure 2.3). Printed by the Columbia Phoenix Press in 1867, the broadside is an early harbinger of what will mature into a pervasive, if not systematic, element of print culture that will shape much overlooked southern ephemera for almost a century. Such early fundraising broadsides show that the culture surrounding

# JANNEY'S HALL.

### FOR THE BENEFIT OF
## THE LADIES' MEMORIAL ASSOCIATION.

THE

# Columbia Varieties

Will give another of their select entertainments on THIS
(Friday) EVENING, March 1, for the benefit of the LADIES'
MEMORIAL ASSOCIATION, and would say to the public that the
company have endeavored to get up one of the best Programmes
that they possibly could for the occasion. The Hall is in good condition, and the seats very comfortable. Reserved seats can be pro-
cured without any additional charge.

# NEW AGONIES.

## Friday Evening, March 1.

### PROGRAMME.

PART I.

Overture—Piano............................JOSEPH DENCK
Song.....................................LITTLE JAKE
Trio—Guitars and Piano......RAWLS, PEARSON and DENCK

PART II.

**MEDLEY--PIANO,** - - - - J. Denck.

### Intermission of Ten Minutes.

# MINSTRELS.

PART III.

Hungarian National March............................BAND
Organ Gal...................................E. HEISE
Carrie Vaughn...............................LITTLE JAKE
New York Fashions.......................J. SCARBOROUGH
Finale.......................................COMPANY

PART IV.

Stump Speech............................J. SCARBOROUGH
Jig...........................................E. HEISE

## THE GAL WID DE WATERFALL.

## POLKA GROTESQUE.

## GYMNASTIC EXERCISES.

PRICE OF ADMISSION 50 Cents.        NO HALF PRICE.

Doors open at quarter to 7.  Rocket to commence at 7½ o'clock.

J. HART DENCK, - - - Musical Director
J. SCARBOROUGH, - - - General Manager

A portion of the Hall reserved for Colored People.

COLUMBIA PHOENIX PRINT.

Figure 2.3: "Janney's Hall. For the Benefit
of the Ladies' Memorial Association."
Image courtesy of the South Caroliniana
Library, University of South Carolina.

monument boosterism was an attempt to reestablish antebellum power dynamics. By ensnaring African Americans into the economic structure of southern culture, these fundraisers attempted to mimic and replace the economic and racial divisions of the slave system.

Granted, Eric Lott has argued that "the minstrel show was less the incarnation of an age-old racism than an emergent social semantic figure highly responsive to the emotional demands and troubled fantasies of its audiences." However, what Lott calls the "reactionary nostalgia" of the Reconstruction-era minstrel show is here intimately tied to the memorialization of those who fought and died to defend, at least in part, the very institutions that proliferated slavery and racial hierarchy in the United States.[13] That the recently freed, though still too often beleaguered, Black population was encouraged to join in a segregated witnessing of the festivities is instructive insofar as it reveals the essentially racist power dynamics that underwrote the early productions of Confederate Memorial Day and contextualizes these festivities as an early desire to solidify and reaffirm the South's recently disrupted social norms. The use of minstrel shows and racial subjugation highlights that white southern resistance to Reconstruction early on used monuments and the culture of their production as a form of maintaining the continuance of a white supremacist culture during and immediately after Reconstruction. While it's difficult to determine how or if African Americans were involved with such fundraising endeavors, Cox points out that Black southerners "perhaps unwillingly" participated in the monument celebrations "as they provided the workforce that put the monuments into place."[14] Though beyond the scope of this essay, the racialized labor of Reconstruction and Jim Crow southern communities is yet another lens through which we might read how the production and maintenance of Confederate monuments reinforce racial hierarchies and white supremacist ideology in the United States.

Race, gender, and age are each important elements to consider when assessing how monuments have been read and received. Cox and Cynthia Mills have both demonstrated that white women were essential to the establishment of Confederate monuments.[15] Kirk Savage has read monumental sculpture in the United States along racial lines, and broadsides such as the one discussed above show that fundraising for memorial celebrations and monuments considered and perhaps attempted to manipulate Black southern communities.[16] However, children were perhaps the most important audience that those who erected the monuments hoped to influence, and appeals to southern youth appear in the promotional literature. As Cassandra Jackson argues elsewhere in this collection, Confederate monuments are not merely about the past but represent a historicized "desire for ideological futurity," and engaging with southern youth in such materially explicit ways functioned pedagogically to ensure that future generations would internalize the ideals and perpetuate the legacy of the Lost

# An Appeal to the Patriotic and Loyal Boys and Girls of Clarendon County

**No braver or truer men ever lived than "The Boys in Grey" who marched away to war in 1861--1865 from Clarendon County.**

Many of them never came back and few, very few, are living now. You boys and girls are the descendants of those splendid heroes, and it is your privilege and pleasure as well as your duty to help in the erection of this beautiful monument.

We want *every* child to give, no matter how small the contribution, for we want every child to feel that he or she has a part in the monument.

Then we have decided to call the last week in February

*Confederate Monument Week*

and every school in the county is

earnestly requested during that week to raise money for the monument. Entertainments may be held and contributions solicited from everybody in the community.

When the monument is unveiled all the schools will be invited to attend and a committee of children from the three schools sending in largest amount in proportion to enrollment will have the honor of helping in the ceremony by pulling the cords that let the veil fall from around it.

The monument will be built of South Carolina granite and was designed and will be carved by talent from South Carolina.

The teachers will please send the contributions raised by their schools and the number of their pupils to **Mrs. F. O. Richardson, treasurer, Manning, S. C.**

Mrs. Joseph Sprott, Chairman; Miss Ria Lee Bowman, Miss Gussie Appelt, Secretaries; Mrs. F. O. Richardson, Treasurer; Mrs. D. M. Bradham, Mrs. C. B. Geiger, Miss Edna Brockinton.

THE HERALD, MANNING, S. C.

2.4: *An Appeal to the Patriotic and Loyal Boys and Girls of Clarendon County.* 1914. Image courtesy of the h Caroliniana Library, University of South Carolina.

Cause. One particularly interesting broadside encouraged children to donate money for the raising of a local monument (see Figure 2.4). Styled *An Appeal to the Patriotic and Loyal Boys and Girls of Clarendon County*, it reminds children that they are "the descendants of those splendid heroes, and [that] it is [their] privilege and pleasure as well as [their] duty to help in the erection of this beautiful monument."[17] The language of the circular, which was printed by the local newspaper office, emphasizes the desire to make future generations emotionally and financially invested in the practice of public memorialization, ensuring that the Lost Cause and its many monuments have a long half-life. One of the effects of the pattern of regularly recurring monument campaigns, erections, and celebrations is that each successive group of children who read these circulars and was exposed to the experience of fêting and memorializing was yet another generation of young people educated with a prescribed bias toward the Confederacy and indoctrination in the Lost Cause.

Attention to historical advertisements, broadsides, circulars, and newspaper accounts is important when evaluating the cultural force of Confederate monuments in the present because they show us how these objects reinforce white supremacist beliefs by virtue of their very quotidian nature. Their associations with the news, social events, and grade school activities parallel and reinforce their establishment within the landscape. Because they are seen every day, they have become simultaneously invisible and ever-present, like racism itself. David Currey has argued that Confederate soldier monuments, which peaked between 1903 and 1914, were not just a solace but also provided a model for southerners to mold the individual character of a new generation.[18] These ephemeral print promotional tracts highlight a level of boosterism involved in the production of the monuments, detail the various tropes used to pursue committees to keep building ever more monuments, and broaden our understanding of who the stakeholders were. In reconstructing these relationships between stonemasons and reporters, we find a nexus of regional businesses that benefited from the South's simultaneous desire to reimagine both the past and the future. Additionally, by tracing the connections between promoters and the public, especially the Ladies' Memorial Association, the United Daughters of the Confederacy, and local schools, we find social connections linked to education and domesticity that helped to ingrain the Lost Cause into the very fabric of everyday life.

While promotional literature reveals how the monuments came to be and allows us to study the different rhetorical traditions promoters leveraged to encourage communities throughout the South to erect statues to the Confederacy, the primary means through which people learned about the monuments and their unveilings were newspapers, commission reports, and commemorative pamphlets. Much of the reporting of monumental ceremonies follows a set pattern, and the bulk of the reports share a variety of rhetorical figures and literary tropes. Invocations, prayers, and jeremiads situate the reporting in American performative traditions such as convocations, sermons, and orations. The set oratorical programs of the celebrations give the commentaries an attachment to colonial history and are often guised in antiquarian trappings that operate to make the Confederacy an ancient and honorable tradition, something that is somehow of a piece with the narrative of the national founding and in some cases might even precede and/or supersede the American Revolution and the US Constitution. In legitimating the Lost Cause as a foundational and usable past, such reporting makes quick work of transforming presentist cultural and racial grievances into a standard historical repertoire, thus cloaking the racism of the present in the narrative trappings of history and tradition.

Among the earliest monuments to mark the transition from the cemetery to a site of government authority, the Columbia Confederate monument offered South Carolina an opportunity to structure the end of Reconstruction as a grand celebration and a public day of thanksgiving. Unveiled on May 13, 1879, the Confederate monument on the South Carolina State House grounds is an early example of the South's quick and deliberate response to the end of Reconstruction. Earlier monuments to Confederate soldiers appeared in cemeteries. Their physical presence among the dead denied them any explicit power over the state and explicitly carried the connotation of mourning. However, after Reconstruction, the consistent and deliberate erection of Confederate monuments on courthouse and statehouse grounds signified the renewed faith in Confederate principles and ensured that faith in the Lost Cause would remain. Defended and enshrined in these larger-than-life figures that embody what John J. Winberry has described as "one of the few distinguishing landscape features" of the South, the symbolic event of unveiling the Confederate statue was a culturally symbolic act rife with religious connotations of resurrection and new life.[19] The various public orations and prayers, along with their subsequent printings and reprintings, offer documentation of how the original audience interpreted these monuments and thereby reveal the foundational tenets of post-Reconstruction, neo-Confederate aesthetics, and the nascent tenets of the Lost Cause.

At these events, local ministers, veterans, and state and federal government officials offered public prayers and allegorical sermons, which were commonly preached prior to the unveiling of the monument. In addition to the appropriation of colonial antiquarianism found in the act of reporting, the prayers generally worked to make the Lost Cause sacrosanct, as if it was a new covenant and a new testament. For the unveiling of the Confederate monument in Columbia in May 1879, the *Columbia Register* reports that General John S. Preston compared the South to the Israelites' flight out of Egypt, to the plight of the Athenians under Sulla, to Brutus assassinating the tyrant Julius Caesar, and to the shattered strings of the harp of Memnon, the king of Ethiopia.[20] Preston goes on to argue that all liberty-loving people across time, from the Aegean to the Jordan and in Rome, were working toward like ends. The oration is a rhetorical hodgepodge, the metaphors are poorly mixed, and the allusions crisscross in ways that are difficult to follow or make coherent. However, rather than nitpick the lackluster literary quality of these celebrations, I think we learn more about the monuments and the psychology of the South by taking them at face value. Similar to how the South attempted to make historical and religious arguments in support of slavery during the antebellum period and arguably a precursor to current white nationalist appropriations of classicism, the prayers, orations, and reporting on the monuments' unveilings worked to associate the Confederacy with a broad array of cultural antecedents. There is a glut of overwrought style to these events, a desperate striving and grasping to associate the Confederacy with every conceivable tradition and mythology in the hope of finding something onto which to successfully graft the Lost Cause.

The secular speeches are often varied, yet most pull from the classical tradition for their metaphors as they strive to contextualize the Confederate soldiers in a *longue durée* of heroism reaching back to Homer, Hesiod, Thucydides, and Virgil, moving its way through the Crusades, the English Civil War, and the American Revolutionary War, thereby cloaking the Confederate narrative of the American Civil War and its Lost Cause in a transhistorical epic tradition. Several speeches at the Columbia monument unveiling refer to Sparta, and this seems to have set a precedent that other towns in the state would follow for the next two decades. References to both the *Iliad* and the three hundred Spartans against the Persians at Thermopylae are especially popular in dedicatory speeches not only in Columbia but in every small town in South Carolina that erects a monument to the Confederate dead. For example, the *Fort Mill News* reporting on the monument built by L. D. Childs goes off on a tangent about the three hundred but then waxes poetical in drawing from Persian mythology, apparently not understanding that the Spartans were fighting against the Persians.[21] It doesn't seem to matter who a given hero was fighting for so long as he was valorous, and herein lay the point: if these orators can adequately confuse history so that at the end of the day we only see "heroes," then what they were fighting for becomes irrelevant. It becomes that much easier to celebrate Confederate soldiers and forget why they fought in the first place. In so doing, the orators and the monuments accomplished what Hubbard feared: the celebration of a cause that attempted to destroy the nation, the valorization of traitors, and the defense of a fundamentally racist society.

The most extreme of these myths, and the most laborious and certainly the most powerful for white southern audiences, was Christianity, and no small effort went into equating the Confederate soldier with Christ. Again, going back to the unveiling of the Columbia monument, the *News and Courier* of

Charleston, South Carolina, reports that, during a speech in honor of the Ladies' Memorial Association, the monument itself supersedes the image of Christ on the cross by virtue of the white women then in attendance on the State House grounds: "In humble reverence, that not even at the Cross and Tomb of the Son of God did women kneel with a surer trust in the Divine Truth for which He died, than these women do here kneel today, by the monument their hands have raised in testimony of the truth for which the Confederate Soldier died."[22] What truth and for whom is not stated. All that matters in the ritual is that the Lost Cause is domesticated by virtue of the white women who raised the funds to erect the statue and that the statue's erection is associated with divine will. Once it was successfully compounded by the force of Christianity, it is small wonder that the Confederacy became such an enduring myth in its own right. When we consider that hundreds of these rituals were performed throughout the South over the course of decades, and when we consider the role that regional printing had in encouraging and disseminating these ideas, then we can begin to map how Lost Cause ideology became so pervasive over the course of the twentieth century.

## THE WOMEN'S MONUMENT AND THE LATER AESTHETIC RATIONALE FOR THE LOST CAUSE

The cultural movement of monuments from cemeteries to the town court-house signifies the growing temerity throughout the South to reestablish white supremacy and enshrine the idea of the Confederate soldier under the aegis of civil government. While most towns and county seats could only afford a single monument, state capitols, with their broader influence and greater access to resources, became centers for extensive and varied memorialization. The South Carolina Confederate soldier monument is an early example of the growing trend to symbolically align state government with the Confederacy, and it was by no means the last. Installed in April 1912, thirty-three years after the soldier monument, the Confederate women's monument originally faced south on the south side of the capitol complex and thus reinterpreted the Confederacy for the next generation of South Carolinians.

Along with the erection of monuments, the practice of collusion between editors and sculptors carried on well into the twentieth century, and on April 12, 1912, F. Wellington Ruckstuhl published a long essay titled "Sculptor Interprets the Memorial" in *The State*, a Columbia, South Carolina, newspaper, in which he explains the "Aesthetic Secrets" of his "beautiful monument in everlasting bronze."[23] Ruckstuhl had originally intended on creating a grand monument to Confederate women to be installed in Richmond; however, on March 25, 1909, Captain William E. Gonzales, editor of *The State*, wrote asking Ruckstuhl "what sort of a monument [he] could furnish to South Carolina for $15,000." Ruck-stuhl accepted the offer and set off for Paris to work on the project.

Ruckstuhl seems in part to have written the article out of concern that South Carolinians might not understand the abstract nature of his sculpture, noting "if the masses do not, at first, understand, [the artist] should not in any manner apologize for his work, but he should explain it to the people."[24] Whatever his exact motives, the article is similar to earlier reports on Confederate monuments in South Carolina insofar as it has the effect of prescribing the intended reading of the monument. Like the orations and prayers offered at the unveiling of the soldier monument in 1879, Ruckstuhl invokes both the classical tradition and the fundamental religiosity of postbellum representations of the Confederacy. Additionally, he also indirectly aligns the memory of the Confederacy with Anglo-American imperialism of the late nineteenth century, showing how the monuments were often adapted to recontextualize the Confederacy with new and emergent trends in the national consciousness.

Just as the presence of white women in the audience at the unveiling of the soldier's monument was used to position Christianity as an underlying force of Confederate values and motivation, so too does Ruckstuhl inscribe religion into his monument to Confederate women. In defending his sculpture, Ruckstuhl is intent on showing that it would have been ineffective to depict Confederate women in any historical act of labor on behalf of the Confederacy. His extensive defense on this point betrays the tension arising in the early twentieth century of those who had a living memory of the Civil War and desired an accurate representation of their suffering against those who understood that if the memory of the Confederacy was to have an enduring force over the national consciousness, it would need to be abstracted and updated to address broader sympathies of filiopietism, liberty, and domesticity. Ruckstuhl explains that his choice of an abstract woman was born out of a fear that an image of a Confederate woman in the act of labor such as "sewing a Confederate battle flag" or "ministering to the suffering soldier" would, after a time, become obsolete and therefore "ridiculous."[25] Instead, he argues that he "decided to lift her to the plane of the most high of all her characteristic activities carried on during and after the war—that of consulting Holy writ and losing herself in the lofty contemplation of her warwork . . . meditating over the past as well as the future of her country." In addition to coopting Christianity as a fundamental tenet of the Confederacy, the monument effectively obfuscates the material contributions of southern white women during and after the war.

By divorcing the Confederacy from the material and political history of the war and striving to attach it to classical art and religion, Ruckstuhl is self-consciously attempting to protect the memory of the Confederacy and extend its appeal by associating it with a racialized, abstract ideal of femininity. Like the soldier's monument, the women's monument is described within a long Western aesthetic tradition in order to attach the memory of the Confederacy to established ideals of beauty and democracy from ancient Athens to the present. To accomplish this, Ruckstuhl compares his monument to the Jupiter of Phidias, the Hermes of Praxiteles, the Venus de Milo, Michelangelo's Medici Tombs, the monuments to Bismarck and "Emperor William" in Berlin, and most importantly to the "colossal monument to Queen Victoria in London."[26] In so doing, he attempts to associate his work with two contemporary trends of liberal humanism and national imperialism. The association with Queen Victoria was timely. Ruckstuhl was evidently inspired by the recent monument to the late British monarch, and he further emphasizes the connection by comparing the face of his sculpture with those of "Queen Victoria, Empress Eugenie, and the Russian Czarina—a fighting beauty and a beautiful fighter." Ruckstuhl's desire for his audience to associate his abstracted representation of the Confederate woman with imperial aristocracy emphasizes his association of Confederate memory with political force and exposes power and violence as the central themes and values of his monument.

## POSTCARDS AND THE CIRCULATION OF MONUMENTS

It is relatively easy to accept the connection between newspaper and regional job printing and their effect on local and regional opinions about Confederate monuments in the South, and while the limited national reach of some magazines drew advertising dollars from northern firms, it might be a bit harder to accept the greater national reach of these monuments. However, there was an emergent print technology developing alongside the spread of Confederate monuments that was capable of disseminating images of them across space in mass numbers: the postcard. Postcards emerged during Reconstruction, proliferated during the Columbian Exposition of 1893, and were thus coincidental with the changing political state and the steady production of Confederate monuments. Barry Shank has argued that postcards are "flexible social tools" that "mark the networks of numerous competing class functions," emblematic of the "genre based aesthetics of mass culture," and an indicator that "social networks were no longer limited geographically."[27] As such, they have the ability to function as a mobile simulacrum of a place and a totem of what that place symbolizes. Just as the "card itself became the message," so too did the image on the card become the place and all that it stood for.[28] During the same period that monuments were proliferating, dozens of editions of postcards representing each monument in Columbia were being printed and mailed throughout the nation (see Figures 2.5 and 2.6). As a result, the Confederate aesthetics and Lost

A 12531   Confederate Monument, Columbia, S. C.

Figure 2.5: Rotograph
Company, "Confederate
Monument, Columbia, S.C.,"
1905. Image courtesy of the
South Caroliniana Library,
University of South Carolina.

Cause ideology of the region became inscribed onto the act of sending a familiar missive and thereby entered the national imaginary and received the stamp of the national infrastructure of the post office. The result was that postcards transformed Confederate ideology and aesthetics into a tourist attraction. The federally sponsored extension of the thread of imaginary connection between the sender and the addressee transforms the act of memorialization, and the dissemination of the monument as a piece of tourist ephemera links the idea of a place to the monument. When the postcard is received, the recipient is introduced to Columbia as the Confederate soldier's monument, the monument to Wade Hampton, the Confederate women's monument, or an aerial photo of children forming a living Confederate flag on the capitol steps.

It would be remiss of me to discuss postcards of Confederate monuments without comparing them to the related, though far more explicit, genre of lynching postcards that became popular at the same time and for

Figure 2.6: Curt Teich
and Company, "Women's
Monument, Columbia, S.C.,"
1935. Image courtesy of the
South Caroliniana Library,
University of South Carolina.

WOMEN'S MONUMENT, COLUMBIA, S. C.                    113539

similar reasons. William Drake has argued that "the postcard contains a multi-dimensional system of communication [and] in this 3"x5" microcosm, held in our hand, an entire system of artistic, psychological, and literary interpretation resides."[29] We can extend the psychological underpinnings of such images by considering Susan Sontag's argument that lynching postcards "force us to think about the extent of the evil unleased specifically by racism" and that the viewing of the mobs of white spectators surrounding dead and mutilated Black individuals "makes us the spectators, too," which was precisely the point of such postcards for the original audience who viewed and disseminated them.[30] Likewise, the dissemination of images of Confederate monuments through the post reifies the monument, making it a synecdoche for the place itself and extending these ideals throughout the republic, thereby normalizing the Lost Cause in the national imagination and completing the task of transforming traitors into patriots.

While the federal post office outlawed the sending of lynching postcards through the mail service in 1908, forcing their trade underground and limiting their means of circulation to interpersonal exchange networks, the mailing of postcards of Confederate monuments remains acceptable and allows the ideas and values of the Confederacy to circulate through federal channels.[31] Just as Wendy Wolters has argued that it is impossible to reverse the "race, gender, and sexuality that accompanied the original production of the photographs and the lynchings themselves," so too is it impossible to remove the racist, white supremacist intentions of the Confederate monuments.[32] While I am by no means arguing that postcards of Confederate monuments are as violent or as powerful as lynching postcards, comparison of these two genres of the form allows us to understand how ephemeral print culture enabled and encouraged racist sentiments to foster a sense of community across regional lines. Both Wolters and Dora Apel remind us that local photographers and printers set up impromptu equipment to develop, print, and sell cards at the lynchings as they occurred, thereby linking the ritual of violence to the material and economic structures of communication technology that allow belief systems to circulate in print.[33] Apel has further argued that "statement[s] about community values and civic pride made by such postcards cannot be underestimated," and Robert Snyder has pointed out that "encoded in lynching cards for generations to come were messages that community virtues were protected."[34] The monuments, like the lynchings, are a value statement, and mailing postcards of monuments perpetuated and normalized the Lost Cause and had the potential to extend those values beyond regional borders, adding an element of mobility to an edifice that would otherwise seem to be static.

## MODERN REVISIONS AND ADDITIONS

While we tend to think of monuments as unchanging, and while much of their force comes from their monolithic structure and imposition on the landscape, there are cases in which their movement in space and their meaning over time have been revised to adapt them to and protect them from the changing national climate regarding racism and white supremacy. Perhaps less well known than the presence of the monuments themselves is the fact that, as the South Carolina State House complex has expanded, the positions of some of the monuments have changed. Now, the women's monument has been moved farther south and turned toward the north so that it faces the southern side of the capitol building. The mutability of the monuments becomes all the more evident when we understand that their development over time has allowed them to be recontextualized just as their original production was intended to recontextualize the Civil War and the South's response to Reconstruction. Thomas J. Brown has considered the juxtaposition of the soldier and women's monuments and argued that "beneath the important tensions, the Lost Cause maintained some consistent emphases from the Soldier monument to the women's monument" and that "white supremacism was the most obvious continuity."[35] The extension of white supremacism across these two generations is later transmuted into a twentieth-century neo-Confederate aesthetics and apologetics of the Lost Cause that becomes all the more powerful when we realize that revision is an integral rather than accidental element of its structure. While earlier monuments operate on a level similar to what Toni Morrison has identified as an "effort to talk about" an "Africanist presence" with a "vocabulary designed to disguise the subject," later monuments and their attempts to address the history of slavery and the Black experience in the United States have been a mix of hostility and compromise.[36]

As the generations who remembered the Confederacy aged and died, new work had to be done to keep its traditions alive. This essay does not admit space to account for the Dixiecrats or the Republican Party's southern strategy at any length. Suffice it to say that the reaction to the civil rights movement in the middle of the twentieth century required that new heroes be added to the array of monumental sculpture designed to define and influence the populace. Neo-Confederate monuments and the perpetuation of racist ideology masquerading as patriotism functionally extend and augment statues to the soldiers and women of the Confederacy. W. J. T. Mitchell has theorized how iconography bridges the gap between the physical world and the mind, arguing that "the whole matrix of analogies (particularly ocular metaphors) that govern representative theories of the mind . . . helps us to see the reciprocity and interdependence" between physical and mental object, between monuments and cultural beliefs.[37] The statue of Strom Thurmond is a case in point. Installed in 1999, while Thurmond was still alive, the statue faces the monument to Confederate women, standing between it and the capitol and linking the conservative movement of the twentieth century with the Confederacy. M. Christine Boyer has described such spaces of public display and ritual as "rhetorical topoi . . . those civic compositions that teach us about our national heritage and our public responsibilities and assume that the urban landscape itself is the emblematic embodiment of power and memory."[38] The three monuments—the Confederate soldier, Thurmond, and the Confederate women—draw a line through the state capitol. They mark and guard it, and they make painfully clear the values of state government in South Carolina.

Marc Augé reminds us that a monument, "as the Latin etymology of the word indicates, is an attempt at the tangible expression of permanence or, at the very least, of duration. Gods need shrines, as sovereigns need thrones and palaces,

Figure 2.7: Cameron Howell, photograph of the Richard Greener Statue, *Daily Gamecock*. Image courtesy of University of South Carolina Communications.

to place them above temporal contingencies. They thus enable people to think in terms of continuity through the generations."[39] It is this transhistorical force that Confederate monuments strive for, and, paradoxically, their movement around and addition to the urban geography of the capitol is part of what helps them to endure. Additionally, the power of what they omit works to exclude and alienate and is just as forceful as their power to indoctrinate. The desire to repress and control the Black presence in South Carolina's history, be it antebellum, Confederate, or modern, is also at the heart of what these monuments represent. They express how the state has historically chosen to reckon with its own historical ties to slavery. The spectral haunting of slavery in South Carolina allows for the space surrounding these monuments to manifest itself as a site of antebellum nostalgia and Jim Crow violence. The disembodied memory of slavery in the establishment and maintenance of the State House complex underwrites projects such as the African American Memorial and the careful placement of plaques that identify that yes, the enslaved were once here, without attempting to manifest their historical presence in any individual way. Savage has pointed out that "before 1860 there are no known images whatsoever of African Americans, slaves or freemen, in marble or bronze" and that sculpture's "obsession with ideal human form made the whole subject of slavery extremely difficult for sculptors to represent."[40] The hesitancy to sculpt Black persons is tantamount to erasure.

The University of South Carolina has recently become a space that is actively trying to counter the white supremacist narratives of Confederate memorialization.[41] Representations of race in the South have historically skewed toward a reinforcement of white supremacist power dynamics and often imagine Black people as enslaved. Additionally, where monuments appear is also important, and though a state institution, the university does not have the same force of civil government that the State House monuments embody. A 2013 monument for the Black students who entered the university during Reconstruction is modest at best, obscure and difficult to find, and does not represent the students in physical form. More recently, the names of campus buildings have created further tension among the campus community, the board of trustees, the state legislature, and the surrounding community.[42]

One attempt at compromise has come in the form of erecting monuments and statues in honor of specific African Americans. On February 22, 2018, a statue of Richard Greener—the first Black professor at the University of South Carolina during Reconstruction, who also served as librarian—was unveiled outside the university's Thomas Cooper Library and offers a substantial, prominent, and positive representation of Black intellectualism during Reconstruction (see Figure 2.7). Unencumbered by a white presence, well-dressed, and carrying an armful of folio-sized books, the Greener statue represents a historical Black man in fully human terms and places him in a prominent setting in a space of higher learning. As beautiful and powerful as it is, the Greener statue is also a memorial to Reconstruction's failed promise, and as such, it raises several new questions. Is the Greener statue a supplement to or a replacement of the Confederate monuments on the capitol and on campus? Are we merely going to maintain separate, parallel, perhaps even competing traditions of South Carolina's history? Is this a way forward, or is it yet another in a long line of US compromises concerning race and national identity? Given that South Carolina's Heritage Act makes it illegal to remove any public monuments without a two-thirds majority vote in the state legislature, it seems unlikely that any Confederate monuments will be removed in the near future. I hope that, in performing a recovery of the ephemeral, promotional, and periodical literature, we might be able to shed some light on the obscure structural forces that have allowed these monuments and the alternate history they represent to perpetuate Lost Cause ideology and pervade the national imagination.

## NOTES

1. Thomas H. Hubbard, *The Lost Cause: Address Delivered before the Commandery of the State of New York, Military Order of the Loyal Legion of the United States, at the Regular Meeting, Held December 11, 1912, at Delmonico's*, 3.

2. Hubbard, *Lost Cause*, 11.

3. Hubbard, *Lost Cause*, 13.

4. Charles Reagan Wilson, *Baptized in Blood: The Religion of the Lost Cause, 1865–1920* (Athens: University of Georgia Press, 1980), 8; and C. Vann Woodward, *Origins of the New South, 1877–1913* (Baton Rouge: Louisiana State University Press, 1971), 156, 249.

5. Gary W. Gallagher, "Introduction," in *The Myth of the Lost Cause and Civil War History*, ed. Gary W. Gallagher and Alan T. Nolan (Bloomington: Indiana University Press, 2000), 1–10; and Rollin G. Osterweis, *The Myth of the Lost Cause, 1865–1900* (New York: Archon Books, 1973).

6. Gaines M. Foster, *Ghosts of the Confederacy: Defeat, the Lost Cause, and the Emergence of the New South, 1865–1913* (New York: Oxford University Press, 1988), 8.

7. Karen L. Cox, *Dixie's Daughters: The United Daughters of the Confederacy and the Preservation of Confederate Culture* (Gainesville: University Press of Florida, 2003), 3, 4.

8. Carl F. Kaestle and Janice A. Radway, "A Framework for the History of Publishing and Reading in the United States, 1880–1940," in *Print in Motion: The Expansion of Publishing and Reading in the United States, 1880–1940*, ed. Carl F. Kaestle and Janice A. Radway (Chapel Hill: University of North Carolina Press, 2009), 10–11; Richard Ohmann, "Diverging Paths: Books and Magazines in the Transition to Corporate Capitalism," in Kaestle and Radway, *Print in Motion*, 102; and Reda C. Goff, "The Confederate Veteran Magazine," *Tennessee Historical Quarterly* 31, no. 1 (Spring 1972): 48.

9. Douglas J. Butler, *North Carolina Civil War Monuments: An Illustrated History* (Jefferson, NC: MacFarland and Company, 2013), 144.

10. Southern Marble and Granite Company, "A Few Confederate Monuments Erected by the Southern Marble & Granite Co. Spartanburg, S.C." (1912).

11. Evander McIvor Law to Samuel E. White, "Confederate Monument Association, Fort Mill," folder 1, South Caroliniana Library, University of South Carolina.

12. L. D. Childs to Spratt, November 17, 1891, "Confederate Monument Association, Fort Mill," folder 1, South Caroliniana Library, University of South Carolina.

13. Eric Lott, *Love and Theft: Blackface Minstrelsy and the American Working Class* (New York: Oxford University Press, 1993), 6, 7.

14. Cox, *Dixie's Daughters*, 174n7.

15. Cox, *Dixie's Daughters*; and Cynthia Mills, "Introduction," in *Monuments to the Lost Cause: Women, Art, and the Landscapes of Southern Memory*, ed. Cynthia Mills and Pamela H. Simpson (Knoxville: University of Tennessee Press, 2003), xv–xxx.

16. Kirk Savage, *Standing Soldiers, Kneeling Slaves: Race, War, and Monument in Nineteenth-Century America* (Princeton, NJ: Princeton University Press, 1997).

17. *An Appeal to the Patriotic and Loyal Boys and Girls of Clarendon County* (Manning: The Herald, 1914).

18. David Currey, "The Virtuous Soldier: Constructing a Usable Confederate Past in Franklin, Tennessee," in Mills and Simpson, *Monuments to the Lost Cause*, 133–48.

19. John J. Winberry, "'Lest We Forget': The Confederate Monument and the Southern Townscape," *Southeastern Geographer* 23, no. 2 (November 1983): 119.

20. *South Carolina Monument Association: Origin, History, and Work, with an Account of the Proceedings at the Unveiling of the Monument to the Confederate Dead, and the Oration*

*of Gen. John S. Preston, at Columbia, S.C., May 13, 1879* (Charleston: News and Courier Bookpresses, 1879).

21. *Fort Mill News*, December 22, 1891.

22. *News and Courier*, May 14, 1879; and *South Carolina Monument Association*, 37.

23. F. Wellington Ruckstuhl, "Sculptor Interprets the Memorial," *The State*, April 12, 1912, 4.

24. Ruckstuhl, "Sculptor Interprets."

25. Ruckstuhl, "Sculptor Interprets."

26. Ruckstuhl, "Sculptor Interprets."

27. Barry Shank, *A Token of My Affection: Greeting Cards and American Business Culture* (New York: Columbia University Press, 2004), 125, 126, 127–28.

28. Shank, *Token of My Affection*, 133.

29. William Drake, "Representation: Re-Collecting Mythology in an Age of Showing and Telling" (PhD diss., Pacific Graduate Institute, 2001), 10.

30. Susan Sontag, *Regarding the Pain of Others* (New York: Farrar, Straus, and Giroux, 2003), 91.

31. Dora Apel, *Imagery of Lynching: Black Men, White Women, and the Mob* (New Brunswick, NJ: Rutgers University Press, 2004), 30.

32. Wendy Wolters, "Without Sanctuary: Bearing Witness, Bearing Whiteness," *JAC* 24, no. 2 (2004): 409.

33. Wolters, "Without Sanctuary"; and Apel, *Imagery of Lynching*, 30.

34. Apel, *Imagery of Lynching*, 30; and Robert Snyder quoted in Apel, *Imagery of Lynching*, 30.

35. Thomas J. Brown, *Civil War Canon: Sites of Confederate Memory in South Carolina* (Chapel Hill: University of North Carolina Press, 2015), 124.

36. Toni Morrison, *Playing in the Dark: Whiteness and the Literary Imagination* (Cambridge, MA: Harvard University Press, 1992), 50.

37. W. J. T. Mitchell, *Iconology: Image, Text, Ideology* (Chicago: University of Chicago Press, 1980), 16, 17.

38. M. Christine Boyer, *The City of Collective Memory: Its Historical Imaginary and Architectural Entertainments* (Cambridge, MA: Massachusetts Institute of Technology Press, 1994), 321.

39. Marc Augé, *Non-Places: Introduction to an Anthropology of Supermodernity*, trans. John Howe (New York: Verso, 1995), 60.

40. Savage, *Standing Soldiers*, 8.

41. In response to student concerns, the University of South Carolina established a Presidential Commission on University History to address the legacy of racism on campus, and one goal is to consider the renaming of buildings. See Jessica Holdman, "'The Strom' Center, 15 Other USC Building Names Proposed for Possible Removal," *Post and Courier*, February 26, 2021, https://www.postandcourier.com/columbia/the-strom-center-15-other -usc-building-names-proposed-for-possible-removal/article_a1ea4f4e-77a3-11eb-970b-0307a1b8e4ea.html; and Lauren Sausser, "Group to Tackle Controversial Names on University of South Carolina Campus Buildings," *Post and Courier*, February 17, 2018, https://www .postandcourier.com/health/group-to-tackle-controversial-names-on-university-of-south -carolina-campus-buildings/article_e404acf6-1281-11e8-abbc-7b5cd5739a55.html.

42. Sausser, "Group to Tackle." While the Presidential Commission on University History is working to compile a list of names to be removed from buildings, the list would then have to be reviewed by the Board of Trustees before facing a vote in the legislature.

# Bibliography

Apel, Dora. *Imagery of Lynching: Black Men, White Women, and the Mob*. New Brunswick, NJ: Rutgers University Press, 2004.

*An Appeal to the Patriotic and Loyal Boys and Girls of Clarendon County*. Manning, SC: The Herald, 1914.

Augé, Marc. *Non-Places: Introduction to an Anthropology of Supermodernity*. Translated by John Howe. New York: Verso, 1995.

Boyer, M. Christine. *The City of Collective Memory: Its Historical Imaginary and Architectural Entertainments*. Cambridge, MA: Massachusetts Institute of Technology Press, 1994.

Brown, Thomas J. *Civil War Canon: Sites of Confederate Memory in South Carolina*. Chapel Hill: University of North Carolina Press, 2015.

Butler, Douglas J. *North Carolina Civil War Monuments: An Illustrated History*. Jefferson, NC: McFarland & Company, 2013.

Childs, L. D. Letter to Spratt, 17 November 1891. "Confederate Monument Association, Fort Mill." Folder 1, South Caroliniana Library, University of South Carolina.

Cox, Karen L. *Dixie's Daughters: The United Daughters of the Confederacy and the Preservation of Confederate Culture*. Gainesville: University Press of Florida, 2003.

Currey, David. "The Virtuous Soldier: Constructing a Usable Confederate Past in Franklin, Tennessee." In *Monuments to the Lost Cause: Women, Art, and the Landscapes of Southern Memory*, edited by Cynthia Mills and Pamela H. Simpson, 133–48. Knoxville: University of Tennessee Press, 2003.

Drake, William. "Representation: Re-Collecting Mythology in an Age of Showing and Telling." PhD diss., Pacific Graduate Institute, 2001.

*Fort Mill News*, December 22, 1891.

Foster, Gaines M. *Ghosts of the Confederacy: Defeat, the Lost Cause, and the Emergence of the New South, 1865–1913*. New York: Oxford University Press, 1988.

Gallagher, Gary W. "Introduction." In *The Myth of the Lost Cause and Civil War History*, edited by Gary W. Gallagher and Alan T. Nolan, 1–10. Bloomington: Indiana University Press, 2000.

Goff, Reda C. "The Confederate Veteran Magazine." *Tennessee Historical Quarterly* 31, no. 1 (Spring 1972): 45–60.

Holdman, Jessica. "'The Strom' Center, 15 Other USC Building Names Proposed for Possible Removal." *Post and Courier*, February 26, 2021. https://www.postandcourier.com/columbia/the-strom-center-15-other-usc-building-names-proposed-for-possible-removal/article_a1ea4f4e-77a3-11eb-970b-0307a1b8e4ea.html.

Hubbard, Thomas H. *The Lost Cause: Address Delivered before the Commandery of the State of New York, Military Order of the Loyal Legion of the United States, at the Regular Meeting, Held December 11, 1912, at Delmonico's*. New York, 1912.

Kaestle, Carl F., and Janice A. Radway. "A Framework for the History of Publishing and Reading in the United States, 1880–1940." In *Print in Motion: The Expansion of Publishing and Reading in the United States, 1880–1940*, edited by Carl F. Kaestle and Janice A. Radway, 7–21. Chapel Hill: University of North Carolina Press, 2009.

Law, Evander McIvor. Letter to Samuel E. White. "Confederate Monument Association, Fort Mill." Folder 1, South Caroliniana Library, University of South Carolina.

Lott, Eric. *Love and Theft: Blackface Minstrelsy and the American Working Class*. New York: Oxford University Press, 1993.

Mills, Cynthia. "Introduction." In *Monuments to the Lost Cause: Women, Art, and the Landscapes of Southern Memory*, edited by Cynthia Mills and Pamela H. Simpson, xv–xxx. Knoxville: University of Tennessee Press, 2003.

Mitchell, W. J. T. *Iconology: Image, Text, Ideology*. Chicago: University of Chicago Press, 1980.

Morrison, Toni. *Playing in the Dark: Whiteness and the Literary Imagination*. Cambridge, MA: Harvard University Press, 1992.

*News and Courier*, May 14, 1879.

Ohmann, Richard. "Diverging Paths: Books and Magazines in the Transition to Corporate Capitalism." In *Print in Motion: The Expansion of Publishing and Reading in the United States, 1880–1940*, edited by Carl F. Kaestle and Janice A. Radway, 102–15. Chapel Hill: University of North Carolina Press, 2009.

Osterweis, Rollin G. *The Myth of the Lost Cause, 1865–1900*. New York: Archon Books, 1973.

Ruckstuhl, F. Wellington. "Sculptor Interprets the Memorial." *The State*, April 12, 1912.

Sausser, Lauren. "Group to Tackle Controversial Names on University of South Carolina Campus Buildings." *Post and Courier*, February 17, 2018. https://www.postandcourier.com/health/group-to-tackle-controversial-names-on-university-of-south-carolina-campus-buildings/article_e404acf6-1281-11e8-abbc-7b5cd5739a55.html.

Savage, Kirk. *Standing Soldiers, Kneeling Slaves: Race, War, and Monument in Nineteenth-Century America*. Princeton, NJ: Princeton University Press, 1997.

Shank, Barry. *A Token of My Affection: Greeting Cards and American Business Culture*. New York: Columbia University Press, 2004.

Sontag, Susan. *Regarding the Pain of Others*. New York: Farrar, Straus, and Giroux, 2003.

*South Carolina Monument Association: Origin, History, and Work, with an Account of the Proceedings at the Unveiling of the Monument to the Confederate Dead, and the Oration of Gen. John S. Preston, at Columbia, S.C., May 13, 1879*. Charleston: News and Courier Bookpresses, 1879.

Southern Marble and Granite Company. "A Few Confederate Monuments Erected by the Southern Marble & Granite Co. Spartanburg, S.C." 1912.

Wilson, Charles Reagan. *Baptized in Blood: The Religion of the Lost Cause, 1865–1920*. Athens: University of Georgia Press, 1980.

Winberry, John J. "'Lest We Forget': The Confederate Monument and the Southern Townscape." *Southeastern Geographer* 23, no. 2 (November 1983): 107–21.

Wolters, Wendy. "Without Sanctuary: Bearing Witness, Bearing Whiteness." *JAC* 24, no. 2 (2004): 399–425.

Woodward, C. Vann. *Origins of the New South, 1877–1913*. Baton Rouge: Louisiana State University Press, 1971.

# CHAPTER 3

# SOUTH BY SOUTHWEST

### Confederate and Conquistador Memorials Crossing/Closing Borders

### —Spencer R. Herrera

On June 12, 2016, upon winning a Tony Award for Best Original Score for his musical *Hamilton*, Lin-Manuel Miranda recited a sonnet, which he dedicated to his wife and the victims of a shooting massacre that left forty-nine people dead at a gay nightclub in Orlando, Florida. The sonnet reads in part: "When senseless acts of tragedy remind us / That nothing here is promised, not one day. / . . . / And love is love is love is love is love is love is love is love cannot be / killed or swept aside."[1] The beautiful words "love is love is love is love is love is love is love is love cannot be / killed or swept aside" reflect a poetic truth with which it is almost impossible to argue. Love is love is love, and who can say otherwise? The love we feel for one another "cannot be killed or swept aside." Unfortunately, however, the ones whom we love can be killed. And, as the sonnet reminds us, "nothing here is promised, not one day." Truer words have never been spoken.

On August 3, 2019, a racist and delusional gunman from Dallas was in search of a large concentration of Mexicans he could murder with his WASR-10 assault-style rifle. He found his target in the border town of El Paso, Texas.[2] He stumbled upon a Walmart, located only four miles from the US-Mexico border, where many Mexican nationals and Mexican Americans shop. He killed twenty-three people and injured twenty-three more.

If love is love is love, then the converse must also hold true. Hate is hate is hate. Hate kills the promise of tomorrow, and it leaves a bloody stain on our history. Unfortunately, many of the violent acts committed against people of color in our country are poorly documented or made into a historical footnote. This is especially true of how we publicly commemorate our nation's history as told through historical markers, monuments, and memorials. The aesthetic designs, inscriptions, and locations of these public figures and places often work together to sanitize our darkest moments in history by simplifying the historical record through a dichotomic lens of a dominant narrative versus a subaltern one, of those who control the narrative versus those whose narrative gets told by others. To this end, seldom do we examine the complex layers of our historical landmarks, national founders, or heroic figures with a critical eye. Instead, we bestow their names upon buildings and public places, celebrate their birthdays with recognized holidays, and dedicate monuments and memorials in their honor. By doing so, we vow to memorialize these designated hallowed places and historical figures into the fabric of our national identity.

However, when we memorialize such people and places, the questions arise: for whom are we preserving these memories, and for what purpose? As Arthur Danto reasons, "we erect monuments so that we shall always remember, and build memorials so that we shall never forget."[3] Oftentimes, however, these physical markers do little to validate why such places and people should be honored in the first place, or why we should continue to revere them even after years of historical distancing, which should have enabled us to create a sense of social justice in hindsight. This questioning of what and who we honor has been a slow-developing dialogue that has gained traction in recent years with the divisive rhetoric surrounding the ethical legitimacy of Confederate monuments and memorials across the United States.

Unfortunately, the call to remove Confederate monuments and memorials has been rejected by many people who support the southern cause and what they feel represents their heritage. Despite the nostalgic desire to safeguard this southern patrimony, of the more than 1,700 Confederate monuments that exist across the country, 110 of them were removed from 2015 to 2018.[4] This anti-Confederate monument movement only began in earnest after a self-identified white supremacist shot and killed nine Black people at a historically Black church in Charleston, South Carolina, in June 2015. In the aftermath of this mass murder, photos emerged of the shooter posing with the Confederate flag, which spurred a nationwide movement to begin removing public tributes to Confederate heroes. Unfortunately, this is the kind of individual who finds inspiration in Confederate symbolism to imbue our country with racism and hate.

Texas, a perennially politically conservative state, led this monument removal movement with thirty-one Confederate symbols taken down over a three-year period after that horrific massacre.[5] Yet, despite this trend, Texas still has at least 180 registered Confederate monuments and well over two hundred if we count schools, government buildings, and street names. Even in the farthest stretches of the state, Confederate symbols play a part in the local lore and representation of white supremacy.

In the westernmost part of the Confederacy, in El Paso, Texas, there is a small patch of land where a set of four historical markers record the people and places that have influenced the area. These four historical markers span a period

of over three hundred years. One dual-sided marker memorializes two Confederate officers. The second is dedicated to the Camino Real, the Royal Road
from Mexico City to Santa Fe, New Mexico, upon which Spanish and Mexican convoys traveled with people and goods. The third memorial is missing its
inscription, and it is unclear who or what it memorializes.[6] The fourth marker is
dedicated to Don Juan de Oñate, a Mexican-born explorer of Spanish parentage
known as the "Last Conquistador," who led the first permanent colony through
present-day El Paso on the colonists' way to northern New Mexico, where they
commandeered a Pueblo village for their settlement.

When one thinks of Confederate monuments and memorials, El Paso is not
what comes to mind. This far west Texas town, although officially part of the
Confederacy, was far removed, geographically and culturally, from the Deep
South. Yet in a discreet, tucked-away corner, right next to the border fence that
separates the United States and Mexico, sits the dual-sided memorial dedicated
to two local Confederate agents, Captain James W. Magoffin and Major Simeon
Hart.[7] This memorial, along with the other historical markers commemorating Hispanic (Spanish and Mexican) contributions to the Southwest, creates a
unique geographic and cultural-historical dialogue not only for the region but
for the country. These markers located in this border contact zone demarcate a
space like no other in this nation. Whereas Confederate monuments and memorials are almost always about the past, this space, if framed in a new way, without
the Confederate and Oñate memorials, could create a strong message of hope
for the future. For the moment though, they are stuck in a loop of historical
erasure, waiting for society to progress past its racially divisive cultural legacy
and to recognize the value of this historically significant geographic location.

When one visits this area and reads the inscriptions on each marker, it is easy
to see how these four small markers, situated together, make an odd ensemble.
The Oñate marker and the Camino Real marker make historical and geographic
sense, although the Oñate marker does come with its own historical and political controversies.[8] However, the Confederate dual-sided memorial distorts any
united message that this statuary quartet was designed to convey. These markers are situated for interpretation as a unit. They are positioned in a half circle
facing each other as if in historical and cultural dialogue. But with the blank
marker positioned between the Camino Real and Oñate markers, the conversation is disrupted. Despite the incomplete marker and distorted messaging,
these four markers are still joined, albeit incongruently, by the space they share.
I argue that it is this space that needs to be reevaluated and reimagined into a
new space with a new memorial that will never allow us to forget how this place
marks where East meets West and North meets South. It has been a place of
movement for over a millennium. It is much more than the site where someone

established a flour mill or crossed the river on the way to their final destination. This space is one of the major geographic, cultural, and historical contact zones of the Americas.

If we ever hope to better understand how diversity is a strength of this country and that our American immigrant story did not begin at Plymouth Rock but at the Oñate Crossing, then we must first come to grips with this particular contact zone. Mary Louise Pratt defines contact zones as "social spaces where disparate cultures meet, clash, and grapple with each other, often in highly asymmetrical relations of domination and subordination—such as colonialism and slavery, or their aftermaths as they are lived out across the globe today."[9] When we consider this definition, we can see how this space epitomizes a contact zone. The question becomes: how do we stop ignoring its message and instead use it to build something meaningful out of the culture clash? Until we can do this, the memorials at this space will continue to close borders, not cross them.


## THE BORDER MARKER QUARTET


Adjacent to where the Rio Grande is funneled through a canal, nestled between Ciudad Juárez to the south and I-10 and the University of Texas at El Paso (UTEP) campus to the north, and less than two miles west of downtown El Paso, sits what is popularly known as the Oñate Crossing (see Figure 3.1).[10] Oñate led a caravan of settlers and soldiers through northern Mexico and arrived at the Rio Grande in April 1598. With the help of local Indians, his expedition located a manageable place to cross the river with their wagons and livestock in tow. This ford, which also opens up to a pass between the mountains, connected Mexico to New Mexico along the road called El Camino Real de Tierra Adentro. The settlement along the river's banks became known as El Paso del Norte, or the Pass to the North. These four memorials are located on this small piece of land, connecting two countries.

Today, an abandoned Mexican restaurant, formerly the Hart residence, occupies the space next to the memorials. An inactive decorative water fountain sits adjacent to them. Construction fencing traverses the property, although the memorials are accessible. There is a small homeless camp of several tents nearby. And the border fence with Ciudad Juárez in the background stands within a stone's throw of the memorials. This is where the four memorials lie in collective ruin as their façades begin to fade, and they lose the luster they once had (see Figures 3.2 and 3.3).

The first historical marker to the left as one approaches the space from the US side is made of granite. It was erected by the state of Texas in 1964. It is

Figure 3.1: Spencer R.
Herrera, photograph of
Oñate Crossing State
Historical Sign at the
US–Mexico border.
Image courtesy of
Spencer R. Herrera.

the most aesthetic piece of the group considering it is made of polished stone.
However, its inscription is beginning to wear due to time and the harsh desert
elements. One fascinating aspect about this marker is that it is two-sided. The
side with the text facing the El Paso direction of this border space is dedicated
to Magoffin. His name is in large text, and in smaller text above it reads "Hometown of Texas Confederates." The inscription reads:

> Born Kentucky. Trader in Mexico. Special U.S. Army agent in Mexican War, 1846–47.
> Established trading post at Magoffinville about 1850. Named state agent with
> Simeon Hart to receive U.S. property surrendered at Ft. Bliss, Mar. 1861 prior to Civil
> War. This and other military stores obtained through his long standing contacts in
> Mexico supplied the Confederate Forces in the Arizona–New Mexico campaign
> 1861–62. Made State Brig. Gen. 1861. Left here with Confederate evacuation 1862. As
> Capt. C.S.A. business ability utilized to obtain military supplies in Texas, Mexico—
> State Senator 1863–65. Buried in San Antonio.[11]

Figure 3.2: Spencer R. Herrera, photograph of Oñate Crossing from Spur 1966 with Ciudad Juárez in the background. Image courtesy of Spencer R. Herrera.

Figure 3.3: Spencer R. Herrera, photograph of Oñate Crossing. Image courtesy of Spencer R. Herrera.

Magoffin was influential in the development of early El Paso. His legacy extends beyond his contribution to the Civil War; yet his memorial focuses mostly on his involvement with the Confederate cause. It is strange considering the geographic location of this marker and Magoffin's minor role in the war that there is a memorial dedicated to his Confederate contribution. The Magoffin family name is easily one of the most recognizable in El Paso. There are several places that bear his name, including an auditorium at UTEP, a historic district in the city, apartment housing, and streets. Yet, strangely, the only memorial in the city dedicated to him does not specify his accomplishments outside of the Mexican-American War, which was founded on manifest destiny, and the Civil War. As made clear by its inscription, the focus is on his identity as a captain in the Confederate States of America (CSA) Army. To ignore his other contributions to society and make his Confederate involvement the reason for his memorial is to give precedence to the message of white supremacy.

The other side of this same granite memorial, facing the direction of Ciudad Juárez in this border space, is dedicated to Hart. The inscription reads:

> Born New York moved to El Paso 1861, founded Hart's Mill that ground out 100 barrels flour a day and sold to buyers from Arizona to San Antonio. When the Civil War came, he was the main source for securing military supplies for the Arizona–New Mexico campaign. In 1862, Hart joined the C.S.A. army and was made chief purchasing agent for the War Department west of the Mississippi. His extensive contacts in Mexico and Europe and his knowledge of markets made him able to render great service to the Confederacy, which could only exist by trading valuable cotton for war goods through foreign countries. Through his arrangements for supplies, a Union plot to invade Texas across the Rio Grande was thwarted early 1863. Buried in Evergreen Cemetery.[12]

Although Hart's influence and historical presence do not meet the level of Magoffin's, he too is recognized throughout El Paso, with his name donning an elementary school, public housing, and a historical section near the border. Yet again, despite his contributions to the development of El Paso, his side of the memorial also focuses on his service to the Confederate cause. The message behind this dual-sided memorial, and for those who established it, is clear: these two men were Confederate agents first and foremost. They are banded together because of their white supremacist heritage. Despite any positive contributions they may have made to help develop the El Paso region before the Civil War, the purpose of these markers is to never forget their loyalty and service to the Confederate cause, which was to enslave Black people to economically exploit their labor.

The second historical marker, moving in a clockwise direction, made of stone and cement with a cast aluminum plaque atop, is dedicated to the Camino Real. It was erected in 1983 by the Texas Historical Commission. The inscription reads:

> For more than 200 years, the Camino Real, or Royal Road, was the major route for transporting commercial goods from Mexico City and Chihuahua to Santa Fe and Taos. First traveled by Juan de Oñate during his 1598 expedition to New Mexico, the Camino Real followed the San Elizario, Socorro, and Ysleta Road, crossed the Rio Grande west of present downtown El Paso, and continued north into New Mexico. When the Rio Grande was established as the U.S.-Mexico boundary in 1848, this section of the old Camino Real became part of the United States.[13]

This marker pays tribute to the road that has connected travelers from Mexico City to Santa Fe for over four hundred years, beginning with Spanish colonizers, then Mexican merchants and migrants, and eventually people from other parts of Latin America. And before it was given this name by the Spanish settlers, various groups of Indigenous people had traversed this path for hundreds of years, trading precious items such as turquoise, animal hides, and parrot feathers.

The third historical marker, made of cement, is blank. The theme of its original dedication is not clear. Due to age, weather, or possibly vandalism, its plaque and inscription are now absent. The irony of the missing dedication on this marker speaks to the need to reimagine what and who should be memorialized in this space. This missing inscription is an invitation to build something new, a memorial that honors the space and the many unnamed people who have passed through it, making history in their own right, but who have not been recognized for their historical and cultural contributions.

The fourth historical marker, made of cement, is dedicated to El Paso del Rio del Norte. It was erected in 1936 by the state of Texas when the state legislature created a commission to celebrate the one hundredth anniversary of Texas's independence from Mexico. The inscription reads:

> On May 4, 1598, Don Juan de Oñate, Adelantado and Captain-General, Governor of New Mexico, first named El Paso del Rio del Norte.
>
> Through this old pass, the lowest snow-free feasible route from the Atlantic to the Pacific through the Rocky Mountains, extend today the great trunk lines of telegraph and railroad. The city of El Paso marks the place and perpetuates the name.[14]

It is for this reason that this place bears the name of Oñate Crossing. Since before Ellis Island became synonymous with immigration to the US and the Statue of Liberty called for the huddled masses, people of Spanish and Mexican descent have been crossing this river from the Rio Bravo side to the Rio Grande side. And although the historical record and a small marker credit Oñate for locating this place, Indigenous people had crossed this river ford, in both directions, for an untold period before Europeans set foot in the Americas. And it would be another 250 years before Anglo American manifest destiny would wrestle this area away from Mexico.

## MAGOFFIN AND HART: TWO CONFEDERATE AGENTS FOR THE SOUTH(WEST)

Magoffin was born in 1799. He was originally from Kentucky, and like many others in that era, he immigrated from the Appalachian region to Texas.[15] In his early twenties, he moved to Matamoros in northern Mexico to pursue trade interests. He was heavily involved in commerce between Matamoros, the Texas coast, and New Orleans, particularly in exchanging cotton for finished goods. By the mid-1830s, he had moved his family and business enterprise to Chihuahua, where he switched his focus to the lucrative trade routes between Chihuahua, Santa Fe, and St. Louis. In the record predominantly written by white historians, Magoffin is noted for developing a reputation as a respected and successful businessman and gracious host to visitors at his home, becoming known as Don Santiago.[16]

By 1836, Texas had seceded from Mexico, and tensions between the US and Mexico had increased. In 1846, President James K. Polk, who needed someone with Magoffin's experience in Mexico, asked Magoffin to serve as an envoy on behalf of the US in its forthcoming campaign to invade Mexico. Magoffin was instructed to join General Stephen W. Kearny's expedition, which was en route to wrestle New Mexico away from Mexico. Sufficiently fluent in Spanish, Magoffin went ahead of the caravan to speak with New Mexico governor Manuel Armijo. It is unclear what Magoffin told him, but Armijo ordered his troops to withdraw from Santa Fe.[17] For this reason, some historians credit Magoffin with facilitating the "bloodless conquest of Santa Fe."[18] Upon return to El Paso, Magoffin was arrested by Mexican authorities, most likely for treason, and imprisoned in Chihuahua until the end of the Mexican-American War in 1848.[19] After the Mexican-American War, he became a supplier to the US Army, gaining trade acumen that would serve him well during the Civil War.

In February 1861, Texas voted in favor of secession from the Union. Most Mexican Americans in El Paso at the time showed little interest in taking sides in this conflict.[20] The majority of the Anglo Americans in El Paso, however, were pro-Confederacy. Most were not enslavers, but they were staunch supporters of Jefferson Davis, the president of the Confederacy, who enslaved as many as 113 Black people and was quoted as saying, "We recognize the negro as God and

God's Book and God's Laws, in nature, tell us to recognize him—our inferior, fitted expressly for servitude."[21] Considering such deep-seated racist views, Anglo citizens of El Paso who were pro-Confederate and supportive of Davis should be linked to the white supremacist movement of that time. They also strongly supported Davis because he was in favor of building a southern transcontinental railroad, which was of economic and political importance to the isolated far west Texas region and its merchants. However, to build such a railroad and to develop agricultural and textile goods that could be delivered via this new route would require cheap, if not free, labor. Indentured servitude, masked as cheap Mexican and Indigenous labor, was one option available to them. Growing the enslaved trade market to far west Texas would have been an even more lucrative scenario for the pro-Confederate constituency. Economic greed and profit lines supported by acts of white supremacy and Black enslavement made for a logical motive for Confederate support in El Paso, which eventually saturated the area.

After Texas seceded from the Union, US troops were ordered to abandon Fort Bliss. All military property was then turned over to Magoffin and Hart, the authorized Confederate agents for the region.[22] As a Confederate agent, Magoffin mainly provided supplies for the Confederate Army in New Mexico. He supplied John W. Baylor and Henry H. Sibley's missions on their marches into New Mexico. Unfortunately for the Confederacy, the Battle at Glorieta Pass, registered as one of the eleven Class I Civil War battles, in which the South attempted to gain control of the Southwest and secure access to the Pacific, failed. After this significant blow to the Confederacy in New Mexico, nearly all of Magoffin's family left El Paso for San Antonio, though his wife, Dolores Valdés Magoffin, moved across the river to stay with her family in Mexico. After regaining control of the region, the Union government in New Mexico auctioned off Magoffin's land in El Paso. He eventually received a pardon for his role as a Confederate agent in September 1867 and had his citizenship restored. Magoffin remained in San Antonio, where he later died. His son, Joseph, eventually was able to reclaim the family's lost property.

It is fair to say that James W. Magoffin was more than just a Confederate sympathizer. He was an agent of the South who supplied the Confederacy with the provisions to outfit and feed soldiers in its objective to secure the Southwest. However, his historical and political footprint, based on the prevalent use of his name in El Paso, clearly has not been limited to his role in the Confederacy. He was a successful businessman who promoted trade, at the time, across three countries: the US, Texas, and Mexico. He helped to establish Fort Bliss, a major US Army base that still exists today. And he founded Magoffinville, the future site of El Paso. And yet, despite his diverse contributions to the border region, his lone memorial, albeit small in size and located in an obscure location, is dedicated to his service to the Confederacy.

Despite the positive reception that Magoffin seemed to enjoy in El Paso, evidenced by numerous places bearing his name, we should look deeper into his history and motivations before we grant him the status of being such a heroic and important figure in El Paso's history. He has been painted as a generous host who had good relationships with Mexicans, particularly wealthy men with whom he could conduct business. But other studies have indicated that Magoffin was merely acting out of self-interest by serving as a spy for the US as it was preparing to forcefully take New Mexico from Mexico as part of the Mexican-American War.[23] As an active agent for manifest destiny, he aided in Mexico's loss of New Mexico, which was part of a domino effect in which Mexico eventually lost the rest of its northern territory.[24] As for helping to establish what eventually became Fort Bliss, it was, once again, in the self-interest of protecting his business assets from any perceived threat after the war with Mexico and Indian raids. Interestingly, this military post was established at Magoffinville in 1854 on the order of then-US secretary of war Jefferson Davis. Thus, the pro-Confederate relationship with Davis had begun well before the Civil War. Therefore, although Magoffin did indeed contribute to the founding of El Paso, his motives were questionable and clearly served his business and political interests.

Hart, like Magoffin, made his way to El Paso as an adult. He was born in Highland, New York, on March 28, 1816, and grew up in St. Louis, Missouri. He immigrated to the Southwest in 1848, served as an adjutant in a Missouri Calvary unit, and participated in the Mexican-American War. He married the daughter of a wealthy Mexican flour miller from Chihuahua. He then established his own flour mill and residence in present-day El Paso, adjacent to the Oñate Crossing location. The residence is now an abandoned Mexican restaurant called La Hacienda.

Before the Civil War, in 1850, Hart signed a contract to provide flour to local Army posts for eleven cents per pound.[25] Due to his business acumen and real estate holdings, he reported the value of his assets in the 1860 census to be $350,000, making him the wealthiest man in the area. He had much to gain or lose, depending on the outcome of the Civil War. Winning would have meant continued contracts to support the Confederate Army with flour and other government-related deals that would have certainly increased his wealth. Losing meant financial disaster. El Pasoans with southern sympathies had their properties seized and sold by Union forces. In Hart's case, this included his flour mill, dwelling houses, corrals, ranch houses, machinery, and stables, which sold for $3,000. It took several years, but after a long struggle, Hart recovered his property from W. W. Mills, a pro-Union El Pasoan and political enemy of Hart's, who accepted a payment of $10 in 1873.

Like Magoffin and many Anglo Americans of the region, Hart was a staunch proponent of secession. In a local election, Hart's political enemies, brothers

Anson and W. W. Mills, cast two of the scarce votes in opposition to secession. After the vote, Hart shouted, "Champagne for the secessionists and the noose for all Unionists."[26] Just like Magoffin, Hart was much more than a Confederate sympathizer; he was a fierce opponent of maintaining the Union. As a business-man with interests in securing more trade for the region and expanding his flour manufacturing contracts, Hart supported the Confederacy's expansion to the Southwest. However, unlike most others in El Paso, he was one of the few enslavers in the area.[27] Thus, the noose would have been an acceptable "reward" for anti-Confederate obstructionists who challenged his enslaver mindset.

Hart, like Magoffin, was a Confederate agent in the region, securing prop-erty and goods for the South. As a purchasing agent, Hart was also in charge of gathering feed corn and flour for Sibley and the Confederate Army as they planned to push Union forces into Colorado. He even produced at his mill some fifty thousand pounds of flour to supply Sibley's men. Hart also had $40,000 to $50,000 on hand to purchase corn, flour, salt, beef, soap, and beans from mer-chants in the Mexican states of Chihuahua and Sonora.[28] Although these items were plentiful in Mexico, the Mexicans refused payment in Confederate script.[29] The Confederate loss of the Southwest, via the Battle of Glorieta Pass, falls mostly on the poor leadership of Sibley. But some blame should be allocated to Hart due to his inability to gather the necessary supplies to provision the Confederate Army in the deserts of the Southwest, where soldiers relied heavily upon purchasing agents like Hart because there were scant natural resources to support them otherwise.

Hart died in 1874, and his body was buried on the grounds of his residence and mill. His and his wife's bodies were later exhumed and reinterred elsewhere to make way for highway construction.[30] His former residence, which became the now defunct La Hacienda restaurant, and his shared Confederate memorial still remain at the Oñate Crossing.

## OÑATE: THE LAST CONQUISTADOR

Oñate has a complex and controversial history in New Mexico. He was born in Zacatecas, Mexico, in 1550 to Spanish parents. He was married to Isabel de Tolosa Cortés de Moctezuma, a descendant of the famous conquistador Hernán Cortés and the Aztec emperor Moctezuma.[31] He is credited with colonizing New Mexico for the Spanish crown. With authority granted to him by King Phillip II of Spain, Oñate took formal possession of New Mexico for Spain on April 30, 1598. The historic and symbolic ceremony included a Catholic mass, the reading of the toma, and the performance of a play.[32] By May 4, his expedition, which included at least five hundred men, women, and children, seven thousand head of livestock, and eighty-plus wagons and oxcarts, had begun to cross a section of the Rio Grande that Oñate described as "the pass of the river and the ford," which today is two miles west of downtown El Paso.[33] It was the best place within miles that enabled them to cross the river safely with wagons. The markings of a heavily used foot trail by local Indians provided evidence that it was a good place to cross. They were assisted in their crossing by a friendly group of Manso Indians. Eventually, on July 11, the expedition reached the northern Pueblo of Ohkay Owingeh, approximately thirty miles north of present-day Santa Fe. Here, Oñate and his men displaced native people from their homes to settle their colony, renaming the centuries-old Indigenous village San Juan de los Caballeros.

Hispanophiles still celebrate the influence of Spanish and Mexican colonizers who settled New Mexico. Colonizers established Santa Fe, the first capital city in the present-day United States, in 1610, introduced the Spanish language and the Catholic faith across the Southwest, and helped establish a Mestizo Hispanic population that eventually grew throughout the Southwest. However, that is only one side of the story. It is important to remember that, although Oñate declared New Mexico for the Spanish crown, there were already thousands of American Indians occupying these lands before the settlers arrived.

When the Oñate expedition arrived at the new territory in 1598, there were an estimated eighty thousand Pueblo Indians living in New Mexico, not to mention other Indigenous groups of people excluded from this number.[34] By 1679, less than one hundred years later, that population had been severely reduced to seventeen thousand. There is no way to describe this dramatic change other than to call it a genocide. Many of these people died from European-introduced diseases for which they had no immunity. Others perished due to a lack of resources, forced to share with or relinquish their shelter, food, and water to the invading settlers. And an untold number were killed. Oñate's brutal force was directly responsible for the murder of hundreds of Indigenous people, for which he is still remembered today by many Pueblo people. The most documented of these atrocities, described in Spanish written records and American Indian oral history, took place at Acoma Pueblo, sixty miles west of Albuquerque.

In late 1598, a group of Spanish soldiers, on their way to Zuni Pueblo, sought provisions from Acoma Pueblo and were denied their request. After one of the soldiers stole two turkeys, a bird sacred to the Acoma people, and violated an Indian woman, Acoma men responded by killing Captain Don Juan Zaldívar and twelve other men.[35] In retaliation, a group of seventy soldiers armed with a cannon, led by Don Vicente Zaldívar, the slain captain's brother, returned to Acoma on January 21, 1599, to punish the Acoma people and send a message to other Pueblos considering rebellion. When the battle ended, eight hundred Acoma men, women, and children had been slain. Eighty men and children were taken as prisoners, stood trial, and were found guilty.[36] Men over twenty-five had one foot cut off and were sentenced to twenty years of personal servitude to the Spanish colonists.[37] Young men between the ages of twelve and twenty-five received twenty years of personal servitude.[38] Young women over twelve years of age were given twenty years of servitude. Sixty young girls were sent to Mexico City to serve in the convents there, never to see their homeland or families again. And two Hopi men caught at the Acoma battle had their right hands cut off and were set free to spread the news of Spanish retribution.[39]

The Spanish crown denounced Oñate's ruthless military response as it was also attempting to convert the Pueblo people to Christianity. In 1606, Oñate was ordered to return to Mexico City until the allegations of his war crimes against the Indians and other misdeeds could be settled. He resigned from the governorship in 1607, and in 1613, he was found guilty of his crimes and banished from the New Mexico colony and Mexico City. He went to Spain where he died in 1626.[40] The penalty of exile is hardly sufficient punishment for the level of his atrocities. And yet despite his well-documented misdeeds, Oñate has a number of statues and public places named in his honor, including a statue in Española, New Mexico, and El Paso, a park in Albuquerque, trail plaques across the state of New Mexico, and a high school in Las Cruces, New Mexico. The statue at the entrance to the El Paso airport, the largest bronze equestrian statue in the world at thirty-six feet high, was designed in his honor. However, the official name of the statue was changed to "The Equestrian" in response to the negative press clouding the construction and public unveiling of such a large and expensive statue dedicated to a convicted war criminal.

Despite all the controversy surrounding taxpayer properties that bear the name of Oñate and the mostly unsuccessful calls for removal of his memorials from the public eye, there is one location that has been completely overlooked. One could say the Oñate Crossing has been ignored to the point of creating a historical obsolescence. That is to say that we, as a society and educational system, do not commemorate this physical space as a significant marker of transcontinental migration well before the inception of the United States. Just like the mass murderer who massacred innocent people in El Paso, the general public and mass media continue to paint Hispanic immigration to the US as an invasion at worst and as a recent phenomenon at best.

I argue that this crossing of cultures and peoples, which is of great historical significance, has not so much been accidently overlooked as it has been purposely neglected. This key historical landmark has not been endowed with the public commemoration that it deserves due to its close proximity to Mexico, specifically Ciudad Juárez, which has been plagued by poverty and crime. Xenophobes and misguided nationalists do not want to be reminded that an untold number of migrants have passed through this natural ford, both before and after the Rio Grande became the dividing boundary between the two countries.

To be clear, Oñate is at best a controversial figure who does not deserve to be honored with public admiration through numerous places bearing his name. However, his contribution to the colonization of New Mexico and the introduction of a Spanish/Mexican cultural heritage cannot be ignored, nor should it. This border space that bears his name is an extremely significant transnational historical landmark. The Oñate Crossing is the unheralded Ellis Island of the Southwest: it has a longer history than Ellis Island but has yet to receive its due recognition. To reiterate the argument of this essay, it is the place that matters more, not the person.

## MEMORIALIZING THE RACIST PAST AND REMAKING A COMPLEX FUTURE

The double-sided Confederate historical marker dedicated to Magoffin and Hart was erected in 1964. And just like this double-sided marker that points to two countries in two directions, there are two points of view one can take on why state officials chose to erect this Confederate marker, and many others, during the early 1960s. Some historians argue that there was a big push in the early 1960s to commemorate the Civil War Centennial. But this timing also coincides with the civil rights movement, specifically the Civil Rights Act of 1964. Thus, although the reason for the proliferation of Confederate symbolism in the early 1960s is debatable, I contend that erecting a memorial in 1964 to two individuals that focuses on their roles in helping to expand the Confederacy and neglects their contributions to society in general is a reaffirmation of white supremacy as a reaction to the threat of its demise.

This act of public commemoration pays tribute to larger questions of white supremacy and some Anglos' fear of losing power to ethnic groups in the region and country. To this point, Jane Dailey argues, "Most of the people who were involved in erecting the [Confederate] monuments were not necessarily erecting a monument to the past, but were rather, erecting them toward a white supremacist future."[41] In this light, perhaps the turbulent sixties should be divided into halves with the early 1960s being designated as the segregationist sixties. The year when this small Confederate memorial was erected, 1964, affirms this point. A comprehensive study of Confederate statues and monuments across the US published by the Southern Poverty Law Center in 2016 shows huge spikes in monument construction twice during the twentieth century: first, in the early 1900s, and then, in the 1950s and 1960s.[42]

Both of these periods were ripe with tension and racial violence due to the struggle for civil rights. In the early 1900s, after the Reconstruction period, southern states enacted Jim Crow laws to disenfranchise Black Americans and legalize segregation efforts. In the middle part of the twentieth century, the

civil rights movement, seeking equal rights afforded by the Constitution, nulli-
fied such segregation. Granted, 1961 represented the centennial anniversary of
the start of the Civil War. As such, it was common for many towns across the
South and other places with southern sympathies to erect monuments to their
Confederate forefathers. However, once again, it was no accident that the bitter
memory of the mythic Lost Cause of the Confederacy, even after one hundred
years, coincided with a continued, orchestrated political and socioeconomic
effort to disenfranchise Black Americans and, when possible, turn a blind eye to
racialized violence committed against them.

1964 did not just mark a centennial period of this country's biggest war in
terms of casualties. It also symbolized a major turning point in US race relations, rooted in the argument that all human beings are created equal. Considered the most significant civil rights legislation since Reconstruction, the Civil
Rights Act, signed into law by President Lyndon B. Johnson, "prohibited discrimination in public places, provided for the integration of schools and other
public facilities, and made employment discrimination illegal."[43] The Magoffin-
Hart double-sided Confederate marker, along with the rest of the Confederate
monuments erected during this period, is a veiled symbol of white supremacist
backlash against the landmark civil rights legislation. In fact, one US senator
from Texas voted for the Civil Rights Act, while the other voted against it.[44] And
of the twenty-three votes cast by Texas's members of Congress, eighteen were
against it.[45] One of those negative votes was cast by Representative Edgar Foreman of Texas's 16th Congressional District, representing far west Texas from El
Paso to the Permian Basin.

From the perspective of many white southerners, Confederate monuments
and memorials provide a sense of nostalgia while paying tribute to Confederate
values and heritage, however ill-placed those ideas are. In a general framework,
philosopher George Schedler defines the purpose of monuments as "markers or
statues whose purpose is to pay homage to the conduct or character—usually
courage or leadership—of some person or group. Minimally, a monument is
either a marker with an inscription or a statue with no inscription designed to
recall with affection, or at least with approval, something or some person."[46] The
Confederate memorials, for those who erected and respect them, certainly fit this
description in a broad sense. But aside from a monument's dedication and its
political and historical messaging, we should also consider the significance of its
location and how that can convey an even more complex, if not mixed, message.

According to John J. Winberry, there are four common locations and purposes for Confederate monuments: a) battlefield monuments commemorating
troops, b) cemetery monuments commemorating the dead, c) courthouse or
urban monuments commemorating those who served from a particular county,
and d) large, impressive monuments raised on the grounds of state capitols

across the South.[47] The Confederate memorial marker at the Oñate Crossing does not fit any of these common locations. The Oñate Crossing is not a battlefield, nor a cemetery, nor a courthouse, and it is not on capitol or municipal grounds. Perhaps at one time, when La Hacienda restaurant was bustling with business, people would have visited the markers to learn more about El Paso's past and appreciate the historical connection between Hart's Mill and the Oñate Crossing. However, despite any historical or geographic link, the Confederate historical marker is still an odd fit for this border zone.

Aside from the monument's geographic location, there are other elements to consider when we attempt to gauge the historical significance of this Confederate marker. Some have claimed that the standard-bearer monument of an unknown Confederate soldier atop a column, commonly located at a county courthouse, often faces north; the soldier, in his stoic pose, awaits the invading Union Army ready to defend his southern home. Winberry shows that this is true about half the time.[48] When we consider this, it is clear that a monument's dedication, geographic location, and directional positionality are all strategic and purposeful. This last component is especially true for the four small memorial markers at the Oñate Crossing. However, instead of facing north toward the US or south toward Mexico, they face each other in an open half semicircle.

The positionality of these memorials at the Oñate Crossing is significant because they are creating a historical dialogue with each other. This dialogue, made possible through public commemoration, takes place in a space that I have argued is the most significant historical contact zone in the country as it connects the US with Mexico and the rest of Latin America through a crossing that has undoubtedly seen millions of migrants and immigrants cross in both directions. However, although the location and positionality of the markers work together to create a powerful message, it is the actual messaging of the markers that lacks complexity and depth, and this is where the unmarked historical marker comes into play.

The unmarked historical marker is the simplest one, bearing no artistic rendering or design. It is a plain cement marker without a plaque or inscription. There is no faded inscription visible to the naked eye. The plaque might have broken off or been vandalized, or perhaps it was never completed and installed. I argue that this incomplete marker, unlike the others, despite its designer's intent, does not represent the past but the future. However, we, the residents and citizens of the Southwest and, by extension, the rest of the US, need to be able to first imagine a monument worthy of honoring a future when our diversity is respected and celebrated—not just the diversity of significant historical figures but also of everyday people, places, origins, ethnicities, religions, and philosophies. The Oñate Crossing is the ideal location for such a monument because it represents a space of movement and migration, in all directions, of leaving and returning.

After we can imagine it, then we can build it. But before that, we must cease treating this space as a transitory historical black hole. The Oñate Crossing is a highly significant cultural heritage landmark. Yet, out of all of the institutions and organizations that share some legal claim to that abandoned lot, including the US Department of Homeland Security, the US Bureau of Reclamation, the Texas Department of Transportation, UTEP, the city of El Paso, the Mexican government, and private landowners, none have come close to successfully transforming this piece of land into its fullest potential as a sacred space.

What's missing is the sanctification of this space. Kenneth E. Foote contends that:

> Sanctification involves the creation of what geographers term a "sacred" place—a site set apart from its surroundings and dedicated to the memory of an event, person, or group. Sanctification almost always involves the construction of a durable marker, either some sort of monument or memorial or a garden, park, or building that is intended to be maintained in perpetuity. . . . Formal consecration is a prerequisite of sanctification. That is, there must be a ceremony that includes an explicit statement of the site's significance and an explanation of why the event should be remembered. Sanctification demonstrates most clearly the relationship of landscape and memory.[49]

Although the Oñate Crossing markers are dedicated to the memory of people and place, they have not aged well, in message or physical durability. In addition, we can say that this place has not been made or treated like a sacred site for three reasons. One, it does not follow Foote's prescribed notion of a sacred site because the relationship between these markers and their memories has not been made clear for the general public. Indeed, I have shown the (mis)connection between the markers and related histories here. Secondly, it does not adhere to the popular Hispanic notion of what a sacred site is, even though that is the predominant population of the area. According to Levi Romero, the New Mexico Centennial poet laureate, in *Sagrado: A Photopoetics across the Chicano Homeland*, a sacred place is where two or more gather in the name of community.[50] Locals or visitors seldom visit this tucked-away place, but when they do, it is certainly not to embrace their shared community. Lastly, this space cannot be considered sacred yet because "sanctification can ensue when communities are struck by accidents and tragedies such as natural disasters, fires, explosions, crashes, and other accidents."[51] This particular space has not seen such tragedies, at least in recorded history.

Unfortunately, however, the city of El Paso did witness such a tragedy when a racist gunman massacred twenty-three innocent people in his deranged plan to stem the tide of what he viewed as a Hispanic invasion of this country. He, and others like him, do not know or appreciate the region's history. Nor do they care to learn the facts because such complexities would refute their perverted versions of the truth. The best result that could come from this tragedy, other than serious gun reform, is for residents to unite and build something that memorializes the lives lost and allows them to move forward without ever forgetting their past. Makeshift memorials with flowers, pictures, and words of encouragement at the site of the tragedy in a Walmart parking lot may be cathartic but are only a momentary outpouring of emotions.[52] A permanent memorial designed to honor these victims, formally consecrated and made into a sacred space, should be placed at the Oñate Crossing to replace the outdated and poorly planned Confederate and Oñate markers.

Seldom do we successfully memorialize people who merit public recognition in an appropriate manner and at the right place. For this reason, Foote notes, "Relatively few tragedies result in sanctification."[53] There are several reasons why this is the case, but he argues that "the most important is whether the tragedy touches a single, relatively homogenous, self-identified community, one that comes to view the tragedy as a common, public loss." El Paso is predominantly Mexican and Mexican American, but it is heterogeneous in many ways as it also includes Anglo, Black, American Indian, and Asian American communities. Additionally, it is home to Fort Bliss, one of the largest US Army bases in the country, which houses a diverse population of soldiers and civilian support staff. And of course, it straddles the border and shares this space with its sister city of Ciudad Juárez. It is this heterogeneous diversity from which El Paso draws its strength and resiliency.

Although this place cannot be considered a sacred site in its current state, it thus has the potential to be transformed into one and to commemorate not just the memory of the past but the possibility of creating a better future. For, as Foote shows, the new sacred site "is transformed into a symbol intended to remind future generations of a virtue or sacrifice or to warn them of events to be avoided."[54] Any time innocent people are murdered solely because they are different from the one(s) perpetrating the violence, we know that we must make concrete and lasting change to never repeat such tragedies. The creation of a permanent and sacred place dedicated to the healing of those wounds is an essential step in this process.

## CONCLUSION

As this chapter demonstrates, the two-sided memorial marker dedicated to two Confederate agents, erected in 1964 in this southwest border space, is a white supremacist reaction to the Civil Rights Act of the same year. The Civil War, as has been well documented, was the most destructive and divisive war this country has ever seen. The Confederate memorial in El Paso, and others elsewhere in the country, does not teach us how to repair divisions; it was not intended as such. But with the construction of a new memorial in this border contact zone to stand in place of the blank marker and replace the Confederate and Oñate markers, we can create something truly monumental. With a monument designed for and dedicated to the power of crossing borders, both geographic and cultural, in addition to memorializing the memory of the lives lost due to racist and xenophobic violence, this space has the potential to be transformed into a powerful symbol of what this country was designed to represent. El Paso, the city where cultures and communities come into contact and intersect, can become more than just a place people pass through, as its name suggests. It can also develop into a destination where people gather in the name of community. For now, although these historical markers do not cross borders, a new monument as proposed here can demonstrate the potential and power to transcend them.

## NOTES

1. "Lin-Manuel Miranda's Sonnet from the Tony Awards," *New York Times*, June 12, 2016, www.nytimes.com/2016/06/13/theater/lin-manuel-mirandas-sonnet-from-the-tony-awards .html.

2. According to recent data, El Paso County is 81.8 percent Hispanic, which makes it one of the largest Hispanic cities in the United States ("Population," City of El Paso, accessed July 24, 2020, http://www.elpasotexas.gov/economic-development/business-services/data-and -statistics/population).

3. Arthur C. Danto, "The Vietnam Veterans Memorial," *The Nation*, August 31, 1985, 152.

4. Brigit Katz, "At Least 110 Confederate Monuments and Symbols Have Been Removed Since 2015," *Smithsonian Magazine*, June 8, 2018, https://www.smithsonianmag.com/smart -news/least-110-confederate-monuments-and-symbols-have-been-removed-2015-180969254/.

5. Katz, "At Least 110."

6. In an effort to uncover this information, I contacted the El Camino Real de Tierra Adentro Trail Association (CARTA), a historic preservationist, and an environmental consulting firm, all of whom had worked at the site. None were able to provide a definitive explanation of the blank monument. Spencer R. Herrera, email message to CARTA, July 25, 2019; CARTA secretary, email message to Troy Ainsworth, July 25, 2019; and Spencer R. Herrera, email message to Ama Terra, July 25, 2019.

7. In this essay, I use the terms *monuments*, *memorials*, and *markers* interchangeably. However, I define the Confederate piece as a memorial because it memorializes the lives of James W. Magoffin and Simeon Hart with the dates and places of their births and deaths. The other two inscribed pieces I call markers or historical markers because they lean toward marking the history of that place.

8. Don Juan de Oñate was accused by the Spanish crown of "several violations including the use of excessive force during the Acoma rebellion, the hanging of two Indians, the execution of mutineers and deserters, and adultery. He was fined, banned from Mexico City for four years, and banished from New Mexico forever." Today, by many, he is viewed as a war criminal ("Juan

de Oñate," New Mexico History, last modified January 10, 2013, http://newmexicohistory.org/
2013/01/10/juan-de-onate/).

9. Mary Louise Pratt, *Imperial Eyes: Travel Writing and Transculturation* (New York:
Routledge, 2008), 7.

10. This space goes by two different names depending on the source: the "Oñate Crossing"
or "Hart's Mill." The space I am analyzing is the Oñate Crossing, which is confirmed in
D. Dobson-Brown and R. Feit, "El Paso del Norte: A Cultural Landscape History of the Oñate
Crossing on the Camino Real de Tierra Adentro 1598–1893, Ciudad Juárez, Mexico and El
Paso, Texas U.S.A." (AmaTerra Environmental, 2018), prepared for the National Park Service–
National Trails Intermountain Region. Hart's Mill is adjacent to this space.

11. Capt. James W. Magoffin, 1964, granite memorial, Oñate Crossing, El Paso.

12. Maj. Simeon Hart, 1964, granite memorial, Oñate Crossing, El Paso.

13. The Camino Real, 1983, stone and cement historical marker, Oñate Crossing, El Paso.

14. El Paso del Rio del Norte, 1936, cement historical marker, Oñate Crossing, El Paso.

15. When Texas was part of Mexico, officially the state of Coahuila y Texas, many Anglo
immigrants came to settle the area as part of the Moses and Stephen F. Austin colony,
invited by the Mexican government. However, over time, many Anglo settlers, mostly from
the Appalachian region, came illegally without permission, which eventually led them to
outnumber the local Mexican residents in Texas.

16. See Martin Donnell Kohout, "Magoffin, James Wiley," Texas State Historical Association,
last modified December 6, 2019, http://www.tshaonline.org/handbook/online/articles/fma13;
and Rex W. Strickland, *Six Who Came to El Paso: Pioneers of the 1840s* (El Paso: Texas Western
Press, 1963).

17. There is some speculation, but no clear proof, that Magoffin bribed Manuel Armijo to
flee New Mexico instead of putting up resistance. It is worth noting that Magoffin and Armijo
were also related through marriage.

18. See Thomas Hart Benton and John S. Jenkins regarding Magoffin's role in the "bloodless
conquest." Benton, *Thirty Years' View; or, A History of the Working of the American Government
for Thirty Years, from 1820 to 1850* (New York: Appleton and Company, 1854); and Jenkins,
*History of the War between the United States and Mexico, from the Commencement of Hostilities
to the Ratification of the Treaty of Peace* (Auburn, NY: Derby and Miller, 1850).

19. "James Wiley Magoffin," Texas Historical Commission, accessed July 24, 2020, https://
www.thc.texas.gov/historic-sites/magoffin-home/history/james-wiley-magoffin.

20. W. H. Timmons, *James Wiley Magoffin: Don Santiago—El Paso Pioneer* (El Paso: Texas
Western Press, 1999), 75.

21. William C. Davis, *Look Away! A History of the Confederate States of America* (New York:
Free Press, 2002), 137.

22. Timmons, *James Wiley Magoffin*, 76.

23. According to Howard R. Lamar, who wrote the foreword to Susan Shelby Magoffin's
diary *Down the Santa Fe Trail and into Mexico* (1962), "In 1830 James further entrenched
himself in the economic and social life of the northern provinces by marrying Dona Maria
Gertrudes Valdez de Beremende, who came from a prominent Chihuahua family." Lamar
quoted in Cameron L. Saffell, "A Reexamination of the 'Bloodless Conquest' of Santa Fe,"
*New Mexico Historical Review* 91, no. 3 (Summer 2016): 285. The nuanced language is worth
mentioning here as it appears that Magoffin viewed marrying into a rich Mexican family as a
business opportunity. This point is further supported by the fact that, after his first wife passed
away, he married her sister Dolores.

24. As a result of the Mexican-American War and the Treaty of Guadalupe Hidalgo (1848),
Mexico ceded 55 percent of its territory, including parts of present-day Arizona, California,

New Mexico, Texas, Colorado, Nevada, and Utah, to the United States. It had lost most of Texas after the Texas Revolution in 1836, which was backed by the United States and its volunteer mercenaries.

25. W. H. Timmons, "Hart, Simeon," Texas State Historical Association, accessed July 24, 2020, http://www.tshaonline.org/handbook/online/articles/fhaak.

26. Strickland, *Six Who Came*, 39.

27. Timmons, *James Wiley Magoffin*, 75.

28. Timmons, *James Wiley Magoffin*, 79.

29. Timmons, *James Wiley Magoffin*, 80.

30. One could argue that Hart was not as important as historical revisionists made him out to be. The mausoleum that housed his and his wife's remains was destroyed by highway construction. Their bodies lie in an unmarked grave somewhere in El Paso. See Timmons, "Hart, Simeon."

31. "Juan de Oñate," New Mexico History.

32. Marc Simmons, *The Last Conquistador: Juan de Oñate and the Settling of the Far Southwest* (Norman: University of Oklahoma Press, 1991), 100. *La toma* stated that the Spanish crown was taking formal possession of all territory north of the Rio Grande on behalf of King Phillip. The play was a version of *Moros y cristianos*, a didactic play used to teach Indians about the repercussions of war against the Spaniards. Essentially, they would suffer a similarly ill fate as the Moors.

33. Simmons, *Last Conquistador*, 101.

34. Ramón A. Gutiérrez, *When Jesus Came, the Corn Mothers Went Away: Marriage, Sexuality, and Power in New Mexico, 1500–1846* (Stanford: Stanford University Press, 1991), 92.

35. Gutiérrez, *When Jesus Came*, 52–53.

36. Gutiérrez, *When Jesus Came*, 53.

37. Gutiérrez, *When Jesus Came*, 54.

38. Gutiérrez, *When Jesus Came*, 53.

39. "Juan de Oñate," New Mexico History.

40. Gerald F. Kozlowski, "Oñate, Juan de," Texas State Historical Association, last modified August 3, 2017, http://www.tshaonline.org/handbook/online/articles/fono2.

41. Quoted in Miles Parks, "Confederate Statues Were Built to Further a 'White Supremacist Future,'" NPR, August 20, 2017, https://www.npr.org/2017/08/20/544266880/confederate-statues-were-built-to-further-a-white-supremacist-future.

42. "Whose Heritage? Public Symbols of the Confederacy," Southern Poverty Law Center, accessed July 24, 2020, https://www.splcenter.org/20190201/whose-heritage-public-symbols-confederacy.

43. "Civil Rights Act (1964)," Our Documents, accessed July 24, 2020, https://www.ourdocuments.gov/doc.php?flash=false&doc=97.

44. "H.R. 7152 Passage," GovTrack.us, accessed July 24, 2020, https://www.govtrack.us/congress/votes/88-1964/s409.

45. "H.R. 7152. Civil Rights Act of 1964. Adoption of a Resolution (H. Res. 789) Providing for House Approval of the Bill as Amended by the Senate," GovTrack.us, accessed July 24, 2020, https://www.govtrack.us/congress/votes/88-1964/h182. It is worth mentioning that, in 1966, just two years after this landmark civil rights legislation, Texas Western College, later renamed the University of Texas at El Paso (UTEP), won the National Collegiate Athletics Association's men's basketball national championship, becoming the first team with an all-Black starting lineup to do so. The Texas Department of Transportation's recently constructed spur connecting the UTEP campus and the Oñate Crossing is named in the team's honor Spur 1966. It is ironic that this spur celebrating Black history leads to the Confederate monument at the Oñate Crossing.

46. George Schedler, "Are Confederate Monuments Racist?," *International Journal of Applied Philosophy* 15, no. 2 (January 2001): 288.

47. John J. Winberry, "'Lest We Forget': The Confederate Monument and the Southern Townscape," *Southeastern Geographer* 23, no. 2 (November 1983): 108.

48. Winberry, "'Lest We Forget.'"

49. Kenneth E. Foote, *Shadowed Ground: America's Landscapes of Violence and Tragedy* (Austin: University of Texas Press, 1997), 8.

50. Spencer Herrera, Robert Kaiser, and Levi Romero, *Sagrado: A Photopoetics across the Chicano Homeland* (Albuquerque: University of New Mexico Press, 2013), xi.

51. Foote, *Shadowed Ground*, 15.

52. Walmart did construct a permanent memorial to honor the victims. However, I argue that any memorial located in a retail parking lot, no matter how aesthetically pleasing, is not sufficient to honor their memory and is even less capable of inspiring a better future.

53. Foote, *Shadowed Ground*, 15.

54. Foote, *Shadowed Ground*, 8.

## Bibliography

Benton, Thomas Hart. *Thirty Years' View; or, A History of the Working of the American Government for Thirty Years, from 1820 to 1850*. New York: Appleton and Company, 1854.

The Camino Real. 1983. Stone and cement historical marker. Oñate Crossing, El Paso.

Capt. James W. Magoffin. 1964. Granite memorial. Oñate Crossing, El Paso.

CARTA Secretary. Email message to Troy Ainsworth. July 25, 2019.

City of El Paso. "Population." Accessed July 24, 2020. http://www.elpasotexas.gov/economic -development/business-services/data-and-statistics/population.

Danto, Arthur C. "The Vietnam Veterans Memorial." *The Nation*, August 31, 1985.

Davis, William C. *Look Away! A History of the Confederate States of America*. New York: Free Press, 2002.

Dobson-Brown, D., and R. Feit. "El Paso del Norte: A Cultural Landscape History of the Oñate Crossing on the Camino Real de Tierra Adentro 1598–1893, Ciudad Juárez, Mexico and El Paso, Texas U.S.A." AmaTerra Environmental, 2018.

El Paso del Rio del Norte. 1936. Cement historical marker. Oñate Crossing, El Paso.

Foote, Kenneth E. *Shadowed Ground: America's Landscapes of Violence and Tragedy*. Austin: University of Texas Press, 1997.

GovTrack.us. "H.R. 7152. Civil Rights Act of 1964. Adoption of a Resolution (H. Res. 789) Providing for House Approval of the Bill as Amended by the Senate." Accessed July 24, 2020. https://www.govtrack.us/congress/votes/88-1964/h182.

GovTrack.us. "H.R. 7152 Passage." Accessed July 24, 2020. https://www.govtrack.us/congress/ votes/88-1964/s409.

Gutiérrez, Ramón A. *When Jesus Came, the Corn Mothers Went Away: Marriage, Sexuality, and Power in New Mexico, 1500–1846*. Stanford: Stanford University Press, 1991.

Herrera, Spencer R. Email message to Ama Terra. July 25, 2019.

Herrera, Spencer R. Email message to CARTA. July 25, 2019.

Herrera, Spencer R., Robert Kaiser, and Levi Romero. *Sagrado: A Photopoetics across the Chicano Homeland*. Albuquerque: University of New Mexico Press, 2013.

Jenkins, John S. *History of the War Between the United States and Mexico, from the Commencement of Hostilities to the Ratification of the Treaty of Peace*. Auburn, NY: Derby and Miller, 1850.

Katz, Brigit. "At Least 110 Confederate Monuments and Symbols Have Been Removed Since 2015." *Smithsonian Magazine*, June 8, 2018. https://www.smithsonianmag.com/smart-news/least-110-confederate-monuments-and-symbols-have-been-removed-2015-180969254/.

Kohout, Martin Donnell. "Magoffin, James Wiley." Texas State Historical Association. Last modified December 6, 2019. http://www.tshaonline.org/handbook/online/articles/fma13.

Kozlowski, Gerald F. "Oñate, Juan de." Texas State Historical Association. Last modified August 3, 2017. http://www.tshaonline.org/handbook/online/articles/fon02.

"Lin-Manuel Miranda's Sonnet from the Tony Awards." *New York Times*, June 12, 2016. www.nytimes.com/2016/06/13/theater/lin-manuel-mirandas-sonnet-from-the-tony-awards.html.

Maj. Simeon Hart. 1964. Granite memorial. Oñate Crossing, El Paso.

Nava, Margaret M. *Remembering: A Guide to New Mexico Cemeteries, Monuments, and Memorials*. Santa Fe: Sunstone Press, 2006.

New Mexico History. "Juan de Oñate." Last modified January 10, 2013. http://newmexicohistory.org/2013/01/10/juan-de-onate/.

Our Documents. "Civil Rights Act (1964)." Accessed July 24, 2020. https://www.ourdocuments.gov/doc.php?flash=false&doc=97.

Owley, Jessica, and Jess Phelps. "Understanding the Complicated Landscape of Civil War Monuments." *Indiana Law Journal* 93, no. 5 (2018): 15–33.

Parks, Miles. "Confederate Statues Were Built to Further a 'White Supremacist Future.'" NPR, August 20, 2017. https://www.npr.org/2017/08/20/544266880/confederate-statues-were-built-to-further-a-white-supremacist-future.

Pratt, Mary Louise. *Imperial Eyes: Travel Writing and Transculturation*. New York: Routledge, 2008.

Saffell, Cameron L. "A Reexamination of the 'Bloodless Conquest' of Santa Fe." *New Mexico Historical Review* 91, no. 3 (Summer 2016): 277–308.

Schedler, George. "Are Confederate Monuments Racist?" *International Journal of Applied Philosophy* 15, no. 2 (January 2001): 287–308.

Simmons, Marc. *The Last Conquistador: Juan de Oñate and the Settling of the Far Southwest*. Norman: University of Oklahoma Press, 1991.

Southern Poverty Law Center. "Whose Heritage? Public Symbols of the Confederacy." Accessed July 24, 2020. https://www.splcenter.org/20190201/whose-heritage-public-symbols-con federacy.

Strickland, Rex W. *Six Who Came to El Paso: Pioneers of the 1840s*. El Paso: Texas Western Press, 1963.

Texas Historical Commission. "James Wiley Magoffin." Accessed July 24, 2020. https://www.thc.texas.gov/historic-sites/magoffin-home/history/james-wiley-magoffin.

Timmons, W. H. "Hart, Simeon." Texas State Historical Association. Accessed July 24, 2020. http://www.tshaonline.org/handbook/online/articles/fhaak.

Timmons, W. H. *James Wiley Magoffin: Don Santiago—El Paso Pioneer*. El Paso: Texas Western Press, 1999.

Winberry, John J. "'Lest We Forget': The Confederate Monument and the Southern Townscape." *Southeastern Geographer* 23, no. 2 (November 1983): 107–21.

# CULTURAL PRODUCTION

Reading Literary and Cultural Texts
as Confederate Monuments
and Counter-Monuments

Figure 4.1: This image, taken from a postcard, captures the unveiling and dedication of Silent Sam on June 2, 1913. "[Unveiling of the Confederate Monument, June 2, 1913]," 1913, Orange County, North Carolina Postcard Collection (P052), North Carolina Collection Photographic Archives. Image courtesy of the Wilson Library, University of North Carolina at Chapel Hill.

# CHAPTER 4

# WEAPONIZING SILENT SAM

Heritage Politics and *The Third Revolution*

—Danielle Christmas

## SAINTING SOLDIERS AND WHIPPING WENCHES

On June 2, 1913, on the main street of downtown Chapel Hill, Julian Carr, then commander of the North Carolina Division of the United Confederate Veterans, dedicated a statue on the grounds of the University of North Carolina (UNC) in honor of "the precious blood of the student Confederate soldier" (see Figure 4.1).[1] Carr's Chapel Hill audience can be forgiven for overlooking the ostensible context of honoring the Confederacy, given his appeal to the memorialized soldiers' "high and holy . . . duty" as Dixie "Knights of the Holy Grail" who, like Christ before them, "served for the reward of serving . . . suffered for the reward of suffering . . . endured for the reward of enduring . . . [and] fought for the reward of duty done." His speech was the equivalent of a public petition to UNC's martyred Knights Templar, and the statue in their name deservedly held campus pride of place.

While the Civil War may have seemed secondary to Carr's main remarks, his pause for what he described as a "rather personal . . . allusion" belies efforts to downplay the significance of race to the politics of neo-Confederate memory, at least in the case of Silent Sam.[2] Specifically, Carr described an encounter that occurred just after the war ended, and his recounting is infamous in practically every contemporary account of the monument's installation. In this memory, nearly fifty years past, Carr came across "a negro wench" a mere "one hundred yards from where we stand"; recalling the woman's insolence toward "a Southern lady," he told of discharging the "pleasing duty" of having "horse-whipped" the woman "until her skirts hung in shreds." Interpretations of this story tend to overlook the crucial implications of its conclusion: perceiving Carr's intentions, the victim of his assault "rushed for protection to these University buildings

99

where was stationed a garrison of 100 Federal soldiers," though to no avail. Rather than finding protection, her whipping was done "in the immediate presence of the entire garrison." Carr went on to describe having "slept with a double-barrel shot gun under his head," presumably to guard against retaliation for his defiance of Yankee authority, signaling his unwillingness to compromise what is right and just, even in the face of grave risk. As he saw it, a disrespectful Black woman needed punishment, and he, the great Confederate hero, "less than ninety days" after Appomattox, was one of the few brave enough to see to it.

Carr's 1913 recollection of this 1865 incident is important not only for what it reveals about the racial subtext of Confederate monument culture. After all, his story is only relevant if we understand this reassertion of Confederate identity—in the form of Carr's "horse-whipping" resistance, as with Silent Sam's installation—to be in some way a corrective to a postwar perversion of the white southern social order. More than this, with Silent Sam as the postscript to his story, Carr and his audience have finally removed the imprint of Yankee surveillance from an institution where federal agents attempted to undermine southern control. Silent Sam, during his tenure, physically reclaimed Confederate space so as to make clear the consequences for any Black women (or men) who would be so naïve as to expect sanctuary on this newly consecrated Confederate ground. For every Black and Brown person who felt Silent Sam as a threatening presence over his century-long reign, we might conclude that the monument was doing the symbolic work for which it was erected.

The purpose of this essay is not to recount the life and afterlife of Silent Sam; a number of serviceable summaries of that story, from the monument's installation in June 1913 to its toppling in August 2018, are already readily available.[3] Nor will I discuss in any detail the ongoing *Sturm und Drang* associated with the issue, aside from the brief observation that the conflict did not end when the statue was removed from the site where Carr dedicated it. Among other plot points, a not-negligible number of university instructors threatened to withhold grades in response to costly and tone-deaf proposals for the disposition and preservation of the dispossessed Confederate statue, and, in an unusual exception to academic and southern gentility, Chancellor Carol Folt's resignation was involuntarily "accelerated" (plainly put, she was fired) when, in January 2019, she yielded to the collective exasperation and had the monument's base removed. After more than one hundred years, Carr's concrete soldier and his perch had been fully erased from UNC grounds, leaving a moral and political morass in its wake.

The case of Silent Sam and his ideological quagmire is an interesting case but not a unique one. As one of many such sites in the battle over Confederate monuments, it brings into relief the prevailing assumptions about what motivates the kind of people who effectively protected Silent Sam for one hundred years.

My aim in this essay is to use my skills as a literary scholar to understand the place of storytelling, in news as well as novels, to offer a more authentic evaluation of the stakes associated with the fight to preserve Confederate monuments like Silent Sam. And more than this, I intend to draw particular attention to these stakes as characterized by those who would most violently, in prose and in person, defend them. Reading white nationalist media, like the *Daily Stormer*, against neo-Confederate fiction, like Gregory Kay's *The Third Revolution*, I aim to make a compelling and clear case for an ideological discourse that I call *heritage politics*, a strategy that frames the removal of Confederate monuments and the ethnic cleansing of white Americans as two sides of the same coin.

Carr's account of horse-whipping a Black woman just ninety days after Robert E. Lee's surrender is a fundamental part of the story of one of North Carolina's best-known Confederate monuments. And yet despite Carr's transparent and unequivocal linking of Jim Crow-era Confederate memory with prewar southern racial politics, the contemporary debate over these monuments has, in effect, been distilled down to an argument over the true motives of Carr's audience, the men and women of Chapel Hill who endured the heat of a June day. Did these men and women suffer the North Carolina heat in order to celebrate the richness of southern culture—its music, food, and family values—and to honor the fallen boys and men who fought to preserve it? Or was his audience, attentive and uncomfortable for the better part of an hour, primarily interested in memorializing a return to antebellum-era racial authority, reinstituted under the pedestaled gaze of a freshly uniformed young white man in a jaunty hat, rifle in both hands, and army-issue canteen sitting on his hip? Put another way, I seek to understand whether today's neo-Confederate enthusiasts, the ideological inheritors of Carr's attentive and sweaty listeners, attribute their passion to collective pride in a mint juleps-and-magnolias conception of a southern past or, alternatively, to an abiding longing for the power structures that scarred the Black hands of those who mixed their bourbon cocktails and whipped the Black backs of those who pruned their magnolia bushes.

That the material culture behind the former (pride) is contingent on the fruits of the latter (oppression) is obvious, however often the fact is ignored—but this is not my primary interest. Instead, my concern is a fallacy in the media's macro-narrative of neo-Confederate efforts to claim public space. What I am suggesting is that the debate as it is presently framed in the mainstream media presumes a fundamental compatibility between the identity of Carr's 1913 audience and the subject-positions of the men and women who now defend the Silent Sam monument, his sculpted brethren, and his rebel flag. Often, these neo-Confederate defenders are imagined as gray-haired Civil War reenactors, dedicated Sons of Confederate Veterans and United Daughters of the Confederacy who have inherited, by virtue of upbringing and enculturation, the traditions of Carr's

United Confederate Veterans. The modern media narrative does acknowledge that the relatively polished and calculating agents of the "alt-right"—a fancy self-descriptor for white nationalist intellectuals, influencers, and literati—are rhetorical allies of these sons and daughters. Nevertheless, most of the journalists who would indict the defenders of these monuments as neo-Confederate hillbillies still take for granted that these neo-Confederate enthusiasts, and not their "alt-right" proponents, are the primary ideological opponents with whom Silent Sam's dismantlers and their activist allies are principally arguing.

## CONFEDERATE MONUMENTS: THE MAINSTREAM MEDIA EDITION, OR, "NUTTY LIBERALS" AND RACIST "RAGE PARADES"

In the November 2018 issue of the *Washington Post Magazine,* under a dramatic headline—"Sins of the Fathers"—Paul Duggan asked how, though "the Confederacy was built on slavery . . . can so many Southern whites still believe otherwise?"[4] The story was accompanied by an image of the individual whom Duggan had chosen as his interlocutor, a stand-in for the willfully ignorant southern whites in question: a certain Frank Earnest who, "sport[ing] a thatch of chin whiskers straight from a daguerreotype," could easily be taken for the reincarnation of Stonewall Jackson. Living up to his Confederate costumery, Earnest was described as "chief of heritage defense for the Virginia Sons of Confederate Veterans." Unsurprisingly, the biographical profile describes an eccentric character—one who had visited the National Museum of African American History and Culture wearing "an array of Confederacy-themed lapel pins, including two replicas of the flag" and who was devoted to protecting "the legacy of his rebel ancestors under constant assault by 'nutty liberals.'" For Duggan, however, Earnest represented a larger problem, the "persistence of monument defenders" who "against all moral logic . . . cling to debunked nostalgia," to a "gauzy fiction of the Lost Cause, which soft-pedals the atrocities of slavery and accentuates Confederate grievance and gallantry."

Duggan's account of his ultimately unsuccessful ten-month effort to change Earnest's mind offers an entertaining perspective on the larger drama surrounding Confederate monuments. When it comes to providing insight into what is at stake in these struggles, however, his article and others like it fall short. Frank Earnest is a flesh-and-blood anachronism, a representative of a demographic and value system about which a typical *Washington Post Magazine* reader would likely be curious. In his explication of this value system, Duggan's article distinguishes Earnest's heritage crusade from the attendees of the Unite the Right rally in Charlottesville, Virginia—held almost exactly a year before the protests that brought down Silent Sam—asserting that the 2017 protesters were there only "nominally in support of the endangered [Robert E.] Lee sculpture."[5] Frank Earnest, for his part, dismissed the "Charlottesville chaos" as "two opposing groups of radical crazies": the Unite the Right crowd who "besmirched Old Dixie by co-opting" the monument protest, in conflict with liberal counterprotestors, a group of "silly progressives [who] are ignorant of the truth about the noble secessionist cause." But however telling this reductive summary of the Charlottesville events may be, Duggan failed to make the key point that it is precisely what he described as the "ethno-fascist" agenda and the sentiment behind the racist "rage parade" that have elevated the debate over the monuments to a national concern. And however interesting the Frank Earnests and their Dixie romance revisionism may be, they are most accurately understood as outliers among the most influential voices defending Confederate monuments.

Duggan's investigation of neo-Confederate psychology fits the arc of media accounts of public debates over monuments like Charlottesville's Robert E. Lee and Chapel Hill's Silent Sam. Thus, on the one hand and from the left, these accounts describe a contest between historically dishonest, unapologetic racists on one side and culturally sensitive, intellectually honest progressives on the other side. On the other hand and from the right, the clash is felt to be one of historically informed traditionalists proud of their culture against agenda-driven outsiders hostile to white southern culture—that is, a fight between proud white southerners and the judgmental elites who would shame them.

Without ascribing to the press or its readership the status of "elites," the charge of unrestrained—if deserved—criticism can hardly be denied. The *Washington Post* might counter claims of bias for printing Nina Silber's article "Worshiping the Confederacy Is about White Supremacy—Even the Nazis Thought So" by pointing out that it was relegated to a section of the paper reserved for guest writers' interpretive "analyses."[6] However, it is difficult to defend against charges of editorial bias with articles like Karen L. Cox's "The Whole Point of Confederate Monuments Is to Celebrate White Supremacy" representing the range of the "analysis."[7] My acknowledgment of journalistic bias where I find it is not necessarily a critique. I am in fact reminded of an amusing *New York Times* editorial in which Paul Krugman suggested that "facts have a well-known liberal bias"; as he pointed out, a fact that supports a progressive argument is no less true for its partisan value.[8] Likewise, however unworthy of indictment, liberal bias is no less present for its denial. Thus, it can hardly be denied that the *Post* and similar outlets that have been churning out such headlines as "Unsure about Confederate Statues? Ask Yourself If You Support White Supremacy" and "The Fragile Statues of Whiteness" are, for the most part, depicting those who support the monuments as inveterate or, most generously, uninformed racists.[9]

The most prominent conservative counterpart of the *Post* is Fox News, and Christopher Carbone's coverage serves as a prime example. In his Fox News article about aggrieved members of the United Daughters of the Confederacy (UDC) fighting to protect the vilified vestiges of a proud white southern history, Carbone describes their modest effort to "denounce hate groups and affirm [the value of] . . . Confederate memorial statues and monuments."[10] To represent the polemical counterpoint, Carbone matches the UDC's genteel restraint with a UNC graduate student named Maya Little, painted as a belligerent Confederate monument "vandal" who "says the Daughters need to stop acting as if they're the victims." While the *Post* would undoubtedly have told the UDC story differently, its version would have featured the same basic premise of traditionalists opposed to progressives, with one or the other side being racist, ignorant, northern, southern, intellectual, elitist, and so on depending on the ideological orientation of the story. This us-against-them framing, whatever its merits, elides the silent players, the self-marginalized third parties, despite the fact that it is the latter who are quietly shaping the terms of the debate.

I call attention to the shallow narrative here precisely because, as opposed to the nihilistic critics that attack and undermine mainstream journalists, these same men and women regularly (if not regularly enough) provide crucial information in a time of disinformation, struggling to overcome political obfuscation and working in the face of unrelenting ad hominem assaults. Simply put, this is not a good time to be a journalist in the United States. My aim here is to trace the implications of the fact that, even at its most dispassionate, press coverage of the recent conflicts over monuments from Charlottesville to Chapel Hill, in media outlets from the *Washington Post* to Fox News, frames the issue in superficial binary terms as "traditionalists versus outsiders." I am arguing that this oversimplification injures readers, not only depriving them of political insight but actually furthering the agenda of a political movement that most members of the ideological mainstream, conservative or liberal, find objectionable.

## THE *DAILY STORMER*: HERITAGE POLITICS EDITION, OR, "FIRST THEY CAME FOR THE CONFEDERATE MONUMENTS"

Whichever of these accounts prevails, then, conventional press coverage of Confederate monument conflicts amounts to two sides of the same coin. The conflict is one between liberals cast as either enlightened crusaders or cultural bullies, and conservatives cast as either inflexible racists or preservers of culture. Again, this is the mainstream view; as might be expected, the white nationalist press has a somewhat different perspective. Among these media outlets, the *Daily Stormer* in particular, as the leading white nationalist voice for the millennial set, offers valuable insight into an alternative—and, I argue, in fact more accurate—conception of what is at stake in the debates over the future of public Confederate monuments.

The path to the *Daily Stormer*'s coverage leads, as it happens, through Carbone's Fox News colleague Tucker Carlson, who is notorious for his claims that, for example, white supremacy "is a hoax" being nefariously used to "divide the country and keep a hold on power."[11] Carlson, who has for several years hosted one of the most-watched news programs on what is consistently ranked the most-watched cable news network, has used this pulpit to present his own version of the Confederate monuments debate.[12] According to Carlson, "fanatics on the left" are trying to reduce the Confederate heroes honored by the monuments to "racist villains," and the removal of monuments represents the first step in a "radical" agenda to "tear down" the rights of freedom-loving Americans.[13]

Carlson's characterization of critics of the monuments as pseudo-Marxist radicals matters a great deal more than does the reporting of Carbone and conservatives like him. Although they are ostensibly waging the same battle to defend Confederate monuments, Carlson uses his prime time platform to normalize the alt-right talking point that this battle is not about social values (i.e., the aforementioned constructs of southern racists versus an ethical intelligentsia, or cultural traditionalists versus smug elites). Instead, Carlson and the *Daily Stormer* alike insist that what is at stake in the conflict over the preservation of monuments is freedom and dignity—which his listeners can easily infer to be white freedom and dignity—in what, for them, amounts to a fanatical assault on group identity.

Carlson's screed invites his viewers into a fringe media discourse that is most rhetorically robust on platforms like the *Daily Stormer*, and the ideological bridge from one to the other is not accidental. The link between Carlson and the *Daily Stormer* has in fact been affirmed by the site's founder, Andrew Anglin, who once described Carlson's broadcast as "basically *Daily Stormer: The Show*" and the Fox News host himself as "literally our greatest ally."[14] The statistics confirm this impression; thus, one media observer calculated that "Carlson had been featured in 265 articles on the *Daily Stormer* between November 2016 and November 2018."[15]

While Carlson does the hard work of mainstreaming this racial alarmism, the *Daily Stormer* is unparalleled in its ability to articulate issues in ways that serve its white nationalist agenda. Thus, for example, Anglin's response to what he described as an attempt by South Carolinians to "kike-over their own so-called 'heritage law'" by adding Reconstruction-era Black victims to a Confederate monument is more than simple racial vitriol,[16] for he concludes with a gesture toward David Lane's fourteen-word slogan—"We must secure the existence of our people and a future for white children"—that, for many of his sympathizers, is the central precept of white nationalist ideology. In Anglin's words, the fact that the South Carolina monument has been "defaced" in this way symbolizes a threat to "providing a future for" white children, clear evidence that the very "existence of our [white] people" represents the stakes in play.

Readers of the *Daily Stormer* with less fluency in alt-right ideology and needing a less subtle warning can find it in "First They Came for the Confederate Monuments . . ." by a writer pseudonymously identified as John Chrysostomos.[17] The article's moral pronouncements are buttressed by the spiritual ethos of his namesake, an early church father and Catholic saint beloved by white nationalists for his impassioned antisemitic screeds describing Jews as "robbers," "wild beasts," and "demons."[18] This pseudonym imbues the article with a prophetic tone, especially when coupled with the titular gesture at Martin Niemöller's famous confessional poem about German cowardice in the face of Nazi violence. In Chrysostomos's discussion of an attempt to remove a William McKinley statue from public display in Arcata, California, white people are recast as the victims of a new Nazi oppression. With his rhetorical sleight-of-hand, the author asserts that there is an ongoing assault on white southern culture that represents the initial stage in an ethnic "cleansing," not of Jews but of white Americans.[19] The piece ends with a dire warning that this dispute "should be yet another wakeup call to whites . . . that we should be united by our race and stand together." This reads as a plea to the lay historian who, with *History Channel* hindsight, imagines himself shrewder than the bystander-victims of Niemöller's poem, the moral cowards who were complacent in the face of mounting Nazi violence.

Despite the irony of the *Daily Stormer* using Niemöller's words to make an empathic appeal for Holocaust victims—the white man's brethren in this parable of genocidal persecution—Chrysostomos is in fact addressing the site's most important reading demographic: he is speaking to the ideological newbie, as yet predisposed against murderous antisemitism, who feels the removal of monuments as more an existential critique of their own white personhood than additional evidence of a global Jewish plot. (The *Stormer* saves its *Protocols of the Elders of Zion*-reminiscent rhetoric for its more seasoned readership, those least likely to view allusions to Jewish ethnic cleansing with anything but glee.)[20] In short, the removal of Confederate monuments is a recruitment opportunity, and related *Stormer* articles are cumulative invitations to join the fight. These alarmist appeals are effective precisely because they promise to explain and affirm escalating white angst, diagnosing the problem—white cultural and biological erasure—while testifying to white virtue. By the end of this particular article, in the spirit of cultural induction, Chrysostomos may not have fully indoctrinated the white nationalist neophyte but, by wielding the ethos of a celebrated antihate poem, he will undoubtedly have inspired cautious concern and, in small part, contributed to the normalization of the new American hate. In the totality of its writing, the *Daily Stormer* is effective at taking the anxious and insecure reader engaging in a curious flirtation with white nationalism and weaponizing Confederate monuments to project worst-case survival scenarios that are the stuff of racial nightmares.

This white nationalist reframing serves as a kind of rhetorical ground zero for what I call heritage politics. That is, the white nationalist ideology typified by the *Daily Stormer* is dressed up in the cloak of regional pride and southern sentimentality embodied by the United Daughters of the Confederacy. Such a political slippage effectively inoculates the white nationalist project against its moral critics, staging it instead as a rhetorical debate over competing notions of mainstream history and culture. In point of fact, these debates—racism versus progressivism, traditionalism versus neo-carpetbagger colonialism, and so on—are no less charged than the nightly news would suggest. Heritage politics reframes what is at root an argument in favor of a white ethno-state into a diversionary debate over symbols that represent something more than history and cultural pride. This rhetorical shift amounts to taking what is, in truth, a debate over a white nationalist project of racial exclusion and extermination and reframing it as a moral argument about cultural signifiers. In this way, white nationalists have glossed their advocacy for an American ethno-state with the familiar dog whistle of a new "culture wars," crafting a viciously racist discourse into palatable fodder for a CNN segment face-off that will invariably conclude with a good-willed "let's agree to disagree."

This short explication has raised the ways in which sentiment is deployed on behalf of heritage politics in the media and would name those disingenuous figures (Tucker Carlson, Andrew Anglin) who have labored on its behalf, but a close reading of the *Daily Stormer* alone is insufficient to explain the ideological journey from disaffected reader to ethno-state advocate. We would be served to understand the *Daily Stormer* as a gateway and white nationalist subculture as the dynamic landscape that brings its vitriol to life. And while the media representations of neo-Confederate characters like Frank Earnest gesture at the sincerity that underpins his activism, we must look elsewhere for a more multidimensional picture and dig deeper into white nationalist cultural production to grasp a more nuanced idea of the imaginative landscape that would render epithet-driven *Daily Stormer* prophecy into plausible potentiality. The anxiety-filled reader cautiously contemplating the prophetic accuracy of white nationalism is left with an urgent question: what is the future of history if eliminating Confederate monuments is one step on the path to exterminating white people? And the outsider, filled with a different anxiety around Trump-era racial unrest, is left with an urgent question of her own: what narrative framing paints so convincing a portrait of racial precarity and its relationship to Confederate symbols that a growing number of white Americans believe them to be symbols worth killing and dying for?

## GREGORY KAY'S *THE THIRD REVOLUTION*: A SPECULATIVE TALE OF "HERITAGE NOT HATE"

Thus far, I have demonstrated the way in which threats to dislocate monuments like Silent Sam are used to cultivate white nationalist alarmism over an encroaching, if amorphous, existential threat to white Americans. Neo-Confederate fiction is an important tool in the rhetorical arsenal, providing shape and texture to the ostensible racial threat, both naming and disarming the enemy over a library of multivolume epics. According to Southern Poverty Law Center (SPLC) researcher Heidi Beirich's examination of far-right hate groups, white nationalist (including neo-Confederate) novels are exerting an influence by "reaching the highest levels of power" and "impact[ing extremist] policy."[21] This literature richly details the dystopian future that writers like Anglin only gesture at, describing the imminent risks should white readers fail to heed his clarion call and avert disaster. To demonstrate how this politics connects the news media with the movement's aesthetic culture, I consider the ways in which the neo-Confederate subgenre of the white nationalist canon corroborates and consolidates heritage politics. Kevin Hicks describes the rich arc of neo-Confederate mythology in "Literature and the Neo-Confederacy," encompassing more than a century of literary culture ranging from familiar Lost Cause romances like Thomas Dixon's *The Clansman* (1905) to more forgotten agrarian works like Allen Tate's *The Fathers* (1938), and from contemporary alarmist fiction like Ellen Williams's *Bedford, a World Vision* (2000) to its most violent and alarmist iterations in Lloyd Lenard's *The Last Confederate Flag* (2000). I will consider here just one of these novels, Gregory Kay's *The Third Revolution* (2004), among the more salient examples of the fetishistic fixation on Confederate monuments.[22] This novel invokes heritage politics to provide a convincing account of the threat to white personhood and reveal the sentimental logic that seamlessly ties the preservation of Confederate symbols to white survival.

Kay's book, the first in a popular and, in the words of the SPLC, "militantly racist" tetralogy, adds to its pairing of Confederate symbols and fear of white genocide a generous helping of pathos.[23] As the plot progresses, the removal of Confederate monuments leads directly to the kind of apocalyptic race war that the leading voices of contemporary white extremism promise should the liberal assault on Confederate memory continue. Such a worldview clarifies the urgency of neo-Confederate activism while offering insight into a seductive narrative rationale that is convincing a growing number of white men and women, people with common sense, of the virtuous exigency of ethnic separatism, however violently achieved.

A former chairman of the West Virginia chapter of the League of the South, Kay knows his audience, both the converted and the curious. The league, founded in 1994 by neo-Confederate activist Michael Hill, is organized around the premise that "cultural as well as political secession is the only practical, the only realistic, and the only moral choice."[24] The group describes its mission as organized advocacy for "heritage not hate,"[25] while asserting that its members are dedicated to white southern "survival" and working "to advance the cultural, social, economic, and political well-being and independence of the Southern people, by all honorable means."[26] This mission statement, like so much white nationalist writing, simultaneously reveals and conceals its racial message.

Michael Hill poses a challenge to soldiers like Kay: with "few practical solutions" to the "tyranny" that oppresses white southerners, it makes sense that the federal government "would want our guns and ammunition" in an effort to stop resisters from "shooting back."[27] Hill would like his league brothers and sisters to understand that, in exigent circumstances, "when politics fail to provide safeguards for the people's lives, liberty, and property, then the people must seek extra-political solutions. Got any ideas where to begin?" Kay's oeuvre is his full-throated "yes"; whether the league consolidated or simply energized Kay's militancy, *The Third Revolution* reads as a speculative response to this rhetorical call to arms.

With so grave a charge, Kay is not interested in starting or ending his novel with lyrical yearning, however much sentimentality is its essential engine. The back cover copy sets the tone with an alert declaring in large print that "It's the 21st Century and the South is rising again!"[28] A story of resistance and revolution, the novel fulfills this promise. The title of *The Third Revolution* refers to the projected culmination of, first, the colonial rebellion against Britain in 1776 and then the Confederate rebellion that Lost Cause historians consider the second revolution in 1861.

In the novel, the seed of this third separatist revolution is a protest on the grounds of the South Carolina State House over the removal of a Confederate flag set over a Confederate soldier monument. A Black policeman attacks the white protesters, killing some and injuring others. It is during the ensuing riot that we encounter the novel's protagonist, fellow officer Frank Gore. From the outset, Frank's dispassionate racial politics and law-and-order pedigree are intended to lend credibility to his opinions and actions; he is depicted as harboring no ideological biases. It is from this perspective of a clear-thinking lawman that Frank observes media coverage that inaccurately and unfairly blames the Ku Klux Klan for the rioting.

Kay's target audience presumably envisions a Klan made up of white gentiles with a reputation for politically incorrect racial politics. But when that fact is glossed over, and the Klansmen are depicted as the target of government scapegoating, the perpetrators and their victims are quickly brought into relief. The Klan, in its status as an underdog in the bloody fight against fascist abuse, inevitably benefits from any comparison to its oppressors, and its unsavory racial

politics benefit from this same moral rehabilitation. If there is merit to the prov-
erb that "the enemy of my enemy is my friend," then Frank Gore, the reader's
ethical proxy, is firmly on the side of Team Klan.

Over the course of the novel, the injustice associated with the deadly riot effectively radicalizes Frank, and he eventually joins a paramilitary band of revolution-
aries known as the Confederate Army Provisional (CAP). These freedom fight-
ers are pursued by an alphabet soup of federal agencies including ATF (Bureau
of Alcohol, Tobacco, Firearms, and Explosives), DHS (Department of Homeland
Security), and the FBI. The sheer scale of the government's effort to suppress the
CAP group is as much an indicator of its threat to the status quo as it is the righteousness of its cause; the group is an organized expression of conscience, with
machine guns in hand, and something that a totalitarian regime cannot tolerate.

The protagonist who, through four novels, becomes the beacon of a separatist nation, does not embark on this path with guns blazing. In fact, the scene
in which Frank is moved to radical action has the mawkishness of a Hallmark
movie. While he is in the hospital recovering from the injury received during the
riot, his grandmother visits and encourages him to confront the false media narrative that is scapegoating the Klan. Dramatizing this call to conscience, she takes
from a locket "a small piece of dirty disreputable-looking red cloth" and tells him
that it is far more than it seems: "That's a piece of the company Battle Flag that
my own grandfather died carrying at Shiloh, fighting the Yankee invaders. Those
stains? That's his blood, Frankie; his blood, my blood, and *your* blood."[29]

This revelation evokes in Frank "a strange warmth coursing through his
body," a sense of connectedness with the "unseen eyes [of his forefathers] upon
him."[30] "Granny" makes clear to Frank what he is just starting to understand;
"tapping his chest gently over his heart," she insists that "*this* is your heritage. . . .
It's in here, in the heart and in the blood. Bred in the bone, like the old folks used
to say." The locket and its cloth contents are "just a symbol" of this flesh-and-
bone heritage, "a reminder, so that we never forget who we are!" The symbolism
is thick as Frank's grandmother invokes the Civil War with a blood-soaked family relic for him as he recovers in the hospital from his own blood sacrifice on
behalf of defenders of the Confederate flag. When his grandmother associates
the remnants of her family flag with the heritage that she calls upon her grand-
son to embody, she is invoking this "symbol" and "reminder" in the context of
the material threat to white southern heritage represented by the monument.
Frank's audience can be expected to conflate his family, its legacy, and southern
heritage markers, particularly those who encounter the novel at a charged historical moment when the debate over Confederate flags and monuments has,
outside the confines of fiction, served as a predicate for violence.

As the story proceeds, the government continues to meet the low expectations set by its deceitful account of the riot. Frank is moved by his grandmother's

bedside plea, and he speaks up to tell the truth about what happened at the statehouse, though to no avail and at great personal cost. He is put on forced leave from the police force and eventually framed for multiple murders because of his resistance to the official government narrative. In other words, some faceless regime is so invested in maligning supporters of the Confederate flag that it is willing to bring about the ruin of a patriotic white man, and a police officer at that. The fact that this premise alone—the persecution of a patriotic white police officer—reads as totally believable to an increasingly radicalized readership, while striking cultural outsiders as the height of absurdity, is emblematic of the conceptual chasm that exists between dueling notions of "reality" in US racial discourses.

Where Frank's persecution is concerned, the outsized reaction of the government is its own proof; the unstained, full-sized contemporary rendering of Frank's locket-sized legacy is a metaphysical threat to the regime's survival. Even for a reader immune to southern sentimentality, the meaning is clear: resistance to oppression must include protecting Confederate monuments and flags in all their transcendental power. In the novel, as in heritage politics, the stakes of protecting the flag are less about some romantic notion of a shared regional history than about a symbol with the unique power to render a prevailing oppressor vulnerable. The fact that the novel's version of the government has staked so much on the removal of Confederate symbols and what is characterized as the total decimation of southern heritage helps to clarify the stakes of the dispute over the monuments for Kay's characters as well as his real-world compatriots. For them, the fight to protect the flag is one for total survival, and so existential a threat as racial extinction calls white men and women of conscience to marshal and defend all existential weapons, whether battle flags or battle monuments, on behalf of this survival.

Over his four-hundred-page journey, Frank falls in league with a white journalist named Samantha Norris and, with her, takes up the revolutionary cause of the Confederate Army Provisional. As the reader leaves Frank in this first phase of his four-volume story, Frank launches into a monologue, addressing his fictional audience, as well as his reading audience, directly. In his videotaped address, Frank sets the stage for the next volume by recalling his initial disinterest in revolution, again showing himself to be a man of peace and good sense. His radicalization, he asserts, was not at first a matter of politics; he and Samantha "fled to the Confederate Army Provisional simply in order to stay alive."[31] The opponents of their resistance, Frank says, are "the armed forces who have sought to kill us . . . [and] slaughtered civilians who dared demand their rights"; they are, ultimately, the same forces that are responsible for the death of Frank's grandmother, the person who is so important to his ethical formation at the beginning of the novel. Frank's radicalization is attributed to both "the Federal

Government and its shameless lackeys" and to his inborn "patriotism."[32] As he puts it, in the face of "un-Godly persecution . . . no patriot will allow tyrants and despots to hold sway over their country, for any reason."[33]

Given the novel's lengthy account of Frank's targeted persecution—a catalog of criminal behavior that is more than sufficient to merit his "snarl[ing]" mono- logue—it is easy to disregard the nostalgic texture of his address.[34] Neverthe- less, Frank's romantic appeal to "this South of ours, this beautiful Dixie Land" reminds his sympathizers, and Kay's readers, that his revolutionary movement is not simply a response to only a year, or even a decade, of organized govern- ment assaults on southern heritage.[35] Rather, Frank's land "has been trodden under the heel of the tyrants in Washington for a century and a half, and that heavy tread has beaten down the Southern man until it's made us think that's the way it should be."

With this gesture back to the 1860s defeat of the Confederacy, before the "century and a half of tyranny" began, Kay would have his reader consider all that white southerners suffered by this loss.[36] Over the intervening decades, a 150-year long eulogy to the Lost Cause, the white southern man has been deni- grated through such reform efforts as forced integration, the undermining of Jim Crow laws, and the Voting Rights Act. The repeated "treading" upon the white southern man is intended to leave him so poisoned as to "think that's the way it should be." This invocation of the famous Gadsden flag motto ("Don't Tread on Me") renders Frank's message simultaneously local and transregional, urgent but timeless. Christopher Gadsden was, like Frank, a South Carolin- ian, and his flag was the equivalent of a colonial-era meme, with the symbolic power to galvanize his fellow colonists to wage the first revolution.[37] As Gads- den exhorted his fellow Americans to resist the "tread" of British tyranny, so also Kay, through Frank, asks his white readers, northerners and southerners alike, to understand Frank's indignity as the shared burden of all who would resist the ostensible erasure of the white past and assault on the white pres- ent. In this novel, as in the *Daily Stormer*, this macronarrative of erasure and assault is foregrounded by the displacement of a very different rebel flag. The distillation of white personhood to this sacrosanct flag, a fabric incarnation of a neo-Confederate blood-and-soil ethos, is not just an asset to the narrative of heritage politics but is its essential foundation.

## CONCLUSION, OR, "TIME TO RISE AGAIN"

Novels like *The Third Revolution* offer insight because they personalize issues that the new generation of white nationalists would depersonalize with euphe- mism and statistics.[38] Not only does Gregory Kay's book demonstrate the inner logic that links Confederate heritage with white survival, but it is also, for some, a key step on the path toward embracing white nationalist ideology. The *Daily Stormer* pulls in readers with memes and what may generously be called crudeness, while the fiction appeals to readers' emotions by richly rendering the dystopian reality just around the bend, forcefully making the case that violence is the only means to reverse what will soon be irreversible.

Within the canon of white nationalist literature, neo-Confederate fiction occupies a singular place. Southern cultural oppression is a compelling parable for the existential problem that defines contemporary white nationalism. When imaginatively set to paper by writers like Kay, these epics of oppression propose, as something historically legitimate and fully rational, the age-old "southern solution" of regional secession. Given different rhetorical framing, the southern solution has been drained of sentimentality and recast by the Andrew Anglins of the subculture to serve the ethnic separatist purposes of his movement, adding polemical polish to the robust heritage narratives so masterfully offered in neo-Confederate fiction. Kay and his media peers use the tangible threat of Confederate monument removal as a catalyst for alarm, leading their anxious white audience naturally and necessarily to an equally tangible answer: it is time to answer Anglin's call to provide "a future for white children," it is time for whites to "unite and stand together" with Chrysostomos, and—after Kay's arduous literary exercise in pathos and politics—it is time to follow Gore's example and "rise again." It is, in other words, time for a third revolution.

## NOTES

1. Julian Shakespeare Carr, "Unveiling of Confederate Monument at University. June 2, 1913," folder 26, Julian Shakespeare Carr Papers, Southern Historical Collection, Louis Round Wilson Special Collections Library, University of North Carolina at Chapel Hill.

2. Carr, "Unveiling of Confederate Monument."

3. For brief and accurate summaries of this history, see Kristina Killgrove, "Scholars Explain the Racist History of UNC's Silent Sam Statues," *Forbes*, August 22, 2018, https://www.forbes.com/sites/kristinakillgrove/2018/08/22/scholars-explain-the-racist-history-of-uncs-silent-sam-statue/#5b46c725114f; and Colin Warren-Hicks, "A Look at the Long and Controversial Life of 'Silent Sam,'" *News and Observer*, August 23, 2017, https://www.newsobserver.com/news/local/counties/orange-county/article168816697.html. For a more comprehensive evaluation of the Silent Sam narrative over time, the *Daily Tar Heel*, a student-run daily newspaper that serves as an archive of campus life, hosts a comprehensive database of related articles at https://www.dailytarheel.com/section/silent-sam-monument.

4. Paul Duggan, "Sins of the Fathers," *Washington Post Magazine*, November 28, 2018, https://www.washingtonpost.com/news/magazine/wp/2018/11/28/feature/the-confederacy-was-built-on-slavery-how-can-so-many-southern-whites-still-believe-otherwise/.

5. Duggan, "Sins of the Fathers."

6. Nina Silber, "Worshiping the Confederacy Is about White Supremacy—Even the Nazis Thought So," *Washington Post*, August 17, 2017, https://www.washingtonpost.com/news/made -by-history/wp/2017/08/17/worshiping-the-confederacy-is-about-white-supremacy-even-the -nazis-thought-so/.

7. Karen L. Cox, "The Whole Point of Confederate Monuments Is to Celebrate White Supremacy," *Washington Post*, August 16, 2017, https://www.washingtonpost.com/news/ posteverything/wp/2017/08/16/the-whole-point-of-confederate-monuments-is-to-celebrate -white-supremacy/.

8. Paul Krugman, "Facts Have a Well-Known Liberal Bias," *New York Times*, December 8, 2017, https://www.nytimes.com/2017/12/08/opinion/facts-have-a-well-known-liberal-bias.html.

9. Examples include Blain Roberts and Ethan J. Kyle, "Unsure about Confederate Statues? Ask Yourself If You Support White Supremacy," *The Fresno Bee*, August 16, 2017, https://www .fresnobee.com/opinion/readers-opinion/article167609442.html; and David Shorter, "The Fragile Statues of Whiteness," *Huffington Post*, August 28, 2017, https://www.huffpost.com/ entry/the-fragile-statues-of-whiteness_b_59981418e4b033e0fbdec456.

10. Christopher Carbone, "Confederate Monuments: This 124-Year-Old Women's Group Is Fighting to Keep Them Around," Fox News, August 12, 2018, https://www.foxnews.com/us/ confederate-monuments-this-124-year-old-womens-group-is-fighting-to-keep-them-around.

11. Brian Stelter, "Tucker Carlson Wrongly Tells His Viewers the Country's White Supremacy Problem 'Is a Hoax,'" CNN, August 7, 2019, https://www.cnn.com/2019/08/07/ media/tucker-carlson-white-supremacy-reliable-sources/index.html.

12. Dominic Patten, "Fox News Tops Cable Ratings Again in Q2 Despite Well-Watched Dem Debates on MSNBC; Tucker Carlson Up, Rachel Maddow Down," *Deadline*, July 2, 2019, https://deadline.com/2019/07/fox-news-ratings-top-cable-tucker-carlson-rachel-maddow -cnn-down-msnbc-second-quarter-1202641256/.

13. "Tucker on Fate of Slaveholders Washington, Jefferson: 'If That's the Standard, Nobody Is Safe,'" *Fox News Insider*, August 15, 2017, https://insider.foxnews.com/2017/08/15/ tucker-carlson-washington-jefferson-slave-holders-memorials-go-next.

14. Joseph Bernstein, "Data Shows Tucker Carlson Is the *Daily Stormer*'s Favorite Pundit," *BuzzFeed News*, November 28, 2018, https://www.buzzfeednews.com/article/josephbernstein/ tucker-carlson-fox-news-daily-stormers-favorite-pundit.

15. Bernstein, "Data Shows."

16. Andrew Anglin, "North [*sic*] Carolina: Monument Honoring White Hero to Be Defaced with Blacks," *Daily Stormer*, November 25, 2018, URL inactive.

17. John Chrysostomos, "First They Came for the Confederate Monuments . . . ," *Daily Stormer*, April 2, 2018, URL inactive.

18. John Chrysostom, *Discourses against Judaizing Christians*, trans. Paul W. Harkins (Washington, DC: Catholic University of America Press, 1999), 10–11.

19. Chrysostomos, "First They Came."

20. *The Protocols of the Elders of Zion* is a fabricated collection of twenty-four chapters, or "protocols," that detail a plot by Jewish "elders" to manipulate the world economy, take over global media, and foster transnational unrest. First published in Russia in 1903, the *Protocols* has been widely translated despite its proven inauthenticity. In its century-long US publication history, its debut is particularly notable: in 1920, auto manufacturer Henry Ford serialized the forged document in his newspaper, the *Dearborn Independent*, eventually collecting and disseminating 500,000 copies of the complete *Protocols*. The tract remains a ubiquitous point of reference in white nationalist subculture. See Stephen E. Bronner, *A Rumor about the Jews: Antisemitism, Conspiracy, and the* Protocols of Zion (New York: Oxford University Press, 2000).

21. Ian Allen, "Inside the World of Racist Science Fiction," *New York Times*, July 30, 2018, https://www.nytimes.com/2018/07/30/opinion/inside-the-world-of-racist-science-fiction.html.

22. Kevin Hicks, "Literature and the Neo-Confederacy," in *Neo-Confederacy: A Critical Introduction*, ed. Euan Hague, Heidi Beirich, and Edward H. Sebesta (Austin: University of Texas Press, 2008), 226–52. Among the novels Hicks discusses are Thomas Dixon, *The Clansman* (New York: Grosset & Dunlap, 1905); Allen Tate, *The Fathers* (New York: G. P. Putnam's Sons, 1938); Ellen Williams, *Bedford, a World Vision* (Belleville, Ont.: Guardian Books, 2000); and Lloyd Lenard, *The Last Confederate Flag* (Baltimore: AmErica House, 2000).

23. "*First Freedom*'s Final Issue," Southern Poverty Law Center, June 29, 2018, https://www.splcenter.org/hatewatch/2018/06/29/first-freedom's-final-issue.

24. "Welcome to The League of the South," The League of the South, accessed October 10, 2019, https://leagueofthesouth.com.

25. Helen Taylor, "The South and Britain: Celtic Cultural Connections," in *South to a New Place: Region, Literature, Culture*, ed. Suzanne W. Jones and Sharon Monteith (Baton Rouge: Louisiana State University Press, 2002), 341.

26. "Welcome to The League of the South."

27. Michael Hill, "When Politics Fail," The League of the South, accessed October 10, 2019, https://leagueofthesouth.com/when-politics-fail/.

28. Gregory Kay, *The Third Revolution* (self-pub., CreateSpace, 2004), back cover.

29. Kay, *Third Revolution*, 21.

30. Kay, *Third Revolution*, 21.

31. Kay, *Third Revolution*, 402.

32. Kay, *Third Revolution*, 401.

33. Kay, *Third Revolution*, 402.

34. Kay, *Third Revolution*, 401.

35. Kay, *Third Revolution*, 402.

36. Kay, *Third Revolution*, 402.

37. Rob Walker, "The Shifting Symbolism of the Gadsden Flag," *New Yorker*, October 2, 2016, https://www.newyorker.com/news/news-desk/the-shifting-symbolism-of-the-gadsden-flag.

38. For an explication of the distinction between the "old" and "new" white nationalists, see Carol M. Swain, *The New White Nationalism in America: Its Challenge to Integration* (New York: Cambridge University Press, 2004).

## Bibliography

Allen, Ian. "Inside the World of Racist Science Fiction." *New York Times*, July 30, 2018. https://www.nytimes.com/2018/07/30/opinion/inside-the-world-of-racist-science-fiction.html.

Anglin, Andrew. "North [*sic*] Carolina: Monument Honoring White Hero to Be Defaced with Blacks." *Daily Stormer*, November 25, 2018. URL inactive.

Bernstein, Joseph. "Data Shows Tucker Carlson Is the *Daily Stormer*'s Favorite Pundit." *BuzzFeed News*, November 28, 2018. https://www.buzzfeednews.com/article/joseph bernstein/tucker-carlson-fox-news-daily-stormers-favorite-pundit.

Bronner, Stephen E. *A Rumor about the Jews: Antisemitism, Conspiracy, and the* Protocols of Zion. New York: Oxford University Press, 2000.

Carbone, Christopher. "Confederate Monuments: This 124-Year-Old Women's Group Is Fighting to Keep Them Around." Fox News, August 12, 2018. https://www.foxnews.com/us/

confederate-monuments-this-124-year-old-womens-group-is-fighting-to-keep-them
-around.

Carr, Julian Shakespeare. "Unveiling of Confederate Monument at University. June 2, 1913."
Folder 26, Julian Shakespeare Carr Papers, Southern Historical Collection, Louis Round
Wilson Special Collections Library, University of North Carolina at Chapel Hill.

Chrysostom, John. *Discourses against Judaizing Christians*. Translated by Paul W. Harkins.
Washington, DC: Catholic University of America Press, 1999.

Chrysostomos, John. "First They Came for the Confederate Monuments . . ." *Daily Stormer*,
April 2, 2018. URL inactive.

Cox, Karen L. "The Whole Point of Confederate Monuments Is to Celebrate White Supremacy."
*Washington Post*, August 16, 2017. https://www.washingtonpost.com/news/posteverything/
wp/2017/08/16/the-whole-point-of-confederate-monuments-is-to-celebrate-white
-supremacy/.

Dixon, Thomas, Jr. *The Clansman: A Historical Romance of the Ku Klux Klan*. New York:
Grosset & Dunlap, 1905.

Duggan, Paul. "Sins of the Fathers." *Washington Post Magazine*, November 28, 2018. https://
www.washingtonpost.com/news/magazine/wp/2018/11/28/feature/the-confederacy-was
-built-on-slavery-how-can-so-many-southern-whites-still-believe-otherwise/.

"*First Freedom*'s Final Issue." Southern Poverty Law Center, June 29, 2018. https://www.spl
center.org/hatewatch/2018/06/29/first-freedom's-final-issue.

Hicks, Kevin. "Literature and Neo-Confederacy." In *Neo-Confederacy: A Critical Introduction*,
edited by Euan Hague, Heidi Beirich, and Edward H. Sebesta, 226–52. Austin: University of
Texas Press, 2008.

Kay, Gregory. *The Third Revolution*. Self-published, CreateSpace, 2004.

Killgrove, Kristina. "Scholars Explain the Racist History of UNC's Silent Sam Statue."
*Forbes*, August 22, 2018. https://www.forbes.com/sites/kristinakillgrove/2018/08/22/
scholars-explain-the-racist-history-of-uncs-silent-sam-statue/#5b46c725114f.

Krugman, Paul. "Facts Have a Well-Known Liberal Bias." *New York Times*, December 8, 2017.
https://www.nytimes.com/2017/12/08/opinion/facts-have-a-well-known-liberal-bias.html.

The League of the South. "Welcome to The League of the South." Accessed October 10, 2019.
https://leagueofthesouth.com.

Lenard, Lloyd E. *The Last Confederate Flag*. Baltimore: AmErica House, 2000.

Patten, Dominic. "Fox News Tops Cable Ratings Again in Q2 Despite Well-Watched Dem
Debates on MSNBC; Tucker Carlson Up, Rachel Maddow Down." *Deadline*, July 2, 2019.
https://deadline.com/2019/07/fox-news-ratings-top-cable-tucker-carlson-rachel-maddow
-cnn-down-msnbc-second-quarter-1202641256/.

Roberts, Blain, and Ethan J. Kyle. "Unsure about Confederate Statues? Ask Yourself If You
Support White Supremacy." *The Fresno Bee*, August 16, 2017. https://www.fresnobee.com/
opinion/readers-opinion/article167609442.html.

Shorter, David. "The Fragile Statues of Whiteness." *Huffington Post*, August 28, 2017. https://
www.huffpost.com/entry/the-fragile-statues-of-whiteness_b_59981418e4b033e0fbdec456.

Silber, Nina. "Worshiping the Confederacy Is about White Supremacy—Even the Nazis
Thought So." *Washington Post*, August 17, 2017. https://www.washingtonpost.com/news/
made-by-history/wp/2017/08/17/worshiping-the-confederacy-is-about-white-suprem
acy-even-the-nazis-thought-so/.

"Silent Sam Monument." *Daily Tar Heel*. https://www.dailytarheel.com/section/silent-sam
-monument.

Stelter, Brian. "Tucker Carlson Wrongly Tells His Viewers the Country's White Supremacy Problem 'Is a Hoax.'" CNN, August 7, 2019. https://www.cnn.com/2019/08/07/media/tucker -carlson-white-supremacy-reliable-sources/index.html.

Swain, Carol M. *The New White Nationalism in America: Its Challenge to Integration*. New York: Cambridge University Press, 2004.

Tate, Allen. *The Fathers*. New York: G. P. Putnam's Sons, 1938.

Taylor, Helen. "The South and Britain: Celtic Cultural Connections." In *South to a New Place: Region, Literature, Culture*, edited by Suzanne W. Jones and Sharon Monteith, 340–62. Baton Rouge: Louisiana State University Press, 2002.

"Tucker on Fate of Slaveholders Washington, Jefferson: 'If That's the Standard, Nobody Is Safe.'" *Fox News Insider*, August 15, 2017. https://insider.foxnews.com/2017/08/15/tucker-carlson -washington-jefferson-slave-holders-memorials-go-next.

Walker, Rob. "The Shifting Symbolism of the Gadsden Flag." *New Yorker*, October 2, 2016. https://www.newyorker.com/news/news-desk/the-shifting-symbolism-of-the-gadsden-flag.

Warren-Hicks, Colin. "A Look at the Long and Controversial Life of 'Silent Sam.'" *News and Observer*, August 23, 2017. https://www.newsobserver.com/news/local/counties/orange -county/article168816697.html.

Williams, Ellen. *Bedford, a World Vision*. Belleville, Ont.: Guardian Books, 2000.

# CHAPTER 5

# "WASTING THE PAST"

Albion Tourgée, Confederate Memory, and the Politics of Context

## —Garrett Bridger Gilmore

> Education teaches the dominant class how to make the subjection of the class
> it is inclined by temperament and interest to oppress, more complete.
> —Albion W. Tourgée[1]

In 2009, then-graduate student in the Department of History at the University
of North Carolina at Chapel Hill (UNC) Adam H. Domby recovered a speech
on the dedication of the Confederate monument, colloquially known as Silent
Sam, from the university's archives. Delivered by Julian Carr, prominent North
Carolina white supremacist, politician, and industrialist, the 1913 speech came
at a high point in a national trend in commemorating Confederate monuments.
The monument erected at UNC depicted a student-aged soldier and was paid
for with funds raised by the United Daughters of the Confederacy and the university. One passage in particular struck a nerve for many Chapel Hill community members reading the speech a century later:

> 100 yards from where we stand, less than 90 days perhaps after my return from
> Appomattox, I horse-whipped a negro wench, until her skirts hung in shreds,
> because upon the streets of this quiet village she had publicly insulted and maligned
> a Southern lady, and then rushed for protection to these University buildings where
> was stationed a garrison of 100 Federal soldiers. I performed the pleasing duty in
> the immediate presence of the entire garrison, and for thirty nights afterwards slept
> with a double-barrel shot gun under my head.[2]

While nothing is known about the unnamed victim of Carr's assault, awareness
of this story of violence clarified for many the meaning of allowing Silent Sam
to remain in its place of prominence on UNC's campus. The Lost Cause myth of

Confederate heroism and honor embodied in the figure of the young Confederate soldier was at its root a celebration of white violence and Black disempowerment.

In August 2018, anti-racist members of the UNC community tore Silent Sam from its pedestal in the culmination of years of organizing to have the statue removed by the university. This act violated North Carolina law mandating the preservation of Confederate monuments, a law passed alongside measures to limit voting access as part of the ongoing retrenchment of white political power in the North Carolina legislature.[3] In December 2018, the UNC Board of Governors released a plan for the preservation of the Confederate monument that included the construction of an educational center to house the statue that would cost $5.3 million to build and $800,000 annually to operate.[4] This effort to preserve Silent Sam in a museum-like educational space represented an extreme form of the logic of contextualization: this symbol of white supremacy would be preserved but surrounded by interpretive materials providing information about the real history of the era it commemorated. Contextualization largely makes sense as a function of a public university's mission to educate. By providing accurate historical context, the facts of history come to replace the myths and falsehoods of popular historical memory.

Details on the historical voices and perspectives that would constitute Silent Sam's contextualization were absent from the 2018 proposal that was ultimately rejected, yet the Board of Governors was specific in its proposal to provide security for the statue. The board proposed creating a "mobile force platoon" of officers specially trained to break up student protests that would operate across all University of North Carolina campuses.[5] This proposal sparked outrage over the amount of resources that would be dedicated to the re-erection of the Confederate monument (which had been torn down four months earlier) and the expansion of police power on the university's campus. The proposal to expand police power within the university system was especially galling to students and community members in light of the UNC Police Department's pattern of surveilling, harassing, and arresting students (on charges more often than not dismissed by judges) while giving white supremacists (many armed and having specifically threatened violence against students and professors) protection and cover during rallies and protests on campus.[6] In a process of terrible historical symmetry, the same violence that was celebrated at Silent Sam's erection emerged from its institutional slumber to strike down an anti-racist community movement in the name of civil order, preservation of property, and respect for history. In reality, the end of the conversation would be brought about not by contextualization but by the threat of a crackdown on those moving the conversation forward.

The events surrounding Silent Sam's removal force us to consider contextualization as a unique mode of administrative response to conflicts over signs and symbols of white supremacy. Such administrative responses are distinct from academic research and critical discourses that take place within universities among faculty, staff, students, and community members. Contextualization as a pretext for the preservation of symbols of white supremacy should be understood as a crucial tactic for the operation of what James M. Thomas calls university "diversity regimes": "a set of meanings and practices that institutionalizes a benign commitment to diversity, and in doing so obscures, entrenches, and even intensifies racial inequality by failing to make fundamental changes in how power, resources, and opportunities are distributed."[7] The removal of Silent Sam has exposed an important contradiction in the competing systems of values and discourses that make up the contested ground of US universities: research undertaken within universities in fields like history, geography, sociology, and literary studies increasingly calls into question the social and political function of universities and the value of the apparently universal education and knowledge universities produce. Shaped by my own training in such critical conversations, I am guided by Lisa Lowe's argument that "even as it proposes inclusivity, liberal universalism effects principles of inclusion and exclusion . . . [and] that the uses of universalizing concepts of reason, civilization, and freedom effect colonial divisions of humanity."[8] Such scholarship challenges long-held liberal humanist underpinnings of the university as a space of free inquiry and consequently of social progress and instead often exposes how universities have fostered and benefited from white supremacy like any other US cultural institution. If we apply such critical insights to contextualization as an administrative response, we see that contextualization presupposes that there are real and meaningful differences between current historical contexts and past ones. Contextualization furthermore supposes that our ability to understand past contexts can transform the political power of signs and symbols like monuments that survive their immediate context of production. Contextualization imagines that closure of a present conflict about the meaning of a monument can be wrought through the production of a narrative of historical closure, even if contextualization is intended to spark further conversation. The past, as it were, is past, and everyone stands to gain equally from understanding it.

The strategy of contextualizing white supremacist icons within existing and expanding structures of university administration and policing might be best understood as a particularly insidious torsion of the rhetoric of diversity and inclusion through the process of "staging difference . . . the performance of racial inclusiveness for the sake of institutional impression management, rather than for producing a racially equitable campus."[9] UNC professor of geography Danielle Purifoy identifies this dynamic in her reflection on Silent Sam's removal, connecting the overt violence of Silent Sam's neo-Confederate supporters with the "smiling violence of many mostly white administrators and faculty at white schools across this country—who place an economic and social chokehold on the parameters of our political and intellectual existence on campus as they titillate themselves publicly with proclamations of diversity and inclusion."[10] In the case of Silent Sam, contextualization posits white supremacy as an idea among others, re-assimilating white supremacy into the structure of the university under the guises of historical objectivity and the requirement of tolerance for a diversity of ideas.

The dual impulse to historically contextualize and violently police reveals clear fault lines within the operating logic of university diversity regimes. On the one hand, contextualization promises to proliferate knowledge (about slavery and the rise of Jim Crow) apparently for anti-racist ends (disavowal of similarity with these earlier eras). On the other, the expansion of permissible ideas within the institutional discourses of the university (in the form of the acknowledgement of violence in the university's past) necessitates a consolidation of power around the edges of that information (in the form of the normalization of violence in the university's present). The material investments in policing attached to UNC's initial plans for contextualization starkly reveal that "while violence characterizes exclusion from the universality of the human, it also accompanies inclusion or assimilation into it."[11] Permissible knowledge about the reality of white supremacy in the past cannot be transformed into impermissible action directed against white supremacy in its institutional forms in the present. The university arrests the students whose labor and presence on campus serve as the justification of the university's existence in a "diverse" society.

As white supremacy concedes ground on certain symbolic fronts, it entrenches along others, and so as Adam H. Domby puts it, "fact checking is not enough when addressing lies that undermined democracy."[12] Against the assumption of historical difference between a racist past and a diverse present that underwrites contextualization as an administrative attempt to accommodate white supremacy within the governing paradigm of diversity and inclusion, we must understand any form of preservation of Confederate monuments as active perpetuation of white supremacy and anti-Blackness in institutional spaces. To wrestle with the lingering implications of Carr's dedication, then, requires interrogating how institutions like universities perpetuate white supremacy through inaction, compromise, and equivocation. Carr's speech depicts an act of domination over not only his unnamed victim but also, and perhaps more importantly for the political logic of the Lost Cause, over federal authority represented as an occupying military force. In a rehearsal of the failures of Reconstruction in microcosm, Carr's acts of violence are met with inaction. Carr challenges the authority of the federal government through public acts of anti-Black violence, but it is the federal troops' lack of response that provides the real evidence of Carr's white power. As Reconstruction wore on and wore down, white apathy and hostility in the rest of the country would become one of the largest obstacles for Black southerners in their fight for legal and social inclusion. Responding to Carr's legacy requires interrogating the role passivity, disavowal, and institutional inertia have played in fostering white supremacy in the United States, so we can better imagine ways to build new institutions in which meaningful anti-racist transformation might become possible.

If Carr's celebration of the permissibility of racist violence speaks across the century to our own time, the novels of his contemporary Albion W. Tourgée offer one way we might begin to consider compromise and half-measures, especially those undertaken in the name of preserving abstract notions of social order that already works for everyone, as important tools for the expansion of white supremacy. Tourgée captures the turmoil of Reconstruction and its abandonment by the federal government in his best-selling novel *A Fool's Errand* (1879), an important if largely forgotten piece of nineteenth-century American literary and political history. A white Ohio-born lawyer, judge, politician, and author who lived in Greensboro from 1865 to 1880, Tourgée moved to North Carolina hoping to transform the South by putting into practice the ideals of individual liberty, free labor, and equality before the law. Tourgée left North Carolina having nearly destroyed his marriage and finances in a losing battle to keep control of the state government out of the hands of ex-Confederate politicians. Originally published anonymously in November 1879, *A Fool's Errand* appeared in an expanded second edition in 1880 bearing Tourgée's name and accompanied by a twelve-chapter appendix entitled *The Invisible Empire*, which provided documentation for Tourgée's influential and controversial account of the Ku Klux Klan in the novel.

Centered on the failed Reconstruction career of Comfort Servosse, a loosely fictionalized version of Tourgée himself, *A Fool's Errand* explores how ideals of equality and justice alone failed to interrupt the re-emergence of white supremacy in North Carolina after the Civil War. Describing his optimism in this era later in life, Tourgée would write, "I believed in many things then. . . . I believed in the United States as the flower of liberty, security and equal right for all. I believed the abolition of Slavery was all that was required to establish ultimate equality for and in right, opportunity and security before the law."[13] As he reflects in *A Fool's Errand*, such "formal" changes did not address the material reality of white supremacy: "Slavery as a formal state of society was at an end: as a force, a power, a moral element, it was just as active as before. . . . as a form of society it could be abolished by proclamation and enactment: as a moral entity, it is as indestructible as the souls on which it has left its mark."[14] Beyond revealing acts of violence from the antebellum and Reconstruction eras that help us challenge major facets of Lost Cause mythology, Tourgée's novel interrogates how white supremacists made sense of the violence they committed and, most importantly, how they turned the language and logic of post-emancipation politics into tools for the re-consolidation of power. *A Fool's Errand* therefore offers a lesson in dynamics of institutional and interpersonal politics through which extralegal violence and Lost Cause historical memory worked together to build institutions whose white supremacy consisted not only in the beliefs of its members, but in the very structures and logics through which institutional action and inaction could be defined. In the remainder of this chapter, I situate *A Fool's Errand* in its early Jim Crow-era historical context, outline some of the ways that Tourgée's political vision offers insight into twenty-first century conversations about racism and institutional power, and then finally offer readings of scenes from *A Fool's Errand* in which Tourgée dramatizes the interplay between fabricated historical memory and the normalization of white supremacy within Reconstruction-era political institutions.

Situating Tourgée's novel historically is complicated by the fact that so much of the literary life of Lost Cause mythology emerged as a response to the success of works like *A Fool's Errand*. As Carolyn L. Karcher writes in the afterword to her 2016 study of Tourgée's post-Reconstruction writing career, "the process of rescuing Tourgée from the oblivion to which the triumph of white supremacy consigned him in his lifetime has been long, bumpy, and arduous."[15] The novel's runaway success in 1879–80 helped raise awareness about the increasing disenfranchisement and economic re-enslavement of Black citizens in the South among northern voters. *A Fool's Errand* galvanized Republican voters, who rallied behind James Garfield in the 1880 presidential election, momentarily recommitting the federal government to the defense of the economic and political freedom of freedmen and -women in the South. Tragically, Garfield was assassinated less than a year into his first term, and his vice president, Chester A. Arthur, proved uninterested in interfering in southern politics. For a second time, Tourgée's grand hopes for racial equality in the country were squashed. The rise of Jim Crow wiped away many of the new political protections for Black North Carolinians that Tourgée had championed.

As his political program withered away under Jim Crow rule, Tourgée's literary legacy was also subject to white supremacist attacks. Writing in the aftermath of the initial defeat of Reconstruction governance in North Carolina, Tourgée used fictional narratives to expose the relationship among organized clandestine white supremacist violence, the historical memory used to justify it, and the constitutionally illegitimate operation of state institutions like courts and legislatures then in the hands of former Confederates. In the early twentieth century, literature and film celebrated the apparent virtues of white supremacist political rule that Tourgée spent his adult life fighting against. North Carolinian Thomas Dixon's novels *The Leopard's Spots* (1902) and *The Clansman* (1905) were literary responses to Tourgée's novels and politics, and their success helped close the book on Tourgée's public reputation.[16] When they were adapted by D. W. Griffith into *The Birth of a Nation* (1915), these narratives birthed both modern cinema and the modern Ku Klux Klan. The massive popular success of Lost Cause narratives among white audiences found academic support among white historians whose early twentieth-century output consistently presented slavery as a largely peaceful and harmonious social system and Reconstruction as a period of northern- and Black-led destruction of civil society in the South.

While his racist contemporaries like Thomas Nelson Page and Dixon promoted Lost Cause mythology by writing novels that imputed heroism to ex-Confederates and Klansmen to "imply different views of what the postbellum South should strive for . . . [through] views of the future [that] are narratively linked to the past," Tourgée exposes how such violence and the questionable historical memory that justified it delayed and diminished transformation in the material, political, and social status of newly recognized Black citizens.[17] While Tourgée stages scenes wherein his protagonist resists and counters incipient Lost Cause mythmaking and other smaller-scale narratives of white southern virtue and innocence, *A Fool's Errand* is provocatively pessimistic about the efficacy of mere debunking and insists on the necessity of building and sustaining power to foster and defend racial equity. Arriving before the explosion of Lost Cause mythology in the final years of the nineteenth century, Tourgée's novel helps us read Confederate monuments within their institutional contexts by doing more than simply naming white supremacist violence and offering a historically accurate counternarrative to the Lost Cause. Instead, Tourgée illustrates how this violence was, in essence, put into institutional context by its practitioners: interpreted within the language and logic of free labor and local sovereignty that allowed racial exploitation and violence to continue unabated.

In the final years of his life, as Dixon's star rose alongside the entrenchment of his narrative of Reconstruction, Tourgée remained an unapologetic defender of Reconstruction's founding promises and staunch in his appraisal of its failure. When a former classmate suggested that *The Leopard's Spots* and *A Fool's Errand* were "on the same footing as equally biased, but equally valid, representatives of opposing viewpoints," Tourgée responded in frustration that Dixon's novels were useless as historiography but valuable for their insight into the mind of Jim Crow-era white elites.[18] Tourgée balked at the suggestion that his and Dixon's novels were equally accurate—because equally biased—accounts of Reconstruction, going so far as to point out that for men like Dixon the pretense of historical accuracy meant nothing outside of its rhetorical usefulness in maintaining power. "He is right," Tourgée wrote sarcastically of the air of historical authority put on by Dixon and other Lost Cause mythmakers, "indubitably right not because he has studied a matter, but because he cannot be wrong."[19] Tourgée highlights that what is really at stake in Dixon's work is an exercise of

racial authority; his novels are monuments to white supremacy's power to produce and maintain its own truths. We can read *A Fool's Errand* as an object lesson in the peril of such moral and epistemological equivocation that continues
to structure disparate university responses to racist violence and symbols and
anti-racist community defense.

Tourgée provides a challenge to the idea that correct knowledge and moral
beliefs lead to just outcomes through the animating concept of foolishness. Distinct from ignorance, which suggests a lack of knowledge, foolishness suggests
both a naïve idealism and a credulity about the intentions of political adversar-
ies that leave the subject vulnerable to manipulation and exploitation. This credulity is a central feature of Tourgée's political thinking in *A Fool's Errand*; Tourgée refers to Servosse as "the Fool" throughout the novel. At the novel's climax
after the Klan has been disbanded in North Carolina without its members facing consequences for their violent lawlessness, Servosse wonders at the seeming
lack of contradiction between such extreme terror and the patterns of everyday
life. "Were they deliberately savage and vicious," Servosse asks himself, "or was
he in error?"[20] This is a moment of crisis for Servosse's liberal ideals and his
belief that an interest in human equality and justice is universal. "Was there any
absolute standard of right," he continues, "or were religion and morality merely
relative and incidental terms? Was that right in Georgia which was wrong in
Maine?" Tourgée's rhetorical questions imply a negative response, thereby gal-
vanizing readerly support for the reinvigoration of federal intervention in the
southern states. Yet a recognition of facts on the ground was not enough to be
transformative; Tourgée sought real changes to the way federal and state governments interacted in order to use the force of the federal government to combat white supremacist violence and fraud happening at the state level.

The flawed idealism of Tourgée's nineteenth-century Fool anticipates limitations in the twentieth-century liberal ideal of colorblindness, "a transcen-
dent goal of equality before the law, regardless of race."[21] We can understand
university diversity regimes as embodying colorblind frameworks within academic administrative and promotional contexts. In the twentieth century, the
ascendance of racial liberalism professing the same ideals as Tourgée—equality
before the law and individual sovereignty within the market—would transform
Black political demands into partial reforms of existing institutions without
fully addressing core economic and legal disparities that produce and maintain
racial hierarchies within the United States. The apparent success of midcentury
civil rights reforms produces in our own time a sense of white self-satisfaction
and colorblind racism that relegates racial violence to the past without addressing its lingering manifestations. As Charles Mills frames this colorblind logic in
the field of political theory, "in a perfectly just society, race would not exist, so
we do not . . . have to concern ourselves with matters of racial justice in our own

society."[22] Tourgée addressed analogous concerns in his own time, writing in 1888 that readers in the United States "esteem slavery as simply a dead, unpleasant fact of which they wish to hear no more, and regard any disparaging allusion to its results as an attempt to revive a defunct political sentiment."[23]

The issue in both Tourgée's time and our own is not necessarily the nonrecognition of race (indeed, diversity regimes work in part through public displays of racial difference) but rather a definition of race that denies the ways racial categories have been and continue to be produced as positions of power and not merely signs of identity. Tourgée's understanding that colorblind justice was only an aspiration that required taking "the realities of racism into account" in order to produce real equity sets him apart from white liberals who would take up the mantle of colorblindness in the twentieth century and from diversity regimes within institutions today.[24] As was the case with civil rights reforms in the twentieth century whose limited gains still require active defense from revanchist state and federal legislation, within this arrangement, the new social compact that would be formed was a revised form of white political dominance rhetorically committed to equality before the law but functionally in the service of the expansion of white power within new state and economic formations. As Tourgée puts it,

> Reconstruction was a failure so far as it attempted to unify the nation, to make one people in fact of what had been one only in name before the convulsion of civil war. It was a failure, too, so far as it attempted to fix and secure the position and rights of the colored race. They were fixed, it is true, on paper, and security for a certain sort taken to prevent the abrogation of that formal declaration. No guaranty whatever was provided against their practical subversion, which was accomplished with an ease and impunity that amazed those who instituted the movement.[25]

This lip service to equality before the law did not prevent the maintenance of white power through exclusionary reforms and outright fraud and violence justified as defenses of those political institutions. Servosse's trajectory in *A Fool's Errand* demonstrates the competing forms of knowledge and political conviction that defined the era and shows how certain forms of racial knowledge were forcibly made inoperative through the use of public speech and public silence to manipulate institutions in defense of white power. Tourgée explores the bad faith deployment of democratic and communitarian ideals that helped to resecure white supremacy in the South by normalizing the class and racial interests of former enslavers and their supporters. Through violence and coercion, white supremacy was reasserted as defense of reconstructed state institutions and was thereby laundered into accordance with the low bar set by national expectations.

Though ultimately committed to a vision of a racially egalitarian society based on liberal ideals of free labor and robust public democracy that differ from current conversations about the material ground of racial justice, *A Fool's Errand* nonetheless illustrates how rhetorical equivocation between racist and anti-racist positions minimizes the appearance of social conflict while heightening the stakes thereof. There are lessons to be learned not only from the content of Tourgée's novels but also in the history of their political impact, though these lessons come from autopsies of failure, not analyses of successes. To bring Tourgée's *A Fool's Errand* to bear on the present, we should approach it in terms of what Lowe describes as a *past conditional temporality*, "a space of productive attention to the scene of loss, a thinking with twofold attention that seeks to encompass at once the positive objects and methods of history and social science, and also the matters absent, entangled and unavailable by its methods."[26] In his novels, Tourgée was able to capture in narrative and essayistic form compelling versions of historical events and thorough political analysis thereof and therefore offer a compelling archive by which we might understand the complex reality of the Reconstruction era in North Carolina. More telling for our own moment, though, is the failure of such compelling evidence to secure the future for the liberal political regime it sought to instantiate. Alongside a historical lesson in the ways extralegal power subverted democracy in the South is a political lesson in the necessity of concerted efforts to build and wield power to protect democratic institutions.

Tourgée challenges his readers to consider the ways that liberal political institutions could be manipulated for illiberal ends along the color line. As Tourgée further wrote in his letter on Dixon, "I realize [now] the terrible truth that neither Education, Christianity nor Civilization, mean justice or equality between man and man, when one is white and the other is colored."[27] Tourgée's framing here suggests that the category of race itself disrupts the universal concepts that had initially motivated Tourgée's entry into Reconstruction politics. Disillusioned after Reconstruction's failure, Tourgée nonetheless kept up a radical if largely failure-prone fight for justice within the terms of US political institutions. Running through Tourgée's writing is a tacit recognition that political institutions mask coercive power and that this power defined the fundamental reality of social relations. For example, in "Shall White Minorities Rule?," an essay published nine years after *A Fool's Errand*, Tourgée addresses arguments that posed the disenfranchisement of Black citizens as a necessary step in preserving the integrity of electoral democracy. Rejecting the paternalistic framing of the "Negro problem" as a question of "What shall we do with the Negro?," Tourgée instead casts the issue as a question of an uncertain exercise of oppressive power: "is it not about time that we asked ourselves, 'What will the Negro permit us to do with him?'"[28]

In *A Fool's Errand*, Servosse's foolishness results from his misapprehension of other white people's willingness to take seriously the experiences of their Black contemporaries and to question their understanding of how their idealized political institutions operate. Tourgée depicts this reluctance in letters between Servosse and a northern politician (ironically referred to as the "Wise Man"). Responding to Servosse's complaints about violence against Black communities and their white allies, the Wise Man offers a list of legal reasons why the federal government cannot intervene in local politics before offering an impractical suggestion: "instead of whining over the wrongs they suffer at the hands of the rebels, they should assert themselves, and put down such lawless violence."[29] In order to wash his hands of responsibility for the violence in North Carolina, the Wise Man suggests that Black southerners simply fight back. "If people are killed by the Ku-Klux," he concludes, "why do they not kill the Ku-Klux?" What appears initially to be a question of concern for the integrity of federal and state institutions is revealed to be, in reality, a matter of disinterest in violent oppression.

For Tourgée, then, a key question faced by white Americans was what kinds of violence and domination the government would implicitly authorize through inaction. Elsewhere in "Shall White Minorities Rule?," Tourgée reflects:

> The arguments advanced in support of [white minority rule in the South] thus far are identical with those adduced in favor of slavery and the slave trade, nullification, secession, rebellion, Ku-Kluxism—all varying phases, let us not forget, of the same idea. They are argued by the same class of our people, with the same unanimity, the same positiveness, the same arrogant assumption of infallibility as of old. They not only boastfully admit that for a decade and a half they have nullified the law and defied the national power, but boldly proclaim their determination to continue to do so as long as they may see fit.[30]

Similarly, in *A Fool's Errand*, Tourgée presents white supremacist resistance to Reconstruction as a sustained campaign of counterrevolution that was marked by its conscious manipulation of northern credulity and the nation's desire for the appearance of civic normalcy. Rather than waging a second war against federal authority, Tourgée argues, the South used a rhetoric of concern for individual rights and civic responsibility to claim a moral high ground in rhetorical contests over the essence of southern political identity. They could thereby "turn against the enemy the weapon by which he had sought to secure their degradation, and by means of it . . . accomplish a degradation of their oppressor."[31] At the end of the Reconstruction era, what appeared to be a political consensus in the South that the federal government was bound to respect was in reality a coerced silence when Black southerners "became . . . incapable of organizing a successful opposition to the will of a majority of the white race."[32] The issue was not a lack of an oppositional political will, but the lack of power to make that will legible within and across state institutions.

One facet of white supremacy's unquestioned power was its ability to entertain certain kinds of oppositional narratives in order to create opportunities for apparent debunking that could further pass off racist historical memory as objective historical truth. We can see this exercise of power in comfort with nuance in the treatment of the Ku Klux Klan in novels written by Tourgée's contemporaries. As Brook Thomas points out, popular white authors like Dixon and Page portray the Klan as comprised of "morally suspect people, who often become scalawags," thereby affecting a double equivocation.[33] These authors preserved their portrayal of the Klan's "heroism" by containing its sins within unsavory figures who in turn could be further used in the service of Lost Cause mythmaking through their connection to unscrupulous, power-hungry Reconstruction-era Republicans. The pretense of nuanced context in such propagandistic narratives appears to give credit to multiple views on the subject; but, in reality, the posture of moderation obscured the fact that political power of the time remained in the hands of men like Carr and Dixon who had supported the subversion of the very institutions they now defended. As Reconstruction wears on in *A Fool's Errand*, Tourgée recounts how the forces of white supremacy turn the logic of legislation meant to protect Black southerners against already victimized communities.

These inversions illustrate not only the totality of the white supremacist takeover of state governments but also an opportunistic appropriation of the emerging logics of civil rights law. As Robyn Wiegman has argued, "the distinctiveness of southern white supremacist identity since the Civil War hinges on a repeated appeal to the minoritized, injured 'nature' of whiteness . . . [that produces] the threat of its own extinction as the justification and motivation for violent retaliations."[34] We see this rhetoric of victimization at work in legislative measures that take place toward the end of *A Fool's Errand* after former Confederates successfully take over the state legislature:

> The Legislatures of the several States were in session, and most of them passed immediately an act of amnesty and pardon for all who had committed acts of violence in disguise, or at the instigation of any secret organization; and in the excess of their zeal, and lest it should be supposed that they desired to screen only their friends, they extended their mantle of forgiveness so as to cover apparently the innocent as well as the guilty; those who sought no pardon, as well as the kneeling suppliants. In short, they pardoned not only the perpetrators of these outrages, but, in a reckless determination to forgive, *they even pardoned the victims!*[35]

Critical here is the epistemological violence produced by the pardoning process. Pardoning relies on a logic of contextualization; guilt is reassessed in light of a more complete understanding. Here, a political regime won through the violent suppression of political participation uses ill-gotten power to grant itself legitimacy purely through the pretension of equitable, deliberative governance. Racial power is consolidated through a conceptual leveling between disparate kinds of political organization: white-controlled legislatures equate Klan violence with defensive measures taken by the Klan's victims. This subversion of the intention of laws passed to use the power of the state to protect Black citizens from racist violence legitimizes extralegal white supremacist violence through the state power of the pardon. Additionally, and perhaps as importantly, this moment illustrates how white supremacy leverages real and imagined injury to catalyze its growth. The state, empowered by the extralegal violence that shaped its membership and ideology, absorbed the meaning of that violence and turned it against its victims. Noting that the legislature refused to pardon actions undertaken by the Republican governor to protect Black North Carolinians from Klan violence, Tourgée sourly remarks, "there are some things which can not be forgiven, even in an era of 'reconciliation'!"[36] While the Klan worked as an open secret at its peak, its dissolution prompted new forms of misrepresentation and moral equivocation that allowed the values of white supremacy to continue unabated in the life of the state.

In *A Fool's Errand*, Tourgée portrays Klan violence and its institutional aftereffects as the effort of "the whole South . . . having one common thought, one imperial purpose, one relentless will."[37] We can identify, in Tourgée's framing of a single, dominant narrative, the rise of Lost Cause mythology. But we can also see throughout the novel smaller acts of mythmaking that instilled former Confederates and the world they sought to recreate with a sense of inherent rightness and social authority. This "network of smaller fabrications that underpinned the larger Lost Cause myths about the South," as Domby calls it, allows us to question the dynamic relationship between truth and power that still defines struggle over monuments to the Confederacy.[38] A consequence of Domby's thesis that individual and local acts of historical exaggeration, fraud, and reinvention coalesced into what we now experience as broad, society-wide Lost Cause myths is that distinct modes and moments of historical fabrication entail distinct kinds of reception and response. *A Fool's Errand* offers us the opportunity to consider foolishness as one such response.

The central impasse faced by Servosse and his co-strugglers in *A Fool's Errand* is not simply the fact that the empowered classes in the South valued white social control over other political ideals but that the ability to meet that manipulation with the exercise of community power (including violence) appears to likewise constitute a violation of civic norms. Tourgée tries to make this contradiction visible to readers by treating white supremacy as a sincerely held belief, not a marker of ignorance or cynicism that can be met through public debate and democratic processes. Before the Civil War, the South "had ruled, until the right to dominate had seemed almost inherent; and finally, when their will was thwarted by an aroused majority, earnestly believing themselves to be oppressed beyond endurance, they flew to arms, and contested with marvelous courage and tenacity for the right to sever the compact which bound them to the other."[39] The Black race, he writes, "was earnestly and devoutly regarded by [whites] as inherently and unutterably inferior and degraded, so that even its generic name had become an epithet of scorn and contempt." Meeting this challenge required a similarly sincere and dedicated intervention of force. Servosse explains to a Black neighbor, "when a part of the country rebels, and runs wild for a time, it ought to have the rank wood, the wild growth, cut away without mercy. They ought to be held down, and pruned, and shaped until they are content to bear 'the peaceable fruits of righteousness.'"[40]

The complexity of Tourgée's theoretical framing of the relationship among history, truth, power, and politics leads to striking moments of narrative tension within *A Fool's Errand* that help us map out the reemergence of white supremacy as a political force from discrete acts of violence and inventions of historical memory. Frequently, characters know of a danger to themselves or others but lack either the power (in the case of the novel's freedmen) or courage (in the case of the novel's white moderates) to buck the expectations of the community. At the center of the novel are two murders that Tourgée depicts through incomplete, multiperspective retellings that are finally unified through a Black character's account. As Brook Thomas argues, Tourgée's narrative experimentation "while giving an African American the privilege of revealing the truth . . . also reminds us that his testimony will never be heard in court."[41] Servosse's position is particularly complicated as he both understands the broader political dynamics shaping his experience in Verdenton and lacks traditional outlets for producing political change based on that knowledge. In *A Fool's Errand*, knowledge is dangerous, as evidenced by the fate of Uncle Jerry, one of the novel's Black political leaders, who is lynched for spreading the truth about the murder of John Walters, a local white Republican. Reflecting on Uncle Jerry's platform of organized Black self-defense, Tourgée writes, "he had an idea that his race must, in a sense, achieve its own liberty, establish its own manhood, by a stubborn resistance to aggression,—an idea which it is altogether probable would have been the correct and proper one, had not the odds of ignorance and prejudice been so decidedly against them."[42] Without a base of power, which Tourgée understands here to be constituted by generations of accumulated wealth, training, and normalization, a politics, no matter how just or how grounded in reality, "may be heroic; but it is the heroism of folly, the faith—or hope, rather—of the fool."

While dangerous to the novel's Black characters, this faith in ideals proves more complicated for Tourgée's white protagonist. In many of the novel's most striking scenes, Servosse refutes attempts made by his white supremacist peers to assimilate him into their institutions. In these moments, Tourgée most trenchantly reflects on the uselessness of knowledge without power and exposes how political institutions express power relations that may not square with official ideology by appealing to the same ideals they subvert and seducing white contractors into racist social arrangements. Early in the novel, for example, former enslavers goad Servosse into speaking in defense of Black suffrage at a political meeting as a pretext for assaulting him. Though framed as an invitation to participate in a free democratic process, Tourgée presents this as a moment of cynical coercion. During the meeting, the main speaker decrying President Johnson's Reconstruction plan confronts Servosse:

> I see there is a man on the ground who has lately come among us from one of the Northern States, who has been here all day listening to what we have said, whether as a spy or citizen I do not know. It is currently reported that he has been sent down here by some body of men at the North to assist in overturning our institutions, and putting the bottom rail on top. I understand that he is in favor of social equality, n----r witnesses, n----r juries, and n----r voters. I don't know these things, but just hear them; and it may be that I am doing him an injustice. I hope I am, and, if so, that an opportunity will now be given for him to come forward and deny them. If he has come among us as a *bona-fide* citizen, having the interest of our people at heart, now is a good time for him to let it be known.[43]

The result of Servosse's speech reveals his misunderstanding of what his neighbors take bona fide citizenship to entail. For them, "the interest of our people" lies in continuing white political and economic dominance, but Servosse operates as if they are genuinely interested in adjusting to the reality of the Confederacy's defeat. Servosse's position is, from a modern perspective, fairly conservative. He appeals to the self-interest of his new white neighbors to accept the inevitability of Black suffrage and encourages them to actively grant voting rights to a portion of the Black population in order to satisfy the low bar set by presidential expectations.

The important dynamic here is that Servosse seeks to build consensus among his neighbors despite the bad faith invitation to participate in their conversation. He seeks their consent regarding changes to the social contract: to allow certain classes of newly freed Black men to enter into it in however limited a fashion. "It makes no difference whether you accept the terms now offered or not," he begins, "in this respect—yes, it may make this difference: it is usually better to meet an unpleasant necessity half way than wait till it forces itself on you."[44] Servosse is unable to foresee that the refusal of consent in this political process can—and will—exceed traditional political institutions. In large part due to his underestimation of how committed to white supremacy his North Carolina neighbors are, Servosse fails to anticipate how extralegal violence will shape the operation of apparently race-neutral Reconstruction political institutions. When he leaves the meeting, he is warned of an ambush planned by men upset by the speech that he had been forced into making. Servosse confronts for the first time what he realizes fully at the end of his time in the state, "it was not personal hostility or antipathy" that motivated white supremacist attacks on the Black community and their white supporters, "but [the victim's] public character and affiliations."[45] Realizing this disjuncture between private and public personhood, Servosse chooses his political commitments to racial egalitarianism (however limited his specific prescriptions might seem now) over the opportunity to save his reputation by adhering to the terms of the local racial contract.

While much of the political discussion in *A Fool's Errand* is essayistic, Tourgée also uses narrative passages to illustrate how individuals use stories to square extralegal action (in this case, violence in defense of white supremacy) with officially recognized social norms. In a striking scene that follows soon after Servosse's entry into local politics, Tourgée introduces a counterpoint to Servosse's preference for principle over personal reputation. Tourgée stages a conversation between Servosse and his neighbor Judge Nathan Hyman that further dramatizes the negotiation of white complicity and silence with regard to the racial contract. Hyman is essentially a moderate who is unwilling to reject the racial status quo despite professed misgivings about the violence required to maintain white supremacy. Hyman's character illustrates the perils of socially functional white ignorance: he relives the old status quo as a painful memory even as Servosse's wife, Metta, explains in a letter to her sister, "[Hyman] is a queer old gossip, who is so anxious to be on good terms with everybody that he has hard times to keep anybody on his side."[46] Hyman is then Servosse's opposite, exclusively interested in avoiding interpersonal conflict by defending the status quo whereas Servosse welcomes controversy as a necessary means of political change.

Over the course of a single conversation, Tourgée presents Hyman's apparently apolitical character as part and parcel of white supremacy's diffuse social power. Hyman progresses from an abstract defense of southern institutions to a personal defense of his own character before finally settling on a concrete defense of white supremacy as a social good, all without seemingly contradicting himself. Encountering Metta home alone one day, Hyman asks to borrow some of the Servosses' abolitionist literature, "just to see what hurt us."[47] When he returns a few days later, Hyman discusses his reading with Comfort. Hyman recounts his reading experience:

I had no notion of being angry; though, now I come to think on't, I can't imagine why I am not. There's certainly hard things enough in those books about me and my people to make any man mad. But the truth is, Colonel, it seems to be all about the past,—what is all over and done with now,—so that I seem to be reading of somebody else, and some other time than my own. Do you know, Colonel, that I never read any 'abolition' books before, only some of the milder sort? And I am of the notion now, that our folks made a mistake in keeping them out of the South.[48]

Tourgée builds an argument about white supremacy and its relationship to miscognition through the ensuing conversation between Hyman and Servosse. Hyman seeks to repair old rifts quickly, opining that, if an open exchange of ideas had taken place between North and South, the war might have been avoided. Servosse disagrees, "Each party distrusted the other's sincerity, and despised the other's knowledge. War was inevitable: sooner or later is must have come. Why, even now we can not agree in regard to the incidents flowing from emancipation."[49] To Servosse, a resolution to the sectional disagreement cannot be had through the mere exchange of ideas between two white men sitting in their parlor. Servosse and Hyman cannot simply speak for their section and call a truce; rectification requires expanding the terms of the social body, not negotiating new forms of intrawhite civility within its old terms.

At this point early in his tenure in North Carolina, Servosse admits he "can not see why the South should not have seen its own interest to have lain in the way of gradual emancipation long ago."[50] Hyman responds he "never could make out what *interest* [the North] had in the matter at all."[51] In this exchange, each man's understanding of the terms of the racial contract comes into view through this sectional defamiliarization. Hyman proceeds to defend the South through an intensive focus on individual agency and moral virtue. He complains abolitionists were "fanatics," who "made too much . . . out of the abuses of slavery." He admits "it *was* abused . . . and many bad things done by bad men under cover of it; but they might have credited us with honesty, at least. We were not all cruel and unjust." Hyman here deploys a language of individual morality to neutralize the evils of slavery as an institution. If it were properly contextualized, he suggests, outsiders would see that slavery was not so bad.

Servosse entertains these generalizations, but he defends the apparent abolitionist misunderstanding as a natural reaction to the slave society's intense persecution of dissent. The racial contract in the plantation South was so rigid and the gulf between white and Black so wide that any step outside its bounds provoked violent response. Hyman makes a parallel point without admitting the basic inequity of the arrangement or his own role in the system. "We did feel bound to protect the institution," he explains, "Not only our interests, but the safety of society as we honestly thought, depended on its continuance, unimpaired and perfect, until something else should take its place, at least. As long as the n----r was *here*, we were all satisfied that he must be a slave."[52] Hyman speaks to a lack of vision or imagination, suggesting that imagining a world other than the slave system was impossible. Of course, many residents of the South *did* imagine other possible worlds, including the millions of people this system and its beneficiaries like Hyman held in captivity. Hyman does show a moment of insight into the cultivated forgetting his position entails, remarking to Servosse that "you and I are getting back to human nature again in our anxiety to excuse our respective sides," though it is clear that he is the only one feeling anxiety, as Servosse has spent most of the conversation encouraging Hyman to expand on his own ideas, and that these returns to truisms about human behavior address only his own anxiety. Defense by abstraction can take Hyman only so far.

Hyman's role in the conversation turns abruptly from these generalizations as he informs Servosse that he has a particular reason to feel this anxiety: he is a character in one of the abolitionist books. The book's authors, a pair of abolitionist ministers who had traveled through the area some years before, accuse Hyman of setting them up for an ambush and beating. Hyman objects to the representation of his role in the book and tries to convince Servosse that the violence (which he does not deny happened) done in defense of the institution of slavery does not make him a bad person. He repeatedly provides caveats and explanations attesting to his own character, even as the evidence unfolds to the contrary:

> I didn't quarrel with him (you know I never quarrel with anybody, Colonel), an' I presume I did tell him I was his friend. I'm everybody's friend, an' always have been. I didn't want him to get in trouble, an' didn't want no harm to come to him. That's all true, an' I've no doubt I said so to him. But I did *not* approve his doctrine, nor sympathize with his sentiments; nor did I tell him so, though he says I did in the note. I never thought of such a thing.[53]

Hyman is depicted in the book as having led the ministers into an ambush by telling them to change the location of a planned meeting. Hyman insists if they had gone to their original destination "they would have been strung up to a tree, certain."[54] He feels insulted that he is blamed by the authors for having had a role in the actions of the mob that violently disrupted the meeting and ran them out of town.

Servosse is sympathetic to Hyman's embarrassment but does not let him off the hook for his implication in the system of violence that produced the situation in which Hyman found himself. Hyman's personal character is of little consequence given the outcome of the situation, and while he tried to avoid "trouble," he did nothing to distinguish himself from the mob. Hyman insists on the purity of his own moral agency despite the anecdote's evidence to the contrary. "You don't pretend to justify such proceedings, Squire?" asks Servosse once Hyman is done with his story.[55] Hyman's response cuts to the heart of the issues Tourgée is raising here:

> I don't really see what there is to make such a fuss about. . . . Here was a peaceable community, living under the protection of the Constitution and laws of the country; and these men, who had no business or interest here, came among us, and advocated doctrines, which, if adopted, would have destroyed the constitution of our society, and perhaps have endangered our lives and families.[56]

He expresses admiration of the mob's restraint, praising them for not killing the minister as they perhaps ought to have done. Pushed to take sides, Hyman abandons his apologetic approach and reveals the commitments underlying his apparently neutral position.

Servosse then confronts the violence at the heart of Hyman's abstractions and his insistence on personal exceptionalism: "It is just such intolerance as this, Squire, which makes it next to impossible for the South to accept its present situation. You all want to shoot, whip, hang, and burn those who do not agree with you. It is all the fruit and outcome of two hundred years of slavery: in fact, it is part and parcel of it."[57] Hyman responds that he and the men were simply defending themselves and their institutions. Servosse's response shows Tourgée thinking systematically at his finest level. "Protected yourself *against* your institutions," Servosse corrects Hyman.[58] His point here is that the revolutionary potential so feared by enslavers is baked into the system; a structure of violence begets retaliatory violence as a necessary counterbalance. By suppressing ideas critical of slavery, enslavers maintained the precarious balance of power achieved only through the unidirectional violence of enslavement. When confronted with alternatives, they position themselves through narratives as aggrieved and provoked victims, so as to rationalize the violence needed to maintain "peace" in their community.

Against Hyman's argument that his community has the right to defend itself, Servosse argues, "no community has any right to have, cherish, or protect any institution which can not bear the light of reason and free discussion."[59] With this statement, Servosse pushes for a broader conception of community, a radical but necessary proposition in a time when formerly enslaved people suddenly became potential members of political and social life. Hyman retreats to the force of majority opinion, but Servosse shuts down this line of thought:

> The arguments you use are the arguments of intolerance and bigotry in all ages. Even men who wish to be liberal-minded, like you, Squire, are blinded by them. You thought it was fair to whip those ministers for preaching what they deemed God's word *because* the bulk of the community did not agree with them. That was the very

same argument which would have been used to justify Tom Savage and the others, if they had succeeded in giving me a flagellation a while ago, as they attempted to do. The principle is the same. I had disagreed with my neighbors, and advocated strange doctrines. By your reasoning they had a right suppress me by violence, or even by murder if need be.

Hyman cannot face this reality and excuses himself, insisting, "I want to get along peaceably now, and I am sure our people want to do the same. We may be a little hot-blooded, and all that; but we are not mean."[60] Tourgée underscores how little effect the conversation has had on Hyman as the chapter closes. "[Hyman] lighted his pipe, and went home," Tourgée writes, "evidently thinking that his connection with this *ante bellum* barbarity had somehow increased his importance in the eyes of his new neighbors."

Only much later in the novel, when his Republican son is captured and "whipped . . . just like a n----r" by Klan members, does Hyman face the reality that white identity is forged through violence and power, not honor and ideals.[61] Even as he bemoans the fate of his son, though, Hyman makes excuses for the offending neighbors "with the impulses of a life still strong upon him to make excuse for that people whose thought he had always indorsed hitherto, and whose acts he had always excused, if he could not altogether approve."[62] Servosse arranges for Hyman's son to flee the state and live with the same northern minister Hyman had allowed to be whipped before the war. Through these conversations with Hyman, Tourgée reveals how the posturing of openness to new ideas and alternative perspectives can be used in the service of equivocating disparate levels of social power. In thus resolving this character's arc, Tourgée signals a generations-long timeframe for the changes in attitude and institutions he envisioned for bringing about a regime of free labor in the South. While holding out hope for this eventual transformation, Tourgée acknowledges that it would require sustained local attention and effort that was unlikely without the support of outside forces to match the forces of white supremacy within and without official institutions.

Reading *A Fool's Errand* in the twenty-first century requires recognizing there can be no triumph in a critical return to Tourgée's novel without understanding how the novel seeks to discomfit readers sympathetic to its political ideals. Tourgée's drive to understand white supremacy and critique its manipulation of liberal conceptions of political discourse like self-determination and individual freedom walks a tightrope seldom tread by white writers in his time or in ours, in part because they do not map onto traditional narratives of historical and personal transformation. As Hyman's character shows, the drive to proliferate context and generate discourse about difference without an underlying commitment to transformation leads to moral equivocation and the consolidation of preexisting power relations. Tourgée largely manages to clearly understand the forces motivating the white supremacists in his work—the overarching desire to maintain white power—without naturalizing this logic as an inherent racial trait or presenting it as a legitimate idea among others within the liberal democracy he hoped to foster.

These moments of reflection on the relationship between extralegal violence and their effect on political institutions resonate with Julian Carr's staging of his act of violence. In our time, seeing the violence in narratives like Carr's or Hyman's can be easy, but understanding and acting on the networks of power these narratives tap into proves more challenging. Efforts to simply contextualize statues refuse the truth of the connections that Carr speaks to between past and present. To relegate men like Carr to some dead history whose power is removed through the annotation of monuments and buildings does a disservice to those in the past who fought against white supremacy and to all people whose lives are shaped by institutions rooted in the era of Reconstruction. Carr's speech and its meditation on institutional contexts then raises questions about what value there is in knowing history if such knowledge only serves as a fig leaf for inaction in the face of ongoing inequity.

## NOTES

1. Albion W. Tourgée to E. H. Johnson, 1902, in *Undaunted Radical: The Selected Writings and Speeches of Albion W. Tourgée*, ed. Mark Elliott and John David Smith (Baton Rouge: Louisiana State University Press, 2010), 369.

2. Julian Shakespeare Carr, "Unveiling of Confederate Monument at University. June 2, 1913," folder 26, Julian Shakespeare Carr Papers, Southern Historical Collection, Louis Round Wilson Special Collections Library, University of North Carolina at Chapel Hill.

3. In 2016, the United States Fourth Circuit Court of Appeals ruled that the North Carolina Republican Party, following changes to federal preclearance authorized by the Voting Rights Act, passed election laws that "target[ed] African Americans with almost surgical precision" and that "the State took away [minority voters'] opportunity because [they] were about to exercise it."

4. University of North Carolina at Chapel Hill, *Recommendation for the Disposition and Preservation of the Confederate Monument*, December 3, 2018, https://bot.unc.edu/files/2018/12/Final-Report.pdf, 5.

5. University of North Carolina at Chapel Hill, *Recommendation for the Disposition and Preservation of the Confederate Monument Appendices*, December 3, 2018, https://bot.unc.edu/files/2018/12/12_03_18-Report-Appendices.pdf, 4.

6. Defend UNC–Take Action Chapel Hill, *Cops and Klan Go Hand-in-Hand*, Summer 2019, https://archive.org/details/copsklanunc.

7. James M. Thomas, "Diversity Regimes and Racial Inequality: A Case Study of Diversity University," *Social Currents* 5, no. 2 (August 2017): 141.

8. Lisa Lowe, *The Intimacies of Four Continents* (Durham, NC: Duke University Press, 2015), 6.

9. Thomas, "Diversity Regimes," 150.

10. Danielle Purifoy, "Shrieking Sam," *Scalawag*, January 14, 2019, https://www.scalawag magazine.org/2019/01/silent-sam-essay/.

11. Lowe, *Intimacies of Four Continents*, 6.

12. Adam H. Domby, *The False Cause: Fraud, Fabrication, and White Supremacy in Confederate Memory* (Charlottesville: University of Virginia Press, 2020).

13. Tourgée to E. H. Johnson, 357.

14. Albion W. Tourgée, *A Fool's Errand: A Novel of the South during Reconstruction* (Long Grove, IL:Waveland Press, 1991), 380–81.

15. Carolyn L. Karcher, *A Refugee from His Race: Albion W. Tourgée and His Fight against White Supremacy* (Chapel Hill: University of North Carolina Press, 2015), 333.

16. Mark Elliott, *Color-Blind Justice: Albion Tourgée and the Quest for Racial Equality from the Civil War to Plessy v. Ferguson* (New York: Oxford University Press, 2006), 22.

17. Brook Thomas, *The Literature of Reconstruction: Not in Plain Black and White* (Baltimore: Johns Hopkins University Press, 2016), 124.

18. Karcher, *Refugee from His Race*, 317.

19. Tourgée to E. H. Johnson, 357.

20. Tourgée, *Fool's Errand*, 317.

21. Elliott, *Color-Blind Justice*, 35.

22. Charles Mills, *Black Right/White Wrongs: The Critique of Racial Liberalism* (New York: Oxford University Press, 2017), 35.

23. Albion W. Tourgée, "The South as a Field for Fiction," in Elliott and Smith, *Undaunted Radical*, 204.

24. Elliott, *Color-Blind Justice*, 35.

25. Tourgée, *Fool's Errand*, 377.

26. Lowe, *Intimacies of Four Continents*, 40–41.

27. Tourgée to E. H. Johnson, 358.

28. Albion W. Tourgée, "Shall White Minorities Rule?," in Elliott and Smith, *Undaunted Radical*, 119.

29. Tourgée, *Fool's Errand*, 235.

30. Tourgée, "Shall White Minorities Rule?," 113.

31. Tourgée, *Fool's Errand*, 323.

32. Tourgée, *Fool's Errand*, 326.

33. Thomas, *Literature of Reconstruction*, 157.

34. Robyn Wiegman, "Whiteness Studies and the Paradox of Particularity," *boundary 2* 26, no. 3 (Fall 1999): 117.

35. Tourgée, *Fool's Errand*, 317.

36. Tourgée, *Fool's Errand*, 318. Republican governor William Woods Holden was impeached by the North Carolina legislature in 1870 for actions undertaken to combat Klan violence. He was pardoned by the North Carolina State Senate in 2011.

37. Tourgée, *Fool's Errand*, 323.

38. Domby, *False Cause*.

39. Tourgée, *Fool's Errand*, 320.

40. Tourgée, *Fool's Errand*, 115.

41. Thomas, *Literature of Reconstruction*, 158.

42. Tourgée, *Fool's Errand*, 225.

43. Tourgée, *Fool's Errand*, 58–59.

44. Tourgée, *Fool's Errand*, 65.

45. Tourgée, *Fool's Errand*, 233.

46. Tourgée, *Fool's Errand*, 51.
47. Tourgée, *Fool's Errand*, 85.
48. Tourgée, *Fool's Errand*, 89.
49. Tourgée, *Fool's Errand*, 90.
50. Tourgée, *Fool's Errand*, 90.
51. Tourgée, *Fool's Errand*, 91.
52. Tourgée, *Fool's Errand*, 91.
53. Tourgée, *Fool's Errand*, 92–93.
54. Tourgée, *Fool's Errand*, 93.
55. Tourgée, *Fool's Errand*, 94.
56. Tourgée, *Fool's Errand*, 94.
57. Tourgée, *Fool's Errand*, 94–95.
58. Tourgée, *Fool's Errand*, 95.
59. Tourgée, *Fool's Errand*, 95.
60. Tourgée, *Fool's Errand*, 96.
61. Tourgée, *Fool's Errand*, 200.
62. Tourgée, *Fool's Errand*, 201.

## Bibliography

Carr, Julian Shakespeare. "Unveiling of Confederate Monument at University. June 2, 1913." Folder 26, Julian Shakespeare Carr Papers, Southern Historical Collection, Louis Round Wilson Special Collections Library, University of North Carolina at Chapel Hill.

Defend UNC–Take Action Chapel Hill. *Cops and Klan Go Hand-in-Hand*, Summer 2019. https://archive.org/details/copsklanunc.

Domby, Adam H. *The False Cause: Fraud, Fabrication, and White Supremacy in Confederate Memory*. Charlottesville: University of Virginia Press, 2020.

Elliott, Mark. *Color-Blind Justice: Albion Tourgée and the Quest for Racial Equality from the Civil War to Plessy v. Ferguson*. New York: Oxford University Press, 2006.

Karcher, Carolyn L. *A Refugee from His Race: Albion W. Tourgée and His Fight against White Supremacy*. Chapel Hill: University of North Carolina Press, 2016.

Lowe, Lisa. *The Intimacies of Four Continents*. Durham, NC: Duke University Press, 2015.

Mills, Charles. *Black Right/White Wrongs: The Critique of Racial Liberalism*. New York: Oxford University Press, 2017.

Purifoy, Danielle. "Shrieking Sam." *Scalawag*, January 14, 2019. https://www.scalawagmagazine.org/2019/01/silent-sam-essay/.

Thomas, Brook. *The Literature of Reconstruction: Not in Plain Black and White*. Baltimore: Johns Hopkins University Press, 2016.

Thomas, James M. "Diversity Regimes and Racial Inequality: A Case Study of Diversity University." *Social Currents* 5, no 2 (August 2017): 140–56.

Tourgée, Albion W. *A Fool's Errand: A Novel of the South during Reconstruction*. Long Grove, IL.: Waveland Press, 1991. First published 1879 by Fords, Howard, and Hulbert (New York).

Tourgée, Albion W. "Letter to E. H. Johnson." In *Undaunted Radical: The Selected Writings and Speeches of Albion W. Tourgée*, edited by Mark Elliott and John David Smith, 356–78. Baton Rouge: Louisiana State University Press, 2010.

Tourgée, Albion W. "Shall White Minorities Rule?" In *Undaunted Radical: The Selected Writings and Speeches of Albion W. Tourgée*, edited by Mark Elliott and John David Smith, 112–22. Baton Rouge: Louisiana State University Press, 2010.

Tourgée, Albion W. "The South as a Field for Fiction." In *Undaunted Radical: The Selected Writings and Speeches of Albion W. Tourgée*, edited by Mark Elliott and John David Smith, 203–11. Baton Rouge: Louisiana State University Press, 2010.

University of North Carolina at Chapel Hill. *Recommendation for the Disposition and Preservation of the Confederate Monument*, December 3, 2018. https://bot.unc.edu/files/2018/12/Final-Report.pdf.

University of North Carolina at Chapel Hill. *Recommendation for the Disposition and Preservation of the Confederate Monument Appendices*, December 3, 2018. https://bot.unc.edu/files/2018/12/12_03_18-Report-Appendices.pdf.

Wiegman, Robyn. "Whiteness Studies and the Paradox of Particularity." *boundary 2* 26, no. 3 (Fall 1999): 115–50.

# CHAPTER 6

# REDEEMING WHITE WOMEN IN/ THROUGH LOST CAUSE FILMS

## —Maria Seger

That Spike Lee's critically acclaimed film *BlacKkKlansman* (2018) opens with scenes grabbed from *Gone with the Wind* (1939) and *The Birth of a Nation* (1915) is no coincidence. These direct references to blockbuster Lost Cause films set up *BlacKkKlansman*'s meta meditation on the role of film in the persistence of white supremacy across the twentieth and twenty-first centuries. *BlacKkKlansman* chronicles the work of Ron Stallworth (played by John David Washington), the first Black detective in Colorado Springs, who attempts to infiltrate and take down the Ku Klux Klan (KKK). In speaking back to these Lost Cause films through this plot, *BlacKkKlansman* significantly revises white women's role in perpetuating Confederate ideology. The film imagines a more active, less symbolic role for white women in the figure of Connie Kendrickson (played by Ashlie Atkinson), the wife of Felix Kendrickson (played by Jasper Pääkkönen), a local KKK member. Whereas white women in Lost Cause films often serve as passive yet culturally powerful symbols, in *BlacKkKlansman*, Connie becomes the agent of violent white supremacist power. Perhaps because of the cultural assumption of white women's perceived innocence, the KKK men choose Connie to plant a bomb at a Black power rally. When her plans are foiled, she leaves the bomb in the wheel well of the car of Patrice Dumas (played by Laura Harrier), the president of the Black Student Union at Colorado College.

In the film's climax, Ron arrives at Patrice's house to stop Connie. When two white cops arrive on the scene quickly thereafter, Connie predictably claims that Ron is sexually assaulting her, in the spirit of *The Birth of a Nation* that the KKK earlier watched to get motivated for their impending terrorism. Believing her, the white cops tackle and handcuff Ron before his partner, Flip Zimmerman (played by Adam Driver), appears to verify his identity. Felix and his KKK conspirators accidentally blow themselves up when they detonate the bomb that Connie planted in Patrice's wheel well, while Connie ends up the sole person incarcerated for the attack.[1] Thus, *BlacKkKlansman* references Lost Cause films to challenge Confederate and neo-Confederate ideology, exposing in the process the paradoxical position white women have held in white supremacist projects. The film deconstructs the myth of white women's innocence and their so-called need for white men's protection. Yet it also shows how white men grant white women agency only when that agency is used in the service of white supremacy. In the end, the film suggests that the misogyny of white supremacy means that white women will always be left holding the bag for their complicity.

Importantly, *BlacKkKlansman* demonstrates that this contemporary predicament about white women's role in preserving white supremacy can be traced back to earlier memorializations of the Confederacy. As historians like Stephanie McCurry and Drew Gilpin Faust have argued, Confederate ideology has always struggled with the tension between, on the one hand, requiring white women's social and political support, and on the other, embracing a brand of white supremacy that depends upon men's supremacy.[2] The so-called redemption of the South embodied in Confederate monuments—whether literal or literary—has frequently centered on white men.[3] Following southern studies scholars Karen L. Cox and Tara McPherson, through a reading of the canonical Lost Cause films *The Birth of a Nation* and *Gone with the Wind*, I shift the focus to white women, specifically locating their imagined role in their own redemption in their negotiation of their relationship to property through narratives of lynching and sexual violence.[4] Doing so allows us to see how white masculine victimization was built on constructing and then displacing white feminine victimization. Though these two films were released in different cultural moments—the reactionary 1910s and the liberal 1930s—they nonetheless employ the generic conventions of romance and the traditional lynching narrative to demonstrate the ongoing problem of white masculine fragility.[5] This fragility caused (and continues to cause) both violent enforcement and violations of the boundaries of and intersections among race, class, and gender.[6]

In *The Birth of a Nation*, twin narratives of Black men's sexual pursuit of white women are ultimately corrected by white men's acts of extralegal violence that restore their sole ownership—figured as protection—of white women. As the threatened and then revenged or restored property of white men, the main white women characters, Flora Cameron (played by Mae Marsh) and Elsie Stoneman (played by Lillian Gish), trade economic and political power for sociocultural power through self-sacrifice or marriage. In this way, the South's redemption occurs through white women's elimination (in the case of Flora) or containment (in the case of Elsie). In essence, these white women also redeem themselves by eagerly embracing their status as white men's literal and figurative

property. They accomplish this process rhetorically through the generic conventions of lynching and romance narratives.[7]

Decades later, *Gone with the Wind* inverts the lynching narrative, depicting
poor white men's robbery and attempted sexual assault of an elite white woman
as rectified by a loyal, submissive Black man's intervention and elite white men's
revenge. Once again, then, elite white men commit acts of extralegal violence
to claim ownership of elite white women—this time, not against the threat of
Black men, who have been rendered docile, but of poor white men challenging
antebellum class boundaries in a postbellum climate of economic precarity for
all. As the figure of the white southern lady, the protagonist Scarlett O'Hara
(played by Vivien Leigh) surrenders herself as property in marriage. However,
unlike in *The Birth of a Nation*, Scarlett marries to maintain ownership of her
family's plantation and expands her economic and political power. At film's end,
Scarlett's continued devotion to Rhett Butler (played by Clark Gable), especially
after a scene of what I'm interpreting as marital sexual violence, reveals the disturbing extent to which the South's redemption rests in white women's inter-
nalizing their status as property in marriage, articulated through the generic
conventions of romance.[8] Ultimately, narratives of white women's redemption
depend upon using their agency to further their constraint, from early Lost
Cause films to today's neo-Confederate imaginary.[9]

## WHITE WOMEN AS PROPERTY/OWNERS

In drawing on both the literal and figurative connotations of the term *property*,
my argument implies that redemption in the Lost Cause imaginary exceeds
"righting" the traumatic rupture of the Civil War in a purely theological, heroic,
or avenging manner. Indeed, *redemption* also connotes the idea of economic
recovery, reclamation, and freedom.[10] (It's no coincidence that both sets of connotations link to notions of white masculinity.) This explains why the acts of
violence that the Lost Cause imaginary endorses assume a moral equivalence
to types of property, ranging from exclusive sovereignty over states to white
women and Black people (insofar as they also register as types of property in
this imaginary).[11] The *Oxford English Dictionary* defines the word *property* in
three ways relevant to this discussion: 1) "A (usually material) thing belonging
to a person, group of persons, etc.; a possession; (as a mass noun) that which
one owns; possessions collectively; a person's goods, wealth, etc."; 2) "The fact
of owning something or of being owned; (esp. in legal contexts) the (exclusive)
right to the possession, use, or disposal of a thing; ownership; proprietorship";
and 3) figuratively as "A means to an end; a person or thing to be made use of;
an instrument or tool."[12] In Lost Cause films, white women become the literal

possessions of white men, in the sense of the first and second definitions, especially when exclusivity is in question, through acts of suicide, marriage, and
sexual violence. Moreover, Lost Cause films make white women property in
the third definition by instrumentalizing them (and depicting them instrumentalizing themselves) for redemptive white supremacist ends, rendering them
figurative property. In imagining white women in this way, these popular Lost
Cause films attempt to make their fantasy a reality—through their immense
cultural influence—in an era of white women's increasing economic, political,
and sexual agency.[13]

Indeed, white women's increasing autonomy and activism necessitated a
reconsideration of their role in the South's redemption. Lost Cause films narratively shored up white supremacy not only by using the generic elements of
romance but also by enacting and revising the traditional lynching narrative;
these generic patterns functioned hand-in-hand. (Re)imagining the lynching
narrative allowed Lost Cause films to regulate white women's relationship to
property, while adhering to romance genre conventions allowed them to contain white women's agency by depicting white women willingly renouncing
their autonomy and requesting white men's protection, welcoming their status
as property. Put simply, white women's role in redeeming the South was to freely
give themselves over to white men so that white men could get on with the "real"
work of redeeming the South through anti-Black violence. White women were
to be the mythical reason for—but not the agents of—this anti-Black violence.
Confederate memorialization advancing white supremacy required, then, a
careful rhetorical negotiation: neutralize white women as economic and political agents by imagining their self-constraint, their assumption of their natural
role as sexualized, endangered possessions through which white men's masculinity could be reconstructed post-defeat. In this formulation, a white woman's
authentic passivity was her greatest virtue. Using generic elements of romance
and lynching narratives, Lost Cause films venerate white women *choosing* symbolic cultural power by embracing their status as white southern ladies in order
to convince their white women audiences to do the same. Given the historic and
continued popularity of these canonical films across the nation, this rhetorical
strategy seems to have succeeded.

While southern studies scholars have analyzed Lost Cause literature's
nostalgia, denial, and negotiation of modernity, literary studies methods have
not yet been significantly brought to bear on this body of work, perhaps because
the texts' racism is so abhorrent.[14] Yet, if we want to understand the power of
Confederate (and neo-Confederate) white supremacy, we have to understand
its cultural forms and discourses. What generic conventions and patterns do
these texts use, and why? What discursive and rhetorical projects are revealed
through close reading their scenes and passages? How do they undertake the

cultural work of memorialization in specifically literary ways? In southern studies, Cox examines film's role in Lost Cause culture more broadly, while McPherson considers the significant position of white women in Lost Cause literature.
Cox shows that, between 1915 and 1945, a majority of films set in the South were
set in the Old South, extending and reinforcing the Lost Cause myth in US
culture. This proves, as Cox argues, that Lost Cause ideology was not merely
a southern project. After 1915, she writes, "a consensus of opinion . . . favored
the dominant southern narrative of the Civil War," and thus, Lost Cause films
expressed the nation's perception of the South rather than the South's perception of itself.[15] This insight seems especially important to understand when we
consider the enduring significance of *The Birth of a Nation* and *Gone with the
Wind* across the US, in film circles, neo-Confederate circles, and beyond.

McPherson turns her attention to the figures of the white southern lady and
the younger white southern belle, "mythologized image[s] of innocence and
purity."[16] Within Lost Cause ideology, the white southern lady, she writes, has
become disconnected "from the violence for which she was the cover story"—
the lynching of Black men. The hyperfeminized white southern lady served as
the "discursive symbol" for the South because, McPherson argues, the region
was responding to its own literal and figurative feminization, in the form of
white men's population loss and military defeat.[17] And while the ideal of the
white southern lady disciplined "white women who were enjoying the new freedoms born of wartime," white women were also complicit, "unwilling to question white privilege, buying into a return to the pedestal on which southern
femininity was properly situated." Indeed, as Cox and McPherson show with
the United Daughters of the Confederacy in particular, white women's position in Lost Cause ideology was a paradox. While they had great visibility and
authority over Confederate memorialization and education, the Lost Cause ideology those projects furthered, writes McPherson, "insisted on their fragility
and need for protection by white men."[18] I extend the investigation of this seeming contradiction through economic and discursive lenses. In Lost Cause films,
white women use their agency to willingly assume the position of venerated but
vulnerable property. Discursively, this ideological positioning develops through
the generic conventions of and intersection between romance and lynching
narratives, both of which, to different extents, constellate femininity/masculin-
ity and vulnerability/protection through the property/owner binary.

## REDEMPTION THROUGH ELIMINATION

Scholarship on *The Birth of a Nation* tends to focus on its revolutionary filmic
qualities, its immense commercial success, and its controversial historical

reception. The film is seldom interpreted as a narrative patterned after and inspiring other Lost Cause narratives. When it is taken up by literary and cultural studies scholars, their work has focused on white women's suffering, containment, and empowerment, sometimes through the lens of psychoanalysis.[19] Building on readings by Amy Louise Wood and Susan Courtney, I argue here that *The Birth of a Nation* attempts to redeem the South by establishing white women's role as property in the white supremacist imaginary through plots of their elimination and containment.[20] The film depicts two parallel narratives that position Black men as sexual aggressors and white men as virtuous avengers, the results of which ultimately restore white women as the property of white men. The first centers on Flora Cameron's suicidal leap from a cliff to avoid the sexual advances of the Black officer Gus (played by Walter Long in blackface), which results in his lynching, and the second focuses on Elsie Stoneman's attempt to avoid the marriage proposals of the Black lieutenant governor Silas Lynch (played by George Siegmann in blackface), which leads to his capture and her subsequent marriage to Ben Cameron (played by Henry B. Walthall). Flora's elimination through suicide and Elsie's containment through (white) marriage demonstrate their shift over the course of the film from threatened to avenged and/or restored property of white men.

The film engages in fantasies of white men's supremacy it hopes to bring to fruition by depicting Flora and Elsie as actively choosing passive and symbolic sociocultural power over and above economic and political power. That is, when Flora and Elsie welcome their status as property, they forfeit their ability to decide, control, or act with regard to themselves, others, and objects, all in the service of the white supremacist redemption of the South. *The Birth of a Nation*—"the most profitable and most watched silent film ever produced"— invites its audience of white women to do the same.[21] While the film has been credited with inspiring the reconstruction of white masculinity through a KKK revival and organized anti-Black violence in major metropolitan areas like Boston and Philadelphia, we must also attend to the prerequisite redemption of white femininity those projects required. For white men and women across the nation, *The Birth of a Nation*, like other Confederate monuments, guided the way to enacting social fantasies. And, significantly, it had the endorsement of the state in doing so: President Woodrow Wilson viewed *The Birth of a Nation* at home, making it the first US film aired at the White House.

*The Birth of a Nation* chronicles two families: the Stonemans, abolitionist northerners, and the Camerons, southern enslavers. Divided into two parts, the film in its first half depicts the Civil War, with the sons of each family enlisting in the Union and Confederate armies, respectively. Elsie Stoneman falls in love with Ben Cameron after caring for him in a Union hospital. She helps to secure him a pardon from President Abraham Lincoln (played by Joseph

Henabery) for his Confederate activities. After depicting Lincoln's assassination, implying the death of conciliatory postwar policies, the film's second half relates the dramatic consequences of the South's Reconstruction. Ben forms the KKK to fight southern white men's political and social oppression by emancipated Black men. He leads the lynching of Gus, the Black militiaman who romantically pursues his sister, Flora Cameron, causing her suicide, and he later rescues his love interest, Elsie, from the clutches of the Black lieutenant governor Silas Lynch. The film concludes with two weddings between white men and women of the Stoneman and Cameron families, including that of Ben and Elsie, signifying the solidified reunion of North and South under the banner of white supremacy.

Employing the generic conventions of the lynching narrative, *The Birth of a Nation* constructs Gus as Black sexual aggressor and Flora as pure and virginal white southern belle to demonstrate the virtue of Flora's subsequent elimination through suicide. In one scene taking place in the woods, the film establishes these roles by juxtaposing shots of Gus aggressively pursuing Flora with Flora playfully pursuing a squirrel. Shots of Gus in his military hat and jacket spying on Flora from behind shrubbery are interspersed with frames of Flora chasing a squirrel into its drey in a nearby tree. Though the same dramatic, foreboding music with a quick tempo and sharp chords plays over both sequences, the film implies a difference between Flora's and Gus's quests. Though Flora's chasing the animal, it's Gus who's hunting, and Flora who's rendered prey. Flora laughs at and interacts with the squirrel, miming it and blowing it kisses, while Gus stares intently and unceasingly at Flora. The film thus contrasts Flora's sexual innocence with Gus's lascivious gaze to make Flora's protection as property necessary and to construct anti-Black violence as defensive. Both facilitate white remasculinization.

Indeed, throughout this scene, the film constructs Flora as property in dispute, a dispute that's no longer resolvable by law or social custom but can only be resolved by violence. Gus finally approaches Flora and says, "You see, I'm a Captain now—and I want to marry—." Gus's pivot to his military rank subtly threatens his (and Black men's more generally) alleged monopoly on violence in the Reconstruction era. Viewers' interpretation of this threat constructs the moral value and legitimacy of Confederate ideology, in that Gus's invocation of military dominance invites a challenge, requiring defense and counterattack. Immediately following Gus's proposal, the film cuts to a close-up of Flora in which she's seen looking around for help and wringing her hands. Gus grabs her arm with both hands, and she strikes him and dashes away. He calls after her, "Wait, missie, I won't hurt yeh." The film allows Gus this line, yet the ensuing two minutes jump between shots of Flora running frantically through the forest, Flora's brother, Ben, finding clues as to her endangerment (her water pail and

Figure 6.1: A publicity still of Flora Cameron (played by Mae Marsh) preparing to jump off a cliff to escape the sexual advances of the free Black militiaman, Gus (played by Walter Long in blackface), in *The Birth of a Nation* (1915). Photograph of Mae Marsh, 1915. Image courtesy of *Wikimedia Commons.*

coat and Gus's military jacket and cap), and Gus nodding and reaching toward Flora as she narrowly escapes him. In this reading, Flora (and white women more generally) becomes the battlefield on which Gus and Ben settle opposing claims to legitimate violence and masculinity—the violence of the federal government or the violence of Confederate white supremacy, the masculinity of Black men or the masculinity of white men.

Flora embraces her status as the literal and figurative property of white men, redeeming herself and the South more generally, by taking her own life to avoid Gus's advances. In this way, the film instrumentalizes Flora through its lynching plot, giving her agency solely to end her agency, and then rewarding her choice as symbolically and narratively important. Indeed, Flora's suicide serves as the inciting incident of the film's second half; the revival of the KKK, the redemption of the South, and the reunion of North and South narratively depend upon it. Climbing to the top of a cliff of rocks, Flora turns back to Gus, saying, "Stay away or I'll jump!" Gus nonetheless pursues her (see Figure 6.1). The film features a side-view long shot of her leap and then a frontal long shot of her body falling and landing on the rocks below, rolling to a stop in a grassy patch. Gus peers over the cliff's edge. Realizing that Flora is likely dead and hearing Ben's voice in the distance, he hurries away from the scene. Ben spots Flora and rushes to her aid. He asks her who has done this to her, and she slowly mouths the word "Gus." Even as she is dying, he quiets her by placing his handkerchief over her mouth. As Ben embraces her from behind, Flora's body goes limp, indicating her death, and the camera focuses on Ben's anger, eyebrows raised, lips pursed, and chest puffed out. Here, the focus of the frame literally displaces the white feminine victimization it has constructed in favor of centering white masculine victimization instead.

Viewers are instructed not so much to grieve the loss of Flora as to applaud it. The intertitle closes the scene with a moral: "For her who had learned the stern lesson of honor we should not grieve that she found sweeter the opal gates of death." Here, the film celebrates ("honor[s]") Flora's choice (she "found [death] sweeter") as the right and necessary exercise of her agency. Flora has avoided becoming a victim of the traditional lynching narrative (she isn't sexually assaulted), yet her fatal jump from the cliff will still inspire Gus's lynching.[22] Indeed, Flora has paved the way for redeeming the South and white men like her brother through her self-elimination. If property is a means to an end, Flora's embrace of the means of suicide results in the end of her valorization as the cultural object that justifies white supremacist lynching, the formation of the KKK, and Jim Crow. Discursively, in Lost Cause rhetoric, Flora's choice of death renders the continuation of Confederate white supremacist violence legitimate and necessary. As Michael Rogin puts it, "The birth of a nation required Flora's blood as well as Gus's."[23]

## REDEMPTION THROUGH CONTAINMENT

Though Elsie doesn't take her own life when facing sexual pursuit by Lynch, she nonetheless functions to extend the model of white women's redemption that *The Birth of a Nation* establishes with Flora. This time, Elsie is contained rather than eliminated through a similar embrace of her status as white men's property. Elsie travels to Lynch's home to seek the release of Ben's father, who has been arrested. The intertitle indicates that she approaches Lynch "ignorant of Lynch's designs on her" (see Figure 6.2). This is Elsie's second instance of political appeal, as she earlier orchestrated Lincoln's pardon for Ben's Confederate activities. That Elsie's political meddling puts her in harm's way is no coincidence: the film implicitly warns white women to let white men handle the direct agential affairs of the South's redemption. As Lynch enters his office, he stares at Elsie in a vignetted closeup. His eyes widen, his eyebrows rise, and a surprised smile grows across his face. As with closeups of Gus, viewers watch Lynch watching Elsie. In employing shots of Black men leering at white women, the film visually encourages its audience to be disgusted by Black men's gazes, not to see scenes from their points of view. Elsie explains Dr. Cameron's plight to Lynch, and Lynch, eager to please, immediately draws up paperwork demanding his release.

To contain her agency, the film punishes Elsie's political action by rendering her vulnerable to the same implicit sexual violence of Black men to which

Figure 6.2: A publicity still of Elsie Stoneman (played by Lillian Gish) attempting to avoid the coercive marriage proposal of the Black lieutenant governor, Silas Lynch (played by George Siegmann in blackface). Photograph of Lillian Gish, 1915. Image courtesy of *Wikimedia Commons*.

it sacrificed Flora. Elsie, relieved that Lynch has agreed to free Dr. Cameron, gathers her coat to leave, but Lynch stops her as an intertitle reads, "Lynch's proposal of marriage." The camera closes in on a vignetted frame of Elsie this time, showing her shock and revulsion through parted lips and widened eyes as she draws in a quick breath. The angle widens to a medium shot of the two facing one another, and Elsie points at Lynch accusingly, threatening him with "a horsewhipping for his insolence." While Flora threatens violence to herself in an attempt to stop Gus's pursuit, Elsie, on the other hand, threatens violence to Lynch. But Elsie cannot perform such an act of violence herself and maintain her white femininity. Thus, the scene encourages Elsie to embrace her status as white men's property to ensure that white men's "protective" anti-Black violence will intercede on her behalf. Here, white women's victimization facilitates white men's victimization (and subsequently, the imagined restoration of masculinity) in the form of a property violation. Lynch replies to Elsie's threat with a subtle warning of his own: he raises the window shade to show her the Black militiamen assaulting white townsfolk in the streets. He says, "See! My people fill the streets! With them I will build a Black Empire and you as a Queen shall sit by my side." But this offer of power isn't tempting enough for Elsie. The political agency she exercises at the beginning of the scene collapses; she's been contained. In this way, the film enacts white supremacist fantasies that white women could never desire Black men and that white women will eventually sensibly reject political agency.

Through the generic conventions of the lynching narrative, the film can be said to instrumentalize Black men as much as white women, rendering them, too, as a kind of figurative property. In this sense, the film shows that abolition has not actually effected emancipation. Directly following Lynch's gesturing to the Black militia gathered outside, Elsie seats herself in a chair, dazed, looking straight into the camera, while Lynch approaches on bended knee, gathering up and then kissing the hem of her dress. She shrieks and throws her arm behind her head and then attempts to escape, but he has locked his office from the outside. Elsie spins in circles, tipsy and off-balance, attempting to convey physical weakness and commotion in a full shot. Lynch slouches down in an armchair, rubbing his legs suggestively, while Elsie puts both of her hands to the sides of her head, mouth agape, turning her eyes away in shock. This part of the scene contains more sexually suggestive elements than Gus's chase of Flora because white supremacy correlates Black men's political, economic, and sexual agency. As with the juxtaposition of shots of Ben's search between Flora and Gus's cat-and-mouse game in the forest, the film intersperses these more sexually provocative shots of Elsie and Lynch with shots of Klan members riding the countryside on horseback. This cross-cutting highlights several cause-and-effect conclusions assumed by the traditional lynching narrative, the most relevant of which is that white women want and need white men's protection from Black men. Both white women and Black men are rhetorically constructed and contained in this narrative patterning. When the film displaces the political and economic threat of Black men onto a sexual threat, it displaces white men's victimization onto white women, then refracts that victimization back onto white men. In the process, the film encourages white women to willingly abdicate political and economic power while rhetorically legitimizing anti-Black violence for sexual rather than political or economic reasons. The upshot of this thinking, unsurprisingly, is power concentrated in the hands of white men.

The scene ends with the reconstruction of white masculinity through white men's triumph over white women's—and by extension their own—victimization by Black men. The KKK, acting on the advice of white spies disguised in blackface who hear Elsie's cries, bursts into Lynch's office, subduing him and freeing Elsie. Ben lifts his hood, embracing a joyfully smiling Elsie in a vignetted frame. The film crystallizes the South's redemption and the nation's reunification under the banner of white supremacy with romance genre conventions: it concludes with the triumphant marriage of Ben and Elsie, an encapsulation of Ben's power and masculinity and Elsie's containment through her willing embrace of her status as property. In the end, *The Birth of a Nation* demonstrates why Lost Cause narratives depend upon lynching and romance storylines to redeem the

South. By encouraging white women to assume the position of property through plots of elimination or containment, Lost Cause narratives fantasize about white men's unquestioned masculinity, supremacy, and monopoly on political and economic power.

The upshot of *The Birth of a Nation* is the realization that neo-Confederate ideology's emphasis on white men's victimization is not a backlash against today's so-called politically correct culture. Rather, the construction of white masculine victimization has strong roots in the eras of Reconstruction and Jim Crow, when white men, through Lost Cause narratives, reimagined themselves as heroes overcoming total domination, connecting themselves to false US origin stories. Thus, *The Birth of a Nation* ultimately captures the paradox of US exceptionalism: white men need gender and racial difference and allegedly tyrannical governments to feel masculine and therefore free.

## REDEMPTION THROUGH SEXUAL VIOLENCE

Scholarly work on *Gone with the Wind*—both the book and the film—has often investigated its adherence to the romance genre, its racist portrayal of Black characters, and its embodiment of Lost Cause ideology.[24] More recently, literary and cultural studies scholars have turned to interpreting the racial and gendered politics of dual scenes of sexual violence (the first in the shantytown and the second in the O'Hara-Butler home). While Danielle Barkley connects Lost Cause ideology to the narrative's foiling of romance genre expectations, Erin Sheley and Deborah Barker highlight issues of sovereignty and property to argue that these scenes of sexual violence reveal the political and economic dimensions of southern white men's Lost Cause ideology.[25] Building on Sheley and Barker's work, I read *Gone with the Wind* in relation to the traditional lynching narrative. Interpreting these scenes of sexual violence not only in light of romance genre conventions but also in light of lynching narratives' patterns allows us to see how *Gone with the Wind*'s depiction of white men perpetrating sexual violence against Scarlett serves as a kind of disciplinary violence that encourages Scarlett to desire to be property, parallel to Flora's elimination and Elsie's containment in *The Birth of a Nation*. Furthermore, analyzing the acts of sexual violence through this literary lens more clearly reveals the film's discursive contribution to the Lost Cause project, the construction of white women as property and white men as victimized and then victorious.

Decades after the premiere of *The Birth of a Nation*, in an arguably more complex racial and economic moment, *Gone with the Wind* inverts the traditional lynching narrative, depicting Scarlett, a white woman who owns significant property, being attacked by poor white men and rescued by loyal, submissive Black men.[26] Despite this revision of aggressors and rescuers, the narrative requires vengeance by elite white men, including her then-current husband Frank Kennedy (played by Carroll Nye), the man she pines for, Ashley Wilkes (played by Leslie Howard), and Rhett Butler, her future husband. Like in *The Birth of a Nation*, then, elite white men commit acts of extralegal violence to reinstitute their sole ownership of elite white women. Unlike in *The Birth of a Nation*, though, ownership of white women need not be saved from the threat of Black men, who have been rendered docile, but from the threat of poor white men challenging preexisting class boundaries in the post-Civil War era of economic precarity.[27] Inversion proves how fundamental the conception of white women as property is to the Lost Cause vision. Even when slavery has been sanitized and romanticized to be "natural" or non-antagonistic, Scarlett must be reduced to property to distinguish between the elite white men who avenge her and the loyal Black men who save her.

On the one hand, Scarlett differs from *The Birth of a Nation*'s Flora and Elsie in that she owns significant property after inheriting her family's plantation, but on the other, Scarlett nonetheless appeals to strategic marriage arrangements to ensure her continued ownership. Thus, Scarlett redeems the South and white women more specifically by surrendering herself as figurative property in the marriage exchange for the sake of maintaining the Tara plantation and its Confederate traditions, even as her real economic and political power increases. In one of the film's final scenes, the inverted lynching narrative partially returns when Rhett attacks Scarlett with sexual violence as revenge for her showing affection for Ashley. Here, marital sexual violence serves as disciplinary violence meant to punish Scarlett for violating the terms of white women as property.[28] After Rhett and Scarlett have separated, Scarlett's closing declaration that she will somehow reunite with Rhett reveals the extent to which, in romanticizing his sexual violence, the narrative forces Scarlett to assume white women's marital position as property, thereby redeeming them in/and the New South.

*Gone with the Wind* chronicles the life of Scarlett, a white southern belle raised on Tara, her family's cotton plantation. On the eve of the Civil War, Scarlett hurriedly marries to make Ashley, the man she longs for and who has married her cousin Melanie Hamilton (played by Olivia de Havilland), jealous. After her first husband dies fighting for the Confederacy, Scarlett stays in Atlanta, causing a scene by dancing with Rhett, a Confederate blockade runner, while she's supposed to be in mourning. As Atlanta burns, Scarlett helps Melanie give birth, and Rhett helps them flee the city. Upon returning to Tara, Scarlett finds it largely deserted and destroyed but for her family and two enslaved people. Just before intermission, she vows to do what she must for her family's survival.

In the film's second half, Scarlett's family works the land themselves but cannot afford to pay the high Reconstruction taxes imposed upon Tara. To come up with the money, Scarlett tricks Frank into marrying her. Later, poor white men attack Scarlett while she's riding alone through a shantytown. When Frank, Ashley, and others raid the shantytown, Frank is killed. Rhett and Scarlett wed shortly thereafter. Following the birth of their daughter, because Scarlett still longs for Ashley, she tells Rhett they'll no longer share a marital bed. Rumors of Scarlett and Ashley embracing plague Rhett, who, in a drunken rage, sexually assaults Scarlett. After a period of separation, Scarlett informs Rhett that she's pregnant, but then falls down the stairs during an argument and miscarries. Their daughter and Melanie also tragically die. Once Ashley is available, Scarlett realizes that she loved Rhett all along. He refuses her, but the film ends with Scarlett returning to Tara, believing that she will one day win Rhett back.

Scarlett's second marriage to Frank both advances and problematizes the notion that *Gone with the Wind* redeems white women by positioning them as property. Set in the Reconstruction era, the film's second half opens with Scarlett's control of Tara in jeopardy due to what the film positions as outrageously unfair Reconstruction taxes meant to dispossess formerly Confederate families.[29] After Rhett denies her the tax money she needs, Scarlett makes a quick calculation to marry Frank, her sister's fiancé, a modest Atlanta merchant whose business is ripe for expansion in the midst of the South's rebuilding. While visiting his store, Scarlett realizes Frank has cleared $1,000—well in excess of the $300 she owes the state—and can afford to increase his lumber business significantly. Thinking out loud about Frank's plans to buy a house in Atlanta for her sister, Scarlett says, "There wouldn't be much help in that for Tara." Then, on a dime, her demeanor changes from investigative to flirtatious, clueing the audience into her plan to "save" Tara by marrying Frank. In doing so, Scarlett's economic and political power appears to be formally subsumed to Frank, who can help her pay the taxes and maintain control, through him, of Tara. But in reality, Scarlett's indirect economic and political power actually increases: she becomes the unofficial manager of Frank's enterprise and even convinces Ashley to join them. The film portrays Scarlett as having the stomach for tough business decisions like using convict labor when Frank and Ashley worry about the ethics of their exploitative capitalism. Thus, while Scarlett's marriage to Frank appears, on its face, to show Scarlett embracing her role as property by giving up ownership of Tara to him in marriage, in actuality, it serves as a convenient cover for her increasing economic and political power.

However, the film quickly disciplines Scarlett for deploying this increased power by subjecting her to an attack as she rides through the local shantytown. Importantly, this scene inverts the traditional lynching narrative depicted in films like *The Birth of a Nation*. Scarlett, having just finished business at the general store that Frank and Ashley own, tells Rhett she's riding out to the lumber mill. Rhett warns her of the danger of doing so: "Through shantytown alone?

Haven't you been told that it's dangerous to drive alone through all that riffraff?" As Scarlett approaches the shantytown, viewers can see that some dirty-faced white men have set a trap for her, stopping her horse and asking her for a quarter. Through force, they take her weapons—her horsewhip and her gun—as she screams for help. As the struggle continues, Scarlett's clothing starts to loosen and her hat falls off, and finally, as with Elsie in *The Birth of a Nation*, she faints, as one of the men looms over her. When Big Sam, the film's Uncle Tom character, comes to save her, he must fight off another opportunistic Black attacker hiding behind her horse and eyeing her limp body. While the Black attacker doesn't touch Scarlett, the standard pattern of the lynching narrative and the film's shots mark the Black attacker's designs as sexual (assault) and the white attackers' plans as primarily economic (theft). Thus, the film subtly inserts the standard lynching narrative even as it overwrites it with the inverse: poor white men threaten elite white women who must be saved by devoted Black men. Moreover, just as *The Birth of a Nation* punishes Elsie for inserting herself into political matters, *Gone with the Wind* narratively teaches Scarlett a lesson about her economic and political independence by making her seem foolish for insisting on riding through the shantytown alone despite Rhett's worry about the danger of the lower classes.

Even in revising the lynching narrative, though, *Gone with the Wind*, like *The Birth of a Nation* before it, continues to position white women as property. The shantytown men's violation of elite white men's ownership in/of white women becomes the justification for extralegal violence.[30] Suffering this attack also convinces Scarlett to embrace her role as property, to accept the protection of elite white men through marriage by relinquishing control of economic and political affairs outside of her household. (This is, in some sense, why Frank must die in the shantytown raid—the power imbalance in their marriage upends this formula—and why the attack "tames" Scarlett enough to subsequently accept Rhett's proposal, a relationship that the film ultimately champions as ideal romantic love.) The extralegal violence against the shantytown men carried out by Frank, Ashley, and other elite white men reestablishes their control of white women as property. As in *The Birth of a Nation*, this vigilante violence happens off-screen, sanitizing it and placing emphasis instead on Scarlett's redemption. While the men are destroying the shantytown and killing its inhabitants, *Gone with the Wind*'s audience watches Scarlett, Melanie, and other white women keeping themselves busy with domestic tasks like sewing and reading while quietly worrying about the violence that's unfolding. Melanie justifies the white men's plan when revealing it to Scarlett, saying, "Ashley and Frank and the others have gone to clean out those woods where you were attacked. It's what a great many of our southern gentlemen have had to do lately for our protection." While the cavalry keeps watch outside the Wilkes home waiting for Ashley and

Figure 6.3: A publicity still of Rhett Butler (played by Clark Gable) towering over Scarlett O'Hara (played by Vivien Leigh). Photograph of Clark Gable and Vivien Leigh, 1939. Image courtesy of *Wikimedia Commons*.

the others to return, Melanie says to the women around the table, "keep on with your sewing ladies, and I'll read aloud." The film shifts between closeups of all four of the women looking extremely nervous, eyes darting from Melanie to the clock to the window. This performance of domesticity narratively emphasizes white women's need for white men's protection. It remasculinizes white men not through the portrayal of their violence, as we might expect, but through the depiction of white women's assumption of passive complicity, of their status as property.

Scarlett's fear after the shantytown attack combined with her guilt about Frank's death in the raid causes her to partially welcome her role as property in her subsequent marriage to Rhett (see Figure 6.3). However, her full dedication to her position as property does not come until after Rhett deploys sexual violence. From the start, their marriage is inherently tumultuous, with Scarlett still pining for Ashley and telling Rhett after the birth of their first child that she no longer desires to have sex with him. When, in one scene, Scarlett physically embraces Ashley and a friend witnesses and gossips about it within their social circle, the betrayal ignites an intense jealousy in Rhett. After a party at Ashley and Melanie's, in which Melanie decides to stand by Scarlett, Rhett drinks to excess and picks a fight with Scarlett. In the ensuing scene, the film implies that, to punish her for her behavior with Ashley, Rhett sexually assaults her. Their argument begins with Rhett saying, "Come in, Mrs. Butler," an important nod to her relation to and ownership by him. Scarlett replies, "You're drunk, and I'm going to bed." He disagrees, pushing her back down into a chair and saying, "You're not going to bed. Not yet. Sit down." The course of their conversation becomes increasingly violent, with Rhett imagining his hands "tear[ing] [her] to pieces" and "smash[ing] [her] skull like a walnut." Scarlett fights back, saying, "Take your hands off me, you drunken fool," and "You'll never corner me or frighten me." But eventually, even though Scarlett escapes the room and makes a break for the stairs, Rhett overpowers her, forcibly kissing her as she visibly struggles to escape his grip. He threatens Scarlett: "You turn me out while you chase Ashley Wilkes, while you dream of Ashley Wilkes. This is one night you're not turning me out." Then, he picks her up and carries her up the stairs as she gasps and tries to wrest herself free to no avail. The extradiegetic music, foreboding with minor chords, plays over a screen that fades to black. As in *The Birth of a Nation*, sexual violence happens off stage.

Horrifically, *Gone with the Wind* justifies Rhett's sexual violence by causally linking it to Scarlett's recommitment to him, implicitly rendering it the discipline she required to fully assume her role as property. Twice, then, the narrative uses threats and acts of sexual violence to cause Scarlett's redemption: first in the shantytown and now in the O'Hara-Butler home. Narratively, Scarlett has been admonished for her resistance to assuming white women's role in the Lost Cause imaginary. This is partly what McPherson means when she says that "the narrative punishes Scarlett for her transgressions, highlighting what happens to independent women in the postbellum (and, by extension, the modern) South."[31] Like *The Birth of a Nation*, in encouraging Scarlett to redeem herself with the plot device of sexual violence, *Gone with the Wind* both threatens and encourages white women to fall into line by willingly ceding their economic and political power for social power as property. In *Gone with the Wind*, Scarlett accomplishes this transformation by desiring Rhett more after the act of marital sexual violence and wanting him back after he leaves her. After the screen fades to black following the scene of Rhett's sexual violence, it reopens on a medium shot of Scarlett waking up in bed, stretching her arms, looking blissfully happy, and humming. The film doesn't allow Scarlett to recognize Rhett's sexual violence as abuse because, ultimately, it can't imagine Scarlett as anything more than property. Read against the grain of the film's romance plot, Scarlett's status as property and Rhett's status as property bearer not only naturalize sexual violence but also property relations that can't be separated from patriarchal white supremacist legal regimes.

In the end, the film's final lines, conveying its cliffhanger ending, connect Scarlett's full (if belated) assumption of her role as property to the redemption of the Confederacy, indirectly fulfilling the generic conventions of the romance plot. After all that has happened between them, Scarlett finally realizes her love for Rhett, but it may be too late. Rhett refuses her plans for reconciliation and decides to return to Charleston. Scarlett seems lost without him, saying, "Rhett, where shall I go? What shall I do?" These lines crystallize Scarlett's development across the second half of the film from property bearer to property—from plantation owner and merchant manager to aimless housewife, lost without a husband to guide her. Rhett, wearing a giant glimmering smile, replies with the film's most famous line: "Frankly, my dear, I don't give a damn." The film allows him triumph in this moment; the extradiegetic music is joyful before returning to melancholy tones. As Scarlett sobs on the stairs, the site at which her sexual assault begins, extradiegetic sound voices dialogue from all the men in her life (her father, Ashley, Rhett, and others) who've emphasized her continual connection to Tara. Due to their influence, she decides to return home. In the film's final lines, she says exultantly about Rhett, "I'll think of some way to get him back. After all, tomorrow is another day." The film ends, then, with Scarlett eagerly embracing her status as property (in the first sentence) thereby reifying the redemption of Confederate white supremacy (in the second sentence). If the audience believes in the Lost Cause narrative, then they likely also believe that Scarlett reunites with Rhett. The generic conventions of the (inverted) lynching, romance, and Lost Cause narratives—here and elsewhere—ultimately rest on Scarlett and other white women's choice to willingly position themselves as white men's property.

## REVIVAL, REMOVAL, RECONTEXTUALIZATION

Reading *The Birth of a Nation* and *Gone with the Wind* in this way has, I hope, revealed that Confederate monuments memorialize white women as much as they do white men because white women's role as complicit property in patriarchal white supremacy is essential to white men's victimization and remasculinization and the redemption of the South more generally. And this need to read such Lost Cause films as Confederate monuments was perhaps never clearer than during the writing of this piece. *Gone with the Wind* stole quite a few headlines in 2020, proving literary Confederate monuments to be both an old *and* a new terrain of ideological battle. In February 2020, for example, Donald Trump attacked the Academy Award winner for best picture, Bong Joon-ho's anticapitalist South Korean film *Parasite* (2019), asking, "Can we get like *Gone with the Wind* back please?"[32] Trump's public admiration of the Lost Cause film signaled a kind of clarity about the patriarchal white supremacist ideologies the film advances. And historically, such discursive investments have been enormously profitable. As Dalton Trumbo, the Hollywood writer eventually blacklisted for his Communist Party affiliation, said before the Hollywood Writers' Congress

in 1943, "The most gigantic milestones of [Hollywood's] appeal to public patron-
age have been the anti-Negro pictures *The Birth of a Nation* and *Gone with the
Wind*."[33] That is to say, Lost Cause narratives sell because anti-Blackness has
always been lucrative, from the early days of Hollywood to today.

But amidst the forced and voluntary removal of a number of Confederate monuments and statues nationwide and an increasingly popular, militant,
and radical Black freedom movement, the profitability of anti-Blackness has
become more complex. Just a few months after Trump's comment, streaming
service HBO Max announced it was pulling *Gone with the Wind* from its collection until it could provide adequate context on the film's racism.[34] This decision was widely seen as a response to a *Los Angeles Times* op-ed calling for the
film's removal penned by John Ridley, screenwriter of *12 Years a Slave* (2013).[35]
Paralleling proposed solutions calling for Confederate monuments' contextualization, *Gone with the Wind* later reappeared in the HBO Max collection
with an introduction outlining the film's white supremacy and cultural influence on perceptions of slavery, Black people, and the South. HBO Max also
posted a panel discussion titled "*Gone with the Wind*: A Complicated Legacy"
in which scholars and filmmakers discuss the film's impacts.[36] It remains to
be seen whether we'll read Lost Cause narratives—among other Confederate
monuments—differently with such recontextualization or whether the conventions of these narratives are, by now, so deeply entrenched in everyday life as to
prohibit audiences' reinterpretations.

## NOTES

Thank you to Ian Beamish, Dine Faucheux, Liz Skilton, and David Squires for their
feedback on early drafts of this essay. Thanks also to Deborah Barker for providing me a digital
copy of her essay.

1. *BlacKkKlansman*, directed by Spike Lee (University City: Universal Pictures Home
Entertainment, 2018), Blu-ray Disc.

2. Stephanie McCurry, *Confederate Reckoning: Power and Politics in the Civil War South*
(Cambridge, MA: Harvard University Press, 2010); and Drew Gilpin Faust, *Mothers of
Invention: Women of the Slaveholding South in the American Civil War* (Chapel Hill: University
of North Carolina Press, 1996).

3. Use of the word *redemption* throughout this chapter always implies the critique of the
notion inherent in the phrase *so-called redemption*.

4. Karen L. Cox, *Dixie's Daughters: The United Daughters of the Confederacy and the
Preservation of Confederate Culture* (Gainesville: University Press of Florida, 2003); Karen L.
Cox, *Dreaming of Dixie: How the South Was Created in American Popular Culture* (Chapel Hill:
University of North Carolina Press, 2011); and Tara McPherson, *Reconstructing Dixie: Race,
Gender, and Nostalgia in the Imagined South* (Durham, NC: Duke University Press, 2003).

5. That these films turn to the generic conventions of romance is probably no coincidence.
Janice A. Radway explains the seeming paradox of white women consuming sexist romance

narratives, many of which include scenes of sexual violence. She suggests that white women consume these fantasies because they portray white men as powerful—violators but also caretakers that fulfill their partners' desires—whereas in the domestic sphere, white women readers were often homemakers who cared for white men who barely noticed them except to treat them like domestic labor. Thus, white women embrace white patriarchy because it restores white men to a masculine ideal rather than rendering them the emasculated victims they imagined themselves to be. Radway, *Reading the Romance: Women, Patriarchy, and Popular Literature* (Chapel Hill: University of North Carolina Press, 1984). According to historian Nina Silber, this pivot to sentimental, romantic narratives was also key to the reunion of North and South after the Civil War. Silber, *The Romance of Reunion: Northerners and the South, 1865–1900* (Chapel Hill: University of North Carolina Press, 1993). By *traditional lynching narrative*, I mean the racist cultural narrative in which, when Black men are accused of the sexual assault of white women, the enormity of the so-called crime outweighs the routine operation of the criminal legal system, resulting in an extralegal lynching. As activists such as Ida B. Wells have shown, white supremacists frequently fabricated this narrative to further Black subjection. Wells-Barnett, *On Lynchings* (Mineola: Dover Press, 2014).

6. Though I don't discuss the role of Black women in detail in this essay, their presence in the form of the stereotypical mammy figure in both films serves to reify and protect white women's femininity. For more on the complimentary roles of the Black mammy figure and the white southern belle in US film, see Cedric J. Robinson, *Forgeries of Memory and Meaning: Blacks and the Regimes of Race in American Theater and Film before World War II* (Chapel Hill: University of North Carolina Press, 2007); and McPherson, *Reconstructing Dixie*.

7. *The Birth of a Nation*, directed by D. W. Griffith (Epoch, 1915), MP4, https://archive.org/details/TheBirthOfANation19151080p.

8. *Gone with the Wind*, directed by Victor Fleming (1939; Burbank: Warner Brothers Pictures, 2009), DVD.

9. I'm following Marissa J. Fuentes and Saba Mahmood in thinking about agency produced by systems of power that isn't harnessed to subvert those systems of power. See Fuentes, *Dispossessed Lives: Enslaved Women, Violence, and the Archive* (Philadelphia: University of Pennsylvania Press, 2016); and Mahmood, *Politics of Piety: The Islamic Revival and the Feminist Subject* (Princeton, NJ: Princeton University Press, 2005). For more on this neo-Confederate phenomenon, see Seyward Darby, "The Rise of the Valkyries: In the Alt-Right, Women Are the Future, and the Problem," *Harper's Magazine*, September 2017, https://harpers.org/archive/2017/09/the-rise-of-the-valkyries/.

10. Economic redemption cannot be disentangled from insecure white masculinity or the protection of white womanhood. As historian Stephanie McCurry argues, while southern white men argued that they went to war to protect and provide for white women, the needs of warfighting itself invalidated their ability to do so. Throughout the war, white women and Black people protected and provided for themselves. McCurry, *Confederate Reckoning*, 94–95.

11. Interestingly, McPherson points out that the land itself is often feminized in Lost Cause ideology. McPherson, *Reconstructing Dixie*, 19. I might extend this claim to say that rendering one feminine and rendering one property were mutually constitutive and reinforcing because of their role in reconstructing white masculinity.

12. *Oxford English Dictionary*, s.v. "Property, n," accessed September 27, 2019.

13. *The Birth of a Nation* and *Gone with the Wind* grossed approximately two billion dollars (adjusted for inflation). Gary W. Gallagher, *Causes Won, Lost, and Forgotten: How Hollywood and Popular Art Shape What We Know about the Civil War* (Chapel Hill: University of North Carolina Press, 2008), 43. For more on the cultural influence of *The Birth of a Nation*, see

Melvyn Stokes, *D. W. Griffith's The Birth of a Nation: A History of "The Most Controversial Motion Picture of All Time"* (New York: Oxford University Press, 2007). For more on the cultural influence of *Gone with the Wind*, see Helen Taylor, *Scarlett's Women: Gone with the Wind and Its Female Fans* (New Brunswick, NJ: Rutgers University Press, 1989). For more on white women's increasing economic agency in this era, see R. Richard Geddes and Sharon Tennyson, "Passage of the Married Women's Property Acts and Earning Acts in the United States: 1850 to 1920," *Research in Economic History* 29 (January 2013): 145–89. For more on white women's increasing political agency in this era, see Elna C. Green, *Southern Strategies: Southern Women and the Woman Suffrage Question* (Chapel Hill: University of North Carolina Press, 1997); and Joan Hoff, *Law, Gender, and Injustice: A Legal History of U.S. Women* (New York: New York University Press, 1991).

14. Will Kaufman begins to apply literary methods in interpreting Lost Cause texts as "freighted with sentiment," showing a "fondness for the old plantation," and featuring loyal enslaved characters. Kaufman, "Literature and the Civil War," in *The Cambridge Companion to the Literature of the American South*, ed. Sharon Monteith (New York: Cambridge University Press, 2013), 42, 47.

15. Cox, *Dreaming of Dixie*, 81–83.

16. McPherson, *Reconstructing Dixie*, 3.

17. McPherson, *Reconstructing Dixie*, 19.

18. McPherson, *Reconstructing Dixie*, 49.

19. Amy Louise Wood argues that the film foregrounds white women's suffering and conceals Black men's misery in order to highlight how the former was "the outrageous price paid for emancipation and black enfranchisement" and how the latter constructed white men as "determined, stoic heroes" who doled out "efficient and honorable justice." Wood, *Lynching and Spectacle: Witnessing Racial Violence in America, 1890–1940* (Chapel Hill: University of North Carolina Press, 2009), 152–53. Susan Courtney locates the film's sexual threats against white women in anxieties about Black men's political and economic gains, which results in the "dramatic containment" of white women through "their victimization and rescue." She argues that the focus on white women's vulnerability stands in for concerns about the frailty of white masculinity; the film focuses the audience's gaze through white women in order to "express white male suffering and loss." Courtney, *Hollywood Fantasies of Miscegenation: Spectacular Narratives of Gender and Race, 1903–1967* (Princeton, NJ: Princeton University Press, 2005), 62–75. Michael Rogin's classic historical, biographical, and psychoanalytic reading of the film connects the extralegal violence deployed against Gus to the oppression of white women: "The sword guards the female genitalia not only to protect the white woman from the black phallus but also to keep her from acquiring a phallus of her own." Indeed, he argues that the film showcases worries not only about Black men's freedom but also about white women's empowerment through readings of Flora's sacrifice and Elsie's binding. Rogin, "'The Sword Became a Flashing Vision': D. W. Griffith's *The Birth of a Nation*," *Representations* 9 (Winter 1985): 176–77. *JSTOR*.

20. Wood, *Lynching and Spectacle*, 152–53; and Courtney, *Hollywood Fantasies*, 62–75.

21. Cox, *Dreaming of Dixie*, 83.

22. Flora's sexual assault is intentionally implied yet unstaged, as is Gus's lynching. The scenes leading up to his lynching juxtapose his KKK "trial" with Flora's family mourning her lifeless body. Wood reads this crosscutting as literally replacing the Black man's body with "the image of wronged white womanhood." Wood, *Lynching and Spectacle*, 157. The reminder of Gus's sexual pursuit of Flora in the moment of his murder supports the rhetoric of white men's protection of white women as property by visually drawing attention to the dead white woman in place of the literal act of murdering the Black man. Later in the film, Lynch's attempted

sexual assault of Elsie also goes unstaged. In the scene in which she approaches him in his office, the film slows the crosscutting, lingering on blank black frames for a few moments before fading in and out of shots of the Klan on horseback, riding across the countryside, and Lynch threatening Elsie. This narrative blankness creates a temporal gap that viewers may fill with generic elements of the lynching narrative (perhaps imagining Lynch's sexual assault of Elsie). Thus, the film continually reaffirms the importance of the traditional lynching narrative to the South's redemption through its sanitization, its unstaged but implied elements.

23. Rogin, "'The Sword Became a Flashing Vision,'" 178.

24. Gary W. Gallagher calls *Gone with the Wind* "the single most powerful influence on American perceptions of the Civil War." Gallagher, *Causes Won*, 45. Cox agrees, saying that the film's "achievement in reinforcing the Lost Cause myth in American culture was matched only by its financial success." Cox, *Dreaming of Dixie*, 94.

25. Danielle Barkley argues that the novel uses romance genre conventions to explore the "desirable, but inaccessible, past," but ultimately foils those conventions in ending with Scarlett and Rhett's failed relationship. Barkley, "No Happy Loves: Desire, Nostalgia, and Failure in Margaret Mitchell's *Gone with the Wind*," *Southern Literary Journal* 48, no. 1 (Fall 2014): 58. *Project Muse.* Erin Sheley suggests that the novel "naturalizes the violent reclamation of sovereignty through lynching, and that the potentially violated female body and the usurped right to property ownership reinforce one another and remain as justifications for violent reassertion of sovereignty." Sheley, "*Gone with the Wind* and the Trauma of Lost Sovereignty," *Southern Literary Journal* 45, no. 2 (Spring 2013): 3. *JSTOR.* Deborah Barker points out that the scenes of sexual violence in *Gone with the Wind* connect Scarlett as white southern belle not only to "white purity and white supremacy" but also to "economic stability," so that when she is threatened, so is the "white southern body politic and economic productivity." Barker, "Reconstructing Scarlett and the Economy of Rape in *Gone with the Wind*," in *New Approaches to* Gone with the Wind, ed. James A. Crank (Baton Rouge: Louisiana State University Press, 2015), 111.

26. The novel, on the other hand, follows the traditional lynching narrative in that the attackers are described as Black men.

27. This inversion makes sense in the Depression era in which the narrative was written and filmed. Elite white men felt threated by poor, landless, migrant white men. Unsurprisingly, this then-contemporary anxiety bled into the film's false depiction of the Reconstruction era and revision of the novel (see previous note).

28. Importantly, marital sexual violence isn't a legal possibility in the Reconstruction or Depression eras. Marital rape became a crime in most states beginning in the 1970s.

29. This common Lost Cause rhetorical tactic positions elite white enslavers as the victims of the Reconstruction era, stripped of their political sovereignty and subject to the plundering of their plantations. Such rhetoric can only follow a Lost Cause depiction of the antebellum era, which rewrites slavery's exclusion and dispossession to encourage white audiences' sympathy for Confederates after the Civil War.

30. See Sheley for more on this formulation's relation to notions of sovereignty. Sheley, "*Gone with the Wind*," 3.

31. McPherson, *Reconstructing Dixie*, 57.

32. "Trump Not a 'Parasite' Fan, Praises 'Gone with the Wind,'" AP News, February 21, 2020, https://apnews.com/672b7e731ec43e40da06b1ff8c8c57ed.

33. Dalton Trumbo quoted in Cox, *Dreaming of Dixie*, 96.

34. Daniel Victor, "HBO Max Pulls *Gone with the Wind*, Citing Racist Depictions," *New York Times*, June 10, 2020, https://www.nytimes.com/2020/06/10/business/media/gone-with-the-wind-hbo-max.html.

35. See John Ridley, "Op Ed: Hey, HBO, *Gone with the Wind* Romanticizes the Horrors of Slavery. Take It Off Your Platform for Now," *Los Angeles Times*, June 8, 2020, https://www .latimes.com/opinion/story/2020-06-08/hbo-max-racism-gone-with-the-wind-movie.

36. Jason Bailey, "*Gone with the Wind* Returns to HBO Max with a Few Additions," *New York Times*, June 25, 2020, https://www.nytimes.com/2020/06/25/movies/gone-with-the-wind -hbo-max.html.

# Bibliography

Bailey, Jason. "*Gone with the Wind* Returns to HBO Max with a Few Additions." *New York Times*, June 25, 2020. https://www.nytimes.com/2020/06/25/movies/gone-with-the-wind -hbo-max.html.

Barker, Deborah. "Reconstructing Scarlett and the Economy of Rape in *Gone with the Wind*." In *New Approaches to* Gone with the Wind, edited by James A. Crank, 110–34. Baton Rouge: Louisiana State University Press, 2015.

Barkley, Danielle. "No Happy Loves: Desire, Nostalgia, and Failure in Margaret Mitchell's *Gone with the Wind*." *Southern Literary Journal* 48, no. 1 (Fall 2014): 54–67. *Project Muse*.

Courtney, Susan. *Hollywood Fantasies of Miscegenation: Spectacular Narratives of Gender and Race, 1903–1967*. Princeton, NJ: Princeton University Press, 2005.

Cox, Karen L. *Dixie's Daughters: The United Daughters of the Confederacy and the Preservation of Confederate Culture*. Gainesville: University Press of Florida, 2003.

Cox, Karen L. *Dreaming of Dixie: How the South Was Created in American Popular Culture*. Chapel Hill: University of North Carolina Press, 2011.

Darby, Seyward. "The Rise of the Valkyries: In the Alt-Right, Women Are the Future, and the Problem." *Harper's Magazine*, September 2017. https://harpers.org/archive/2017/09/ the-rise-of-the-valkyries/.

Faust, Drew Gilpin. *Mothers of Invention: Women of the Slaveholding South in the Civil War*. Chapel Hill: University of North Carolina Press, 1996.

Fleming, Victor, dir. *Gone with the Wind*. 1939. Burbank: Warner Bros. Pictures, 2009. DVD.

Fuentes, Marissa J. *Dispossessed Lives: Enslaved Women, Violence, and the Archive*. Philadelphia: University of Pennsylvania Press, 2016.

Geddes, R. Richard, and Sharon Tennyson. "Passage of the Married Women's Property Acts and Earning Acts in the United States: 1850 to 1920." *Research in Economic History* 29 (2013): 145–89.

Green, Elna C. *Southern Strategies: Southern Women and the Woman Suffrage Question*. Chapel Hill: University of North Carolina Press, 1997.

Griffith, D. W., dir. *The Birth of a Nation*. Epoch, 1915. MP4. https://archive.org/details/TheBirth OfANation19151080p.

Hoff, Joan. *Law, Gender, and Injustice: A Legal History of U.S. Women*. New York: New York University Press, 1991.

Lee, Spike, dir. *BlacKkKlansman*. University City: Universal Pictures Home Entertainment, 2018. Blu-ray Disc.

Mahmood, Saba. *Politics of Piety: The Islamic Revival and the Feminist Subject*. Princeton, NJ: Princeton University Press, 2005.

McCurry, Stephanie. *Confederate Reckoning: Power and Politics in the Civil War South*. Cambridge, MA: Harvard University Press, 2012.

McPherson, Tara. *Reconstructing Dixie: Race, Gender, and Nostalgia in the Imagined South.* Durham, NC: Duke University Press, 2003.

*Oxford English Dictionary.* "Property, *n.*" Accessed September 27, 2019.

Radway, Janice A. *Reading the Romance: Women, Patriarchy, and Popular Literature.* Chapel Hill: University of North Carolina Press, 1984.

Ridley, John. "Op Ed: Hey, HBO, *Gone with the Wind* Romanticizes the Horrors of Slavery. Take It Off Your Platform for Now." *Los Angeles Times,* June 8, 2020. https://www.latimes .com/opinion/story/2020-06-08/hbo-max-racism-gone-with-the-wind-movie.

Robinson, Cedric J. *Forgeries of Memory and Meaning: Blacks and the Regimes of Race in American Theater and Film before World War II.* Chapel Hill: University of North Carolina Press, 2007.

Rogin, Michael. "'The Sword Became a Flashing Vision': D. W. Griffith's *The Birth of a Nation.*" *Representations* 9 (Winter 1985): 150–95. *JSTOR.*

Sheley, Erin. "*Gone with the Wind* and the Trauma of Lost Sovereignty." *Southern Literary Journal* 45, no. 2 (Spring 2013): 1–18. *JSTOR.*

Silber, Nina. *The Romance of Reunion: Northerners and the South, 1865–1900.* Chapel Hill: University of North Carolina Press, 1993.

Stokes, Melvyn. *D. W. Griffith's* The Birth of a Nation: *A History of "The Most Controversial Motion Picture of All Time."* New York: Oxford University Press, 2007.

Taylor, Helen. *Scarlett's Women: Gone with the Wind and Its Female Fans.* New Brunswick, NJ: Rutgers University Press, 1989.

"Trump Not a 'Parasite' Fan, Praises 'Gone with the Wind.'" *AP News,* February 21, 2020. https:// apnews.com/672b7e731ec43e40da06b1ff8c8c57ed.

Victor, Daniel. "HBO Max Pulls *Gone with the Wind,* Citing Racist Depictions." *New York Times,* June 10, 2020. https://www.nytimes.com/2020/06/10/business/media/gone-with-the -wind-hbo-max.html.

Wells-Barnett, Ida B. *On Lynchings.* Mineola, NY: Dover Press, 2014. Parts first published 1892, 1895, and 1900.

Wood, Amy Louise. *Lynching and Spectacle: Witnessing Racial Violence in America, 1890–1940.* Chapel Hill: University of North Carolina Press, 2009.

# CHAPTER 7

# PERFORMING COUNTER-MONUMENTALITY OF THE CIVIL WAR IN NATASHA TRETHEWEY'S *NATIVE GUARD* AND SUZAN-LORI PARKS'S *FATHER COMES HOME FROM THE WARS: PARTS 1, 2, AND 3*

## —Stacie McCormick

For me, narrating counter-histories of slavery has always been inseparable from writing a history of the present, by which I mean the incomplete project of freedom, and the precarious life of the ex-slave, a condition defined by vulnerability to premature death and to gratuitous acts of violence.
--Saidiya Hartman[1]

How do we confront the implications of what Saidiya Hartman so eloquently calls "the incomplete project of freedom" extending out from the slave past? In so many ways, these confrontations, especially in the United States, remain vexed because of the preponderance of monuments to the Confederacy peppering landscapes across the country. These monuments to those who fought to keep Black people enslaved function as tangible reminders of the devaluation of Black life and the ongoing ways Black freedom remains contested (as evinced through mass incarceration, challenges to Black voting rights, the overpolicing of Black communities, medical racism, and state-sanctioned violence against Black subjects). In the years leading up to 2014 and in that year in particular, the United States saw the consequences of this perpetual challenge to Black freedom play out in the rising resistance to socially sanctioned violence against Black subjects via killings of Black people with impunity by the police and even armed individuals operating under problematic "Stand Your Ground" laws. Black Lives Matter was formed and gained increasing prominence because its name so forcefully articulated the value of Black life amidst an onslaught of Black death. In correspondence with this moment, US culture saw a drumbeat toward the removal of symbols to white supremacy in the form of Confederate monuments.

It is in this sociocultural milieu that Natasha Trethewey's *Native Guard* and Suzan-Lori Parks's *Father Comes Home from the Wars: Parts 1, 2, and 3* emerge. *Native Guard* is a poetic meditation on a lesser-known Union Army regiment, the Louisiana Native Guard, and *Father Comes Home from the Wars: Parts 1, 2, and 3* dramatizes Black subjects at the conclusion of the Civil War reflecting on the war's meaning. Both works were performed for audiences in premieres in 2014. Moreover, each work writes a history of the present while invoking the past. In this essay, I consider how the counter-narrativizing of the Civil War constitutes a form of counter-monumentality, or direct responses to institutional monuments. This counter-monumentality is rooted in an ethos driven by a desire not to obscure the past but to produce a narrative that makes visible Black subjectivity and the consequences of this history on Black subjects living in the ongoing present. In the production of living monuments to the Black subjects of the Civil War era, Trethewey and Parks produce dynamic narratives that aim to account for Black experience and portray the affective registers that this particular war calls up for Black subjects: intimacy with death, traumas of memory, desires for freedom, and the need to derive unity from fragmentation. The ephemerality of performance distinguishes Trethewey's and Parks's efforts from those that create temporary physical monuments or overtly challenge standing institutional monuments. As such, performance enables them to critique US society and articulate Black subjects' ambivalent relation to the nation in ways that call up Black embodiment and materiality. These enactments of counter-monumentality are necessarily public engagements that constantly revise how narratives about the slave past are told. They amplify public sentiment by bringing various publics into a shared space, materializing a cultural commons where this canonical history can be engaged and challenged.

## PERFORMING COUNTER-MONUMENTALITY

If we understand 2014 as a threshold year for the challenge to systemic racism in US institutions, particularly the criminal justice system and policing, then the years following saw an increased critique of public monuments to white supremacy. Motivated by the scopic violence implicit in the numerous pictures of Dylann Roof, murderer of nine black parishioners of Mother Emanuel church in Charleston, South Carolina, posing against backdrops of Confederate flags and other symbols of the Confederacy, many citizens took to the streets to challenge all manner of monuments to the Confederacy, making the case that these symbols are overt affirmations of white supremacy. The government of South Carolina voted to remove the Confederate flag as its state flag, and Take 'Em Down NOLA gained steam and successfully removed the statue of Robert E. Lee that sat in the heart of New Orleans. Across the US South in cities such as Charlottesville, Virginia, and even on university campuses such as the University of Texas at Austin and the University of North Carolina at Chapel Hill, Confederate statues and tributes to the Confederacy were and continue to be removed from public spaces.

In addition to activist efforts toward removal, we see increasing performances of what contemporary art critics and archaeologists such as James Osborne call "counter-monumentality": "the construction of monuments that are specifically intended to challenge monuments' conventional tropes of scale and celebration."[2] Osborne goes on to theorize counter-monumentality, asserting, "Counter-monuments thus embody qualities quite opposite from conventional monuments: (a) instead of being permanent, they can be fleeting and transitory; (b) rather than glorifying their subject, they problematize it; and (c) as opposed to being a static representation for the viewer to observe, they actively invite and require viewer participation and engagement."[3] Such anti-monumental practices, as Osborne would have it, also highlight the counterintuitive frailty of memory inherent in monuments.

Writers of US literature have drawn upon anti-monumental practices in their reflections on the Civil War and the aftermath of this history across time. Confronting the way the Civil War has been memorialized in public spaces, authors such as Allen Tate, James Lowell, and Kevin Young, in addition to Parks and Trethewey, have taken up the subject, contextualizing it in their contemporary moments. While analyses of how this plays out in US poetry abound, the work of drama and performance in this area demands greater critical attention, particularly as it most thoroughly reflects the possibilities for literary anti-monumental practices. Performance's expressive force documents and urges critique of institutional monuments, especially since, as generations pass, these sentiments toward the past often shift. It also allows for voices marginalized out of the conversation in the early fabrication and installation of the institutional monuments and associated narratives to place themselves in dialectic relation with these objects. This process makes possible a reframing of such tributes to and accounts of the past via the stage or performative practice that interpolates new sentiment embedded within the monuments.

Drawing on discourses that interrogate the unreliability of the historical archive and performance's disruption of that perceived stability, I read Trethewey's and Parks's work through these lenses to uncover how *Native Guard* and *Father Comes Home from the Wars* represent quintessential counter-monuments to the Civil War. These works create a dialogic relationship to monuments and historical discourses that bring into greater view Black experience and respond to the veritable erasure of Black perspectives from Civil War memory and history. In the performance space, these works produce a different archive of public affect that counters archival practices of containment. These living monuments, then, account for repressed histories and are in themselves implicit critiques that raise questions about the meaning of freedom and the reliability of the archive, thereby causing audiences to question all of the history they aren't taught in educational institutions. Michel-Rolph Trouillot highlights the problems of approaching history from a positivist, singular narrative that doesn't account for multiple subjectivities. He also reminds us that present and past are always in dialectical relation and that "the past is only past because there is a present."[4] Hartman also posits that a thinking through of the present requires engagement with the past. The stakes of such a project are critical for Black subjects negotiating what she calls the "afterlives of slavery" whose voices have often been left out of these critical narratives. She explains, "The necessity of trying to represent what we cannot, rather than leading to pessimism or despair must be embraced as the impossibility that conditions our knowledge of the past and animates our desire for a liberated future."[5]

Moving this conversation to the realm of performance, Diana Taylor and Suzan-Lori Parks offer valuable analytics through which to explore possibilities for critically examining the institutional archive. In referring to how performances (cultural, informal, or formal) carry history, Taylor argues that the intangible storehouses of history and memory held within these performances should be read as the "repertoire" as opposed to an institutional archive.[6] Challenging the authority of the written word, Taylor explains that repertoires of performance democratize knowledge and function as vehicles that transmit histories and transform choreographies of meaning across time. When it comes to performing and representing slavery (especially in theater), questions of time are thrown into critical relief in many ways. First, the stage is a fluid temporal space where histories are constantly performed again and again with audiences suspended in time during the performance. Yet, with each performance, a new experience is produced, so that no two performances are presented in the exact same way. Moreover, the stage, with its transtemporal capacity to "play" with time, makes it a dynamic space in which to stage slavery. Slavery is itself an event that cannot be contained by a conventional understanding of time. Calvin Warren generatively offers the framework of "black time" as an alternative temporality of slavery, which he elaborates as "time without duration; it is a horizon of time that eludes objectification, foreclosing idioms such as 'getting over,' 'getting through,' or 'getting beneath.'"[7] In positing a new mode for understanding time in relation to slavery, Warren refuses a static demarcation of past and present, beginning and end.

Theorizing this possibility, Parks places the stage and Black drama firmly within this repertoire, arguing that the stage is the ideal place to "make history." She writes,

> And the history of History is in question too. A play is a blueprint of an event: a way of creating and rewriting history through the medium of literature. Since history is a recorded or remembered event, theatre, for me, is the perfect place to "make" history—that is, because so much of African-American history has been unrecorded, dismembered, washed out, one of my tasks as playwright is to— through literature and the special strange relationship between theatre and real-life—locate the ancestral burial ground, dig for bones, find bones, hear the bones sing, write it down.[8]

Trethewey's *Native Guard* and Parks's *Father Comes Home from the Wars* harness the performance space to "make" counter-histories of the Civil War, thereby intervening in narratives that have historically marginalized Black subjects out of the conversation.

## "WHERE NO MONUMENTS EXIST TO HEROES"

Described by director Susan Booth as "poetry with the urgency of action," Trethewey's book of poetry *Native Guard* received its first theatrical treatment when the Alliance Theatre in Atlanta, Georgia, staged the poems in 2014 as part of the National Civil War Project.[9] The work was also staged in 2018 at the Atlanta History Center, just steps away from its collection of Civil War artifacts. Trethewey's *Native Guard* is a blend of her reckoning with multiple traumatic pasts: her own childhood in Mississippi—being a product of a then-illegal interracial marriage—the murder of her mother, and the obscure history of the Louisiana Native Guard, one of the Union's first official Black units. *Native Guard* confronts received histories of the Civil War past and yields new insights on the histories that aren't taught in school or memorialized in public space. It was on a trip with her grandmother to Ship Island on the Mississippi Gulf Coast that Trethewey learned of the Louisiana Native Guard. After viewing the monuments to Confederate soldiers, another visitor informed her about the Louisiana Native Guard and its role on the island. There was, however, no marker of the group's imprint on this history and the landscape. Trethewey describes the absence of any public recognition of the Louisiana Native Guard and the relative national amnesia about Black participation in the Civil War as one of the first wounds that propelled her to become a poet, with the second wound being the death of her mother.[10] In *Native Guard*, these wounds converge to offer audiences a critical lens into the political and personal implications of confronting traumatic histories.

Underlying the principle of counter-monumentality that is at the heart of Trethewey's work is the issue of space and place, especially in terms of how physical monuments shape the landscape. It is significant, then, that *Native Guard's* early iterations were performed in the city of Atlanta, a central hub of commercial exchange during the Civil War. Beyond Atlanta's being the location of Stone Mountain's Confederate memorial, we can read the city of Atlanta as a site unto itself, a central *theater of war* that gets reconceptualized through Trethewey's work. Chandra O. Hopkins notes that, on the night she attended a 2014 performance, "Atlanta as troubled homeplace was central in the audience/ performer discussion that followed the show."[11] Indeed, Trethewey's genre-defying performance poetry can be read alongside and with the lens of site-specific performance. While site-specific performance is often understood as taking a "space for what it is, without major alteration, and reveal[ing] it in new ways through performance,"[12] Trethewey pushes against these boundaries by asking us to think of cities and urban spaces themselves as specific sites, where history shapes geography.[13] In fact, one key question that is often raised in site-specific performance is "How can performance reveal alternative layers to the reality of the landscape?"[14] Indeed, when history is read into this question, the meaning and its significance shift and deepen to become new questions: *how can performance reveal subterranean histories in the landscape, and how do those obscured histories shape the landscape?*

The question of performance's capacity to engage the landscape and trouble how histories are told became very resonant in *Native Guard's* 2018 run, when the Alliance Theatre staged the performance in the Atlanta History Center due to renovations taking place in its home theatre space, the Woodruff Arts Center. The 2018 performance run also followed the year of the 2017 standoff over Confederate memorials in Charlottesville. Wendell Brock notes the juxtaposition was "a remarkably resonant twist of fate, hearing Trethewey's bone-deep poems next to an exhibit of Civil War memorabilia, which audience members are invited to visit during intermission."[15] The direct engagement with the artifacts, as well as the conversations the Charlottesville conflict laid bare, created a new dynamic for visitors to engage with this history. During this cultural moment, there were numerous calls for the removal of Confederate symbols mounting, especially in the South, where we saw a "backlash from neo-Confederates and other whites concerned that their own history is being erased [that] has been occasionally ugly, and even deadly. . . . many see the public memorials to the breakaway Southern states as little more than celebrations of white suprem-acy."[16] Notably, the 2014 production was held in the last years of the presidency of Barack Obama, who embraced these conversations and the need to grapple with the harm of the valorization of the Confederacy, as most forcefully demonstrated in the eulogy he gave for the nine parishioners killed in 2015 by the racist neo-Confederate Roof. The 2018 production occurred two years into the term of Donald Trump, who notoriously referred to the white supremacists marching in Charlottesville, ideologically resonant with Roof, as "very fine people."[17]

We can then understand the staging of *Native Guard* both in 2014 at the Alliance Theatre and its deepening in 2018 at the Atlanta History Center as an ongoing conversation about the past, how it gets told, and the harm that comes when key voices are left out of the conversation. Trethewey says as much when she stated in an interview that "the book [*Native Guard*] is trying, in many ways, to talk about those things that have been forgotten or erased or somehow left out of the historical record, and I'm very concerned with trying to inscribe, or reinscribe, those things."[18] In this sense, Trethewey is engaging in a counter-monumental practice of reinscription whereby the past is being queried and rewritten from the perspectives of those left out of the dominant narrative.[19] The move from text to performance reinforces the many layers of reinscription and adaptation that undergird *Native Guard*. We might even consider Trethewey's adaptation of her poetry for the stage as a form of Black adaptation that informs Black life. I reference here my thinking with Rhaisa Williams on the subject of Black adaptation.[20] We understand and name the practice of Black adaptation as a counter-discursive praxis endemic to Black culture and writing. As Zora Neale Hurston describes it, key characteristics within Black expressive culture are acts of reinterpretation and modification of language, of movement, and of the canonical, the fixed. As such, our use of the term *adaptation* is deeply informed by Hurston's assertion that, "While he [the Black subject] lives and moves in the midst of white civilization, everything that he touches is re-interpreted for his own use."[21] This adaptive practice is born of the need to survive oppressive structures and limitations that have endeavored to shape possibility for Black folks. It is a testament to Black subjects' capacity for reimagining even under the worst of circumstances.

In the case of Trethewey's stage adaptation of this work of poetry, we see her reimagining and reinterpreting her work for audiences to engage with it in multiple ways. And in the staging of the performance in the Atlanta History Center, she is also reinterpreting the space to make room for Black experience and loss that had yet to be acknowledged in significant ways. Therefore, my analysis shifts between the poetry and the textual dimensions of *Native Guard* as well as to the performance aspects of the work, considering them in conversation with one another as well as the work's reshaping to meet the demands of the moment.

The performance of *Native Guard*, as a reinscription of the Civil War past on the Atlanta landscape, is in and of itself a gesture to history's possible mutability. In the theater space, there are multiple forms of time that come into play: the historical narrative being told as representative of the past and the present experience of audiences witnessing this "past" with each new performance. This speaks to Parks's affirmation that theater creates the space to call into question the "history of History" with the capital *H* being representative of the received histories that are disseminated as authoritative and told from a predominantly white heteropatriarchal lens.

Not only is Trethewey making history with her work, but by staging the poems and bringing to life the voices of those Black soldiers who do not have physical monuments documenting their roles in shaping US history, she is in many ways digging up the bones of the past and bringing their voices into the narrative. The "Second Act" of the performance deepens this because audience members engage in conversation and share their own relationship to Civil War history. When audiences arrived for the 2014 performances, they were prompted to "write a *name*, a *moment*, or an *idea* that you feel needs to be memorialized," and then they were asked to pin their contributions to the theater's walls.[22] These notes functioned as what Hopkins calls "tiny phenomenological emblems" that facilitate the telling of the story. In this sense, members of the audience become cocreators with Trethewey, and the producers construct and represent these counter-histories. These multiracial audiences, then, complicate the singular ways these narratives are often told. Hopkins notes also the ongoing history-making (to signal Parks) that these performances constitute even as it is unclear where their contributions would be stored after the performance, again attesting to history as embedded in power relations and subject to the will of those in charge of formally preserving them.[23]

In addition to the place-based interventions these performances of *Native Guard* make into how we reckon with history and how much of the narrative of Atlanta is in celebration of the Confederate dead at the expense of those Black subjects whose stories were disremembered and unaccounted for (to call up Toni Morrison), Trethewey's poems critique these silences and raise them up in her work. "Southern History," one of the poems, goes right to the heart of the matter in its assailing of educational institutions that promote a false narrative of history. The speaker recalls a moment in a history class when the instructor tells students, "*Before the war, they* [enslaved people] *were happy*," and then goes on to promulgate myths about enslaved people being better off in slavery by presenting the film *Gone with the Wind* (1939) as a "true account" of this era.[24] The speaker rightfully names these proclamations "a lie" that the teacher silently guarded. In using the word "lie," Trethewey challenges history as fact and as truth. "Southern History," in this case, is a myth perpetuated by those who remain sympathetic to the Confederacy and committed to advancing their ideologies in the present. This poem, like many others in the collection, disrupts that effort, forcefully so.

Alongside the challenge to received and misrepresented histories of the slavery era, Trethewey includes the voices of those who have been obscured. "Native

Guard" and "Elegy for the Native Guards," two other poems, account for the interior lives of those Black soldiers who fought in the war whose valor is not raised up in cultural discourse. "Native Guard" is constructed as an epistolary narrative written by an unnamed Black Union soldier. The poem shifts from meditations on slavery and relations between the enslaved and their enslavers in light of the cultural change brought on by the war. There is still the devaluation of Black life, in which the Black soldiers are devalued by being named "supply units" not "infantry" and are made to perform "n----r work."[25] The soldier notes that, even though the Black soldiers' experiences are intertwined with their white counterparts, "some names shall deck the page of history / as it is written on stone. Some will not."[26] Implicitly, the "some will not" gestures to the Black soldiers, and we see this play out in broader culture. The poem confronts the politics of memory and how these practices often deemphasize the contributions of Black subjects in American history.

Correspondingly, "Elegy for the Native Guards" places a contemporary speaker, assumed to be Trethewey, at the site of Ship Island where the Louisiana Native Guard was active. The speaker observes the dilapidated space that is a remnant of itself after Hurricane Camille hit the island. The speaker notes that the United Daughters of the Confederacy were sure to place a plaque for the Confederate dead, but there is no similar acknowledgment of the Native Guards who also died there, to which the speaker asks: "What is monument to their legacy?"[27] This query functions as a critical counter-monumental practice whereby the elegy is deployed as a form of critique as well as memory. Working in the tradition of other poets who have used the elegy to query Civil War history and memory (Robert Lowell and Young, in particular), elegies such as these, Michael LeMahieu writes, "insist that Civil War memory has a legacy of its own. We build monuments and construct memorials but, because memory itself has a legacy, we also question the monuments we have built, revisit the memorials we have constructed."[28] LeMahieu asserts that the querying of monuments and memorials is imperative "lest each new episode of racial violence seem like a moment of the passing present, lest each new barbarity appear banal."[29] Trethewey's elegy and the contemporary performances of *Native Guard* continually confront the question of time and insist that we not draw fine distinctions between the past and present.

Finally, her poem "Monument" brings together past and present in a convergence with her mother's death and her life amidst the invisible legacies of the Civil War—both in the sense of the ongoing terror Black subjects experience from those still fighting for the Lost Cause and in the sense of those whose histories are suppressed in the landscape and not acknowledged when we recount this history. Trethewey's mother, a Black woman, was caught up in these legacies most intimately, having been in an interracial marriage deemed illegal in the 1960s and then being a victim of gendered violence by a second husband who killed her in Stone Mountain, Georgia. Trethewey calls attention to this, saying, "my mother was murdered on Memorial Drive, in the shadow of Stone Mountain, the largest memorial to the Confederacy. So those two things are side-by-side in my psyche."[30] For Trethewey, the present of her mother's death is very much bound up in the past. The past hovers like a shadow against the backdrop of her mother's precarious life and tragic end. As she writes through her mother's experience, she produces a history of the present that complicates notions of history overall.

"Monument" itself is a testament to the instability of memory and how certain histories are neglected—in this case, her own mother's. This bears particularly on Black women who experience racial and gendered oppression. The speaker in "Monument," who we can assume is Trethewey, notes that movement of the ants busily building beds near her mother's grave reflects her own movement in life: "like everything I've forgotten—disappear / into the subterranean—a world / made by displacement."[31] Cemeteries are one of the few testaments to a lived life, now gone. If left untended, they are subject to ruin and decay that ultimately erase the memory of an individual's physical presence in the world. In signaling that she is likely the lone person invested in tending her mother's grave, she acknowledges that the "monument" to her mother's life would possibly be victim to the ants and other insects who discern (through lack of care) that Black life is often disavowed life. What Trethewey offers through her counter-monumental practice is also a kind of "wake work." An analytic developed by Christina Sharpe, wake work is a "mode of inhabiting *and* rupturing this episteme [the afterlives of slavery] with our known lived and un/imaginable lives."[32] At its heart a decolonial practice, wake work names the ways Black subjects navigate their postslavery subjectivities in light of their ongoing sense of unfreedom. In naming her mother's grave a "monument," Trethewey juxtaposes the conventional renderings of Confederate monuments as tributes to white men with her mother's gravesite as an unacknowledged monument, which ruptures epistemological figurations of who is worthy of being publicly memorialized.

*Native Guard* thus functions as an anti-monumental text and performance in its direct challenges to Civil War historical narratives and the problematic ways this history is remembered. The poems present a powerful counternarrative to received histories of slavery and the Civil War era that do not account for Black subjectivity. Additionally, the site-specific performances in Atlanta constitute a challenge to this history in the city central to the Confederacy. The devastation of Atlanta in 1864 marked a major turning point in bringing the military conflict of the Civil War to a close. It is very fitting, then, that *Native Guard* be staged in Atlanta to usher in an era when the monuments to the Confederacy that stand in the city and beyond are being challenged and progressively removed from public space. This signals a significant turning point in the long battle to defeat the ideologies underlying the war that have persisted long after the war has ended.

## WRITING/RIGHTING HISTORY IN *FATHER COMES HOME FROM THE WARS*

As noted earlier, the challenge to public Civil War memory was steadily gaining momentum when it reached its tipping point in 2014, a year into the Black Lives Matter era. In the same way that *Native Guard* constituted an intervention into how the public engages with and remembers this history, Parks's *Father Comes Home from the Wars* explores in greater theatrical depth the mythology around the Civil War and works to pierce this myth by featuring characters with names such as Homer and Ulysses, making plain how the play interrogates the nature of our national storytelling about slavery and the Civil War. It is notable that both works were being performed concurrently in this 2014 moment, affirming this period as a point of contemporary reckoning with all the ways that this past is unresolved and mistakenly told.

Set during the Civil War in the years 1862 and 1863, *Father Comes Home from the Wars: Parts 1, 2, and 3* depicts a community of enslaved characters negotiating the upheaval caused by the war and even considering exploiting this upheaval by escaping. The question of escape centers most squarely on Hero, who has been offered freedom if he fights alongside his enslaver for the cause of the Confederacy. This impossible compromise becomes the primary conflict in Part 1. It is fitting that Hero has to make such a complex choice because we later learn that he should not be understood as a "hero" in the truest sense of the word. He has enacted a number of betrayals, particularly against the enslaved Homer. Most notably, Hero informs his enslaver of Homer's plans to run away and performs the deed of chopping off Homer's foot as instructed by his enslaver after Homer is caught. Hero's enslaver promised freedom for assisting with Homer's capture; however, he never delivered on that promise.[33] In a series of events, Hero's freedom is tied to unconscionable choices. Thus, from the drama's outset, Parks troubles notions of freedom and its costs. We learn in Part 2 that Hero indeed joins his enslaver to fight as a Confederate soldier. There he meets Smith, a Union Army soldier, who has been captured by Hero's enslaver. In this section of the drama, Smith informs Hero that he is passing as white and was formerly enslaved. Smith encourages Hero to join him in running away and fighting with the Union Army, but Hero ultimately refuses. Finally, Part 3 presents a homecoming of sorts for Hero when we learn that his enslaver has died. With his return, Hero also brings with him disorienting pieces of information:

1) he has a new name—Ulysses; 2) he has a new love interest, Alberta, and has been unfaithful to Penny, the wife he left behind; and 3) he has news that the Civil War is over and that the enslaved are now free, a message that he ironically never gets to relay because those on the plantation abandon him after fully absorbing his changed state.

Father Comes Home from the Wars is one of a number of plays in Parks's dramatic oeuvre that trouble history in the sense of the canonical narratives that shape public understanding. Works such as *Topdog/Underdog* (2001), *The America Play* (1994), and *Imperceptible Mutabilities in the Third Kingdom* (1989), to name a notable few, take up the question and implications of whose history gets told.[34] In a longer meditation referenced earlier in this essay, Parks explains that she sees theater as the ideal space to *make* history, which affirms her enduring commitment to asserting history not as fixed but as mutable.[35] In a 2009 interview with Shawn-Marie Garrett, Parks speaks directly to the monumentalizing of historical figures and the need to hold that practice in critical perspective. She states, "Funny how, at the moment we feel that someone will live forever, we carve them in stone. Stone = eternity, although we should remember they're not fixed. History and the historical are mutable, right?"[36] By calling into question the stability of that which we carve in stone, Parks speaks directly to the critical project of counter-monumentality. This practice asserts that carving someone in stone does not ensure that the desired narrative about them or the "history" they are meant to commemorate will remain fixed. Parks is certainly very invested in troubling this, so we should see her plays as working to chip away (literally and figuratively) at the Confederate monuments that perpetuate a singular and problematic narrative about the Civil War. *Father Comes Home from the Wars* is a critical project that goes directly to that effort. Parks notes the many ways she approaches the concept of writing, which she asserts can include "RIGHTING."[37] In this sense, I want to explore what it means for Parks to re-RIGHT the history of the Civil War soldier in *Father Comes Home from the Wars*. To what extent does this RIGHTing counteract the wrongs perpetuated against Black enslaved soldiers who fought alongside their white counterparts?

With respect to the elevation of Black subjects and their contributions to the Civil War, I want to focus primarily on Parks's depiction of Hero and her desire to complicate how we understand Black soldiers who fought on either side of the battle. In Part 1 of the play, when Hero is contemplating whether to join his enslaver in the war, he remarks on the remnants of the soldier's uniform his enslaver gives him. Aware that his enslaver positions him as less consequential in the battle, as signaled by the partial uniform given to him, Hero consults with the character Old Man who tells him that he can transform the "scraps" of the uniform he receives.[38] "A man like you," he says, "can make a wholesome thing out of bits and pieces." This moment illuminates Parks's use of the uniform as a phenomenological signifier of Hero's partially recognized role as a soldier as well as his divided allegiances. Alice Rayner explains that objects on stage actively "participate in the signifying, narrative, and stylistic fictions" of both drama and culture.[39] She finds this particularly compelling in the context of re-presenting history in works such as Parks's *The America Play* (1995). Rayner asserts, "It is through the intersections of objects and their narratives that history can be written, not in terms of authenticity or of recording what may or may not have happened, but in terms of commentary, often ironic, about such recording of history."[40] Through the soldier's uniform and its mutability throughout the play, Parks signals the mutability of historical narrative and the veritable absence of enslaved Black subjects in canonical tellings of the history of the Civil War.

Through the uniform, Parks captures the ethos of Black soldiers during the Civil War who saw this garb as an important symbol of their transition from enslaved subjects to fully recognized US soldiers. Deborah Willis, in analyzing the visual cultural production of the Black Civil War soldier, notes, "As soon as they were given uniforms, from forage caps to weapons, they posed holding their arms. Whether standing alone, or in a group, they held flags, rifles, and banners while looking directly into the camera lens—as if sending a message of undeniable patriotism."[41] These images record Black soldiers embracing the agency of choosing a cause for which to fight that was folded into the question of what the future of the United States would be. They were shaping the country in meaningful ways through their role as soldiers and knew these acts should be documented. Alongside the writing of letters to loved ones left behind (an act that Trethewey's *Native Guard* utilizes as a literary mode of expression), the images deepened understanding of Black Civil War soldiers' courage as well as their assertion of "citizenship and self-representation."[42] Their documentary acts also seem to anticipate how the historical record would go on to obscure their true contributions to the war. Alan Trachtenberg explains that the repression of Black Americans' roles in the Civil War has been long and sustained. He elaborates, "Racial prejudice has been the major cause of the expunging and erasure of the role of blacks in determining their own future. It remains in the interests of some groups vested in continuing and preserving racial inequality to portray African Americans as unable to take command of their own lives, as inherently subordinate."[43] In many ways, the ethos underlying Parks's visual portrayal of the Black Civil War subject maintains consistency with Black soldiers' labor in documenting themselves in their uniforms, a visual statement of personhood, authority, and freedom.

The soldier's uniform takes on many dimensions throughout *Father Comes Home from the Wars*, making it a dynamic signifier that reifies the complexity of what it meant to be a Civil War soldier for Black subjects. The uniform also works as a narrative device to advance Parks's project of "writing/righting" the historical record. When Hero tries on his uniform for the first time, Penny proclaims, "That outfit makes you look better-looking, Hero, I can't lie."[44] In many ways, the uniform facilitates Hero's transition from an enslaved and dehumanized subject to someone with authority. Although the uniform he is wearing is for the Confederacy, Hero has been promised *his* freedom by his enslaver, so even as he fights for the enslaver's cause of maintaining chattel slavery, he is also fighting on behalf of his own cause, which is his personal freedom.

The symbolic meaning of the soldier's uniform undergoes a series of shifts once Hero leaves for battle with his enslaver, the Colonel. Along the way, Hero and his enslaver capture a Union Army soldier named Smith as prisoner. Once out of the Colonel's watch, Smith reveals that he is a biracial man passing as white and that he wants Hero to join him. We see this layering of symbolic meaning with the soldier's uniform when Smith informs Hero that, after his captain died on the battlefield, he took the captain's coat to wear over his own for warmth.[45] This act makes him more valuable as a prisoner because the Colonel erroneously thinks he has detained a Union Army captain. Moreover, this assignation of value as determined by one's clothing reveals the instability of and irrational ways that social value is determined. Smith's trickster act echoes William Wells Brown's Cato, who changes clothes with his enslaver to escape to freedom in *The Escape; or, A Leap for Freedom* (1858).

For Hero, who was brought in to fight on the side of the Confederacy, the uniform's signifying power aids in narrativizing his growing realization of the war's significance for the institution of slavery and his liminal position between these two sides. In a conversation with Smith while the Colonel is away, Hero asks, "How much you think we're gonna be worth when Freedom comes? What kind of price we gonna fetch then?"[46] Smith responds, "We won't have a price. Just like they don't." The thought of not being overtly valued in capitalist terms presents an existential crisis for Hero, which the uniform comes to represent. During this conversation, Smith lets Hero try on his Union Army captain's coat. Hero then imagines freedom. In their last encounter just before he escapes, Smith declares that Hero is a Union soldier in the 1st Kansas Colored infantry and gives him his private's uniform coat.[47] Hero puts on both coats with the Confederate uniform on top. This moment signals his recognition of his complex status and his divided loyalties. It is only in the end that Hero takes a firm side, once he has the confirmation of the Emancipation Proclamation in hand. He removes his Confederate Army coat to reveal to the others his Union Army coat underneath.[48] This final image of Hero in a Union Army coat in many ways represents both the soldiers who fought (whether by coercion or by will) on behalf of the Confederacy *and* those who fought for the Union, from whose cause he is a direct beneficiary. This latter fact is reinforced as Hero wears the

Union Army uniform closest to his body. These multiple shifts in uniforms do a great deal of critical work in reinforcing the notion of history as mutable and communicating the dynamic identities of Black Civil War soldiers.

We can locate the transgressive practice of counter-monumentality within and beyond Parks's troubling of canonical Civil War histories. Performances of the play reveal how Parks is not only "writing/righting" histories of the past but histories of the present. As we saw with Trethewey's *Native Guard*, site-specific performance makes an important intervention in spaces where the conversations raised within the play are the most consequential and crucial. Since *Father Comes Home from the Wars'* 2014 premiere, it is clear that the play speaks to contemporary issues of police violence and mass incarceration. Performances of this play have all carried the subtext that the history of slavery is unresolved and that the project of Black emancipation is unfinished. In fact, the play ends with haunting lines from Odyssey Dog as The Runaways (along with Penny and Homer) insist on leaving, and thus they never hear Hero (now Ulysses) announce that they have been freed by the Emancipation Proclamation. To this act, Odyssey Dog tells Hero/Ulysses, "The Runaways, they still got to run."[49] In many ways, this signals that even though the war has ended, the quest for freedom persists. This perpetual quest for freedom staged through theater signals what I have called elsewhere "performances of fugitivity," which I define as "subversive, radical, and experimental performances of black artistic and political freedom at the site of slavery."[50] It is a critical framework for reading Black subjects' performances of nonbelonging and unfreedom in the present.

At the time that Parks was preparing to present *Father Comes Home from the Wars* in October 2014, US media was populated with images of protest and citizens staring down a militarized police force on the streets of Ferguson, Missouri, in the aftermath of the killing of Michael Brown. Imagery of the confrontation calls up battle. Black citizens took to the streets to make visible the subterranean war on Black communities waged by the criminal justice system. The fight not only reveals the war but also the quest for freedom on the part of the Black protestors. Parks even includes a moment when Hero places his hands over his head in the iconic "hands up, don't shoot" gesture that became synonymous with Michael Brown and accounts of his murder at the hands of police. Sterling K. Brown, who starred as Hero/Ulysses in the 2014 Public Theatre production, recalls the emotionally charged backdrop of the performances and his personal connection to the events because he grew up in St. Louis, Missouri. He says,

And so the resonance that [the question of freedom and self-ownership after slavery] has for me, in particular, being from St. Louis and doing this play in N.Y.C.—the incident with Mike Brown had transpired in Ferguson. The failure to indict happened while we were performing the show. And it was just heart-wrenching on a personal level for me. I go back to this statement from the *Watchmen*: "Who watches the Watchmen?"[51]

Because Parks troubles the question of freedom in her play, it readily speaks to the ongoing problem of socially sanctioned violence against Black subjects who can be killed with impunity by agents of the state.

A more recent February 2020 performance of *Father Comes Home from the Wars* got to the heart of the matter of Parks's play because it was performed in a New York prison. Staged and produced by a program called Rehabilitation through the Arts (RTA), prisoners in Green Haven prison performed the play in simple white T-shirts with the word "slave" or the character's "slave name" written on them.[52] They had to contend with many obstacles to producing the play in a prison, encountering the following prohibitions: no props, such as fake guns; no use of the colors gray and navy, the colors of the Union and Confederate uniforms, because those were also the colors of the uniforms of the prison guards—a deeply ironic confluence; and some lines of the play being removed for fear that they would stir revolt. However, they worked creatively to perform the play. For many of the actors, the resonance was clear. Lenox Ramsay stated that the play, which the cast members selected, "resonated with a lot of us." Melvin Davis, a twenty-nine-year-old serving a twenty-year sentence, elaborated, "When I'm on that stage, I'm not acting. I really want to get away from there because I really want to get away from here.... When you're incarcerated, it's like you're back on the plantation." Numerous thinkers, Michelle Alexander chief among them, have interrogated the links between slavery, the convict leasing system, and the prison industrial complex.[53] Parks's play gives those most deeply impacted by these realities space to articulate those connections and bring them to light. In many respects, the prison industrial complex is an unofficial monument to slavery, the vestige of a system of incarceration that grew out of slavery and continues to imprison Black Americans at an incredibly disproportionate rate.

Finally, one last site where Parks's play has been performed with great resonance was the August 2019 performance I attended in Dallas, Texas, produced by the African American Repertory Theatre. Texas holds much significance for Parks, both in terms of the history of slavery and her personal history. As a child, her father was in the US military, and he was absent for a good deal of time on tours in Vietnam. Parks recalls living in Odessa, Texas, and waiting for her father to return from war.[54] She drew upon this history as she developed what became *Father Comes Home from the Wars*. Moreover, West Texas is the setting for the play and the site where, on June 19, 1865, two months after the Civil War technically ended, enslaved subjects were informed that they were free. This belated announcement serves as the marker for the official recognition of Black subjects as free and has been commemorated each year with Juneteenth celebrations, primarily in Texas but in many places beyond.[55] *Father Comes Home from the Wars* is one of what critics have termed Parks's Juneteenth plays, with *Imperceptible Mutabilities in the Third Kingdom* being the other notable work that explores Juneteenth and notions of belated emancipation. Clearly, the staging of *Father Comes Home from the Wars* in Texas reminds audiences of slavery as an unfinished event. In the production I saw, the producers set up tables with historical images of Black Civil War soldiers and deeper, more complicated narratives of the slave era. This intentional supplementary work calls attention to the producers' awareness of the play as an intervention into received histories of slavery and the Civil War.

Parks's work functions as a counter-monument through its counter-histories of slavery and her complex rendering of the Black Civil War soldier. Like Trethewey, her depiction of Black Civil War soldiers presents a more complicated picture and performs an important disruption to conventional understandings of whose participation in the war was most consequential. Through the imagery of the uniform, Parks visualizes these complexities and raises it to greater public consciousness. In tandem with the phenomenological dimensions of the uniform, performance histories of this play reinforce *Father Comes Home from the Wars'* underlying theme of emancipation as unfinished. Performing this work in spaces like the prison or in Texas, the site of Juneteenth, makes clear its counter-monumental aspects. In many ways, the counter-monumental strategies Parks employs produce a devastating history of the present by calling attention to the ongoing ways freedom has yet to be fully realized for many Black Americans.

## PIERCING THE WOUND

Both *Native Guard* and *Father Comes Home from the Wars* mark the 2014 moment when we saw public and focused resistance to unchecked police violence against Black subjects and challenges to public spaces that house monuments to the Confederacy. It is no mistake that these two issues came together in such powerful ways. Both are animated by the dehumanization of Black people and the ways US society continues to remind Black people that their lives are expendable. As we emerge from the ground-shifting year of 2020, it is evident that the effects of such disregard have forced a racial reckoning that is ongoing. Even as the country grapples with the long shadow of slavery and the underlying white supremacy that continues to shape the nation, there is a backlash to engaging with these truths. The resistance to the teaching of race and racism in US schools has reached a crescendo so that so-called critical race theory has become the proverbial boogeyman in US education. Also, in this same moment, Nikole Hannah-Jones was not offered tenure in conjunction with the faculty position she was offered at the University of North Carolina at Chapel Hill, which many interpreted as a form of retaliation against her longform journalism *The 1619 Project* and its insistence on seeing slavery as foundational to US life and history.[56]

Given these contemporary contexts, I want to return to Trethewey's assertion that one motivating force in her choosing to be a poet was her frustration with historical erasures of Black subjects in US history, particularly Civil War history. It is a powerful reminder of the stakes of the kind of work she and Suzan-Lori Parks have done. For Trethewey, Confederate monuments advance collective amnesia about the realities of this past, resulting in perpetuation of the societal wound of slavery. Trethewey sees these monuments as daily reminders of the "'brutal history of injustice, violence, and oppression' when people who looked like her were enslaved, persecuted, and violated because of the color of their skin."[57] When contextualized this way, counter-monumentality can be read not only as resistance to the monuments but as an effort to pierce the wound that these monuments represent. By piercing the wound and confronting it, Trethewey and Parks facilitate a reckoning long overdue in US society with Civil War history and the many ways we have not yet accounted for its erasures, its inaccuracies, and its damage.

# NOTES

1. Saidiya Hartman, "Venus in Two Acts," *Small Axe* 12, no. 2 (June 2008): 4.

2. James F. Osborne, "Counter-Monumentality and the Vulnerability of Memory," *Journal of Social Archaeology* 17, no. 2 (May 2017): 165.

3. Osborne, "Counter-Monumentality," 167.

4. Michel-Rolph Trouillot, *Silencing the Past: Power and the Production of History* (Boston: Beacon Press, 2015), 15.

5. Hartman, "Venus in Two Acts," 13.

6. Diana Taylor, *The Archive and the Repertoire: Performing Cultural Memory in the Americas* (Durham, NC: Duke University Press, 2003), 20.

7. Calvin Warren, "Black Time: Slavery, Metaphysics, and the Logic of Wellness," in *The Psychic Hold of Slavery: Legacies in American Expressive Culture*, ed. Soyica Diggs Colbert, Robert J. Patterson, and Aida Levy-Hussen (New Brunswick, NJ: Rutgers University Press, 2016), 56.

8. Suzan-Lori Parks, *The America Play, and Other Works* (New York: Theatre Communications Group, 1995), 12.

9. Freda Scott Giles, review of *Native Guard*, by Natasha Trethewey, directed by Susan V. Booth, Alliance Theatre, Atlanta, *Continuum* 1, no. 2 (January 2015): 1.

10. Nara Schoenberg, "Her Mother's Murder Made Her a Poet: Pulitzer Prize Winner Natasha Trethewey's Career Is Tinged with Tragedy," *Chicago Tribune*, November 6, 2018,

https://www.chicagotribune.com/entertainment/books/ct-books-monument-natasha-trethewey
-1111-story.html.

11. Chandra O. Hopkins, "Whispers from a Silent Past: Inspiration and Memory in Natasha Trethewey's *Native Guard*," *Theatre History Studies* 35 (2016): 292.

12. Rachel Bowditch et al., "Four Principles about Site-Specific Theatre: A Conversation on Architecture, Bodies, and Presence," *Theatre Topics* 28, no. 1 (March 2018): E-5.

13. Kevin M. Kruse details how traffic in Atlanta has been shaped by histories of slavery and segregation in the region. Kruse, "What Does a Traffic Jam in Atlanta Have to Do with Segregation? Quite a Lot," *New York Times Magazine*, August 14, 2019, https://www.nytimes.com/interactive/2019/08/14/magazine/traffic-atlanta-segregation.html.

14. Bowditch et al., "Four Principles," E-7.

15. Wendell Brock, "Alliance Reprises Haunting *Native Guard* at History Center," review of *Native Guard*, by Natasha Trethewey, directed by Susan V. Booth, Alliance Theatre, Atlanta, *Atlanta Journal Constitution*, February 1, 2018, https://www.ajc.com/entertainment/arts-theater/review-alliance-reprises-haunting-native-guard-history-center/eDpvEVOCxA3 EEEiVc3efZI/.

16. Richard Fausset, "A Play about Race and Memory, with Fresh Wounds All Around," *New York Times*, January 21, 2018, https://www.nytimes.com/2018/01/21/theater/native-guard-atlanta-history-center-alliance-theater.html.

17. Jonathan Lemire and Julie Pace, "Defiant Trump Insists Anew: Blame Both Sides for Violence," Associated Press, August 15, 2017, https://apnews.com/7654c14b6bd94cf8814fa6a0af8 d1edd/Defiant-Trump-insists-anew:-Blame-both-sides-for-violence.

18. Fausset, "Play about Race and Memory."

19. Hopkins notes that the 2014 performance she attended was very much invested in placing the "living present of racial identity in the South *in dialogue with* the Civil War past." Hopkins, "Whispers from a Silent Past," 294.

20. Stacie McCormick and Rhaisa Williams, "Introduction: Toni Morrison's Artistic Cosmology and Enduring Legacy," *College Literature* 47, no. 4 (Fall 2020): 641–56.

21. Zora Neale Hurston, "Characteristics of Negro Expression," in *Within the Circle: An Anthology of African American Literary Criticism from the Harlem Renaissance to the Present*, ed. Angelyn Mitchell (Durham, NC: Duke University Press, 1994), 86.

22. Hopkins, "Whispers from a Silent Past," 292.

23. Hopkins, "Whispers from a Silent Past," 294.

24. Natasha Trethewey, *Native Guard* (Boston: Houghton Mifflin, 2006), 38.

25. Trethewey, *Native Guard*, 25.

26. Trethewey, *Native Guard*, 28.

27. Trethewey, *Native Guard*, 44.

28. Michael LeMahieu, "Robert Lowell, Perpetual War, and the Legacy of Civil War Elegy," *College Literature* 43, no. 1 (Winter 2016): 117–18.

29. LeMahieu, "Robert Lowell," 118.

30. Natasha Trethewey, "Former Poet Laureate Natasha Trethewey on Why Poetry Unites Us," interview by Erin Vanderhoof, *Vanity Fair*, November 8, 2018, https://www.vanityfair.com/style/2018/11/natasha-trethewey-monument-interview.

31. Trethewey, *Native Guard*, 43.

32. Christina Sharpe, *In the Wake: On Blackness and Being* (Durham, NC: Duke University Press, 2016), 18.

33. Suzan-Lori Parks, *Father Comes Home from the Wars: Parts 1, 2, and 3* (New York: Theatre Communications Group, 2015), 49.

34. There is abundant critical attention to this subject in scholarship. Among many notable works, see Angenette Spalink, "Taphonomic Historiography: Excavating and Exhuming the Past in Suzan-Lori Parks's *The America Play*," *Modern Drama* 60, no. 1 (Spring 2017): 69–88; Harvey Young, "Touching History: Suzan-Lori Parks, Robbie McCauley, and the Black Body," *Text and Performance Quarterly* 23, no. 2 (2003): 134–53; and Laura Dawkins, "Family Acts: History, Memory, and Performance in Suzan-Lori Parks's *The America Play* and *Topdog/Underdog*," *South Atlantic Review* 74, no. 3 (Summer 2009): 82–98.

35. Parks, *The America Play*.

36. Suzan-Lori Parks, "An Interview with Suzan-Lori Parks," interview by Shawn-Marie Garrett, in *Suzan-Lori Parks: Essays on the Plays and Other Works*, ed. Philip C. Kolin (Jefferson, NC: McFarland and Company, 2010), 183.

37. Parks, "Interview," 185.

38. Parks, *Father Comes Home*, 23.

39. Alice Rayner, *Ghosts: Death's Double and the Phenomena of Theatre* (Minneapolis: University of Minnesota Press, 2006), 74.

40. Rayner, *Ghosts*, 75.

41. Deborah Willis, "The Black Civil War Soldier: Conflict and Citizenship," *Journal of American Studies* 51, no. 2 (May 2017): 287.

42. Willis, "Black Civil War Soldier," 289.

43. Alan Trachtenberg quoted in Willis, "Black Civil War Soldier," 303.

44. Parks, *Father Comes Home*, 26.

45. Parks, *Father Comes Home*, 92.

46. Parks, *Father Comes Home*, 95.

47. Parks, *Father Comes Home*, 102–3.

48. Parks, *Father Comes Home*, 145.

49. Parks, *Father Comes Home*, 159.

50. Stacie Selmon McCormick, *Staging Black Fugitivity* (Columbus: Ohio State University Press, 2019), 23.

51. Sterling K. Brown, "Q&A: Sterling K. Brown Reflects on Playing O. J. Prosecutor Chris Darden on TV and a Slave in the *Father Comes Home* Play," interview by Yvonne Villarreal, *Los Angeles Times*, April 27, 2016, https://www.latimes.com/entertainment/arts/la-et-cm-sterling-k-brown-20160427-story.html.

52. Alice Speri, "A Play about Slavery Pushes Boundaries in a New York Prison," *Portside*, March 9, 2020, https://portside.org/2020-03-09/play-about-slavery-pushes-boundaries-new-york-prison?fbclid=IwAR1yWY-5KKDqSFeOn7xCTRXP_nom9YlKXIV4gH2KjSKJNLQ6_1u3NzqUlDA.

53. Michelle Alexander, *The New Jim Crow: Mass Incarceration in the Age of Colorblindness* (New York: New Press, 2012).

54. Suzan-Lori Parks, "The Playwright: Suzan-Lori Parks," interview by Michael Kantor, *American Masters Podcast*, PBS, audio, 1:07:02, https://www.pbs.org/wnet/americanmasters/podcast/playwright-suzan-lori-parks/.

55. It is important to note that, in 2021, Juneteenth was declared a federal holiday. Joseph R. Biden Jr., "A Proclamation on Juneteenth Day of Observance, 2021," *The White House*, June 18, 2021, https://www.whitehouse.gov/briefing-room/presidential-actions/2021/06/18/a-proclamation-on-juneteenth-day-of-observance-2021/.

56. Nikole Hannah-Jones ultimately rejected the offer and accepted another (with tenure) at Howard University.

57. Hannah Sandorf Davis, "The Wounds of Trethewey," Brigham Young University Humanities, accessed July 24, 2020, https://humanities.byu.edu/the-wounds-of-trethewey/.

# Bibliography

Alexander, Michelle. *The New Jim Crow: Mass Incarceration in the Age of Colorblindness*. New York: New Press, 2012.

Biden, Joseph R., Jr. "A Proclamation on Juneteenth Day of Observance, 2021." The White House, June 18, 2021. https://www.whitehouse.gov/briefing-room/presidential-actions/2021/06/18/a-proclamation-on-juneteenth-day-of-observance-2021/.

Bowditch, Rachel, Daniel Bird Tobin, Chelsea Pace, and Marc Devine. "Four Principles about Site-Specific Theatre: A Conversation on Architecture, Bodies, and Presence." *Theatre Topics* 28, no. 1 (March 2018): E-5–E-19.

Brock, Wendell. "Alliance Reprises Haunting *Native Guard* at History Center." Review of *Native Guard*, by Natasha Trethewey, directed by Susan V. Booth, Atlanta History Center, Atlanta. *Atlanta Journal-Constitution*, February 1, 2018. https://www.ajc.com/entertainment/arts-theater/review-alliance-reprises-haunting-native-guard-history-center/eDpvEVOCxA3EEEiVc3efZI/.

Brown, Sterling K. "Q&A: Sterling K. Brown Reflects on Playing O. J. Prosecutor Chris Darden on TV and a Slave in the *Father Comes Home* Play." Interview by Yvonne Villarreal. *Los Angeles Times*, April 27, 2016. https://www.latimes.com/entertainment/arts/la-et-cm-sterling-k-brown-20160427-story.html.

Davis, Hannah Sandorf. "The Wounds of Trethewey." Brigham Young University Humanities. Accessed July 24, 2020. https://humanities.byu.edu/the-wounds-of-trethewey/.

Dawkins, Laura. "Family Acts: History, Memory, and Performance in Suzan-Lori Parks's *The America Play* and *Topdog/Underdog*." *South Atlantic Review* 74, no. 3 (Summer 2009): 82–98.

Fausset, Richard. "A Play about Race and Memory, with Fresh Wounds All Around." *New York Times*, January 21, 2018. https://www.nytimes.com/2018/01/21/theater/native-guard-atlanta-history-center-alliance-theater.html.

Giles, Freda Scott. Review of *Native Guard*, by Natasha Trethewey, directed by Susan V. Booth, Alliance Theatre, Atlanta. *Continuum* 1, no. 2 (January 2015): 1–2.

Hartman, Saidiya. "Venus in Two Acts." *Small Axe* 12, no. 2 (June 2008): 1–14.

Hopkins, Chandra O. "Whispers from a Silent Past: Inspiration and Memory in Natasha Trethewey's *Native Guard*." *Theatre History Studies* 35 (2016): 287–300.

Hurston, Zora Neale. "Characteristics of Negro Expression." In *Within the Circle: An Anthology of African American Literary Criticism from the Harlem Renaissance to the Present*, edited by Angelyn Mitchell, 79–94. Durham, NC: Duke University Press, 1994.

Kruse, Kevin M. "What Does a Traffic Jam in Atlanta Have to Do with Segregation? Quite a Lot." *New York Times Magazine*, August 14, 2019. https://www.nytimes.com/interactive/2019/08/14/magazine/traffic-atlanta-segregation.html.

LeMahieu, Michael. "Robert Lowell, Perpetual War, and the Legacy of Civil War Elegy." *College Literature* 43, no. 1 (Winter 2016): 91–120.

Lemire, Jonathan, and Julie Pace. "Defiant Trump Insists Anew: Blame Both Sides for Violence." *Associated Press*, August 15, 2017. https://apnews.com/7654c14b6bd94cf8814fa6a0af8d1edd/Defiant-Trump-insists-anew:-Blame-both-sides-for-violence.

McCormick, Stacie Selmon. *Staging Black Fugitivity*. Columbus: Ohio State University Press, 2019.

McCormick, Stacie Selmon, and Rhaisa Williams. "Introduction: Toni Morrison's Artistic Cosmology and Enduring Legacy." *College Literature* 47, no. 4 (Fall 2020): 641–56.

Osborne, James F. "Counter-Monumentality and the Vulnerability of Memory." *Journal of Social Archaeology* 17, no. 2 (May 2017): 163–87.

Parks, Suzan-Lori. *The America Play, and Other Works*. New York: Theatre Communications Group, 1995.

Parks, Suzan-Lori. *Father Comes Home from the Wars: Parts 1, 2, and 3*. New York: Theatre Communications Group, 2015.

Parks, Suzan-Lori. "An Interview with Suzan-Lori Parks." Interview by Shawn-Marie Garrett. In *Suzan-Lori Parks: Essays on the Plays and Other Works*, edited by Philip C. Kolin, 181–90. Jefferson, NC: McFarland and Company, 2010.

Parks, Suzan-Lori. "The Playwright: Suzan-Lori Parks." Interview by Michael Kantor. *American Masters Podcast*, PBS. Audio, 1:07:02. https://www.pbs.org/wnet/americanmasters/podcast/playwright-suzan-lori-parks/.

Rayner, Alice. *Ghosts: Death's Double and the Phenomena of Theatre*. Minneapolis: University of Minnesota Press, 2006.

Schoenberg, Nara. "Her Mother's Murder Made Her a Poet: Pulitzer Prize Winner Natasha Trethewey's Career Is Tinged with Tragedy." *Chicago Tribune*, November 6, 2018. https://www.chicagotribune.com/entertainment/books/ct-books-monument-natasha-trethewey-1111-story.html.

Sharpe, Christina. *In the Wake: On Blackness and Being*. Durham, NC: Duke University Press, 2016.

Spalink, Angenette. "Taphonomic Historiography: Excavating and Exhuming the Past in Suzan-Lori Parks's *The America Play*." *Modern Drama* 60, no. 1 (Spring 2017): 69–88.

Speri, Alice. "A Play about Slavery Pushes Boundaries in a New York Prison." *Portside*, March 9, 2020. https://portside.org/2020-03-09/play-about-slavery-pushes-boundaries-new-york-prison?fbclid=IwAR1yWY-5KKDqSFeOn7xCTRXP_nom9YlKXIV4gH2KjSKJNLQ6_1u3NzqUlDA.

Taylor, Diana. *The Archive and the Repertoire: Performing Cultural Memory in the Americas*. Durham, NC: Duke University Press, 2003.

Trethewey, Natasha. "Former Poet Laureate Natasha Trethewey on Why Poetry Unites Us." Interview by Erin Vanderhoof. *Vanity Fair*, November 8, 2018. https://www.vanityfair.com/style/2018/11/natasha-trethewey-monument-interview.

Trethewey, Natasha. *Native Guard*. Boston: Houghton Mifflin, 2006.

Trouillot, Michel-Rolph. *Silencing the Past: Power and the Production of History*. Boston: Beacon Press, 2015.

Warren, Calvin. "Black Time: Slavery, Metaphysics, and the Logic of Wellness." In *The Psychic Hold of Slavery: Legacies in American Expressive Culture*, edited by Soyica Diggs Colbert, Robert J. Patterson, and Aida Levy-Hussen, 55–68. New Brunswick, NJ: Rutgers University Press, 2016.

Willis, Deborah. "The Black Civil War Soldier: Conflict and Citizenship." *Journal of American Studies* 51, no. 2 (May 2017): 285–323.

Young, Harvey. "Touching History: Suzan-Lori Parks, Robbie McCauley, and the Black Body." *Text and Performance Quarterly* 23, no. 2 (2003): 134–53.

# PEDAGOGY

Reading Confederate Monuments
and Counter-Monuments for How They
Teach Belonging and Social Justice

Figure 8.1: Cassandra Jackson, photograph of Confederate Monument in Florence, Alabama. Image courtesy of Cassandra Jackson.

# CHAPTER 8

# REWRITING THE LANDSCAPE

Black Communities and the Confederate Monuments They Inherited

—Cassandra Jackson

As a child, when school was closed, I accompanied my mother to her job at the Lauderdale County courthouse in Alabama. As we walked toward the front door of the building, a sculpture of a Confederate soldier greeted us (see Figure 8.1). He stood on a tall pedestal, leaning on his rifle and yet gazing into the distance with a peculiar intensity. The text on the pedestal beneath him read: "In Memory of the Confederate Dead of Lauderdale County / The Manner of Their Death Was the Crowning Glory of Their Lives." The monument presented a narrative of a noble white South and transformed the defeat of the Confederacy into an honorable sacrifice. But the memorial was far more than a false narrative of the past because viewers' relationship to that narrative shaped their understanding of their place in the social landscape of the present and the future. For those who felt a kinship with the Confederacy, their ability to honor such a figure proved the righteousness of their ancestors' power and their own right to continue that legacy. For me, a descendant of the enslaved, the monument was evidence of my ancestors' subordination and my own because if men who fought for slavery deserved a public space of honor, neither Black lives nor Black stories mattered. The soldier towered over us, reminding us that, even though it was the 1980s, every Black person who entered that courthouse to work or seek justice still had a master.

I would like to say that I fantasized about toppling that statue, that I dreamed of dashing it to the ground and dousing it with red paint that could name the relationship between its white plaster and the invisible Black blood that had soaked the land underneath it. But my resentment was much quieter because it was also accompanied by a belief in the statue's permanence. I knew that the Confederate soldier should not be there, but I also knew that he would still be standing on that etched pedestal long after I was gone. Owen Dwyer argues that monuments suggest "the presence of something governed by geologic processes, beyond the vagaries of time measured on a human scale."[1] He adds that the "producers of monuments cultivate this appearance, seeking through the landscape a means of securing memory, to put it beyond the reach of time by etching it in the land itself." Dwyer's theory explains why, to my child self, the statue's presence seemed as enduring as the indomitable Tennessee River that rolled nearby and the greedy Wilson Dam that harnessed its energy. The monument was not just about the past, but it was also a plan for the future. It was an investment in white supremacist values that spoke as loud as George Wallace, who was still the governor of Alabama in the 1980s: "Segregation now, segregation tomorrow, segregation forever."[2] The monument took up space in a way that not only passed for history but also for posterity, and this was the source of its power.

By the time I was old enough to understand what the monument meant, I already knew that, in that predominantly white rural town, resistance to the monument would likely be futile. But what happens when these monuments fall into the hands of predominantly Black urban communities who have both the desire and the means to resist them? In this essay, I explore those communities' efforts to intervene in the power of the Confederate monuments that they inherited after white flight. While the exact means of resistance are different in each community, their efforts are connected by a common desire to disrupt the illusion of permanence from which these monuments gain their authority and thus disrupt their function as blueprints for the future. Some communities have removed and stored the monuments, the most unambiguous and conclusive means of resisting the power of these memorials. But other communities, which face state laws prohibiting the elimination or alteration of Confederate monuments, have sought creative means of signaling the monuments' temporality. These cities attempt to create contexts that expose the white supremacist ideologies that inform Confederate monuments and juxtapose those ideologies with the present values of their cities. In this way, they challenge the representation of these monuments as timeless, situating them instead as temporal and thus mutable objects.

Though defenders of Confederate monuments often claim that to remove them is to erase history, history most often runs counter to the goals of monuments. As Kirk Savage notes, "The most cherished axiom of the memorial landscape is its permanence, its eternity. That axiom shuts the lid on history."[3] There is no better example of this "shutting the lid" effect than monuments to the Confederacy, which not only mythologize white supremacy but also erase the histories of slavery and Black resistance to oppression. The point of these monuments is not so much preserving history broadly but rather advancing particular narratives through a form that suggests both stability and immutability. James W.

Loewen describes one Confederate monument as "future-oriented," setting up the deeds of the past as goals for the future.[4] Some of the monuments to the Confederacy, most of which were built long after the war in the thick of Black struggles for civil rights, state their desires for ideological futurity explicitly. A Confederate monument in Highland County, Virginia, offers one such example in its inscription: "To the Confederate soldiers of Highland County a loving tribute to the past, the present, and the future."[5] This monument was erected in early 1918, the year following the formation of Black Army units at Camp Lee, Virginia,[6] and during a resurgence of lynching in Virginia in 1917–18, in which three Black men were killed by white mobs.[7] The Clarendon County, South Carolina, memorial erected in 1914 is equally direct in its attempt to map the future: "Unconquered in defeat; Undismayed in divine faith, undiscouraged in hope for the future; Untiring in rebuilding."[8] Loewen sums up this relationship between the landscape and futurity by rephrasing a famous Orwellian quote: "Who controls the present controls the landscape. Who controls the landscape controls the future."[9]

While I find this model useful in thinking about the urgency and means of contesting Confederate monuments, I also want to be careful not to theorize in ways that obscure the very real threat posed to contemporary Black people by forces that project white supremacist ideas into the future. As Evander Price argues, "Future monuments can also be menacing" because they "anticipate, reify, and endeavor to effect an alternative future—one in which the Civil War is simply one lost battle in a greater war extending across centuries."[10] To encounter these monuments while living in Black skin is to be reminded of one's own vulnerability to oppression in a white supremacist culture. The former mayor of New Orleans Mitch Landrieu, who is white, captures the ways in which the bodies we live in determine how we experience these monuments. Comparing his own childhood experience with an imposing equestrian monument to the Civil War general P. G. T. Beauregard to that of his friend Terence Blanchard, a Black musician and composer who also grew up in New Orleans, Landrieu points out that, whenever he saw the statue, he processed it as "*Confederate leader*" and felt a "vague pride" in the European quality that the statue lent the city.[11] Meanwhile, Landrieu adds, the same statue made Blanchard feel "less than" and communicated that "the South had fought a noble war, for honor and independence, and it would rise from defeat to rule by white supremacy." Despite having grown up in New Orleans, Blanchard reported that he never felt "comfortable growing up in the midst of the monuments" and that he never "came to terms with the presence of Confederate tributes in New Orleans."[12] In short, while Landrieu experienced the kind of ownership implied by his use of the term "pride," Blanchard experienced the opposite of ownership—a reminder that, though he was born in this city, it would never be his home. Blanchard's description captures the internal violence these monuments can cause Black people to whom they serve as daily reminders of their alienness.

We should not forget, however, that at the root of that internal violence is also the threat of physical violence. As New Orleans made plans to remove Confederate monuments, officials and contractors received death threats, one contractor's car was burned, and workers had to wear bulletproof vests to remove statues.[13] These threats and acts of violence were not sparked by a burning desire to preserve the past, any more than white supremacists' brutal beating of DeAndre Harris and murder of Heather Heyer in Charlottesville in 2017 were acts intended to protect the past. If Confederate monuments were not about the future of white supremacy, then there would be no reason for contemporary white supremacist groups to gather at them or defend them with violence. These groups are future-facing, intended to ensure their right to dominate over nonwhite people now and forever. Indeed, the fear that Confederate monuments would attract violence as they had in Charlottesville sparked the removal of Confederate memorials in a number of cities. Baltimore removed its Confederate monuments within days of the white supremacist rally at Charlottesville. Not only did the city council vote unanimously to remove the statues, but Mayor Catherine Pugh used her executive powers to remove them unannounced under the cover of night. She later explained, "the statues represented pain, and not only did I want to protect my city from any more of that pain, I also wanted to protect my city from any of the violence that was occurring around the nation."[14] Pugh's handling of the statues called attention to the fact that the ideologies they represent were and would continue to be enforced through violence.

I have chosen to focus on majority-Black cities, not because altering Confederate landscapes should be the exclusive job of Black leaders but rather because so often Black citizens have not had the power to do so despite the weighty implications of white supremacist symbols in Black spaces. In contrast to other cities, such as Dallas, which removed statues soon after the 2017 riot in Charlottesville, many majority-Black cities, including Baltimore, New Orleans, Selma, and Birmingham, began these discussions long before. Indeed, I would argue that the presence of these monuments in predominantly Black cities had an even more damning meaning for the future of their Black citizens. Already victims of redlining and segregation via white flight, urban Black people who walk among monuments to the Confederacy face visual evidence not only of their powerlessness to control space in their own communities but also the impotence of their elected leaders to serve the interests of Black people. This condition bears a striking contrast to my experience and that of other rural Black people who encountered Confederate monuments in white-controlled spaces. Though I encountered white leaders who either ignored or supported the presence of these monuments, I expected little more of them given that they also benefited from the ideologies represented by the statues. In contrast, to move in Black spaces where these statues persist, even in the presence of Black leadership and the absence of white people, is a powerful daily reminder that Black people are not and can never be the proprietors of the land. In essence, these statues represent the long arm of US racism in that white people need not even be present to exert their power over Black people because they control the land that they reside on. The Confederate figures gaze over the land like symbolic masters, demoting Black leaders to overseers who tend other people's property, land and flesh.

Two ideas inform the core of the mission of Black communities seeking to resist Confederate symbology in public space: first, the belief that landscapes can be invested with the power to oppress and empower people and second, the idea that landscapes can be changed and thus so can the power dynamics embedded in the landscape. As Cara Aitchison, Nicola E. MacLeod, and Stephen J. Shaw point out, "If social and cultural geographies teach us anything . . . it is that power can be viewed as contested and fluid. The spatial representation and manifestation of power can change over time, be disrupted across space . . . and even transgressed."[15] While these ideas about change may seem simple and even obvious to some, their subversiveness becomes more apparent in light of the fact that monuments are designed to resist these very ideas, to overwhelm us with their stability, their weight, and the illusion that they are impervious to everything from nature to time. They teach us to accept their presence as a fact, the visual equivalent of background noise, ever-present and not requiring interrogation. Anything that challenges that guise has the potential to displace the meaning of the landscape.

Effectively shifting the meaning of a monument requires that one first interrupt these day-to-day ways of seeing and thus destabilize our understanding of ourselves and our relationship to the physical and social landscape. Bryan Wagner calls such a phenomenon a "disturbance of vision," a term he uses to describe how white characters in Charles W. Chesnutt's novel *The Marrow of Tradition* (1901) encounter visual evidence of the rise of the Black middle class. According to Wagner, seeing buildings that were formerly occupied by white people now being occupied by Black people, for example, causes these characters to experience an "intense cognitive dissonance generated in these moments of apparent ideological collapse."[16] While monument revision has the potential to have this same effect, particularly on those who imagine a site of revision as a challenge to their own values, changes in the landscape do not have to cause complete conceptual disintegration to disturb our vision. Given that living in the US conditions all of us to move in spaces that shape and are shaped by white supremacy, any revision that poses a challenge to that ideology has the potential to disturb our ordinary ways of seeing. By the same token, not all change constitutes a disturbance of vision. To disturb, change must challenge the conventional power dynamics of the landscape and our communities. Successful revisions must be visually disruptive, demanding viewers' attention to the ideological challenge that it offers. Change that goes unnoticed cannot disturb vision. Because of the ways in which monuments take up physical space, they must be met with striking visual alterations that force new ways of seeing. When done successfully, such revisions can disturb the viewer's vision, carving out a space in which to see the monument as temporal and thus challenging dominant cultural ideologies of the landscape.

To return to Baltimore as an example, though the statues were removed, the pedestals at three sites remain standing. The then-mayor suggested that these empty pedestals remain and include plaques explaining what was removed from them and why. But even without plaques, the pedestals, as Martha S. Jones has suggested, "invite reflection, learning, and [serve as] a poignant sign of an ongoing struggle for reconciliation and justice."[17] The pedestals function as a disturbance of vision. They take up space, yet their emptiness reminds us of what is not there. What better symbol for the passing of time and ideas than a pedestal whose former occupant is no longer deemed relevant to the space in which he once resided? The empty pedestals create both a link to the historical past and a powerful departure from it as they also forecast a new future. In 2018, the grove where one of these pedestals stands was rededicated to Harriet Tubman, the woman who escaped enslavement in Maryland, only to return to the slave states to free countless others from bondage.[18] Thus, rather than replacing one statue with another, the city renamed the land upon which it stands, mapping a future that honors the liberation of all people.

Like Baltimore, the city of Memphis removed symbols of the Confederacy from the land and, in that process, left a trail of signs of absence that jarred the eye and thus forced new ways of seeing the landscape. In 2013, the city began changing the names of parks dedicated to Confederates. Anticipating that state officials would block this effort, the Black-led city council passed the name changes—which ordinarily would have been negotiated over the course of three public meetings—in a single public meeting, despite three white council members who abstained from voting.[19] Confederate Park became Memphis Park; Jefferson Davis Park became Mississippi River Park; and Nathan Bedford Forrest Park, named for a Confederate general and founder of the Ku Klux Klan, became Health Sciences Park. Interestingly, the new names were considered temporary names, placeholders until better names could be found. And thus, the metal plates with the names of Confederate leaders were removed, leaving a series of empty frames.[20] Because of Tennessee state laws prohibiting the removal of monuments, the predominantly Black city was unable to legally remove the monuments to Davis and Forrest that stood in these public parks. In 2017, under powerful pressure from a Black-led grassroots organization called Take 'Em Down 901 (a reference to the Memphis area code), the city orchestrated removal by selling two parks to a nonprofit organization, which then legally removed the statues as soon as the sale was complete. As with the empty sign frames, the pedestals that held the Davis statues and the Forrest statue were left barren. Later in 2018, the pedestal that read "Jefferson Davis / President of the Confederate States of America 1861–1865" was also removed, leaving a concrete slab where the nearly twenty-foot monument used to stand. Meanwhile, the pedestal that once held an equestrian statue of Forrest still stands. Removal in this instance is complicated by the fact that Forrest's remains and those of his wife are buried beneath the pedestal. Though the city hopes to eventually disinter the remains (which had been moved to the park from a local cemetery in 1908), a lawsuit over the site, waged by Forrest's descendants, left the site in limbo.

The objects left at these sites function as disturbances of vision, marking absence and highlighting change in ways that acknowledge space as a site of meaning but also present it as malleable and dependent on the will of the people. Indeed, the shifts in the landscape and the visual vestiges of that transformation form a narrative that invites public participation in shaping the space. The slab where the monument to Davis once stood bears no inscription, and no marker of any kind calls attention to what is missing, yet it signifies both endings and new beginnings. Its blankness suggests transition and incompleteness that demand interpretation. The much more substantial empty pedestal that once held a daunting equestrian monument of Forrest is far more arresting, capturing the eye with its astonishing vacancy. A rather unceremonious circle of orange traffic cones and a chain-link fence surround the pedestal. Though this display is intended to be temporary, its symbolism is surprisingly fitting. Indeed, the empty pedestal, fence, and cones draw curious eyes to the site more than the original monument. These elements signify a site in transition, a story not yet fully told. The flimsy fence allows the public to see what is left and to imagine what is to come in the future of this public space. While the remains that lie under the empty pedestal seem to stake a claim on the land, so too does the fence that cages them in, trapping them in the past.

These signs of temporality destabilize ordinary ways of seeing the Memphis landscape and thus make way for new initiatives intended to allow the city to reclaim public spaces for Black citizens. In 2016, the empty frames at two of the city's parks were filled with temporary signs that read Fourth Bluff Project, an initiative designed to make the parks more accessible to all of Memphis's citizens through design and community-led programming.[21] This act of temporary naming served as a poignant gesture of rewriting the landscape in ways that acknowledge the adaptability of the visual scene and encourage community-driven change. To understand the power of such visual interventions as a means of resistance and reclamation, one need only look to the response of the Tennessee General Assembly, which in 2018 retaliated against the city of Memphis by removing the $250,000 budget reserved for its centennial celebration.[22]

This seemingly conventional desire of a municipality to control the meanings of its landscapes had been met with resistance from state legislatures elsewhere as well. Atlanta is also a city dotted with Confederate monuments and located in Georgia, a state where removal is prohibited by law. The city's failed attempts to adequately contextualize one monument pinpoint the elemental role of disturbances of vision in rewriting landscapes. In 2017, Atlanta mayor Kasim Reed created a commission to address what should be done about Atlanta's monuments and street names that honor the Confederacy. The commission recommended changing street names and removing Confederate monuments. While city leaders were able to change street names, the monuments posed a problem that was bigger both literally and figuratively. The city had to consider how it could intervene in the landscape to change its meaning without being able to remove the imposing structures that symbolize that meaning. Was there a way to take possession of the meaning of land without having a legally enforced right to the land? The commission settled on a series of historical markers that would be installed near each monument. As if to remind the city that it had no right to change its own public landscape, Georgia's majority-white legislature, despite already having a law in place since 2001 that prohibited removal of any monument honoring military service, passed additional laws in 2019, the year the markers would go up, creating steep fines for tampering with or obstructing Confederate monuments.

The first markers were put up at Piedmont Park in front of the Piedmont Peace monument. Erected in 1911, the monument commemorates the strange efforts of a group of former Confederate militiamen to embark on a peace mission.[23] In 1879, the group traveled through northern cities, supposedly to spread goodwill and reconcile with the North. The monument depicts a Confederate soldier holding a gun and half-kneeling as he looks up at a large, winged figure, representing the Angel of Peace, who towers over him. She gestures for him to put his weapon down with one hand and holds up an olive branch with the other. Underneath the figures, a plaque reads: "Cease Firing—Peace Is Proclaimed." A larger plaque attached to the pedestal narrates the history of the militia group, their service in the Confederate army, and their reconciliation mission. The text presents the Confederate soldiers not as misguided but rather as dutiful heroes who, "in the conscientious conviction of their duty to uphold the Cause of the Southern Confederacy, offered their services to the Governor of Georgia and were enrolled in the Confederate Army." In addition, it describes their mission to the North as their noble mission to "restore fraternal sentiment" and "heal the

Nation's wounds in a peaceful and prosperous reunion of the states." The text on the plaque is lengthy and thus indicative of the narrative gymnastics required to exonerate and champion defeated rebels.

The two markers installed by the city stand at the edge of a circular landscape on which the monument sits. Though they are not small, they are tiny in comparison to the size of the monument, and both are laden with small texts. One titled "Peace Monument" offers two photographs, a formal group portrait of the militia and another of the public dedication of the monument. Still referring to the militia efforts as a "peace mission," the narrative also inserts language that situates the group's beliefs as an ideology. For example, the marker refers to the group's efforts as an attempt to "promote what they deemed 'the virtues of the Old South.'" It defines the beliefs of "many southern whites" as "lost cause mythology" or the idea that "despite the defeat, the Confederate cause was morally just." Explaining that rising antipathy toward Black people and immigrants in the North led northerners to embrace the Confederates, the text also indicates that this narrative of reconciliation excluded African Americans. The marker concludes, "This monument should no longer stand as a memorial to white brotherhood; rather, it should be seen as an artifact representing a shared history in which millions of Americans were denied civil and human rights." The second marker nearby, titled "Race and Reconciliation," attempts to offer a history of Black responses to the Jim Crow era in which the monument was erected. Recounting the philosophies of W. E. B. Du Bois and Booker T. Washington, the sign summarizes Washington's 1895 speech, often referred to as the Atlanta Compromise, in which he advocated for capitulation to racial segregation to achieve Black economic advancement. Washington gave the speech at Piedmont Park where the peace monument resides.

The question of whether the markers had succeeded in resisting the white supremacist ideologies of the monument sparked controversy immediately. Richard Rose, the president of Atlanta's NAACP branch, in a letter to the city council called them a "profound disappointment" and argued that they failed to "counter the notion of white supremacy."[24] Rose also took issue with the inclusion of Booker T. Washington's accommodationist views on the markers: "If the premise [of the sign] is to repudiate white supremacy, Booker T. Washington should not have been quoted." In response, Atlanta History Center vice president Calinda Lee, who is credited with writing the text, responded that the markers were not "intended to affirm calls for segregated society, or to suggest that anyone should 'encourage the acceptance of white supremacy.'"[25] Lee went on to say, however, that the markers were also "not intended to be rhetorical spaces but, rather, to provide information in as clear and unbiased a manner as possible so that readers can discern for themselves the intentions of those who installed the monuments."

As Rose's comments indicate, the markers are indeed troubling. Not only do they fail to place the monument in its time, but they also seem to reinscribe its permanence in the landscape. Rather than contesting Confederate ideologies, the markers rely on the honorific language of the Confederates: "Gate City Guard," "virtues of the Old South," and "Anglo Saxon values." In addition, the two photographs on the marker—one of the militia in formal regalia and another of a crowd of formally dressed white people attending a dedication ceremony—present the militia and its cause honorifically. Thus, the marker, rather than contesting white supremacist ideology, seems to function itself as a mini-monument to the honor of the Confederacy. Though it refers to southern Lost Cause ideology as a mythology and mentions how narratives of peace and reconciliation excluded Black people and ignored the liberation of Black people as an important result of the war, the monument's focus on narrating the history of the militia in lieu of discussing the violence enacted against Black people in the very historical moment in which the monument was dedicated seems to situate white supremacist ideology as benign. Thus, implicit in the marker's final statement that the monument "should be seen as an artifact" is an admission that it is not situated as an artifact. Indeed, it is a standing public monument so important for its role in the landscape that, in addition to the plaques attached to it, it also requires two markers to narrate its story.

But even if the texts more effectively described the violence of white racism, the markers would fail because they do not disrupt the visual field. As Heidi Beirich, director of the intelligence project at the Southern Poverty Law Center, noted, "A plaque standing next to something that massive and already offensive can't really undo the harm to citizens who are being exposed to it."[26] Ultimately, the textual response to the monument cannot overwhelm the visual spectacle and indeed only seems to call attention to its seemingly rightful place in the landscape. Atlanta's attempt to contextualize the monument raises questions about what sort of context can serve as a meaningful act of resistance and suggests that the physical presence of the monument, the ways in which it takes up public space, may only be countered with similar forces that take up significant space and potentially minimize the monument in comparison or obscure it, a result that Georgia law prohibits. What the markers lack is a disturbance of vision, an anomaly in the day-to-day landscape that requires explanation and interpretation. Such a disruption forces viewers to recognize their role in the present as connected yet still separated from those who erected the monument in a different time but in the same space.

DeKalb County's three-hundred-pound marker placed in 2019 at the site of the county's thirty-foot obelisk dedicated to the Confederacy also tested the limits of markers as a means of resistance. Though officials had originally voted to remove the 1908 monument, they, like the officials in Atlanta, also had to find an alternative because of Georgia law. Unlike the Atlanta plaques, however, the one-inch-thick bronze marker in DeKalb stood next to the monument and provided a scathing condemnation of the ways in which such monuments were used to intimidate Black citizens. After a brief description of the monument's representation of the Lost Cause of the Confederacy and the United Daughters of the Confederacy's sponsorship of the monument, the text offered this explanation:

> Located in a prominent public space, its presence bolstered white supremacy and faulty history, suggesting that the cause for the Civil War rested on southern Honor and States Rights rhetoric—instead of its real catalyst—American slavery. This monument and similar ones also were created to intimidate African Americans and limit their full participation in the social and political life of their communities. It fostered a culture of segregation by implying that public spaces and public memory belonged to Whites. Since State law prohibited local governments from removing Confederate statues, DeKalb County contextualized this monument in 2019. DeKalb County officials and citizens believe that public history can be of service when it challenges us to broaden our sense of boundaries and includes community discussions of the victories and shortcomings of our shared histories.[27]

The statement clarified the purpose of the monument and others like it without equivocation. It also rested on a weighty surface in front of the courthouse, bearing all the gravity of an official declaration. And yet its reference to state law as the reason why the monument still stood made clear that even this bronze marker was a capitulation, an acknowledgment that the citizens of DeKalb County in 2019 had failed to lay claim to the land. The marker indicated a tension between the official authority of the state and itself, a stone that impersonated official meaning.

With the obelisk towering over it, the marker, which looked no different from any other historical marker, made no visual intervention in the landscape. Indeed, like the Atlanta markers, the visual presence of the DeKalb marker reinforced the power of the monument rather than contesting it. It was not just the difference in scale that prevented the marker from having a visual impact. The marker failed to disturb one's vision because of the nature of the visual encounter: the fact that the viewer had to first approach the monument's seeming permanence and enter into its atemporal space to read about its presence after having already adapted to it. The monument remained at the spatial and ideological center, while the plaque reacted in 2019 (as the text reminds us). This failure to intervene in the meanings of the landscape suggests that how we encounter monuments in time and space is part of how they make meaning. Words on an imposing plaque are not enough to shift the meaning of the larger spatial and visual encounter in real time.

DeKalb County officials seemed to understand that the marker's goal to disempower the monument would always be incomplete. As DeKalb County commissioner Mereda Davis Johnson pointed out, "Contextualization of a racist statue represents progress, but not victory."[28] Thus, DeKalb officials made plans to continue the process of altering the landscape by adding a second marker outside the courthouse. This new marker would honor four African Americans who were lynched in DeKalb County.[29] Indeed, one of the reasons officials sought to place a marker that explained the history of white supremacy and Black voter suppression quickly was so that those attending a commemoration service honoring lynching victims would not have to pass by the Confederate monument as they entered the courthouse without the marker present. But can a marker ever function as a successful intervention in the face of the power of a monument? Because markers that honor certain cultural ideals and those that seek to dismantle them look the same, they fail to attract the attention necessary to complicate the meanings of the landscape. In fact, they often include visual evidence of state control in the form of a government seal, and thus, markers function more like an official extension of the site they mark than as a competing force. For example, the DeKalb County government seal pictured on the context marker next to the monument included an image of Stone Mountain, the site of the nation's largest monument to the Confederacy, the Stone Mountain Memorial Carving of Jefferson Davis, Robert E. Lee, and Stonewall Jackson, just nine miles away.[30]

Interestingly, after so many costly efforts to reclaim the landscape without removing the monument, the county took it down in June 2020 after the site attracted new protests in the wake of the death of George Floyd, an unarmed Black man murdered by police in Minneapolis, Minnesota. The city of Decatur complained that the statue threatened public safety and the Superior Court of DeKalb County agreed that the statue caused "friction" between citizens and potential danger if citizens were to forcibly remove it. By deeming the statue a "public nuisance," the court ordered its removal, thus bypassing the state law against removing Confederate monuments.[31] Ultimately, the removal was possible not because of a change in the law but because on-the-ground activists laid claim to the land with their feet. Community members put their bodies on the line to demand that the public landscape reflect the value of Black life. They gave officials little choice but to chart plans for a landscape that would project a future of Black empowerment. In 2021, officials announced plans to place a memorial to the late civil rights activist Congressman John Lewis on the former site of the Confederate monument.[32]

Like DeKalb County, Birmingham, Alabama, removed its Confederate monument during the 2020 uprising. The journey to removal, however, also included phases in which Black officials attempted to change the meaning of

Figure 8.2: Cassandra Jackson, photograph of Confederate Soldiers and Sailors Monument in Linn Park, Birmingham, Alabama. Image courtesy of Cassandra Jackson.

a landmark to white supremacy without removing it. The city of Birmingham built a spectacular addition to its Confederate monument, demonstrating how visual disruption can simultaneously dismantle and construct meaning. Under pressure from activists seeking to remove the fifty-two-foot obelisk dedicated to Confederate soldiers and sailors in 1905, the mayor of Birmingham expressed his personal opposition to the monument and made clear that the city's Parks and Recreation Board had the authority to remove it.[33] In 2015, the board voted to have the city's lawyers explore this possibility.[34] By 2017, the monument was still standing, and Alabama had passed legislation preventing removal without state permission. After the Charlottesville white supremacist riot, the mayor of the majority-Black city ordered that a series of black wooden panels be built around the monument. The panels formed a black wall that enclosed the obelisk, blocking the text of its dedication from view (see Figure 8.2).

The black wall created a startling visual spectacle that exclaimed that something was amiss in the landscape. That the wall was painted black seemed to suggest that it was part of a larger permanent structure rather than a temporary construction project. The wall did not merely alter the monument but instead appeared to be consuming it. The result was the appearance of a new visual display with parts made of stone and others made of wood working curiously in tandem with each other. The blackness of the wall suggested both the defiance associated with the civil rights and Black power movements and the grief that swallowed Black Birmingham when state-sponsored and vigilante terrorist violence tortured Black people and stole Black lives. Because the wall blocked the text on the memorial from view, the barrier made apparent that the subject of grief was not the Confederate soldiers and sailors for whom the monument was built. Indeed, the monument's close proximity to pivotal sites of the civil rights struggle connected the blackness of the wall to the dark history that surrounded it. The monument sat barely four blocks from the 16th Street Baptist Church, where four little Black girls were killed in a bombing committed by white supremacists in 1963, and Kelly Ingram Park, where police turned water hoses and dogs on civil rights protesters in the same year. Ghostly sculptures that narrate the violence that took place there and honor those who sacrificed their bodies and their lives fill Ingram Park. Thus, the curious new structure appeared linked to this haunting.

The wall was a powerful disturbance of vision not because it merely challenged the monument's right to presence but rather because it transformed the original monument into a disquieting visual display that demanded further investigation. At the same time that the wall disrupted, it also reinvented, presenting a new structure whose full meaning was not entirely apparent. We knew what it was not: it was no longer a monument to the Confederacy. And we knew what it gestured toward: Birmingham as a site of civil defiance and tragic heroism. But what the structure was never became quite clear. Was it supposed to be temporary or permanent, a memorial to the past or a sign of the dark pathway forward? This strange alterity was the source of its power because it required inquiry, disrupting our vision in ways that invited us into the fray of interpretation. Thus, the new structure existed with us in the scale of time, compelling interaction rather than reverence.

The state of Alabama fined and sued the city of Birmingham for blocking the statue, and while a lower court sided with the city, the Alabama Supreme Court ruled that the city had broken state law. In late May 2020, activists, also inspired by the police killing of Floyd, gathered at the site of Birmingham's Confederate Soldiers and Sailors Monument. Protestors removed the plywood wall, spray-painted the monument, and attempted to remove it from the site, until the mayor promised that the city would finish the job. Two days later, the city removed the graffiti-covered statue at night, leaving behind a pile of rubble where the obelisk once stood.[35] It is no coincidence that the Birmingham removal, like the DeKalb removal, was sparked by community members who risked their bodies to have a say in the symbology of public space. They demonstrated that, despite the law, the land is always mutable, and the price of change historically and in the twenty-first century is often the risk of Black lives.

The Birmingham monument was one of more than sixty Confederate monuments that came down in 2020 as protests of police violence against Black people rippled throughout the nation and across the globe. Nonetheless, the battle to inscribe new meaning on the landscape continues. As the old monuments came down, twenty new Confederate monuments, including plaques, massive flags, and statues, were erected on private property across the South.[36] If there is a structure that captures the ongoing struggle to rewrite the white supremacist landscape and the ways in which Black freedom depends on that revision, it is Kehinde Wiley's *Rumors of War*, a twenty-nine-foot equestrian monument depicting a contemporary Black man as the rider. Unveiled in New York City's Times Square in 2019 and later moved to its permanent site in Richmond, Virginia, *Rumors of War* dazzles and dismantles by combining a traditional pedestal base and horse with a young Black figure dressed in a hoodie, Nike sneakers, and ripped jeans. The base and horse are nearly identical to a monument to Confederate general J. E. B. Stuart, which was removed on July 7, 2020.[37] But conceptually, Wiley's monument builds on a series of paintings also titled "Rumors of War," in which he presents contemporary Black figures in the style of equestrian paintings and in what he calls a "charged non-space outside of time."[38] The imagery of the sculpture and the paintings produce a peculiar discomfort as viewers struggle to process the aesthetics of power combined with an undeniably Black body. In this way, the sculpture acknowledges both the oppression of the past and the present, while the heroic figure's gaze points us to new possibilities for freedom in the future. Just before the unveiling of the statue, Wiley captured the significance of Confederate monuments and his response with these words:

I'm a Black man walking those streets. I'm looking up at those things [Confederate monuments] that give me a sense of dread and fear. What does it feel like physically to walk a public space and to have your state, your country, your nation say, "This is what we stand by"? No! We want more. We demand more. . . . And today we say yes to something that looks like us. We say yes to inclusivity. We say yes to broader notions of what it means to be an American. . . . Are we ready? . . . Let's get this party started![39]

Wiley's powerful demand for "more" reflects the demands of many Black-led community organizations and municipalities across the country as Black people wonder aloud what it would be like to see their bodies depicted as free in the landscape and the ways in which this would reconfigure not just space but also their relationship to the nation. Black figures etched into the landscape offer an acknowledgment not just of Black people as important actors in the American past but also their role as actors in the American future.

In 2019, I returned to the Confederate monument of my childhood in Alabama with Wiley's question on my mind: what does it feel like to walk among structures that spark fear and dread in your body, knowing that your state and nation have sanctioned that space? As I parked near the monument, I was struck by how nothing had visibly changed at the site since I was a child. The models of cars parked nearby were the only clues that I was in 2019 and not 1979. The Confederate soldier still stood tall as if he had grown from the land as naturally as the grass underneath him.[40] Though a local nonprofit group was raising money to put an additional monument on the same plaza as the soldier, they had yet to raise the funds or receive permissions. The sculpture they imagined would depict two famous Black residents of the town, Dred and Harriet Scott, best known for an 1857 US Supreme Court case in which they sued for their freedom and that of their children. The court famously ruled against the family, setting a dangerous precedent: "the Negro race ... [is] a separate class of persons ... not regarded as a portion of the people or citizens of the Government."[41] But the fact that the Scotts had pleaded their case all the way to the Supreme Court suggested that they had been persistent in their belief that they were worthy of all of the rights and promises of US freedom. I wondered what difference the presence of a monument to the Scotts would have made as I walked into that courthouse as a child. Would my understanding of my place in that space have been different with a Confederate monument on one side of me and Dred and Harriet Scott standing defiant on the other?

As I got out of the car to snap a quick photo, my mother said, "Be careful," and the words hung in the air between us with no need for explanation. I walked onto the plaza, and seconds after I raised my phone to take a photo, a white woman and man walked out of the courthouse and stopped to stare at me. I clicked away, and the man moved on. The woman turned and ducked back into the building, her mouth as wide open as the door she walked through. I could not be sure if she'd forgotten something or if she was headed to the sheriff's office inside to report my presence. But I knew better than to wait to find out. I moved to my car in a few strides, still hearing my mother's warning and sure of just one thing: this land is still not mine.

# NOTES

1. Owen Dwyer, "Memory on the Margins: Alabama's Civil Rights Journey as a Memorial Text," in *Mapping Tourism*, ed. Stephen P. Hanna and Vincent J. Del Casino Jr. (Minneapolis: University of Minnesota Press, 2003), 31.

2. George Wallace, "Inaugural Address of Governor George Wallace, Which Was Delivered at the Capitol in Montgomery, Alabama," Alabama Department of Archives and History, accessed July 24, 2020, https://digital.archives.alabama.gov/cdm/ref/collection/voices/id/2952.

3. Kirk Savage, *Monument Wars: Washington, D.C., the National Mall, and the Transformation of the Memorial Landscape* (Berkeley: University of California Press, 2011), 10.

4. James W. Loewen, *Lies across America: What Our Historic Sites and National Monuments Get Wrong* (New York: New Press, 2019), 198.

5. Thomas J. Seabrook, "Tributes to the Past, Present, and Future: World War I–Era Confederate Memorialization in Virginia," in *Controversial Monuments and Memorials: A Guide for Community Leaders*, ed. David B. Allison (Lanham, MD: Rowman and Littlefield Publishers, 2018), 68.

6. Amina Luqman-Dawson, *African Americans of Petersburg* (Mount Pleasant, SC: Arcadia Publishing, 2008), 29.

7. W. Fitzhugh Brundage, *Lynching in the New South: Georgia and Virginia, 1880–1930* (Champaign: University of Illinois Press, 1994), 282.

8. Robert S. Seigler, *A Guide to Confederate Monuments in South Carolina: Passing the Silent Cup* (Columbia: South Carolina Department of Archives and History, 1997), 18.

9. Loewen, *Lies across America*, 198.

10. Evander Price, "On Creating a Useable Future: An Introduction to Future Monuments," in *Monument Culture: International Perspectives on the Future of Monuments in a Changing World*, ed. Laura A. Macaluso (Lanham, MD: Rowman and Littlefield Publishers, 2019), 258.

11. Mitch Landrieu, *In the Shadow of Statues: A White Southerner Confronts History* (New York: Penguin Books, 2019), 39–40.

12. Quoted in "Confederate Monuments: Crews Remove P. G. T. Beauregard Statue," NOLA.com, May 17, 2017, https://www.nola.com/news/politics/article_3dcd2683-ea62-5860-a158f61f82cd312c.html.

13. See Jeff Adelson, "Threats Cast at Contractors, Workers Linked to Confederate Monument Removals, New Orleans Official Says," NOLA.com, April 14, 2017, https://www.nola.com/news/ article_93458b38-f779-5599-a955-7e5450277628.html; and Jelani Cobb, "The Battle over Confederate Monuments in New Orleans," *New Yorker*, June 20, 2017, https://www.newyorker.com/news/daily-comment/the-battle-over-confederate-monuments-in-new-orleans.

14. Nicholas Fandos, Russell Goldman, and Jess Bidgood, "Baltimore Mayor Had Statues Removed in 'Best Interest of My City,'" *New York Times*, August 16, 2017, https://www.nytimes.com/2017/08/16/us/baltimore-confederate-statues.html.

15. Cara Aitchison, Nicola E. MacLeod, and Stephen J. Shaw, *Leisure and Tourism Landscapes: Social and Cultural Geographies* (New York: Routledge, 2001), 24.

16. Bryan Wagner, "Charles Chesnutt and the Epistemology of Racial Violence," *American Literature* 73, no. 2 (June 2001): 313.

17. Martha S. Jones (@marthasjones_), "Like Our Empty Pedestals in Baltimore, This 'Empty' Space at @DukeU Can Invite Reflection, Learning, and a Poignant Sign of an Ongoing Struggle for Reconciliation and Justice," Tweet, August 23, 2018, https://twitter.com/marthasjones_/status/1032572778870910977.

18. Eric Levenson, "Baltimore Renames Former Confederate Site for Harriet Tubman," CNN, March 12, 2018, https://www.cnn.com/2018/03/11/us/baltimore-harriet-tubman-park/index.html.

19. Doug Stanglin, "Memphis Changes Names of 3 Confederate-Themed Parks," *USA Today*, February 6, 2013, https://www.usatoday.com/story/news/nation/2013/02/06/memphis-parks-confederate-ku-klux-klan/1895549/.

20. Robbie Brown, "Memphis Drops Confederate Names from Parks, Sowing New Battles," *New York Times*, March 29, 2013, https://www.nytimes.com/2013/03/29/us/memphis-drops-confederate-names-from-parks-sowing-new-battles.html.

21. David Royer, "'Fourth Bluff' Signs at Downtown Park Highlight New Project," *Commercial Appeal*, April 15, 2016, https://archive.commercialappeal.com/news/fourth-bluff-signs-at-downtown-park-highlight-new-project-308c4aa0-e7ff-60e1-e053-0100007f7d7d375914801.html/.

22. Associated Press, "Tennessee Lawmakers Punish Memphis for Removing Confederate Statues," NBC News, April 18, 2018, https://www.nbcnews.com/news/us-news/tennessee-lawmakers-punish-memphis-removing-confederate-statues-n866961.

23. Rosalind Bentley, "Atlanta Erecting Markers about Slavery Next to Confederate Monuments," *Atlanta Journal-Constitution*, July 29, 2019, https://www.ajc.com/news/local-govt-politics/atlanta-erecting-historical-markers-next-confederate-monuments/84aZJcUhOA7GparAHNOGCP/.

24. Quoted in Emil Moffat, "Local NAACP President Questions Content of Signs Near Confederate Monuments," WABE, August 21, 2019, https://www.wabe.org/local-naacp-president-questions-content-of-signs-near-confederate-monuments/.

25. Quoted in Rosalind Bentley, "Atlanta NAACP Criticizes Markers Surrounding Confederate Monuments," *Atlanta Journal-Constitution*, August 22, 2019, https://www.ajc.com/news/local/atlanta-naacp-criticizes-markers-surrounding-confederate-monuments/J270cXywg1hiMAlUZQlloO/.

26. Quoted in Nicquel Terry Ellis, "Blocked from Taking Confederate Statues Down, Atlanta, Birmingham, Memphis Try Other Ideas," *USA Today*, March 13, 2019, https://www.usatoday.com/story/news/nation/2019/02/12/confederate-monuments-leaders-cities-removal-alternatives-civil-rights-groups/2525178002/.

27. Tia Mitchell, "Marker Supplies Historical Context for DeKalb's Confederate Monument," *Atlanta Journal-Constitution*, September 17, 2019, https://www.ajc.com/news/local/marker-supplies-historical-context-for-dekalb-confederate-monument/3mGyZ6ITzCEGVgz785O1zJ/.

28. Mitchell, "Marker Supplies Historical Context."

29. Tia Mitchell, "DeKalb County to Acknowledge Lynchings through Historical Marker," *Atlanta Journal-Constitution*, February 4, 2019, https://www.ajc.com/news/local-govt-politics/dekalb-county-acknowledge-lynchings-through-historical-marker/I9YG2Jno8Jhqu41aEdSorO/.

30. "Memorial Carving," Stone Mountain Park, accessed July 24, 2020, https://www.stonemountainpark.com/Activities/History-Nature/Confederate-Memorial-Carving.

31. J. D. Capelouto and Tyler Estep, "DeKalb Judge Orders Confederate Monument to Be Moved by June 26," *Atlanta Journal-Constitution*, June 12, 2020, https://www.ajc.com/news/local/breaking-dekalb-judge-says-confederate-monument-should-removed/L6pwyzbEiLmEQ9w2mXnGmK/.

32. "DeKalb County Memorializes Four Victims of Racial Terror Lynching," Equal Justice Initiative, July 2, 2020, https://eji.org/news/dekalb-county-memorializes-four-victims-of-racial-terror-lynching/.

33. Kelsey Stein, "Activist Asks Birmingham Mayor to Remove Confederate Monument; Decision Falls to Parks Board," AL.com, July 1, 2015, https://www.al.com/news/birmingham/2015/06/activist_again_calls_to_remove.html.

34. Joseph D. Bryant, "Birmingham City Officials Take Steps to Remove Confederate Monument at Linn Park," AL.com, July 1, 2015, https://www.al.com/news/birmingham/2015/07/finding_another_place_birmingh.html.

35. Colin Dwyer, "Confederate Monument Being Removed After Birmingham Mayor Vows to 'Finish the Job,'" NPR, June 2, 2020, https://www.npr.org/2020/06/02/867659459/confederate-monument-removed-after-birmingham-mayors-vow-to-finish-the-job; and "Update: Crews Fully Remove Confederate Monument in Birmingham's Linn Park, Mayor Woodfin Receives Death Threats," WBRC, June 3, 2020, https://www.wbrc.com/2020/06/01/crews-working-remove-confederate-monument-linn-park/.

36. Marc Fisher, "As Confederate Monuments Tumble, Die-Hards Are Erecting Replacements," *Washington Post*, July 25, 2020, https://www.washingtonpost.com/national/as-confederate-monuments-tumble-die-hards-are-erecting-replacements/2020/07/25/44f537ee-cd04-11ea-b0e3-d55bda07d66a_story.html.

37. Henry Graff, "Statue of Confederate Gen. J. E. B. Stuart Removed in Richmond," NBC12, July 7, 2020, https://www.nbc12.com/2020/07/07/crews-begin-removal-jeb-stuart-statue/.

38. Quoted in Phoebe Hoban, "Kehinde Wiley Makes a Statement with New Sculpture in Times Square," *Architectural Digest*, September 30, 2019, https://www.architecturaldigest.com/story/kehinde-wiley-new-sculpture-times-square-new-york-city.

39. Quoted in Hoban, "Kehinde Wiley."

40. In the summer of 2020, the local activist group Project Say Something began holding weekly protests to demand the removal of this monument. The Florence City Council voted to remove the statue and relocate it to a cemetery. Efforts to remove the statue, however, have been blocked by a lawsuit. See Associated Press, "Florence Moving Toward Removal of Confederate Monument," AL.com, October 14, 2020, www.al.com/news/2020/10/florence-moving-toward-removal-of-confederate-monument.html; and Jeremy Jackson, "Legal Advocacy Organization Says Lauderdale County Confederate Monument Lawsuit Carries No Legal Weight," WHNT News 19, August 20, 2020, https://whnt.com/news/racial-justice-movement/legal-advocacy-organization-says-lauderdale-county-confederate-monument-lawsuit-carries-no-legal-weight/.

41. Dred Scott v. Sandford, 60 U.S. 393 (1857).

## Bibliography

Adelson, Jeff. "Threats Cast at Contractors, Workers Linked to Confederate Monument Removals, New Orleans Official Says." NOLA.com, April 14, 2017. https://www.nola.com/news/article_93458b38-f779-5599-a955-7e5450277628.html.

Aitchison, Cara, Nicola E. MacLeod, and Stephen J. Shaw. *Leisure and Tourism Landscapes: Social and Cultural Geographies.* New York: Routledge, 2001.

Associated Press. "Tennessee Lawmakers Punish Memphis for Removing Confederate Statues." NBC News, April 18, 2018. https://www.nbcnews.com/news/us-news/tennessee-lawmakers-punish-memphis-removing-confederate-statues-n866961.

Associated Press. "Florence Moving toward Removal of Confederate Monument." AL.com, October 14, 2020. www.al.com/news/2020/10/florence-moving-toward-removal-of-confederate-monument.html.

Bentley, Rosalind. "Atlanta Erecting Markers about Slavery Next to Confederate Monuments." *Atlanta Journal-Constitution*, July 29, 2019. https://www.ajc.com/news/local-govt-politics/atlanta-erecting-historical-markers-next-confederate-monuments/84aZJcUhOA7Gpar AHNOGCP/.

Bentley, Rosalind. "Atlanta NAACP Criticizes Markers Surrounding Confederate Monuments." *Atlanta Journal-Constitution*, August 22, 2019. https://www.ajc.com/news/local/atlanta-naacp-criticizes-markers-surrounding-confederate-monuments/J27ocXywg 1hiMAlUZQlloO/.

Brown, Robbie. "Memphis Drops Confederate Names from Parks, Sowing New Battles." *New York Times*, March 29, 2013. https://www.nytimes.com/2013/03/29/us/memphis-drops -confederate-names-from-parks-sowing-new-battles.html.

Brundage, W. Fitzhugh. *Lynching in the New South: Georgia and Virginia, 1880–1930.* Champaign: University of Illinois Press, 1994.

Bryant, Joseph D. "Birmingham City Officials Take Steps to Remove Confederate Monument at Linn Park." AL.com, July 1, 2015. https://www.al.com/news/birmingham/2015/07/finding_ another_place_birmingh.html.

Capelouto, J. D., and Tyler Estep. "DeKalb Judge Orders Confederate Monument to Be Moved by June 26." *Atlanta Journal-Constitution*, June 12, 2020. https://www.ajc.com/ news/local/breaking-dekalb-judge-says-confederate-monument-should-removed/ L6pwyzbEiLmEQ9w2mXnGmK/.

Cobb, Jelani. "The Battle over Confederate Monuments in New Orleans." *New Yorker*, June 20, 2017. https://www.newyorker.com/news/daily-comment/the-battle-over-confederate -monuments-in-new-orleans.

"DeKalb County Memorializes Four Victims of Racial Terror Lynching." Equal Justice Initiative, July 2, 2020. https://eji.org/news/dekalb-county-memorializes-four-victims -of-racial-terror-lynching/.

Dred Scott v. Sandford. 60 U.S. 393 (1857).

Dwyer, Colin. "Confederate Monument Being Removed After Birmingham Mayor Vows to 'Finish the Job.'" NPR, June 2, 2020. https://www.npr.org/2020/06/02/867659459/ confederate-monument-removed-after-birmingham-mayors-vow-to-finish-the-job.

Dwyer, Owen. "Memory on the Margins: Alabama's Civil Rights Journey as a Memorial Text." In *Mapping Tourism*, edited by Stephen P. Hanna and Vincent J. Del Casino Jr., 28–50. Minneapolis: University of Minnesota Press, 2003.

Ellis, Nicquel Terry. "Blocked from Taking Confederate Statues Down, Atlanta, Birmingham, Memphis Try Other Ideas." *USA Today*, March 13, 2019. https://www.usatoday.com/story/ news/nation/2019/02/12/confederate-monuments-leaders-cities-removal-alternatives-civil -rights-groups/2525178002/.

Fandos, Nicholas, Russell Goodman, and Jess Bidgood. "Baltimore Mayor Had Statues Removed in 'Best Interest of My City.'" *New York Times*, August 16, 2017. https://www .nytimes.com/ 2017/08/16/us/baltimore-confederate-statues.html.

Fisher, Marc. "As Confederate Monuments Tumble, Die-Hards Are Erecting Replacements." *Washington Post*, July 25, 2020. https://www.washingtonpost.com/national/as-confederate -monuments-tumble-die-hards-are-erecting-replacements/2020/07/25/44f537ee-cd04-11ea -b0e3-d55bda07d66a_story.html.

Graff, Henry. "Statue of Confederate Gen. J. E. B. Stuart Removed in Richmond." NBC12, July 7, 2020. https://www.nbc12.com/2020/07/07/crews-begin-removal-jeb-stuart-statue/.

Hoban, Phoebe. "Kehinde Wiley Makes a Statement with New Sculpture in Times Square." *Architectural Digest*, September 30, 2019. https://www.architecturaldigest.com/story/ kehinde-wiley-new-sculpture-times-square-new-york-city.

Jackson, Jeremy. "Legal Advocacy Organization Says Lauderdale County Confederate Monument Lawsuit Carries No Legal Weight." WHNT News 19, August 20, 2020. https:// whnt.com/news/racial-justice-movement/legal-advocacy-organization-says-lauderdale -county-confederate-monument-lawsuit-carries-no-legal-weight/.

Jones, Martha S. (@marthasjones_). "Like Our Empty Pedestals in Baltimore, This 'Empty' Space at @DukeU Can Invite Reflection, Learning, and a Poignant Sign of an Ongoing Struggle for Reconciliation and Justice." Tweet, August 23, 2018. https://twitter.com/ marthasjones_/status/1032572778870910977.

Landrieu, Mitch. *In the Shadow of Statues: A White Southerner Confronts History.* New York: Penguin Books, 2019.

Levenson, Eric. "Baltimore Renames Former Confederate Site for Harriet Tubman." CNN, March 12, 2018. https://www.cnn.com/2018/03/11/us/baltimore-harriet-tubman-park/index .html.

Loewen, James W. *Lies across America: What Our Historic Sites and National Monuments Get Wrong.* New York: New Press, 2019.

Luqman-Dawson, Amina. *African Americans of Petersburg.* Mount Pleasant, SC: Arcadia Publishing, 2008.

Mitchell, Tia. "DeKalb County to Acknowledge Lynchings through Historical Marker." *Atlanta Journal-Constitution,* February 4, 2019. https://www.ajc.com/news/local-govt-politics/ dekalb-county-acknowledge-lynchings-through-historical-marker/I9YG2Jno8Jhqu41a EdSorO/.

Mitchell, Tia. "Marker Supplies Historical Context for DeKalb's Confederate Monument." *Atlanta Journal-Constitution,* September 17, 2019. https://www.ajc.com/news/local/marker -supplies-historical-context-for-dekalb-confederate-monument/3mGyZ6ITzCEGVgz7 85O1zJ/.

Moffatt, Emil. "Local NAACP President Questions Content of Signs Near Confederate Monuments." WABE, August 21, 2019. https://www.wabe.org/local-naacp-president -questions-content-of-signs-near-confederate-monuments/.

NOLA.com. "Confederate Monuments: Crews Remove P. G. T. Beauregard Statue." May 17, 2017. https://www.nola.com/news/politics/article_3dcd2683-ea62-5860-a158-f61f82cd312c.html.

Price, Evander. "On Creating a Useable Future: An Introduction to Future Monuments." In *Monument Culture: International Perspectives on the Future of Monuments in a Changing World,* edited by Laura A. Macaluso, 253–60. Lanham, MD: Rowman and Littlefield Publishers, 2019.

Royer, David. "'Fourth Bluff' Signs at Downtown Park Highlight New Project." *Commercial Appeal,* April 15, 2016. https://archive.commercialappeal.com/news/fourth-bluff-signs-at -downtown-park-highlight-new-project-308c4aa0-e7ff-60e1-e053-0100007f7d7d-37591 4801.html/.

Savage, Kirk. *Monument Wars: Washington, D.C., the National Mall, and the Transformation of the Memorial Landscape.* Berkeley: University of California Press, 2011.

Seabrook, Thomas J. "Tributes to the Past, Present, and Future: World War I–Era Confederate Memorialization in Virginia." In *Controversial Monuments and Memorials: A Guide for Community Leaders,* edited by David B. Allison, 65–78. Lanham, MD: Rowman and Littlefield Publishers, 2018.

Seigler, Robert S. *A Guide to Confederate Monuments in South Carolina: Passing the Silent Cup.* Columbia: South Carolina Department of Archives and History, 1997.

Stanglin, Doug. "Memphis Changes Names of 3 Confederate-Themed Parks." *USA Today,* February 6, 2013. https://www.usatoday.com/story/news/nation/2013/02/06/memphis -parks-confederate-ku-klux-klan/1895549/.

Stein, Kelsey. "Activist Asks Birmingham Mayor to Remove Confederate Monument; Decision
    Falls to Parks Board." AL.com, July 1, 2015. https://www.al.com/news/birmingham/2015/06/
    activist_again_calls_to_remove.html.

Stone Mountain Park. "Memorial Carving." Accessed July 24, 2020. https://www.stonemountain
    park.com/Activities/History-Nature/Confederate-Memorial-Carving.

"Update: Crews Fully Remove Confederate Monument in Birmingham's Linn Park, Mayor
    Woodfin Receives Death Threats." WBRC, June 3, 2020. https://www.wbrc.com/2020/06/01/
    crews-working-remove-confederate-monument-linn-park/.

Wagner, Bryan. "Charles Chesnutt and the Epistemology of Racial Violence." *American Literature*
    73, no. 2 (June 2001): 311–37.

Wallace, George. "Inaugural Address of Governor George Wallace, Which Was Delivered at the
    Capitol in Montgomery, Alabama." Alabama Department of Archives and History. Accessed
    July 24, 2020. https://digital.archives.alabama.gov/cdm/ref/collection/voices/id/2952.

# CHAPTER 9

# BATTLE OF THE BILLBOARDS

White Supremacy and Memorial Culture in #Charlottesville

—Lisa Woolfork

The two-day white supremacist terror attacks in Charlottesville, Virginia, on August 11 and 12, 2017, sparked global conversation about the resurgence of white nationalism in the United States. On August 11, white supremacists marched with lit torches through the historic grounds of the University of Virginia shouting "blood and soil"[1] and "Jews will not replace us."[2] The mob culminated at the statue of Thomas Jefferson, surrounding a group of students, staff, and community members gathered there to resist them. White supremacists swarmed the assembled counter-protesters, physically converging on them while hurling invectives, punches, lighter fluid, and torches. On August 12, white supremacist violence would escalate with street brawls, parking garage attacks, and ultimately vehicular homicide when a white supremacist drove his car through a crowd of counter-protesters, killing one person and injuring dozens of others. These terror events transformed the public image of Charlottesville from a quaint college town to a hotbed of white supremacist violence and resistance to it. And yet, while the events in Charlottesville may have inspired other communities to remove their Confederate statues, Charlottesville itself has retained them.[3]

Charlottesville's history of erecting Confederate monuments like the Robert E. Lee and Stonewall Jackson statues coincided with a period of intimidation and terrorism from the Ku Klux Klan in the 1920s. On both occasions, the unveiling ceremonies for the statues drew thousands of guests and an air of celebration. Like other towns and cities in the United States at the time, the Klan terrorized the local community by burning crosses and setting off explosions. As one report by the University of Virginia's Citizens Justice Initiative states, "Charlottesville's Confederate monuments occupy a visible position within a larger historical landscape predicated on anti-black violence and entrenched fictions of racial difference."[4]

There is a long, strong, and as yet unbroken strand of white supremacy that keeps Charlottesville tethered to the commemoration of the Confederacy. There is an important contradiction between "Charlottesville," the city or place that was the epicenter of white supremacist violence, and "#Charlottesville," the hashtagged discursive shorthand that inspired national and global solidarity to resist white nationalism. As I argued in a *Huffington Post* op-ed titled "White Supremacy Is Still Welcomed in Charlottesville,"

> #Charlottesville, the hashtag, was a beacon that lit the way for other cities to repel white supremacy. The August 2017 violence prompted actions of solidarity around the country. In Boston, a group of civilians overwhelmed a small showing of rallying white supremacists. Officials in Baltimore quickly and quietly relocated four of their Confederate statues. Activists in Durham, North Carolina, took the matter into their own hands and toppled a Confederate statue. In Orange County, North Carolina, a school division relented to pressure from community members and banned Confederate imagery from its student dress code. And on Monday, in Staunton, Virginia, the school board voted to remove the name Robert E. Lee from the city's only public high school. A former board member cited #Charlottesville as his motivation to support the measure, saying, "I didn't want to be a coward any more."[5]

Many peripheral reverberations of #Charlottesville reveal themselves in community or state actions to remove or relocate Confederate statues. References to #Charlottesville and its battle against white supremacy also appear in television shows such as *The X-Files* reboot (2016–18) on Fox and the CW's *Black Lightning* (2018–present).[6] In *The X-Files*, #Charlottesville is used as an index of global chaos by showing footage of fascist street brawls interspersed with other calamities around the world. These acts of resistance or acts of representation illustrate the degree to which #Charlottesville served as a cultural flashpoint for the practice and specter of contemporary white supremacist violence. As a result, #Charlottesville is an important motivation for action against the commemoration of white supremacist violence that operates within Confederate memory preservation.

Charlottesville as a place, however, was and remains committed to overt and covert forms of white supremacy in its courts, schools, policing, and beyond. This institutional resolve circulates around the maintenance of Confederate statues. To do this, many Confederate defenders seek to shift the discourse around the objects. They work to expunge the white supremacist violence inherent to the statues' construction and current prominent position. The distance between Charlottesville and #Charlottesville as two distinct symbolic regions is the difference between neutralizing white supremacy and taking action to eradicate it. Memorial culture is a significant component of that contradiction. This essay will explore a unique struggle over public memory, rhetoric, discourse, and semiotics that illustrates the tensions still rampant in Charlottesville. My work as a literary scholar is animated by my commitment to dismantling white supremacy in my local community (and elsewhere). My approach to the fallout and my understanding of the gap between Charlottesville and #Charlottesville is informed by practices of literary cognition including close reading and contextualization. I bring this nexus of skills to illuminate what I call the battle of the billboards: a skirmish between white supremacists and anti-racists that played out in plain sight in Charlottesville.

In September 2018, about a year after the deadly Unite the Right rally, the Make It Right Project, a nonprofit anti-racist organization dedicated to removing Confederate statues from select public spaces, rented a billboard in Charlottesville, Virginia. The large sign was placed at the intersection of East High Street and the Route 250 bypass. The location is one of a few places where such signage is allowed in the city, a significant thoroughfare where it would be seen on the way into town via East High Street and out of town, heading to I-64, from the Route 250 bypass. Kali Holloway, the group's director, worked with local organizers from Black Lives Matter and Showing Up for Racial Justice to craft a visual message that would be hard-hitting, direct, and concise.[7] The large sign would feature black and white pictures of the Lee and Jackson statues (on its left and right sides) with brief red text in the middle of a bright yellow background. Original text suggestions included wording that the Make It Right Project had successfully used on billboards in other cities. "Monumental Lies" was the first choice of local organizers. This, they believed, would counter the argument that these statues were neutral. This short phrase also gestured to the narratives that undergirded the statues' historical construction and contemporary defense. "Monumental Lies" indicted the statues as dangerous fallacies while critiquing those who continued to support the monuments in the streets and in local courts.

The obvious critique of "Monumental Lies," however, was too much for the Charlottesville affiliate of the Lamar Company, which owns the billboard space. The company rejected the phrase with little explanation, although organizers assumed that the word *lies* might be seen as inflammatory rhetoric. A few organizers working on the project were frustrated by the billboard company's refusal to post "Monumental Lies" when the same company had advertised a pro-Confederate cause in the same space a year earlier. After several rounds of revision, the group came up with a phrase that the billboard company was willing to post: "Monumental Change Needed."

The phrase was rooted in a robust critique of Lost Cause mythology and its racist artifacts. Still, there was concern that "Monumental Change Needed" was too ambiguous. To counteract this, the Make It Right Project issued a nation-wide press release while local activists held a press conference on the day the billboards were unveiled. Community members, including Black Lives Matter organizers and other activists, spoke about the need to provide a complete story of the monuments. "Charlottesville must remove these racist Jim Crow monuments to the antebellum slave regime also known as the Confederacy. These statues continue to draw racial terror to our community, as white supremacists fight in our streets and in our courts to defend the lies of their 'Lost Cause,'" I said in a radio broadcast.[8] Zyahna Bryant, a student activist who initiated removal efforts by presenting a petition to city council at the age of fifteen, said in the same broadcast, "Confederate monuments and racist imagery do not belong in our public spaces. These statues represent a deeper history of white supremacy that continues to oppress people of color. In toppling these local odes to the Confederacy, protesters and student activists at UNC Chapel Hill and Durham have shown why the removal of these monuments must remain at the forefront of our conversations." Don Gathers, a chair of the Blue Ribbon Commission for the Study of Race and Public Spaces and a cofounder of Black Lives Matter Charlottesville said, "The necessity of getting that message out there continues to exist. . . . We've got to continue to shut down racism in every form and fashion and at every opportunity."[9] For activists involved with the project, the billboard was part of the larger effort to combat current and historical white supremacy in the Charlottesville community.

However, the compromised slogan "Monumental Change Needed" would prove problematic for the anti-racist campaign. The day of the billboard launch, WVIR NBC29 posted a story on Facebook, where it was shared by community members. The story's tagline clearly stated that the billboards called for the statues' removal. Subsequent discussion revealed the cost of the ambiguous phrase. Several anti-racist activists—including those who had worked with the Albemarle County Hate-Free Schools Coalition to remove Confederate imagery from public schools—believed the signs advocated for statue preservation. Even after activists directly involved in the campaign explained the intention, resistance to the billboards remained, as the following comments suggest:

hell nah, this ain't the way to broadcast this shit lol at all especially if they taking it down

I agree. Why aren't there at least huge Xs though the monument pic. Totally wrong visual message.

yeah, i did find it confusing when i saw it. i thought it was pro-statue.

i was actually pissed when i first saw it and was quickly calculating how to tag that shit.

like, it reinforces the images of the statues that we want to take out of public display, so it reinstitutes them, you know?

so now it's like, lee and jackson statues in the parks AND lee and jackson on a billboard on high street. we can't get away from them![10]

Billboards are a pervasive form of flash advertising. Their success depends upon their ability to convey a message in the seconds it takes to passively consume them. Billboards are discursively demanding. They occupy large physical space to make a fleeting yet persuasive impression on those who move past them. I call billboards demanding for the invasive manner in which they wrangle their way into one's private vehicle or public transportation. Billboards are striking informational tools that deposit their message, if not fully, into the consciousness of the driver or passenger who is bounded by a moving vehicle yet still susceptible to outside content. For these reasons, billboard messaging should leave no room for ambiguity. As the Facebook comments above suggest, despite the anti-racist intention of the Make It Right Project, the billboard was ultimately too tepid to fuel the resistance that the activist community had been engaged in long before the billboard appeared. In addition, the billboard required close reading, which is anathema to the messaging tactic of flash advertising. As one anti-racist activist who was initially angered by the billboard explained, "but then i saw the name of the make it right project at the bottom and remembered that they had written something about taking the statues down. i'm not sure everyone knows who make it right is, though."[11]

The ambiguity of the billboard signaled that, among many local anti-racist activists, the message missed its mark. People who had long advocated for the removal of the statues saw the phrase "Monumental Change Needed" and the black and white images of the two contentious statues as promoting the racist imagery rather than seeking to dismantle it. The claim that "we can't get away from them!" is a useful critique. The Make It Right Project's billboard, according to these anti-racist activists, failed to provide a clear, easily accessible challenge to the racist status quo that keeps the statues in place. They argued that the billboard was additionally problematic because the sign extended the reach of the racist statues by replicating their images beyond the site of their physical location in two downtown parks. The billboard was erected with the intention to challenge or even shame the apathy (and rigorous defense, in the case of the Monument Fund) that keeps the statues in the city's public spaces. The sign was meant to be a reference to or reminder of the "monumental change needed" in the parks that had seen white supremacist violence a year earlier. This was likely meant to be a form of quick intervention: a high-impact message to reach the public on their way into or out of the city, something to make people think, a mental tripping hazard for a brain that wouldn't usually stumble into considering these issues as important.

The critique from anti-racist activists not connected to the billboard project shows, however, that rather than promoting statue removal, the visual message (without paying attention to the project's sponsor) was easily received as being pro-statue. In addition, this ambiguity had the additional consequence of extending the statues' range of harm. No longer limited to the confines of two downtown parks, the statues migrated to a busy intersection to stake a space in front of unsuspecting motorists. The billboard's ambiguous wording and prominent unobstructed reproduction of the statues transformed the effort of an anti-racist organization into what was seen by some as an act that merely furthered white supremacy rather than dismantling it.

If anti-racist activists found the billboard's message too vague to inspire the "monumental change" its red letters boldly declared, defenders of the racist statues recognized the billboard's threat immediately. Days after the Make It Right Project's billboard appeared at the corner of East High Street and the Route 250 bypass, another billboard of sorts emerged in the same parking lot. This one was clearly pro-statue. The pro-racist-monument billboard parodied the anti-racist sign. It used every detail of the Make It Right Project's billboard—from the bright yellow background to black and white images of the Lee and Jackson statues—as the foundation for its own sign. It even retained the bold red letters that appeared on the original sign that read "Monumental Change Needed" and kept the anti-racist group's attribution "Paid for by the Make It Right Project." This is where the similarities end.

Using strikethroughs, cropping, and additions, the parody billboard defended the statues by seeking to shift the terrain on which the conflict had been argued. Rather than viewing the statues as imposing relics of a racist past, the updated version of the billboard seemed designed to show urgency in the face of an impending and (for the Confederate statue supporters) unwanted change. The revised billboard looked, for all intents and purposes, like a graffitied version of the original. This aesthetic choice is interesting given the suspicion with which the Make It Right Project's billboard was initially viewed by at least one anti-racist activist who, as I mention above, wanted to "tag that shit." A black handwriting font gave the impression that a giant hand had scribbled over the Make It Right Project's billboard.

In a technique similar to blackout poetry—in which one writes a poem by blacking out words of an existing text, usually with a permanent marker—the word *monumental* in the phrase "Monumental Change Needed" was radically altered. The letters *al* of the word *monumental* were blacked out with a scratch made by what looked to be a rapid back-and-forth motion of a black marker. But the new sign did more than deduct words from the original; it also added a new letter and new words, in the same black handwritten font, to the first version. The subtraction of the letters *al* changed *monumental* to *monument*. The parody billboard also used additional text to clarify its reasons for effectively spoiling the first sign: "Respect All" was scrawled above the updated word "Monuments." The top line of the revised billboard read "Respect All Monuments." The word "NO" was added to the second line of the original billboard's phrase "Change Needed" to declare "NO Change Needed." The parody billboard also made an important change to the images of the two Confederate monuments featured prominently on the original sign. The Make It Right Project's billboard conspicuously displays Charlottesville's statues of Lee and Jackson, including their stately plinths. These figures are so imposing that they comprise about 50 percent of the sign's messaging space. This might be why so many activists assumed that the billboard was defending the monuments rather than challenging them. The parody billboard takes the unusual step of removing Lee and Jackson from their pedestals. In addition, the parody reduces these cropped statues, making them much smaller. If the original billboard gave about 50 percent of the visual space to the statues, the parody yielded no more than 25 percent of its visual field to the contested relics. Significantly, in the revised billboard, the two Confederate generals are neither venerated nor exulted. Instead, they are diminutive, truncated versions of the actual statues that dominate the city's two downtown parks. The revised billboard transforms these contentious objects into two generic men on horseback, toy soldiers.

The transformation of these two massive statues into small figurines—absent the veneration signified by their huge stone platforms—that appear rather meekly on either side of the parody billboard is a vital change. It might be assumed that the parody billboard wanted to minimize the visual effect, the knee-jerk reaction that the statues had come to mean to many in Charlottesville. An uncontextualized image of the Lee statue, for example, was fraught with the presumption of upholding white supremacist ideology endemic to the Confederacy. To counter the potential negative response, the parody billboard makers simply shrank and diminished (by cropping) the representation of the statues themselves. The reduced version of the statues in the parody billboard are a crucial example of a larger pro-statue argument. The goal in removing Lee and Jackson from their pedestals might have been part of an effort to make them less visually imposing, more quotidian. In this way, one could simply coexist with the white supremacy of the Confederacy in the name of social progress and tolerance.

The Charlottesville Free Press claimed responsibility for transforming the anti-racist billboard into a defense of the Confederacy. A right-wing blog featuring posts against immigration, gay rights, racial diversity, and Black Lives Matter, the Charlottesville Free Press was founded by Mitch Carr, who attended Charlottesville public schools for three years as a child but no longer lives in the city.[12] On September 26, 2018, Carr wrote a blog post explaining why his revised billboard was necessary. The post was titled "Why We Did Our Billboard Parody," and the answer to the question appeared in the first sentence: "The short answer . . . Because standing up to a bully is always the right thing to do." For Carr, the Make It Right Project was part of a larger set of forces arrayed against the South and people like himself. "Elites," Carr says, are responsible for the racial strife in Charlottesville and beyond.[13]

The purpose of his billboard was to resist the cultural constraints of what Carr called "race baiting." His sign was an intervention in the larger and, to him, confusing conversations about multiculturalism. For him, the parody billboard was intended to empower those who saw the sign to vigorously resist being drawn into an elaborate scheme of the "elites." Instead of participating in conversations or even listening to talk about the meaning of the statues, Carr advises his viewers to "Tell the race baiters on both sides to shut up. Tell them you are not listening anymore. On Monday they tell us we need racial diversity, on Tuesday they tell us racial appropriation is racist. Well which is it?"[14] The question is meant to be a rhetorical one, a question that proves the illogic of those who promote racial diversity. The post is riddled with non sequiturs and poor circular reasoning. Carr uses a peculiar and repeated tactic of persuasion to make his case that the statues are not racist. He suggests that those who revere the flag should not be seen as racist if they say they are not racist:

> Those who have a different reverence for the flag based on their heritage of fighting for state sovereignty should be taken at their word, not be compelled to give up their flag or their monuments at the hands of bullies. Everyone should be allowed to honor their past within the law. Reasonable people can disagree and still show mutual respect without advocating revolution in the streets as we have seen in the toppling of statues, most recently in North Carolina.
>
> Finally, to those opposing the statues, try and look at it from the point of view of those who believe that these men were fighting for Virginia against a tyrannical federal government. Take them at their word until they show you evidence to the contrary.

Carr is committed to the idea that reverence for the Confederacy and its symbols can occur without the stigma of racism. White supremacy—the driving factor behind the South's secession from the United States—does not figure into his assessment of the war or the erection of Civil War statues throughout the South in the 1920s. He admits, "It is true that there are white supremacists just as it is true that there are black gangs that commit violence against white people due to their skin color." This racist false equivalence is as far as he is willing to admit that white supremacy exists at all, but as a counterpoint (bizarrely) to interpersonal violence of so-called "black gangs."

Carr seems skeptical of the idea that racism is real. Instead, he reserves his faith in two important narratives: the Lost Cause and civility. The Lost Cause is a massive counter-programming effort begun after the collapse of Recon- struction. This propaganda effectively transformed the story of the South from one of failure to one of gallantry and glory. Textbooks were written to praise Confederate soldiers. Statues of Confederate imagery were raised throughout the South. Margaret Mitchell's *Gone with the Wind* (1936) is the apotheosis of this mythology. Carr firmly believes that the South was a victim of what some euphemistically call the War of Northern Aggression.

In addition to promoting the victimization of white Confederate soldiers— "who fought and died in the south . . . had very little to start with. They (or the bank) owned a few acres of land and did all of the work themselves barely making enough to scrape by"—Carr also believes firmly in civility.[15] He suggests that pro-statue and anti-statue activists should find common ground. He coopts the language and a symbol of diversity and tolerance to do this. Throughout his post, Carr explicitly deploys the notions of civility, tolerance, harmony, and respect to defend the embrace of white supremacist imagery. At various points, he specifically calls for the preservation of the racist statues but using the vocab- ulary of acceptance and even peace: "Stop the fighting over monuments and spend the energy on education so that we can all live in relative harmony"; "I am not asking for anything more than tolerance and respect of others [*sic*] beliefs"; and "All people should be allowed to honor their ancestors and mutual respect needs to be the rule of the day." "Honor" and "respect" are employed often in Carr's defense of the racist monuments. These terms become a way to try to broaden his base of support by using universalizing language with which most people would agree. To gild the lily of his project while simultaneously mak- ing his point as apparent as possible, Carr makes an important addition to his parody of the Make It Right Project's billboard: he places a revised version of the ubiquitous Coexist graphic design in the lower center of the sign. Flanked by Lee and Jackson on either side, Carr's version of Coexist is a pro-Confederate take on the bumper sticker widely adopted by residents in liberal communities throughout the United States.

It is significant that Carr would coopt the Coexist bumper sticker in the ser- vice of his defense of the racist statue. In its most common form, the bum- per sticker is meant to promote tolerance of a variety of religious faiths. Each letter in the word is replaced by an icon representing a world religion. Polish visual artist and poster maker Piotr Młodożeniec entered the original design in a 2000 contest held by the Museum of the Seam, a contemporary art museum

in Jerusalem. The contest theme was "Coexist." Młodożeniec replaced the letter
*C* with the crescent moon associated with Islam; the letter *X* was represented
by the Star of David, an icon of Judaism; the letter *T* was a crucifix representing Christianity. Młodożeniec's design did not win the contest but was featured
on a museum poster that circulated worldwide. His design was quickly taken
without consent by those who wanted to celebrate the message, as did Bono of
the band U2, or profit from it, as did a group of Indiana University students who
built a company that sold products based on Młodożeniec's design.[16] The original Coexist design with three religious icons has undergone many iterations to
become the version most used to express tolerance. In addition to the letters *C*,
*X*, and *T*, the letter *O* is replaced by a peace sign, and the letter *E* is a merging of
symbols for male and female, which represents gender equity and/or LGBTQ
rights. The letter *I* is in standard lowercase, but the dot is replaced by a Pagan/
Wiccan pentacle star. The letter *S* is a yin-yang symbol representing Taoism.

This cluttered version of Młodożeniec's design has been ubiquitous. The
bumper sticker, itself a cooptation of the original, is so pervasive that it has
become a touchstone for controversies regarding liberal and conservative ideologies. Curiously, people across the political spectrum have found something to
critique about it. Those who lean left find the sticker's message of tolerance to be
too shallow, too minimal. As Leah DeCeasare says in her *Huffington Post* piece
"Why Those Coexist Bumper Stickers Bug Me," the sticker "is simply setting the
bar too low."[17] Those on the right, like columnist Anna Githens, are also irritated
by the coexist suggestion. Githens says, "I believe this message, or rather, command, is not only curt and insensitive, but in direct opposition to everything
American."[18] The popularity of this bumper sticker is difficult to underestimate.
The sticker has been so widely adopted that it too has become the subject of
parody, most notably by gun aficionados who replace every letter in the word
*coexist* with a weapon (such as handguns, grenades, AR-15s, or other rifles).

Like many organizations and causes, the Charlottesville Free Press also
revised the Coexist logo. For the most part, Carr uses the popular version as
a focal point for his sign. I believe this was a strategy to connect with Charlottesville motorists and the community at large, which tends to lean liberal. The
Coexist bumper sticker is a common sight on the city's roads and in its parking
lots, especially at churches, Whole Foods, the recycling center, and many coops.
Carr relied on a form of virtue signaling: he could communicate with those
who already had a Coexist sticker on their vehicles. These people believed in the
idea of tolerance enough to put an adhesive decal on their cars. Perhaps Carr's
version was a place to begin persuading them to expand their definition. There
is a significant difference in Carr's Coexist logo, though, one that might prove
challenging for those who support religious or social equality. In Młodożeniec's
design, he replaced the *X* in *coexist* with a Star of David. Most iterations of the

cluttered design retained this symbol as a substitute for the letter $X$. Carr's version did not. Carr removed the Star of David and replaced it with a Confederate flag. The difference is as striking as it is problematic. It is striking because to remove Judaism from the design erases that religion from the place of centrality it had occupied since the design was originally conceived. And it is problematic because it also erases any possible acknowledgment of the clear intention of the neo-Nazis and white supremacists that attacked the community (and chanted slogans like "Jews will not replace us!") on August 11, 2017.

This small revision (changing only one letter) would have drastic consequences for what Coexist should and could signify. If Carr had maintained the typical version of the Coexist bumper sticker, he could have argued that Charlottesville simply needed to practice what it preached. If all these faith traditions can get along with each other (and include symbols of peace and gender equity for good measure), then surely they could extend the same courtesy to two old statues. Instead, Carr made his point less about coexisting as currently demonstrated on the bumper sticker and more about crafting the Confederacy as a valid set of religious or social beliefs on par with Islam or Christianity. Replacing the Star of David with the Stars and Bars is a racist (and anti-Semitic) revision to establish Confederates, neo-Confederates, and the other white supremacists who use that flag as simply belonging to another faith with which to coexist.

It is important to note this strategy for neutralizing the Confederacy. In his statement about his parody billboard, Carr remarks that "I am sure when most people see the billboard, the focus will unfortunately be on the X in the word coexist being a confederate flag. Please allow me to address this first. Fair minded people will also look at the rest of the letters and what they represent. Close minded people will not."[19] It is unclear as to why Carr believes it unfortunate for people to concentrate on the Confederate flag in his billboard. Perhaps he knows that this image is triggering and inflammatory. For this reason, he directs people to ignore it in favor of "the rest of the letters and what they represent."[20] For him, if one is "fair minded," they will understand that the Confederate flag is a neutral object. This has been a pervasive strategy used by Confederate statue and flag defenders in Charlottesville. They refuse to consider the harmful history and persistent effects of these objects in the city's public spaces, despite a city commission of community members declaring this to be true.

This racist parody billboard is one piece of a complex puzzle of racial retrenchment that finds itself embedded throughout Charlottesville. This backward glance is spearheaded by groups like the Monument Fund. It is also sustained by individuals who want to reframe the statues as neutral objects. Central to their vision of historical memory is the notion of "heritage not hate." For them, Confederate nostalgia is not racist. It is not hateful. It is simply an expression of events that occurred in the past. Virginia in particular is amenable to this type of thinking. The state boasts the second highest number of Confederate statues and commemorative plaques in the United States. (Georgia has the most.) Virginia was once the place where the Confederate States of America consolidated its power with Richmond as its capital. That city remains the state's capital and is currently rife with buildings, museums, artifacts, and vast monuments to the Confederacy in its streets and public spaces. In 2019, after her husband landed in hot water for admitting to wearing blackface in medical school, the first lady of Virginia Pamela Northam found herself in a spot of trouble for offering Black students visiting the governor's mansion wads of raw cotton and asking them to imagine themselves to be enslaved. This confluence of past and present, as seen in the troubling undertones of the actions in the governor's mansion and office, reveals the problems that remain in Richmond and the state of Virginia at large in terms of historical and contemporary, if subtle, expressions of white supremacy.

The reverence for the failed white supremacist republic combined with current technologies, laws, and values helps to explain the tenacity with which statue defenders have clung to the past while either coopting the language of liberal progressives or ignoring it altogether. The pro-statue faction wants to eliminate any stigma from the veneration of Confederate symbols. The most efficient route to this goal is to coopt the language of diversity and inclusion. For instance, Carr, who created the parody version of the anti-racist, anti-statue billboard, believes that the Confederate flag is not inherently racist. Instead, he says, "a small minority have hijacked the flag as part of their racist agenda." Carr likely imagines himself wrestling the flag away from those who would use it as racist propaganda as well as those who see the flag itself as part of the white supremacist cause: "Those who have a different reverence for the flag based on their heritage of fighting for state sovereignty should be taken at their word, not be compelled to give up their flag or their monuments at the hands of bullies."[21] It is unclear which "bullies" he's referring to here, but since he's responding to the anti-racist activists who erected the original billboard with his own, it is clear that he is far more comfortable with racist propaganda than anti-racist. Carr continues with a claim that resonates with other forms of Confederate monument defense. He wants Confederate veneration to be included under the larger umbrella of rational contemporary ideas. "Everyone should be allowed to honor their past within the law," Carr observes. "Reasonable people can disagree and still show mutual respect without advocating revolution," a point that is rather ironic for someone who is defending the right to honor a revolt against the United States.

Honoring the past within the confines of the law has long been a challenge for Black people and anti-racist advocates in Virginia. The seeds of white supremacy are deeply planted in the state. From 1619, the arrival of Black people in

Jamestown, to the Enlightenment, to 1817, locating the University of Virginia in a place "nearest to the greatest population of white people," to massive resistance of school desegregation in the 1950s and 1960s, Virginia's towns, cities, counties, and the state as a whole have a robust history of active white supremacy and covert structural racism. Because of this, claims of legal neutrality are often loaded in Virginia and in Charlottesville most particularly. For it is here that theoretically neutral arbiters of the law (like the courts or policing) have been clearly deployed in the promotion and defense of white supremacist causes and logics. These systems in Charlottesville have disproportionately harmed Black people far more than the systems have punished those who promote racist ideas. For example, although Charlottesville's Black population is about 19 percent of the total number of city residents, Black people comprise more than 70 percent of police traffic stops.[22] In terms of white supremacist violence in particular, two young Black men who were victims of the terror attacks on August 12, 2017, found themselves at the mercy of the court after they'd faced that white supremacist violence in the streets. Corey Long was shot at by a white supremacist on camera. He improvised a defense involving a discarded aerosol can and a cigarette lighter. He was eventually convicted for more jail time than the white supremacist that fired his weapon at him. DeAndre Harris was brutally beaten by a group of neo-Nazis and white supremacists in a parking garage less than thirty feet from the police station. Later, one of the white supremacists would harness Virginia's unique legal codes to charge Harris with assault.

There is a strong perception among anti-racists and the Black community more generally that the practice and adjudication of the law are not neutral. For instance, after many years of difficult and rigorous advocacy, a committed group of citizens was finally able to persuade the city to establish a civilian review board to advise, engage, and review the police department. This is one example of favorable developments following the terror attacks of August 2017 that have tried to intervene in the city's structural inequity. In September 2019, heavily armed Virginia state police, accompanied by an armored personnel carrier (a tank), raided a Black family's home in a low-income Charlottesville neighborhood. After handcuffing and detaining family members, no charges or arrests were made, and no explanations were given. Charlottesville's police chief later visited the family to apologize. Such disproportionate contact with law enforcement suggests to many in Charlottesville that the agents of justice are aligned with the racist status quo.

This assumption also holds true for the city judiciary, which plays a significant role in the trial involving the city's Confederate statues. Three months after the deadly terror attack that killed one anti-racist protester and left dozens injured, a Charlottesville judge reinforced the neutrality of the Confederate statues. Judge Robert Moore is presiding over the case that seeks to remove the statues from public space. For him, there is no reasonable contention regarding the racist monuments that attracted the largest white supremacist rally in modern history. In his mind, not only are the statues neutral objects, but they are also innocent objects. In court, Moore clarified his position when he spoke from the bench. As a Charlottesville journalist reported, "'No one had to show up to confront those people,' Moore said, accompanied by groans from those in favor of tearing the statue down. 'The statues didn't cause anything. People did.'"[23] This logic is an iteration of a mode of thinking prevalent in Charlottesville and around the nation. Many of those not actively involved in anti-racist work (be it community organizing, writing, teaching, or other forms of advocacy and reform) hold default positions that maintain the status quo. These points of view include arguments that civility must be preserved at any cost. Typically, these individuals are less susceptible to the harms of anti-black racism. They are often impervious to and/or unaware of the damage of white supremacist violence. As a result, they are more likely to attach themselves to the idea that a statue is just a statue, a pile of chiseled stone, or a harmless work of art. This default position allows fascism to flourish by letting white supremacists and their ideology persist unchecked. This is a form of naturalizing white supremacy.

Naturalizing white supremacy is a disturbing practice in any context. However, to see this unfold from an ostensibly neutral judiciary is additionally problematic. Moore's claim that "no one had to show up to confront those people" blames anti-racist protesters for the deadly rally. Moore does not acknowledge that the white supremacists who arrived in Charlottesville with torches, bats, tear gas, guns, and helmets were drawn to the city for the express purpose of defending the racist statue. Moore's view suggests that fault doesn't lie with the neo-Nazis, white nationalists, and neo-Confederates that attacked community members on August 11, 2017, and marched through the city's downtown streets the following day, killing a counter-protester. He defends the statues and their innocence proclaiming that they "didn't cause anything. People did." This is a similar logic used by gun advocates: guns don't kill people; people kill people. Moore refuses to see that the statues, erected in the 1920s and intended to maintain white supremacy in the public parks in which they were placed, are rooted in a racist history that has lingering effects today. For this reason, many anti-racist activists in Charlottesville have little hope that the case to remove the Confederate statues will end in their favor. The judge is just as much a Confederate statue preservationist as the plaintiffs from the Monument Fund.

The battle of the billboards reveals a deeper, persistent truth about life in Charlottesville. For all the national and international attention given to the city, beyond the glare of the public spotlight that transformed the city into a hashtag, the predominant mode of thinking aligns itself with racism and naturalizing white supremacy. Vigorous debates and discussions continue in this community with brief glimpses of anti-racist progress, but largely, the retrenchment of the status quo prevails.

## NOTES

1. Meg Wagner, "'Blood and Soil': Protesters Chant Nazi Slogan in Charlottesville," CNN, August 12, 2017, https://www.cnn.com/2017/08/12/us/charlottesville-unite-the-right-rally/ index.html.

2. Hawes Spencer and Sheryl Gay Stolberg, "White Nationalists March on University of Virginia," *New York Times*, August 11, 2017, https://www.nytimes.com/2017/08/11/us/white -nationalists-rally-charlottesville-virginia.html.

3. Years of litigation prevented the city of Charlottesville from removing the statues. Pro-Confederate groups invoked an old war memorials law designed to stop Virginia localities from removing Confederate statues once they had been installed. In 2021, the Virginia Supreme Court ruled that the war memorials law did not apply. Charlottesville had the right to remove the statues all along. The Virginia General Assembly has also amended the law to ensure that all other localities in Virginia have the right to remove Confederate statues in their communities as well. With these developments, Charlottesville is currently undergoing a public process to finally remove its statues. See Virginia Bixby, "Dozens Speak in Favor of Removing City Statues: Council Agrees Unanimously," *Daily Progress*, June 8, 2021, https:// dailyprogress.com/news/local/govt-and-politics/dozens-speak-in-favor-of-removing-city -statues-council-agrees-unanimously/article_f0641818-c892-11eb-a29d-f30f60531227 .html; City of Charlottesville v. Payne, 200790 (Virginia Supreme Court 2021), http://www .courts.state.va.us/opinions/opnscvwp/1200790.pdf; and Code of Virginia, "Memorials for War Veterans," Section 15.2–1812, https://law.lis.virginia.gov/vacode/title15.2/chapter18/ section15.2-1812/.

4. Citizen Justice Initiative, University of Virginia, "The Illusion of Progress: Charlottesville's Roots in White Supremacy," 2017, http://illusion.woodson.as.virginia.edu/index.html.

5. Lisa Woolfork, "White Supremacy Is Still Welcomed in Charlottesville," *Huffington Post*, October 9, 2018, https://www.huffpost.com/entry/opinion-charlottesville-arrests-white-suprem acy_n_5bbcaf13e4b028e1fe41b345.

6. *Black Lightning*, season 1, episode 6, "Three Sevens: The Book of Thunder," directed by Benny Boom, written by Charles Holland, aired February 27, 2018, on CW. A review of the episode describes it this way: "Every week, it seems, *Black Lightning* gives me a new reason to love it. This time, it's the fact that they managed to incorporate a story line about the white nationalist protests that rocked Charlottesville, Virginia, last summer. The setting is the same (a politically charged battle between progressive activists and white nationalists over a Confederate statue), the chant is the same (white nationalists shouting 'You will not replace us!'), and so are the details. As TV news anchors report that a woman has been killed by a white nationalist driving his car into the crowd near the statue (as happened to Heather Heyer at last year's Charlottesville protests), Anissa hears someone say that they wish they had the power to stop this madness. Well, Anissa does! She busts out that glam superhero outfit and uses her powers to destroy the statue in one go. Now that's what I like to see from a superhero show: incorporating real-life cultural and political currents, while still using the genre's fantastical elements to act out the kind of catharsis that remains unavailable in the real world." Christian Holub, "*Black Lightning* Recap: 'Three Sevens: The Book of Thunder,'" *Entertainment Weekly*, February 27, 2018, https://ew.com/recap/black-lightning-season-1-episode-6/.

7. See Kali Holloway, "Media Attention Builds around Make It Right Project's Charlottesville VA Billboard Condemning Confederate Monuments," Independent Media Institute, September 4, 2018, https://independentmediainstitute.org/make-it-right-project-puts-up-charlottesville -billboard-supporting-effort-to-take-down-racist-confederate-monuments/. The article includes a photograph of the billboard.

8. Quoted in "Anti-Confederate Statue Billboard Installed on City's Eastern Greenway," NewsRadio WINA, 2018, https://wina.com/news/064460-anti-confederate-statue-billboard -installed-on-citys-eastern-gateway/.

9. Quoted in "Virginia Billboard Calls for Removal of Lee, Jackson Statues," WKYT, September 5, 2018, URL inactive.

10. All comments appear as replies on Nichelle Canteen's sharing of the WVIR NBC29 story on her private Facebook page on September 4, 2018.

11. Nichelle Canteen's sharing of WVIR NBC29 story on her Facebook page.

12. "About Us," Charlottesville Free Press, accessed July 24, 2020, http://charlottesvillefree press.com/about-us/.

13. Mitch Carr, "Why We Did Our Billboard Parody," Charlottesville Free Press, September 28, 2018, http://charlottesvillefreepress.com/why-we-did-our-billboard-parody/.

14. Carr, "Why We Did Our Billboard Parody."

15. Carr, "Why We Did Our Billboard Parody."

16. Phil Edwards, "The Big Fight over Coexist," Vox, June 8, 2016, https://www.vox.com/ 2016/6/8/11867438/coexist-logo-bumper-sticker.

17. Leah DeCeasare, "Why Those Coexist Bumper Stickers Bug Me," *Huffington Post*, October 17, 2014, https://www.huffpost.com/entry/why-the-coexist-bumper-sticker-bugs -me_n_5989772.

18. Anna Githens, "How Coexist Misleads Americans," Renew America, November 20, 2014, http://www.renewamerica.com/columns/githens/141120.

19. Carr, "Why We Did Our Billboard Parody."

20. Curiously, the letters in Carr's version of Coexist are colored by the rainbow flag associated with gay pride. The only exception is the letter *X*, which is the standard red Confederate flag. This is curious because it seems as though, in trying to overload the other symbols with his perception of liberal meaning, he refuses to make the Confederate flag, for all intents and purposes, gay.

21. Carr, "Why We Did Our Billboard Parody."

22. Joshua Eaton, "In Charlottesville, Black Residents 9 Times More Likely to Be Stopped by Police," *Think Progress*, August 23, 2017, https://archive.thinkprogress.org/cville-stop-and -frisk-e884d2504656/.

23. Samantha Baars, "'Trash Bags' Can Stay: Statue Lawsuit Moves Forward," *C-VILLE Weekly*, October 5, 2017, https://www.c-ville.com/statue-lawsuit/#.W1-LwNhKhZo.

## Bibliography

Baars, Samantha. "'Trash Bags' Can Stay: Statue Lawsuit Moves Forward." *C-VILLE Weekly*, October 5, 2017. https://www.c-ville.com/statue-lawsuit/#.W1-LwNhKhZo.

Bixby, Virginia. "Dozens Speak in Favor of Removing City Statues: Council Agrees Unanimously." *Daily Progress*, June 8, 2021. https://dailyprogress.com/news/local/govt-and -politics/dozens-speak-in-favor-of-removing-city-statues-council-agrees-unanimously/ article_f0641818-c892-11eb-a29d-f30f60531227.html.

Boom, Benny, dir. *Black Lightning.* Season 1, episode 6, "Three Sevens: The Book of Thunder." Written by Charles Holland. Aired February 27, 2018, on CW.

Carr, Mitch. "Why We Did Our Billboard Parody." Charlottesville Free Press, September 28, 2018. http://charlottesvillefreepress.com/why-we-did-our-billboard-parody/.

Charlottesville Free Press. "About Us." Accessed July 24, 2020. http://charlottesvillefreepress .com/about-us/.

Citizen Justice Initiative, University of Virginia. "The Illusion of Progress: Charlottesville's Roots in White Supremacy." 2017. http://illusion.woodson.as.virginia.edu/index.html.

City of Charlottesville v. Payne, 200790 (Virginia Supreme Court 2021). http://www.courts .state.va.us/opinions/opnscvwp/1200790.pdf.

Code of Virginia. "Memorials for War Veterans." Section 15.2–1812. https://law.lis.virginia.gov/ vacode/title15.2/chapter18/section15.2-1812/.

DeCeasare, Leah. "Why Those Coexist Bumper Stickers Bug Me." *Huffington Post,* October 17, 2014. https://www.huffpost.com/entry/why-the-coexist-bumper-sticker-bugs-me_n_5989772.

Eaton, Joshua. "In Charlottesville, Black Residents 9 Times More Likely to Be Stopped by Police." *Think Progress,* August 23, 2017. https://archive.thinkprogress.org/cville-stop-and -frisk-e884d2504656/.

Edwards, Phil. "The Big Fight over Coexist." *Vox,* June 8, 2016. https://www.vox.com/2016/6/8/ 11867438/coexist-logo-bumper-sticker.

Githens, Anna. "How Coexist Misleads Americans." Renew America, November 20, 2014. http://www.renewamerica.com/columns/githens/141120.

Holloway, Kali. "Media Attention Builds around Make It Right Project's Charlottesville VA Billboard Condemning Confederate Monuments." Independent Media Institute, September 4, 2018. https://independentmediainstitute.org/make-it-right-project-puts-up -charlottesville-billboard-supporting-effort-to-take-down-racist-confederate-monuments/.

Holub, Christian. "*Black Lightning* Recap: 'Three Sevens: The Book of Thunder.'" *Entertainment Weekly,* February 27, 2018. https://ew.com/recap/black-lightning-season-1-episode-6/.

NewsRadio WINA. "Anti-Confederate Statue Billboard Installed on City's Eastern Greenway." 2018. https://wina.com/news/064460-anti-confederate-statue-billboard-installed-on-citys -eastern-gateway/.

Spencer, Hawes, and Sheryl Gay Stolberg. "White Nationalists March on University of Virginia." *New York Times,* August 11, 2017. https://www.nytimes.com/2017/08/11/us/white -nationalists-rally-charlottesville-virginia.html.

Wagner, Meg. "'Blood and Soil': Protesters Chant Nazi Slogan in Charlottesville." CNN, August 12, 2017. https://www.cnn.com/2017/08/12/us/charlottesville-unite-the-right-rally/index .html.

WKYT. "Virginia Billboard Calls for Removal of Lee, Jackson Statues." September 5, 2018. URL inactive.

Woolfork, Lisa. "White Supremacy Is Still Welcomed in Charlottesville." *Huffington Post,* October 9, 2018. https://www.huffpost.com/entry/opinion-charlottesville-arrests-white -supremacy_n_5bbcaf13e4b028e1fe41b345.

# CHAPTER 10

# TEACHING CONFEDERATE MONUMENTS AS AMERICAN LITERATURE

## —Randi Lynn Tanglen

For twelve years I taught at a small college in a small Texas town that houses the first Confederate monument erected in the state. The 1896 monument in Sherman, Texas, looms large over the majority white community's county courthouse, emphasizing the pedagogical aim of Confederate monuments when they were initially constructed: "The most visible symbols of Confederate culture [were] monuments and flags, both of which were considered important to the edification of southern youth. . . . The majority of monuments erected to the Confederacy were placed in public settings such as courthouse lawns or town squares, where, it was reasoned, they could be observed by children."[1] But the purpose of the monuments was not only to indoctrinate white children to their own racial supremacy but to instill a pedagogy of racial intimidation in Black citizens. It is well documented that most Confederate monuments, like the one in Sherman, were erected decades after the Civil War when southern states were disassembling the rights and freedoms Black Americans had gained during Reconstruction; Confederate soldier monuments personified racial terror by celebrating the Confederate causes of slavery and white supremacy. As essays in this volume detail, well before and certainly in the aftermath of the 2020 Black Lives Matter protests in response to the murder of George Floyd and the 2017 Unite the Right rally in Charlottesville, Virginia, anti-racist activists on campuses such as the University of Virginia and the University of North Carolina at Chapel Hill brought attention to the chilling and pernicious effect campus Confederate monuments have on the educational and lived experiences of Black students and faculty.[2]

In "You Want a Confederate Monument? My Body Is a Confederate Monument," poet and educator Caroline Randall Williams writes, "What is a monument but a standing memory? An artifact to make tangible the truth of the past."[3] Considering the original pedagogical intention of Confederate monuments and the probability that the monument in my Texas community was not going anywhere anytime soon, I started teaching the monument in my US literature courses as a means to critically examine the role of US literature in establishing and maintaining a national culture of white supremacy.[4] In *Playing in the Dark: Whiteness and the Literary Imagination* (1992), Toni Morrison inventories the "black presence" that "hovers in the margins" of early and nineteenth-century US literature: "It is a dark and abiding presence, there for the literary imagination as both a visible and invisible mediating force."[5] In that sense, through racialized erasures, silences, and emphases, US literary history is an "artifact [that] make[s] tangible" the legacies of racism and slavery similarly embodied in the bronze and concrete Confederate soldier statues erected much later on courthouse grounds and college campuses throughout the nation. Much of the canonical and anthologized US literature regularly taught and studied in general education US literature survey and topics courses and even upper division courses for English majors—from Nathaniel Hawthorne to Edgar Allan Poe to Harriet Beecher Stowe—is and can be taught as a type of monument to the Confederate ideology of white supremacy. Likewise, the critiques of earlier Black writers who resisted white supremacy in their writing—such as Harriet Jacobs, William Wells Brown, and Charles W. Chesnutt—are all the more evident and pointed when students study and interact with the concrete evidence of white supremacy in their own backyard.

Historian Donald Yacovone argues that academia has historically promoted "assumptions of white priority, white domination, and white importance" in US educational institutions, from K–12 to college and university levels.[6] He claims that "few teachers and even fewer textbooks connect the nation's slave past to the history of race relations" and that the white professoriate itself has actively "avoided the subject of white supremacy" in our scholarship and especially our teaching and pedagogy. Yacovone's words make me consider the many English education majors in my courses and how the literary studies content and methodological approaches they experience in my classes may be a model for their future Texas public school classrooms and those of surrounding southern states. How can I provide them with the pedagogical questions, models, and content to critically examine white pedagogical supremacy in my own classes and their future classrooms? At institutions such as mine, whose mission promotes "personal growth, justice, community, and service" along with social justice values,[7] I could ask students to consider the role of literature, literary history, and literary criticism in maintaining or resisting assumptions of white racial and cultural supremacy. And as an English professor equipped with the methodological tools of literary and cultural studies, I could provide angles into critically interpreting what Confederate monuments actually meant to Americans in their own day and now in ours.

In this chapter, I will outline a close reading assignment in which students researched the history and reception of the local Confederate monument in Sherman, Texas. This place-based assignment can be built into any number of US literature courses—surveys, topics courses, and seminars—and adapted to any community or campus with a Confederate monument. Even instructors teaching in communities without a Confederate monument could adopt this lens by having students use online resources to research some of the monuments detailed in this volume or a monument highlighted on the Southern Poverty Law Center's interactive, online map.[8] I then explain how I used this assignment in two courses. In one, I used it as a lens for identifying and critically engaging the subtext of white supremacy in the US literature many of my students will one day teach, particularly the popular novel *To Kill a Mockingbird* (1960). In a course for upper-division English majors, the Confederate monument assignment highlighted the present-day relevance and urgency of Chesnutt's critique of Confederate ideology in *The Marrow of Tradition* (1901).

Teaching Confederate monuments as US literature brought about rich class conversations and promoted students' deep thinking about US literature and literary history, but it was not without pedagogical complications. As a white professor teaching at a majority minority campus in the South, teaching the literary politics of white supremacy is fraught with risk. The field of critical pedagogy maintains we "are essentially unfree and inhabit a world rife with contradictions and asymmetry of power and privilege," replicated in institutions of public education, higher learning, and, despite my best efforts, even my own classroom.[9] On a small campus where students take several courses from the same professor, the ability to develop rapport and trust makes it easier to raise issues of racism and white supremacy not only in the literature I teach but in the classroom itself. Over the years, students of color and white students alike have told me this assignment and approach have challenged them to think more critically about literature, systemic racism, and literature's connections to the present day. On the other hand, a handful of Black and white students have criticized me in office hours and end-of-semester evaluations for asking students to critically engage Confederate ideology; they maintain a white professor asking students to read about racial violence and white supremacy is in and of itself a form of racism. While I found such critiques disheartening, I took—and still take—them seriously, and I continue to refine my attempts at practicing an antiracist pedagogy, realizing that "racial competence is a skill that can be learned" and that I am still learning.[10]

## CONFEDERATE MONUMENT RESEARCH AND CLOSE READING ASSIGNMENT

Over the years, I taught several US literature topics courses and seminars that incorporated the history and context of the local Confederate monument as a pedagogical lens. These courses have included classes primarily on nineteenth-century US literature (with an emphasis on protest literature), on social reform literature, and on broad explorations of the themes of literature and social justice. My institution did not offer a US literature survey course in the English department curriculum, but I imagine this assignment and approach could work especially well in a course that emphasizes US literary history. I would usually introduce this assignment about one-third or one-half of the way through the semester, after students had read primary works that introduce the themes of white supremacy such as Frederick Douglass's *Narrative of the Life of Frederick Douglass* (1845) or "What to the Slave Is the Fourth of July?" (1852) and secondary texts already cited in this essay, such as Morrison's *Playing in the Dark* or Yacovone's "Textbook Racism" (2018).[11] By reading these literary and secondary sources before the assignment, students are already familiar with the concept of institutional racism and the role of academia and US literature in upholding such power structures.

I explain to students that we will research the history of the Confederate monument in our community from a social justice perspective to help us think more deeply about the relationship between white supremacy and the literature we are studying. This mini-unit includes research, close reading, and a regular class session at the nearby county courthouse where the monument is located. Most of the students at the residential institution where I taught were not from the local community, and very few of them had been to downtown Sherman, less than a mile from our campus. As much as possible, I connect this assignment to the learning outcomes of the course, such as "students will be able to situate American literature in relevant historical, cultural, and political contexts"; "students will make connections between literary history and the present day and begin to theorize the relationship between literature and historical outcomes"; and "students will be able to comment on the value of collaboration and community in the interpretation of literature and American literary history." I also relate the assignment to the stated mission and social justice values of the college, particularly the college president's Task Force on Diversity and Inclusion. I emphasize the assignment's application of the broader methods of literary studies, such as New Historicism and reception studies, with which most of the English majors and minors in my courses are already familiar. Connecting the assignment to course goals, institutional commitments, and disciplinary approaches helps students see the pedagogical intention and value of an assignment that will take the class away from the direct reading and study of literature for a week or two. Such transparency also makes the students more engaged with and committed to completing the assignment, and I have found most students enjoy the break from typical classroom activities.

After connecting the assignment to course goals, institutional commitments, and disciplinary conventions, I emphasize that the purpose of this assignment is overtly anti-racist, citing the myriad scholars who have established the white supremacist ideology behind the Confederate monuments. Many of these scholars are cited in this article and throughout this volume, and if I were to give this assignment again, I would assign Maria Seger's introduction to this volume along with Cassandra Jackson's essay on the Confederate monument in her childhood community, "Rewriting the Landscape: Black Communities and the Confederate Monuments They Inherited."[12] I make it clear that although it may be appropriate in other classes and disciplines, the purpose of this assignment is not to debate issues such as the "erasure of history" or the heritage politics of the monuments but to help us think more deeply about US literature. I spend a considerable portion of the class period in which I introduce the assignment establishing the pedagogical purpose and parameters of the assignment and the scholarly voices that have already established the racist origins of the monuments in order to anticipate the concerns of students who might worry the assignment will become an opportunity to valorize the Confederacy and the skepticism of students who want to debate the removal of Confederate monuments. I also tell the students that researching the monument will lead us into researching the violent racial history of the community and ask them to come to me outside of class with any concerns regarding the assignment.

Due to time restraints during the semester, I structure the research component of the assignment as guided research. On the course management system, I provide scans of contemporaneous newspaper articles and excerpts from local history books about the monument and its dedication. Depending on the course and its goals, I ask students to read the materials for small-group and class discussion, or I ask them to write a brief summary for a small-group literature circle discussion. I might also lecture on or assign excerpts from books such as Karen L. Cox's *Dixie's Daughters: The United Daughters of the Confederacy and the Preservation of Confederate Culture* (2003) or the Southern Poverty Law Center's "Whose Heritage? Public Symbols of the Confederacy" website to provide a broader national context for understanding the Confederate monument in Sherman; if I were teaching this assignment again, I would assign Brook Thomas's essay in this volume on understanding monuments in the context of the failure of Reconstruction, "Complicating Today's Myth of the Myth of the Lost Cause: The Calhoun Monument, Reconstruction, and Reconciliation."[13]

In their research, the students find that the Confederate monument at the Grayson County Courthouse in Sherman, Texas, erected in 1896, is the oldest Confederate monument in the state and that 93 percent of the nation's Confederate monuments were erected after 1895, and 50 percent after 1903.[14] The bronze statue of a Confederate soldier was purchased with donations raised over six years by the local United Confederate Veterans, with special support from several white women's organizations, including the local chapter of the United Daughters of the Confederacy, Dixie Chapter Number 35.[15] In Texas and all across the South, the United Daughters of the Confederacy raised what today would be millions and millions of dollars to erect the monuments.[16] The Grayson County monument was unveiled on April 21, 1897, San Jacinto Day—the day Texas won its independence from Mexico—a juxtaposition of imperial expansion and the Confederate Lost Cause, both crusades against government and sovereign powers infringing on the rights of the common man or the most holy "right of self-government," as stated in the monument's inscription. For those teaching in the Southwest like I was, Spencer R. Herrera's essay in this volume, "South by Southwest: Confederate and Conquistador Memorials Crossing/ Closing Borders," would provide excellent context on the relationship between Spanish imperial expansion and Confederate ideology.[17] Similar to other monument unveilings throughout the South, Confederate battle flags and American flags were both displayed that day in Sherman, and the program included patriotic hymns; white southerners used the ceremonies "to reclai[m] their identity as patriotic Americans" and to make southern patriotism "synonymous with American patriotism."[18]

An estimated crowd of twenty thousand gathered for the monument's unveiling in Sherman. A local newspaper reported that "Every window was filled with people; the awnings were crowded; the sidewalks were so jammed that passage through them could not be effected, and the streets were literally packing with a surging mass of humanity."[19] The *Dallas News* relayed that "trainloads of Confederate Veterans [from around the state] formed into companies as their trains came in and marched to the courthouse square."[20] At the monument's dedication, after the sheeting fell and the granite and bronze statue was unveiled, the air was filled with gunfire, Rebel yells, and the voices of the United Daughters of the Confederacy singing "In the Sweet Bye and Bye." The events that day, reported in the same article, included speeches by local and state dignitaries and a parade that included "two bands, a fife and drum corps, five camps of United Confederate Veterans, students from five colleges, [and] 1,000 schoolchildren carrying wreaths." My students are always stunned when they learn that among the colleges represented in the bands at the unveiling were students from my institution, Austin College, today known for its "liberal" politics, at

least in contrast with the rest of the county and community—a red county in a
very red state.

After discussing the students' research in class, in the next class session, we
meet at the Confederate monument in downtown Sherman, so students can see
the monument they've researched and *read* the monument in the context of its
location in downtown Sherman. We especially spend time reading the monument's inscription:

> Sacred to the memory of our Confederate dead. True patriots, they fought for
> home and country, for the holy principles of self-government—the only true
> liberty. Their sublime self-sacrifices and unsurpassed valor will teach future
> generations the lesson of high born patriotism, the devotion to duty, of exalted
> courage, of southern chivalry.

Many of my students recall from their medieval literature course these calls
of chivalry as calls to white supremacy: "Read in the context of American medievalism and white supremacy with which it was intertwined, the Sherman monument epitaph imagines Confederate knights possessing 'unsurpassed valor'
and 'exalted courage' whose dedication to protecting white women like the
Daughters of the Confederacy . . . constituted 'southern chivalry' and justified
slavery and racial hierarchy, values entombed when the Confederacy lost the
Civil War."[21] Many of my students are able to see through the rhetoric of chivalry
by linking the inscription to the 1861 words of Alexander Stephens, eventual
vice president of the Confederacy: "Our new government['s] . . . foundations are
laid, its corner-stone rests, upon the great truth that the negro is not equal to
the white man; that slavery subordination to the superior race is his natural and
normal condition."[22] Visiting the monument and seeing the text of its inscription firsthand emphasize the monument's representation of white supremacy
through its connection to the Confederate defenses of slavery and racism.

Students are shocked when they read a more recent inscription on the other
side of the monument indicating the monument had been rededicated in 1996.
Although most students were born well after 1996, the date is still recent enough
to indicate the potency of the monument in the present day; that is, they realize
that the monument is not a relic of the white supremacy of the past but of white
supremacy today. But not all students are surprised by the news of the rededication. By the time we visit the courthouse, many of them had already spent hours
of their own time on Google to learn more about the monument in preparation
for the class visit and had come across news articles about the 1996 rededication. But in their independent research process, they also learn about another
large gathering at the Grayson County Courthouse just thirty-three years after
the original dedication, when another large crowd—a lynch mob—gathered on

the same grounds. Within a few hours, the bronze Confederate soldier would be all that remained of the civic space that he had policed day and night for over three decades.

Because I know students will find information online regarding the 1930 Sherman lynching and race riot as they research the monument, I also provide guided research on the limited information available on this topic.[23] While the murder of George Hughes is known and discussed privately in the community, it has been mostly suppressed; even the article about it on the highly regarded Portal to Texas History refers to the lynching euphemistically as a "riot." On May 5, 1930, a Black farmhand named George Hughes was accused of raping a white woman whose husband, a local farmer, owed him wages. Four days later, on May 9, as jury selection for the trial began, a crowd gathered, filling the courtroom and the courthouse hallways and spilling into the courthouse square. After being advised by the Texas Rangers that the trial could not be held in Sherman "without bloodshed," the judge declared that the venue would be changed. But before a new location could be named, two young white men threw burning cans of gasoline into the courthouse, and a fire quickly spread. Deputies locked Hughes in the courthouse's fireproof vault, and the judge, jury, and law enforcement left the building. Firefighters attempted to control the blaze but were held back by the mob who had cut the water hoses. By late afternoon, "only the walls of the building and the fireproof vault," as well as the Confederate monument, remained on the courthouse grounds. By midnight, the mob had grown to five thousand, and its leaders used explosives to open the vault. Although it is believed that Hughes survived the fire, he did not survive the explosion that crushed the wall of the vault. Black businesses in downtown Sherman were burned, and the Black community literally fled Sherman in the middle of the night. The next day, the governor declared martial law in Sherman until order could be restored. A story about the rioting lynch mob in Sherman made the front page of the *New York Times* the next day. Years later, a local historian would report, almost with approval, that "The names of [those in the mob] who were indicted in the weeks that followed the violence . . . have been carefully excised from the newspaper files in the public library."[24]

I include the information in this article in my classes because it adds an important layer to understanding the white supremacist politics of Confederate monuments and the contexts of literature students will later critically examine in my classes, such as *To Kill a Mockingbird* and *The Marrow of Tradition*. The history of Hughes's lynching helps students see how Confederate monuments allow the antebellum and the present day to "join hands without having to acknowledge each other," resulting in what David W. Blight calls "deflections and evasions, careful remembering and necessary forgetting . . . embittered and irreconcilable versions of experience . . . unresolved legacies" and a fragmented historical memory.[25] The Grayson County monument still stands outside the rebuilt court-house as a prominent feature of the downtown Sherman cityscape, symbolically overlooking the community's government, financial, religious, and social insti-tutions. The monument's 122-year presence at the courthouse is a reminder, as Simon During writes, that "history (or its disappearance) is lived through and in civic spatiality" and of what Michel Foucault would call the disciplinary func-tion of that space "to ensure a certain allocation of people in space . . . as well as the coding of their reciprocal relations."[26] The shadow of the Confederate sen-tinel looms large over the courthouse, those who enter it, and the government functions the courthouse administers, including voting and voter registration across the street and trials at the nearby justice center. Historians note that most Confederate monuments were built when many "states were enacting Jim Crow laws to disenfranchise black Americans."[27] The research and class field trip teach students that the monument, its dedication ceremony, and the later lynching are deeply intertwined events and representative of the community's (and the nation's) ongoing legacies of slavery, racism, and white cultural supremacy.

## READING *TO KILL A MOCKINGBIRD* AS A CONFEDERATE MONUMENT

I recently taught Harper Lee's *To Kill a Mockingbird* through the lens of Confed-erate monuments in a first-year seminar for students from all disciplinary back-grounds, although the class was populated primarily by students planning to major in English with an emphasis in teaching. A critical reexamination of the novel's virtues as a social justice text is timely with the 2015 publication of *Go Set a Watchman*, Lee's earlier version of *To Kill a Mockingbird*, which portrays the older Atticus Finch as an active member of the White Citizens' Council; Joseph Crespino's 2018 account of the relationship between Lee and her father, A. C. Lee, in *Atticus Finch: The Biography*; and Aaron Sorkin's critically acclaimed 2019 Broadway adaptation of the novel.

Most of my students were taught the novel in junior high or high school as a social justice and anti-racist text with an emphasis on Atticus's maxim that "You never really understand a person until you consider things from his point of view . . . until you climb into his skin and walk around in it."[28] Many students in the seminar said *To Kill a Mockingbird* was their favorite book, yet most of them seemed to understand there were themes their teachers would not or pos-sibly were not allowed to address in class, especially related to the rape trial of Tom Robinson and the testimony of Mayella Ewell. Other students, like Scout herself, were confused by the novel's commentary (or lack of commentary) on racialized themes, particularly references to white fears of racial miscegenation, an issue rarely addressed when the novel is taught to younger readers.

Early in our discussions, I ask the class, "Does *To Kill a Mockingbird* deserve its reputation as a social justice and anti-racist novel?" It does not take long for students to notice the sidelined role of Calpurnia and the novel's use of Black characters such as Calpurnia, Zeebo, Reverend Sykes, and Tom to advance plots related to white characters and their concerns. After we finish reading the novel, we research and visit the local Confederate monument at the Grayson County Courthouse and learn about its history and the related lynching of Hughes.

When asked if the novel could be read as a Confederate monument, students first focus on the Confederate "Easter eggs" in *To Kill a Mockingbird*, such as the brief reference to slavery in the origin story of the Finch family in chapter 1, the Confederate pistol Mrs. Dubose supposedly keeps hidden under her shawl, and the school band's performance of "Dixie" during the Maycomb County pageant in chapter 28. But students soon turn to the chapter 15 scene with the lynch mob at the jail as evidence of the novel's unspoken subtext of white supremacy. Most students admit that the first time they read the novel, they did not comprehend the intentions of the mob that threatens Atticus and the children as he guards Tom at the Maycomb jail. Along with learning about the lynching event in Sherman, students also research the history of lynching in the US South and in our community using online resources from the Equal Justice Initiative in Montgomery, Alabama. With this missing context, the significance of that scene and what is at stake for Tom, Calpurnia, and the Black citizens of Maycomb becomes clearer to students originally focused on Scout, Jem, and Atticus's story.

We then look at the earlier conversation between Jem and Atticus after a group of white men visit the Finch family home to warn and threaten Atticus. Jem asks, "They were after you, weren't they?," and Atticus explains, "No son, those were our friends."[29] He also tells Jem that "Way back about nineteen-twenty there was a Klan, but it was a political organization more than anything."[30] Students research the history of the Ku Klux Klan (KKK) in their literature circle groups and find the KKK was indeed a political organization, one responsible for racial violence and terrorism in many southern communities and today identified as a hate group. When Scout asks why her schoolmate's father was in the mob at the jail, Atticus explains: "Mr. Cunningham's basically a good man. . . . he just has his blind spots along with the rest of us."[31] Students instantly identify these words as a version of the insidious "very fine people on both sides" rhetoric that circulated after the 2017 Unite the Right rally in Charlottesville.

At some point in the discussion, I ask students if Atticus seems to support the actual political and social equality of African Americans—or rather, the fairness of the legal and justice systems. According to Atticus in his closing argument, the phrase "all men are created equal" is taken out of context by "Yankee" educators since difference based on class, experience, and character (and by extension, race) should be accepted as natural; this difference and inequality cannot be leveled through institutions such as public schools or the federal government. But, according to Atticus, "In this country our courts are the great levelers, and in our courts all men are created equal."[32] That is, although racial difference and inequality exist in the real world (and perhaps even should), in the courts, at least, guilt and innocence know no racial difference and will certainly come to light. Students eventually, and in some cases very reluctantly, recognize that Atticus is no social justice warrior but rather a genteel mouthpiece for white supremacy.

Although she would not have put it that way, perhaps Lee, on some level, realized this too. The character of Atticus was based on her own father, Alabama newspaperman A. C. Lee. The older Scout, Jean Louise in *Go Set a Watchman*, confronts the aging Atticus: "I remember that rape case you defended, but I missed the point. You love justice, all right. Abstract justice written down item by item like a neat brief. [That case] interfered with your orderly mind, and you had to work order out of disorder."[33] As Joseph Crespino points out, "We know now not only that the Atticus of *Mockingbird* was always too good to be true, but that Harper Lee knew it as well."[34] If students are disillusioned by their hero's racial politics, they are at least comforted by knowing that Lee probably was too.

I admit that asking my students "Is *To Kill a Mockingbird* a Confederate monument?" is a type of provocation, an intellectual exercise in critical rereading to hone our class discussions of literature, race, and social justice. Although I see the pedagogical benefit of framing the novel as a Confederate monument, I do wonder if this approach is a bit heavy-handed. But last semester, through the Southern Poverty Law Center, students found the spread of Confederate monuments spiked twice after the Civil War. Not surprisingly, the first time was during the Jim Crow era, when southern states began enacting laws to disenfranchise Black Americans. The second spike in Confederate monuments began in the late 1950s, with the advances of the early civil rights movement.[35] The best-selling *To Kill a Mockingbird* was published in 1960 and won the Pulitzer Prize in 1961, just as another round of Confederate monuments was being erected and rededicated in the South.

Teaching *To Kill a Mockingbird* as a Confederate monument provided students with an opportunity to critically reread and contend with the assumptions of white supremacy in this American classic, in their own lived experiences, and in the present-day public and political sphere. Students ended up liking these discussions of *To Kill a Mockingbird*, even if it meant experiencing the cognitive dissonance of censuring their favorite book. That said, I'm not sure if I would teach *To Kill a Mockingbird* again. Roxane Gay is critical of the novel: "As for the story, I can take it or leave it. Perhaps I am ambivalent because I am black. I am not the target audience. I don't need to read about a young white girl understanding the perniciousness of racism to actually understand the perniciousness of racism. I have ample firsthand experience."[36]

In this same first-year seminar, we also read Toni Morrison's *The Bluest Eye* (1970), a novel set in the same time period as *To Kill a Mockingbird*, with the precocious Black female narrator Claudia MacTeer as the counterpart to the white Scout.[37] If I'd had time, I also would have included James Baldwin's short story "Going to Meet the Man" (1965), about a young white boy who witnesses a lynching and its formative impact on his psychological development into a vengeful, racist sheriff.[38] This approach to reading a classic social justice novel as a Confederate monument would also work with other texts often taught in US literature courses; certainly Harriet Beecher Stowe's *Uncle Tom's Cabin* (1852) and even eugenicist Charlotte Perkins Gilman's "The Yellow Wall-Paper" (1892) could generate unexpected but rich analyses of literature that perpetuated and still perpetuates the ideologies of white supremacy.[39]

## "THE PRESENT IS WOVEN WITH THE PAST": CONFEDERATE MONUMENTS IN *THE MARROW OF TRADITION*

Understanding the history and politics of the Confederate monument in Sherman also helps students more easily make the connection to how local racial politics serve as a microcosm for the national, as Chesnutt does in his 1901 novel, *The Marrow of Tradition*. Basing his novel on the 1898 race riots in Wilmington, North Carolina, and the 1900 Robert Charles riots in New Orleans, Chesnutt "creat[es] a cast of characters whose past and present histories tied them directly to the social upheavals" of the aftermath of the Civil War and failure of Reconstruction.[40] Chesnutt wrote with the aim of exposing "the unjust spirit of caste which is so insidious as to pervade a whole nation, and so powerful as to subject a whole race and all connected with it to scorn and social ostracism."[41] In other words, he wrote with the social responsibility of unveiling the assumptions of white cultural and racial supremacy. By the time my students read *The Marrow of Tradition* in my literature and social reform class, they are already familiar with historian Jane Dailey's analysis that "Most of the people who were involved in erecting [Confederate] monuments were not necessarily erecting a monument to the past, but were rather erecting them toward a white supremacist future."[42]

Indeed, teaching Chesnutt's novel through the lens of the local Confederate monument allows students to fully appreciate his precept in the novel of "how inseparably the present is woven with the past, how certainly the future will be but the outcome of the present" and to more amply realize the insidious implications of white supremacy in the present day.[43] I have also taught novels such as Frances Ellen Watkins Harper's *Iola Leroy, or Shadows Uplifted* (1892), Pauline Hopkins's *Contending Forces* (1900), or William Wells Brown's *Clotel*

(1853) through the lens of the Confederate monument assignment.[44] These novels feature the experiences of Black women living with the legacies of slavery
and Jim Crow, and classroom discussion is further enriched by Williams's "You
Want a Confederate Monument? My Body is a Confederate Monument" and
Woolfork's "Thomas Jefferson Is the R. Kelly of the American Enlightenment."[45]

The students' study and close reading of the Confederate monument in Sherman make the Confederate culture of the fictitious Wellington in Chesnutt's
novel seem more significant to the novel's plot and more perniciously tied to
its portrayal of a culture of white supremacy. The three instigators of the race
riot—General Belmont, Major Carteret, and Captain McBane—are all Confederate veterans, and Aunt Polly Ochiltree keeps her deceased husband's Confederate pistol hidden among her treasures. Major Carteret's emphasis on family
honor and his wife's insistence on protecting the institution of marriage and her
family legacy are part of the Confederate culture of chivalry and white racial
purity. Because of the students' close reading of the Confederate monument
in Sherman, they more readily comment upon the relationship between Confederate ideology and the assumptions of white supremacy in *The Marrow of
Tradition*, such as when Carteret writes that he's "taking for his theme the unfitness of the negro to participate in government,—an unfitness due to his limited
education, his lack of experience, his criminal tendencies, and more especially
to his hopeless mental and physical inferiority to the white race"; or when we
learn that Carteret "believed in the divine right of white men and gentlemen,
as his ancestors had believed in and died for the divine right of kings"; and
when Belmont raises a toast to "drink with you to 'White Supremacy'!"[46] After
students' research and reading of the local Confederate monument, these words
aren't regarded as the idiosyncratic racist musing of white characters, but as a
reflection of the Confederate white supremacy these characters espouse. The
racist subtext of the inscription on the Grayson County Confederate monument comes into sharp focus when applied to the world of Wellington: "Their
sublime self-sacrifices and unsurpassed valor will teach future generations the
lesson of high born patriotism, the devotion to duty, of exalted courage, of
southern chivalry."

To that end, students also see more directly the relationship among Confederate ideology, the assumptions of white supremacy, and white racial violence. The southern ideology of chivalry (and its attendant defense of white
womanhood) inscribed on the Grayson County monument was the justification for racial violence in Sherman and also in the novel.[47] In the aftermath
of his relative Polly's murder, Carteret says, "It is a murderous and fatal assault
upon a woman of our race,—upon our race in the person of its womanhood,
its crown and flower. If such crimes are not punished with swift and terrible
directness, the whole white womanhood of the South is in danger."[48] Dr. Miller,

a mixed-race doctor, warns a Black citizen that "You'll get into a quarrel with a white man, and at the end of it there'll be a lynching, or a funeral."[49] And in the aftermath of the Wellington race riots, Miller "foresaw the hatreds to which this day would give birth; the long years of constraint and distrust which would still further widen the breach between two peoples whom fate had thrown together in one community."[50] Students note the parallels between the Wilmington race riots, the Sherman lynching and riots, and the 1921 race massacre in nearby Tulsa, which many students end up researching on their own. In all three cases, a false accusation of rape by a white woman led to the devastation of the communities' burgeoning Black business district and middle class.

The relationship between the past and present Chesnutt aims to portray in the novel is more apparent in class discussions and writing assignments because students have researched the Grayson County Confederate monument and the murder of Hughes. This leads to students' raising the issue of present-day racial violence. In their other classes and liberal arts seminars, many students have already read *The New Jim Crow* (2010) and are able to enrich class discussions with Michelle Alexander's connections among slavery, Jim Crow, and police brutality today.[51] The last time I taught Chesnutt's novel—over Zoom during the pandemic—the students, in online responses and Zoom chat boxes, brought up the murder of Botham Jean by an off-duty white female police officer in nearby Dallas and the rhetoric of white womanhood brought up around her highly publicized trial. Although I no longer teach in Sherman, teaching Black authors' critiques of white supremacy through the lens of Confederate monuments has only become more relevant due to paradigm shifts in national conversations about racism and police violence with the 2020 murders of George Floyd, Breonna Taylor, and Ahmaud Arbery. Teaching local Confederate monuments as American literature makes the study of US literature and literary history more relevant to addressing the culture of white supremacy that students read in the headlines and experience firsthand in the community and, sadly, even in our classrooms and institutions of higher learning in general.

In his analysis of nineteenth-century public monuments, Kirk Savage writes, "Public monuments are the most conservative of commemorative forms precisely because they are meant to last, unchanged, forever. While other things come and go, are lost and forgotten, the monument is supposed to remain a fixed point, stabilizing for the physical and the cognitive landscape. Monuments attempt to mold a landscape of collective memory, to conserve what is worth remembering and discard the rest."[52] At the end of each semester, I share this quote with my students and ask them what the Grayson County Confederate monument attempts to conserve and discard. They realize, of course, the monument attempts to conserve the patriotism and southern values of the community's Confederate veterans and their descendants. After reading US literature as Confederate monuments, students also identify the monument's subtext of hiding a legacy of slavery, Jim Crow, and racial terror. The monument discards the Black American experience and history in Grayson County, the community's history of racial terror, and the life and memory of Hughes. I ask them then what US literary history, understood as a Confederate monument, similarly conserves and discards.

As a final reflection essay in all of my courses, I always ask students what they will remember from the class five, ten, or twenty years from now. They all say they will remember what they learned from visiting the Grayson County Confederate monument and how it helped them see the relationship between US literary history and the present day. Students often mention that they realized how little they were taught about US slavery as students in Texas public high schools. But they are eager to take what they have learned into the world. One student wrote, "I found comfort in the knowledge that the problems of today are not of a completely unique nature, they are rather further manifestations of past issues. For example, issues concerning racism and prejudice against Black people stems from the previous history of slavery and the Jim Crow era. This course has truly shown me how important looking at past literature and authors is in beginning the conversation toward finding effective solutions to current issues." Another student, an English education major, wrote: "I'm determined to try and find some way to teach this material to my future students. I probably won't hit them with everything we covered in class, but I want to at least make them aware of how racism exists in the modern world and help prepare them to face it. At least that way I can maybe help the next generation solve the issues we face today."

When I read the words of my students, I am reminded of one of the key assumptions of critical pedagogy—that while educational processes and institutions replicate hierarchies, inequalities, and injustices, including racial prejudice, racism, and the assumptions of white supremacy, the educational experience can also transform individuals so that they, in turn, can transform the world. As bell hooks reminds us, education "is a vocation rooted in hopefulness."[53] Yet, in this era of renewed racial inequality and regalvanized white nationalism, I also think of the last line from *The Marrow of Tradition*: "There's time enough, but none to spare."[54]

## NOTES

1. Karen L. Cox, *Dixie's Daughters: The United Daughters of the Confederacy and the Preservation of Confederate Culture* (Gainesville: University Press of Florida, 2003), 3, 2.

2. See, in this volume, Danielle Christmas, "Weaponizing Silent Sam: Heritage Politics and *The Third Revolution*," in *Reading Confederate Monuments*, ed. Maria Seger (Jackson:

University Press of Mississippi, 2022), 99–117; and Lisa Woolfork, "Battle of the Billboards: White Supremacy and Memorial Culture in #Charlottesville," in Seger, *Reading Confederate Monuments*, 213–29.

3. Caroline Randall Williams, "You Want a Confederate Monument? My Body Is a Confederate Monument," *New York Times*, June 26, 2020, https://www.nytimes.com/2020/06/26/opinion/confederate-monuments-racism.html.

4. Local activists have been working to have the Grayson County Confederate monument removed. See "Protesters Clash over Confederate Monument Outside Grayson Co. Courthouse," News12, last modified June 18, 2020, https://www.kxii.com/2020/06/19/protesters-respond-to-petitions-remove-grayson-countys-confederate-statue-or-leave-it-be/; and "Sherman Attorney Calls for Removal of Confederate Statue from Courthouse Lawn," *Sherman Herald Democrat*, June 16, 2020, https://www.heralddemocrat.com/news/20200616/sherman-attorney-calls-for-removal-of-confederate-statue-from-courthouse-lawn.

5. Toni Morrison, *Playing in the Dark: Whiteness and the Literary Imagination* (New York: Vintage, 1993), 46.

6. Donald Yacovone, "Textbook Racism: How Scholars Sustained White Supremacy," *Chronicle Review*, April 8, 2018, https://www.chronicle.com/article/How-Scholars-Sustained-White/243053.

7. "Mission," Austin College, accessed September 5, 2020, https://www.austincollege.edu/about/fast-facts/mission/.

8. "Whose Heritage? Public Symbols of the Confederacy," Southern Poverty Law Center, last modified August 4, 2020, https://www.splcenter.org/data-projects/whose-heritage.

9. Peter McLaren, "Critical Pedagogy: A Look at the Major Concepts," in *The Critical Pedagogy Reader*, ed. Antonia Darder, Marta P. Baltodano, and Rodolfo D. Torres (New York: Routledge, 2009), 61.

10. Ali Michael goes on to explain: "I define racial competence as having the skills and confidence to engage in healthy cross-racial relationships; to recognize and honor difference without judgement; to notice and analyze racial dynamics as they occur; to confront racism at the individual, group, and systems level . . . to ask for feedback about one's ideas and work; and to raise race questions about oneself and one's practice." Michael, *Raising Race Questions: Whiteness & Inquiry in Education* (New York: Teachers College Press, 2015), 3, 5.

11. Frederick Douglass, *Narrative of the Life of Frederick Douglass: An American Slave, Written by Himself*, in *Narrative of the Life of Frederick Douglass: An American Slave, Written by Himself with Related Documents*, edited by David W. Blight (Boston: Bedford/St. Martin's, 2003), 31–125; Frederick Douglass, "What to the Slave Is the Fourth of July?," in Blight, *Narrative*, 146–71; Morrison, *Playing in the Dark*; and Yacovone, "Textbook Racism."

12. Maria Seger, "Introduction: How and Why to Read Confederate Monuments" in Seger, *Reading Confederate Monuments*, 3–18; and Cassandra Jackson, "Rewriting the Landscape: Black Communities and the Confederate Monuments They Inherited," in Seger, *Reading Confederate Monuments*, 191–212.

13. Cox, *Dixie's Daughters*; Southern Poverty Law Center, "Whose Heritage?"; and Brook Thomas, "Complicating Today's Myth of the Myth of the Lost Cause: The Calhoun Monument, Reconstruction, and Reconciliation," in Seger, *Reading Confederate Monuments*, 21–42.

14. The history of the Grayson County Confederate monument and the murder of George Hughes comes from Graham Landrum, *Grayson County: An Illustrated History of Grayson County, Texas* (Fort Worth: University Supply & Equipment Company, 1960); and Cox, *Dixie's Daughters*, 50.

15. Landrum, *Grayson County*, 90.

16. Karen L. Cox, "Roots of a Bitter Legacy: Determined Women Were the Driving Force behind Confederate Monuments," HistoryNet, January 2018, https://www.historynet.com/bitter-legacy-women-confederate-monuments.htm.

17. Spencer R. Herrera, "South by Southwest: Confederate and Conquistador Memorials Crossing/Closing Borders," in Seger, *Reading Confederate Monuments*, 72–95.

18. Cox, *Dixie's Daughters*, 65.

19. *Denison Sunday Gazetteer* quoted in Carol Morris Little, *A Comprehensive Guide to Outdoor Sculpture in Texas* (Austin: University of Texas Press, 1996), 413.

20. Quoted in Landrum, *Grayson County*, 91.

21. Thomas Blake, "Getting Medieval Post-Charlottesville: Medievalism and the Alt-Right," in *Far-Right Revisionism and the End of History: Alt/Histories*, ed. Louie Dean Valencia-García (New York: Routledge, 2020), 183.

22. Alexander Stephens, "'Cornerstone' Speech," Teaching Tolerance, accessed September 5, 2020, https://www.tolerance.org/classroom-resources/texts/hard-history/cornerstone-speech.

23. The sources I provide students are Landrum, *Grayson County*, and Nolan Thomas, "The Sherman Riot of 1930," Texas State Historical Association, accessed September 5, 2020, https://tshaonline.org/handbook/online/articles/jcso6.

24. Landrum, *Grayson County*, 94.

25. David W. Blight, *Race and Reunion: The Civil War in American Memory* (Cambridge, MA: Harvard University Press, 2001), 5.

26. Simon During, "Editor's Introduction," in *The Cultural Studies Reader*, ed. Simon During (New York: Routledge, 1999), 146; and Michel Foucault, "Space, Power, and Knowledge," in During, *Cultural Studies Reader*, 140.

27. Miles Park, "Confederate Statues Were Built to Further a 'White Supremacist Future,'" National Public Radio, August 20, 2017, https://www.npr.org/2017/08/20/544266880/confederate-statues-were-built-to-further-a-white-supremacist-future.

28. Harper Lee, *To Kill a Mockingbird* (New York: Harper Perennial, 2002), 33.

29. Lee, *To Kill a Mockingbird*, 166.

30. Lee, *To Kill a Mockingbird*, 167.

31. Lee, *To Kill a Mockingbird*, 179.

32. Lee, *To Kill a Mockingbird*, 233.

33. Harper Lee, *Go Set a Watchman* (New York: HarperCollins, 2015), 248.

34. Joseph Crespino, *Atticus Finch: The Biography* (New York: Basic Books, 2018), 173.

35. Southern Poverty Law Center, "Whose Heritage?"

36. Roxane Gay, "Lots of People Love *To Kill a Mockingbird*. Roxane Gay Isn't One of Them," *New York Times*, June 18, 2018, https://www.nytimes.com/2018/06/18/books/review/tom-santopietro-why-to-kill-a-mockingbird-matters.html.

37. Toni Morrison, *The Bluest Eye* (New York: Vintage, 1970).

38. James Baldwin, *Going to Meet the Man* (New York: Dial Press, 1965).

39. Harriet Beecher Stowe, *Uncle Tom's Cabin, or, Life among the Lowly* (New York: Penguin Classics, 1981); and Charlotte Perkins Gilman, "The Yellow Wall-Paper," in *The Yellow Wall-Paper, Herland, and Selected Writings* (New York: Penguin Classics, 2009), 179–96.

40. Nancy Bentley and Sandra Gunning, "Introduction: Cultural and Historical Background," in *The Marrow of Tradition*, by Charles W. Chesnutt, ed. Nancy Bentley and Sandra Gunning (Boston: Bedford/St. Martin's, 2002), 7. See also Gordon Fraser, "Circulation and Resistance: *The Marrow of Tradition* and the 1900 New Orleans Race Riot," *J19* 1, no. 2 (2013): 363–85.

41. Quoted in Bentley and Gunning, "Introduction," 3.

42. Quoted in Park, "Confederate Statues."

43. Charles W. Chesnutt, *The Marrow of Tradition* (Boston: Bedford/St. Martin's, 1999), 114.

44. Francis Ellen Watkins Harper, *Iola Leroy, or Shadows Uplifted* (Boston: Beacon Press, 1999); Pauline Hopkins, *Contending Forces* (New York: Oxford University Press, 1991); and William Wells Brown, *Clotel, or The President's Daughter* (Boston: Bedford/St. Martin's, 2000).

45. Williams, "You Want a Confederate Monument?"; and Lisa Woolfork, "Thomas Jefferson Is the R. Kelly of the American Enlightenment," *Washington Post*, February 15, 2019, https://www.washingtonpost.com/outlook/2019/02/15/thomas-jefferson-is-r-kelly-american-enlightenment/.

46. Chesnutt, *Marrow of Tradition*, 64, 67.

47. Maria Seger highlights the relationship among chivalry, white womanhood, and white supremacy in her essay in this volume, "Redeeming White Women in/through Lost Cause Films," in Seger, *Reading Confederate Monuments*, 142–65.

48. Chesnutt, *Marrow of Tradition*, 156.

49. Chesnutt, *Marrow of Tradition*, 112.

50. Chesnutt, *Marrow of Tradition*, 223.

51. Michelle Alexander, *The New Jim Crow: Mass Incarceration in the Age of Colorblindness* (New York: New Press, 2010).

52. Kirk Savage, *Standing Soldiers, Kneeling Slaves: Race, War, and Monument in Nineteenth-Century America* (Princeton, NJ: Princeton University Press, 1997), 4.

53. bell hooks, *Teaching Community: A Pedagogy of Hope* (New York: Routledge, 2003), iv.

54. Chesnutt, *Marrow of Tradition*, 246.

# Bibliography

Alexander, Michelle. *The New Jim Crow: Mass Incarceration in the Age of Colorblindness*. New York: New Press, 2010.

Austin College. "Mission." Accessed September 5, 2020. https://www.austincollege.edu/about/fast-facts/mission/.

Baldwin, James. *Going to Meet the Man*. New York: Dial Press, 1965.

Bentley, Nancy, and Sandra Gunning. "Introduction: Cultural and Historical Background." In *The Marrow of Tradition*, by Charles W. Chesnutt, edited by Nancy Bentley and Sandra Gunning, 3–26. Boston: Bedford/St. Martin's, 2002.

Blake, Thomas. "Getting Medieval Post-Charlottesville: Medievalism and the Alt-Right." In *Far-Right Revisionism and the End of History: Alt/Histories*, edited by Louie Dean Valencia-García, 179–97. New York: Routledge, 2020.

Blight, David W. *Race and Reunion: The Civil War in American Memory*. Cambridge, MA: Harvard University Press, 2001.

Brown, William Wells. *Clotel, or The President's Daughter*. Boston: Bedford/St. Martin's, 2000.

Chesnutt, Charles W. *The Marrow of Tradition*. Boston: Bedford/St. Martin's, 1999.

Christmas, Danielle. "Weaponizing Silent Sam: Heritage Politics and *The Third Revolution*." In *Reading Confederate Monuments*, edited by Maria Seger. Jackson: University Press of Mississippi, 2022. 99–117.

Cox, Karen L. *Dixie's Daughters: The United Daughters of the Confederacy and the Preservation of Confederate Culture*. Gainesville: University Press of Florida, 2003.

Cox, Karen L. "Roots of a Bitter Legacy: Determined Women Were the Driving Force Behind Confederate Monuments." HistoryNet, January 2018. https://www.historynet.com/bitter-legacy-women-confederate-monuments.htm.

Crespino, Joseph. *Atticus Finch: The Biography*. New York: Basic Books, 2018.

Dailey, Jane. "Baltimore's Confederate Monument Was Never about 'History and Culture.'" *Huffington Post*, August 17, 2017. https://www.huffingtonpost.com/entry/confederate -monuments-history-trump-baltimore_us_5995a3a6e4bod0d2cc84c952.

Douglass, Frederick. *Narrative of the Life of Frederick Douglass: An American Slave, Written by Himself*. In *Narrative of the Life of Frederick Douglass: An American Slave, Written by Himself with Related Documents*, edited by David W. Blight, 31–125. Boston: Bedford/St. Martin's, 2003.

Douglass, Frederick. "What to the Slave Is the Fourth of July?" In *Narrative of the Life of Frederick Douglass: An American Slave, Written by Himself with Related Documents*, edited by David W. Blight, 146–71. Boston: Bedford/St. Martin's, 2003.

During, Simon. "Editor's Introduction." In *The Cultural Studies Reader*, edited by Simon During, 146. New York: Routledge, 1999.

Foucault, Michel. "Space, Power, and Knowledge." In *The Cultural Studies Reader*, edited by Simon During, 134–41. New York: Routledge, 1999.

Fraser, Gordon. "Circulation and Resistance: *The Marrow of Tradition* and the 1900 New Orleans Race Riot." *J19* 1, no. 2 (2013): 363–85.

Gay, Roxane. "Lots of People Love *To Kill a Mockingbird*. Roxane Gay Isn't One of Them." *New York Times*, June 18, 2018. https://www.nytimes.com/2018/06/18/books/review/tom -santopietro-why-to-kill-a-mockingbird-matters.html.

Gilman, Charlotte Perkins. "The Yellow Wall-Paper." In *The Yellow Wall-Paper, Herland, and Selected Writings*, 179–96. New York: Penguin Classics, 2009.

Harper, Francis Ellen Watkins. *Iola LeRoy, or Shadows Uplifted*. Boston: Beacon Press, 1999.

Herrera, Spencer R. "South by Southwest: Confederate and Conquistador Memorials Crossing/ Closing Borders." In *Reading Confederate Monuments*, edited by Maria Seger. Jackson: University Press of Mississippi, 2022. 72–95.

hooks, bell. *Teaching Community: A Pedagogy of Hope*. New York: Routledge, 2003.

Hopkins, Pauline. *Contending Forces*. New York: Oxford University Press, 1991.

Jackson, Cassandra. "Rewriting the Landscape: Black Communities and the Confederate Monuments They Inherited." In *Reading Confederate Monuments*, edited by Maria Seger. Jackson: University Press of Mississippi, 2022. 191–212.

Landrum, Graham. *Grayson County: An Illustrated History of Grayson County, Texas*. Fort Worth: University Supply & Equipment Company, 1960.

Lee, Harper. *Go Set a Watchman*. New York: Harper Collins, 2015.

Lee, Harper. *To Kill a Mockingbird*. New York: Harper Perennial, 2002.

Little, Carol Morris. *A Comprehensive Guide to Outdoor Sculpture in Texas*. Austin: University of Texas Press, 1996.

McLaren, Peter. "Critical Pedagogy: A Look at the Major Concepts." In *The Critical Pedagogy Reader*, edited by Antonia Darder, Marta P. Baltodano, and Rodolfo D. Torres, 61–83. New York: Routledge, 2009.

Michael, Ali. *Raising Race Questions: Whiteness & Inquiry in Education*. New York: Teachers College Press, 2015.

Morrison, Toni. *The Bluest Eye*. New York: Vintage, 1970.

Morrison, Toni. *Playing in the Dark: Whiteness and the Literary Imagination*. New York: Vintage, 1993.

News12. "Protesters Clash over Confederate Monument Outside Grayson Co. Courthouse." Last modified June 18, 2020. https://www.kxii.com/2020/06/19/protesters-respond-to -petitions-remove-grayson-countys-confederate-statue-or-leave-it-be/.

Park, Miles. "Confederate Statues Were Built to Further a 'White Supremacist Future.'" National Public Radio, August 20, 2017. https://www.npr.org/2017/08/20/544266880/ confederate-statues-were-built-to-further-a-white-supremacist-future.

Savage, Kirk. *Standing Soldiers, Kneeling Slaves: Race, War, and Monument in Nineteenth-Century America.* Princeton, NJ: Princeton University Press, 1997.

Seger, Maria. "Introduction: How and Why to Read Confederate Monuments" in *Reading Confederate Monuments*, edited by Maria Seger. Jackson: University Press of Mississippi, 2022. 3–18.

Seger, Maria. "Redeeming White Women in/through Lost Cause Films." In *Reading Confederate Monuments*, edited by Maria Seger. Jackson: University Press of Mississippi, 2022. 142–65.

"Sherman Attorney Calls for Removal of Confederate Statue from Courthouse Lawn." *Sherman Herald Democrat*, June 16, 2020. https://www.heralddemocrat.com/news/20200616/ sherman-attorney-calls-for-removal-of-confederate-statue-from-courthouse-lawn.

Southern Poverty Law Center. "Whose Heritage? Public Symbols of the Confederacy." Last modified August 4, 2020. https://www.splcenter.org/data-projects/whose-heritage.

Stephens, Alexander. "'Cornerstone' Speech." *Teaching Tolerance*. Accessed September 5, 2020. https://www.tolerance.org/classroom-resources/texts/hard-history/cornerstone-speech.

Stowe, Harriet Beecher. *Uncle Tom's Cabin, or, Life among the Lowly.* New York: Penguin Classics, 1981.

Thomas, Brook. "Complicating Today's Myth of the Myth of the Lost Cause: The Calhoun Monument, Reconstruction, and Reconciliation." In *Reading Confederate Monuments*, edited by Maria Seger. Jackson: University Press of Mississippi, 2022. 21–42.

Thomas, Nolan. "The Sherman Riot of 1930." Texas State Historical Association. Accessed September 5, 2020. https://tshaonline.org/handbook/online/articles/jcs06.

Williams, Caroline Randall. "You Want a Confederate Monument? My Body Is a Confederate Monument." *New York Times*, June 26, 2020. https://www.nytimes.com/2020/06/26/ opinion/confederate-monuments-racism.html.

Woolfork, Lisa. "Battle of the Billboards: White Supremacy and Memorial Culture in #Charlottesville." In *Reading Confederate Monuments*, edited by Maria Seger. Jackson: University Press of Mississippi, 2022. 213–29.

Woolfork, Lisa. "Thomas Jefferson Is the R. Kelly of the American Enlightenment." *Washington Post*, February 15, 2019. https://www.washingtonpost.com/outlook/2019/02/15/ thomas-jefferson-is-r-kelly-american-enlightenment/.

Yacovone, Donald. "Textbook Racism: How Scholars Sustained White Supremacy." *Chronicle Review*, April 8, 2018. https://www.chronicle.com/article/How-Scholars-Sustained-White/ 243053.

# CONCLUSION

## Challenging Monumentality, Channeling Counter-Monumentality

### —Maria Seger

"A funny thing happened once a monument was built and took its place in the landscape of people's lives," Kirk Savage writes.[1] "It became a kind of natural fact, as if it had always been meant to be." As the essays in this collection show, reading Confederate monuments for how they make meaning disrupts their claims to inevitability and associated notions of transcendence, neutrality, and permanence. Indeed, engaging the work in this volume encourages us to examine monumentality more broadly and deeply, inspiring questions such as these: What is the work of monuments and memory in US culture? Why is the United States especially predisposed to cultures of monumentality? How do monuments negotiate between the state and its publics? How do monuments function to define who is American and what is America? How do myths and narratives become literally and figuratively monumental, and what ends do they serve when that happens? What's at stake in monumentality's drive to collapse historical complexity rather than augmenting it? If, as Erika Doss has argued, US culture has always had "memorial mania"—what she defines as "an obsession with issues of memory and history and an urgent desire to express and claim those issues in visibly public contexts"[2]—it's ever more pressing for us to examine these pushes to memorialize with the tools of counter-monumentality. Counter-monumentality, whether contesting the authority of a particular monument or the idea of monumentality writ large, rests on interrupting the intransient, glorifying, and static nature of monumentality by privileging ephemerality, critique, and engagement instead.[3] While both monuments and counter-monuments require reading—because, as we've shown, meaning is made in the act of readers' interpretation—the former resists being read while the latter demands it, the former forecloses complexity while the latter opens it up, and the former insists on binaries while the latter dissolves them.

Taken together, I would argue that the writing collected here, whether focused on reading, cultural production, or pedagogy, lights the way to developing strategies for challenging monumentality and channeling counter-monumentality. First, this collection's essays on monumentality taught us to question memorialization's value by demonstrating how to interpret Confederate monuments not only for how they produce meaning but for how they reflect and advance broader structural logics of white supremacy, racial capitalism, and patriarchy, among other ideologies. Brook Thomas and Michael C. Weisenburg read Confederate monuments as texts and in textual contexts. I read popular Lost Cause narratives as Confederate monuments in and of themselves. And Danielle Christmas considered how and why neo-Confederate narratives are taking up the project of Confederate monumentality today.

Then, in the chapters on counter-monumentality, we came to understand its virtues by recognizing that the Confederate monument debate has never been about simply removing monuments but rather about challenging the ideologies underpinning their erection and persistence along with the idea of monumentality itself. Garrett Bridger Gilmore illustrated how a Reconstruction novel can help us identify and call out modern institutional compromising and performative hand-wringing that works in the service of anti-Blackness. Stacie McCormick analyzed two contemporary Black theatrical productions as an inherently counter-monumental mode. Cassandra Jackson examined how, prior to monuments' removal, Black cities contested monumentality in ways that forced a reckoning with nuance. And Lisa Woolfork showed how counter-monumentality can be rendered ineffective when censored, lost in translation, appropriated, or perhaps worse yet, hashtagged.

Finally, two essays in this volume synthesized monumentality and counter-monumentality, if implicitly, by asking whether and how to ethically memorialize and to teach repugnant memorials. Spencer R. Herrera sparked our imaginations about the possibilities of the blank memorial affixed at the intersection of three others that pointed to, upon his *reading* them, the nation's founding in the intertwined racist projects of slavery and settler colonialism. Randi Lynn Tanglen meditated on teaching local Confederate monuments as texts alongside US literary monuments and counter-monuments in order to provide teachers-to-be with a fuller understanding of the extent to which white supremacist ideology suffuses the literal and literary landscapes of their future classrooms.

In undertaking these inquiries, the essays collected here have expertly balanced individual and structural notions of white supremacy as well as the interplay between them, ensuring that we never lose sight of either. On the one hand, contributors recognized that Confederate monuments serve as "archives of [white] public affect, 'repositories of feelings and emotions' that are embodied in their material form and narrative content" and make them ripe for reading.[4] As such, it's no coincidence that the defense of Confederate monuments has been motivated by intense feeling—feeling that has often sparked horrific and spectacular violence, such as at the Unite the Right rally in Charlottesville, Virginia, in 2017. On the other hand, these authors also insisted that Confederate monuments manifest a more systemic white supremacy that reveals anti-Blackness to be at the very core of some of our nation's most fundamental principles and beliefs. Confederate monuments not only attempt to eternally etch myths or narratives about the past into US culture, but they also lay claim to the permanence of US culture itself, a culture "that created and profits from those very myths."[5] The violence this structural white supremacy produces can be subtler, more quotidian, but it's no less lethal.

On the whole, then, the work in this collection jumpstarts the literary and cultural studies contribution to the Confederate monument debate by showing us how and why to read literal and figurative Confederate monuments in our everyday lives, thereby disrupting their "curious power to erase their own political origins and become sacrosanct."[6] But this work also guides us in how we might harness counter-monumentality to resist those broader founding myths and ideologies in US culture that require the exclusion, dispossession, and disavowal of Black people. Indeed, as John Levi Barnard argues, counter-monumentality should cause us to question "monumentalism's assertion of the dominance *and* the permanence of the culture that insists on endlessly constructing . . . monuments to itself."[7] Because when we realize that US culture itself can be contested, destroyed, and toppled just like the monuments to it, we can finally get to work on building an altogether different kind of world.

## NOTES

1. Kirk Savage, *Standing Soldiers, Kneeling Slaves: Race, War, and Monument in Nineteenth-Century America* (Princeton, NJ: Princeton University Press, 1997), 7.

2. Erika Doss, *Memorial Mania: Public Feeling in America* (Chicago: University of Chicago Press, 2010), 2.

3. James F. Osborne, "Counter-Monumentality and the Vulnerability of Memory," *Journal of Social Archaeology* 17, no. 2 (May 2017): 165. See also Quentin Stevens, Karen A. Franck, and Ruth Fazakerley, "Counter-Monuments: The Anti-Monumental and the Dialogic," *Journal of Architecture* 23, no. 5 (2018): 718–39.

4. Doss, *Memorial Mania*, 13.

5. John Levi Barnard, "American Monuments and the Residue of History," *Los Angeles Review of Books*, August 27, 2017, https://blog.lareviewofbooks.org/essays/american-monuments-residue-history/.

6. Savage, *Standing Soldiers*, 7.

7. Barnard, "American Monuments."

# Bibliography

Barnard, John Levi. "American Monuments and the Residue of History." *Los Angeles Review of Books*, August 27, 2017. https://blog.lareviewofbooks.org/essays/american-monuments -residue-history/.

Doss, Erika. *Memorial Mania: Public Feeling in America*. Chicago: University of Chicago Press, 2010.

Osborne, James F. "Counter-Monumentality and the Vulnerability of Memory." *Journal of Social Archaeology* 17, no. 2 (May 2017): 163–87.

Savage, Kirk. *Standing Soldiers, Kneeling Slaves: Race, War, and Monument in Nineteenth-Century America*. Princeton, NJ: Princeton University Press, 1997.

Stevens, Quentin, Karen A. Franck, and Ruth Fazakerley. "Counter-Monuments: The Anti-Monumental and the Dialogic." *Journal of Architecture* 23, no. 5 (2018): 718–39.

# AFTERWORD
## —Joanna Davis-McElligatt

In her meditation on the poetics of monumentalization, the Mississippi poet Natasha Trethewey describes her work as "try[ing] to decipher / the story it tells, / this syntax of monuments / flanking an old courthouse."[1] That is also my work here.

I write these words in the wake of two American revolts—the international uprisings during the summer of 2020 in response to the murder of George Floyd and the white supremacist insurrection at the US Capitol in January 2021. Holed up in my home while the COVID-19 pandemic raged around me, I watched the summer's uprisings unfold on cable news and Twitter. I've never felt more imperiled by the force and weight of white supremacy than I did while struggling to help my nine-year-old son comprehend the eight-minute and forty-six-second video of Floyd's killing. How could I possibly explain how badly Floyd's daughter must miss his strong hands around hers? I can't describe to my son the sound of Floyd's laughter, so how could I make it clear to him that the timbre of his dying voice crying out "Mama! Mama!" is a monument to the sacred power of love? Whose mother possesses the language to make her child understand that her love is not and has never been enough to keep them together in this place? No, I explained to my son while we wept: we are not safe in this country, and our ancestors were not safe either. But listen, my darling boy, there have always been people trying so hard to keep us alive. Don't forget, I said, that right now in this moment *we are surviving*. Because he wanted and needed to do something, we taped three screen-printed signs to the kitchen windows—in large black block letters they announce: JUSTICE NOW! BLACK LIVES MATTER; UNITE! BLACK LIVES MATTER; and JUSTICE FOR GEORGE FLOYD BLACK LIVES MATTER—which we intended to be a monument that means *Black people are alive and living in here*. The terror I felt in the earliest days of the pandemic gradually yielded to an exhilarated pride as activists defaced and tore down and lobbied for the removal of monuments to the Confederacy in Richmond, Charleston, Louisville, Jacksonville, Birmingham, Mobile, Raleigh, Washington, DC—and so many other places. Look, I said to my son as we watched each one fall, these are the people trying so hard to keep us safe. As the summer faded into autumn, I'd ask my partner every morning, "Are they still protesting?" And he'd say, "Yes—everywhere." There was so much strength in their movement.

Yet each night in bed, unable to sleep, I'd watch videos of protests on my phone, bearing witness in quiet horror as peaceful Black Lives Matter activists were pepper-sprayed, beaten with batons, brutalized with shields, corralled and disappeared off the street in broad daylight by state agents without identification. The uprisings were met with fierce opposition from the Trump administration, and in June 2020, it began deploying federal law enforcement to cities where protests had resulted in property destruction or where Confederate monuments had been removed. On June 1, Trump authorized the teargassing and dispersal of peaceful agitators so that he could walk from the White House to St. John's Episcopal Church. Standing awkwardly in front of the church—a monument to God's mercy on earth—Trump held up a small Bible in his hand, glowering at the camera. Reporters asked him if he planned to authorize the use of military force against US citizens by calling in the National Guard. Without a hint of irony, he replied, "We have the greatest country in the world. We're going to keep it nice and safe."[2]

The white supremacist insurrection at the US Capitol had been harbingered by Donald Trump's escalating rhetoric over the summer and in the months leading up to the election. As white supremacists, fascists, and white nationalists stormed the building and raised gallows, forcing members of Congress and the vice president into hiding, media talking heads noted with outrage over and over again that the mob had dared stage an assault on the People's House, as if it had been designed as a monument to *our* freedom—as if slave coffles hadn't passed by the Capitol grounds on their way to the auction block, as if the African enslaved hadn't been the ones who'd hewn the logs, laid the bricks, and set the frames in place. Even as the chaos surged in real time, photographs and video footage circulated of police officers removing barricades and taking selfies with neo-Nazis, nurturing alliances with Oath Keepers, Three Percenters, Proud Boys, and other militia groups—so much so that, in the aftermath, reporters and lawmakers would wonder if the attack had been coordinated with the help of law enforcement and military sympathizers. While far rightists escalated their attacks against the Capitol, Trump refused to send in the National Guard. Instead, he responded directly to the insurgents in a video message: "We love you," he said. "You're very special."[3]

In several photographs circulating on Twitter and in news media, a white man in a black jacket and brown vest waved the Confederate flag in front of portraits of the abolitionists John C. Calhoun and Charles Sumner and a bust of the disgraced President Richard Nixon. Though no one had ever managed to carry the Confederate flag into the building as a monument to white supremacist insurrectionist rule—not even, apparently, during the Civil War—Mississippi had slipped the Confederate battle flag into its own state flag beginning in 1894. In that form, the Confederate battle flag had appeared in the Capitol for over a hundred years, until January 11, 2021—five days *after* the insurrection—when Mississippi's newly designed magnolia flag was raised. As of this writing, the Confederate flag-waving quisling has yet to be identified, but his impudence should serve as a stark reminder that the white supremacist, nativist, and racist systems and ideologies that propagate white supremacist and white nationalist symbologies persist even after those symbols are removed from public view. In the aftermath of the revolts— the uprisings and the insurrection—we might be prompted into increasingly critical examinations of our interactions with and the proliferation of the symbols, systems, and ideologies of white power in both digital and material spaces.

The Confederate monument in Denton, Texas, where I now live, was removed on June 25, 2020, not quite a year after I'd relocated here. Its removal is a testament to twenty years of struggle and agitation by activist Willie Hudspeth. Nearly every Sunday afternoon for years, Hudspeth would sit in a chair between the monument and the nearby courthouse, inviting people to discuss signs that read: PLEASE MOVE STATUE TO CONFEDERATE MUSEUM GOD SAID LOVE EVERYBODY, WHERE IS THE BLACK HISTORY ON THE SQUARE, and SAY NO TO RACISM MOVE THE STATUE. I first noticed the statue one summer afternoon while exploring and walking with my family through the square, the town's historical and quaint business district. As we turned the corner and neared the path that led to the front entrance of the courthouse, I caught a glimpse of an imposing ivory sculpture with a wide arch, on top of which was perched a man holding a gun. As we got closer, I positioned my body so that I could examine the front of the monument—it read OUR CONFEDER-ATE SOLDIERS in block letters along the arch, the dates 1861 and 1865 etched into its pillars. Erected on the Denton Courthouse lawn in 1918 by the United Daughters of the Confederacy, the original monument, as I eventually learned, contained water fountains at the bottom of each pillar, one marked WHITE and the other COLORED, which were removed following the end of de jure segregation. In the moment that I fully ascertained what I was seeing, I was immediately and violently reoriented in both space and time. It became clear that the county square was, in fact, organized around the courthouse, a symbol of white power. How could I have missed that? I could see clearly how the Confederate monument was positioned so that the arches aligned with the doors of the courthouse, both framing it and protecting it. At twelve feet tall, the monument was designed to be ostentatious, highly visible, and specifically threatening to Black people. I realized that the town where I'd moved had been designed to intimidate my ancestors and that in the present moment I, too, was intended to be reminded that the city was not mine and had not been built for anyone who looked like me. From the imposing courthouse to the ivory Confederate soldier to my child's elementary school in a predominantly Black and Latinx section of town that had until recently been named for Robert E. Lee, I was reminded everywhere that we were not welcome.

My family hasn't yet been to the square to see the empty space left behind by the monument, but I know that an absence always signifies a presence. I also know that its removal changes nothing fundamental: I will still have to confront the racist ideologies and systems that animate our world. I understand that, going forward, the time we spend on the square will still take place beneath the specter of the courthouse, haunted by the peril of incarceration and the reek of early death. We will still be walking and shopping on land stolen from the Wichita and Caddo peoples, violently occupied by settlers. I am still living in the afterlife of slavery. Yet I also know that the statue's removal is both an ending and an opening—something like an invitation. Absences offer us a tentative place to begin, to reimagine our civic responsibilities, to oppose and rewrite the history of this place—*our space now*—and to have the courage to imagine new futures.

As a miserable coda to his failed presidency, on January 18, 2021—Martin Luther King Jr.'s birthday—Trump's 1776 Commission released its report, which remained available for exactly two days; the commission was disbanded and the report removed from the White House website immediately following President Joe Biden's inauguration. Established as a response to Nikole Hannah-Jones's *The 1619 Project* for the *New York Times*, the commission's report claims that intellectual work seeking to hold the United States accountable for its long and violent history of white supremacist rule "tramples honest scholarship and historical truth, shames Americans by highlighting only the sins of their ancestors, and teaches claims of systemic racism that can only be eliminated by more discrimination."[4] The commission goes on to suggest that "scholars, students, and all Americans must reject false and fashionable ideologies that obscure facts, [and] ignore historical context," especially those narratives that "tell America's story solely as one of oppression and victimhood rather than one of imperfection but also unprecedented achievement toward freedom, happiness, and fairness for all."[5] As I sifted through the lies and half-truths in the commission's report, I found myself at the end of the day returning to the essays in this collection. In *Reading Confederate Monuments*, I discovered careful history work, new ways to think within and beyond structures of white supremacy, and modes of resistance. This text isn't a monument that means *Remember this*. This text, instead, asks us to *Grapple with this* and *Take this on* and *Struggle through this*. Instead of offering us words etched in stone, the essays compiled here offer us a syntax of Confederate monuments, a way of resisting them and the structures that support their emplacement, and a way of moving beyond and into a more just and ethical future without them.

# NOTES

1. Natasha Trethewey, "Meditation at Decatur Square," in *Monument: Poems New and Selected* (Boston: Houghton Mifflin Harcourt, 2018), 176.
2. Ben Gittleson and Jordyn Phelps, "Police Use Munitions to Forcibly Push Back Peaceful Protestors for Trump Church Visit," ABC News, June 2, 2020, https://abcnews.go.com/Politics/national-guard-troops-deployed-white-house-trump-calls/story?id=71004151.
3. Salvador Hernandez, "Trump Is Justifying His Supporters' Attempted Coup with More Lies About the Election," *BuzzFeed News*, January 6, 2021, https://www.buzzfeednews.com/article/salvadorhernandez/trump-video-supporters-coup.
4. Michael Crowley, "Trump's '1776 Report' Defends America's Founding on the Basis of Slavery and Blasts Progressivism," *New York Times*, January 18, 2021, https://www.nytimes.com/2021/01/18/us/trump-1776-commission-report.html.
5. Kevin M. Kruse, "The Trump Administration's Thinly Veiled Rebuke of 'The 1619 Project' Is a Sloppy, Racist Mess," MSNBC, January 20, 2021, https://www.msnbc.com/opinion/trump-administration-s-thinly-veiled-rebuke-1619-project-sloppy-racist-n1254807.

## Bibliography

Crowley, Michael. "Trump's '1776 Report' Defends America's Founding on the Basis of Slavery and Blasts Progressivism." *New York Times*, January 18, 2021. https://www.nytimes.com/2021/01/18/us/trump-1776-commission-report.html.

Gittleson Ben, and Jordyn Phelps. "Police Use Munitions to Forcibly Push Back Peaceful Protestors for Trump Church Visit." ABC News, June 2, 2020. https://abcnews.go.com/Politics/national-guard-troops-deployed-white-house-trump-calls/story?id=71004151.

Hernandez, Salvador. "Trump Is Justifying His Supporters' Attempted Coup with More Lies about the Election." *BuzzFeed News*, January 6, 2021. https://www.buzzfeednews.com/article/salvadorhernandez/trump-video-supporters-coup.

Kruse, Kevin M. "The Trump Administration's Thinly Veiled Rebuke of 'The 1619 Project' Is a Sloppy, Racist Mess." MSNBC, January 20, 2021. https://www.msnbc.com/opinion/trump-administration-s-thinly-veiled-rebuke-1619-project-sloppy-racist-n1254807.

Trethewey, Natasha. "Meditation at Decatur Square." In *Monument: Poems New and Selected*, 176. Boston: Houghton Mifflin Harcourt, 2018.

# SUGGESTIONS FOR FURTHER READING

## CIVIL WAR MEMORY

Blair, William A. *With Malice toward Some: Treason and Loyalty in the Civil War Era.* Chapel Hill: University of North Carolina Press, 2014.

Blight, David W. *Race and Reunion: The Civil War in American Memory.* Cambridge, MA: Belknap Press, 2001.

Brown, Thomas J. *Civil War Canon: Sites of Confederate Memory in South Carolina.* Chapel Hill: University of North Carolina Press, 2015.

Fahs, Alice, and Joan Waugh, eds. *The Memory of the Civil War in American Culture.* Chapel Hill: University of North Carolina Press, 2004.

Foster, Gaines M. *Ghosts of the Confederacy: Defeat, the Lost Cause, and the Emergence of the New South, 1865–1913.* New York: Oxford University Press, 1987.

Harris, M. Keith. *Across the Bloody Chasm: The Culture of Commemoration among Civil War Veterans.* Baton Rouge: Louisiana State University Press, 2014.

Janney, Caroline E. *Remembering the Civil War: Reunion and the Limits of Reconciliation.* Chapel Hill: University of North Carolina Press, 2013.

Marrs, Cody. *Not Even Past: The Stories We Keep Telling about the Civil War.* Baltimore: Johns Hopkins University Press, 2020.

Silber, Nina. *The Romance of Reunion: Northerners and the South, 1865–1900.* Chapel Hill: University of North Carolina Press, 1993.

## CONFEDERATE LITERARY, POPULAR, AND PRINT CULTURES

Bernath, Michael T. *Confederate Minds: The Struggle for Intellectual Independence in the Civil War South.* Chapel Hill: University of North Carolina Press, 2010.

Cox, Karen L. *Dreaming of Dixie: How the South Was Created in American Popular Culture.* Chapel Hill: University of North Carolina Press, 2011.

Fahs, Alice. *The Imagined Civil War: Popular Literature of the North and South, 1861–65.* Chapel Hill: University of North Carolina Press, 2001.

Gallagher, Gary W. *Causes Won, Lost, and Forgotten: How Hollywood and Popular Art Shape What We Know about the Civil War.* Chapel Hill: University of North Carolina Press, 2008.

Gallagher, Gary W., and Alan T. Nolan, eds. *The Myth of the Lost Cause and Civil War History.* Bloomington: Indiana University Press, 2000.

Hutchison, Coleman. *Apples and Ashes: Literature, Nationalism, and the Confederate States of America.* Athens: University of Georgia Press, 2012.

Kreiser, Lawrence A., Jr., and Randal Allred. *The Civil War in Popular Culture.* Lexington: University Press of Kentucky, 2014.

Marrs, Cody. *Nineteenth-Century American Literature and the Long Civil War*. New York: Cambridge University Press, 2015.

McPherson, Tara. *Reconstructing Dixie: Race, Gender, and Nostalgia in the Imagined South*. Durham, NC: Duke University Press, 2003.

## CONFEDERATE MONUMENTS AND MEMORIALIZATION, THEN AND NOW

Brown, Thomas J. *Civil War Monuments and the Militarization of America*. Chapel Hill: University of North Carolina Press, 2019.

Clinton, Catherine, ed. *Confederate Statues and Memorialization*. Athens: University of Georgia Press, 2019.

Cox, Karen L. *Dixie's Daughters: The United Daughters of the Confederacy and the Preservation of Confederate Culture*. Gainesville: University Press of Florida, 2003.

Cox, Karen L. *No Common Ground: Confederate Monuments and the Ongoing Fight for Racial Justice*. Chapel Hill: University of North Carolina Press, 2021.

Domby, Adam H. *The False Cause: Fraud, Fabrication, and White Supremacy in Confederate Memory*. Charlottesville: University of Virginia Press, 2020.

Green, Hilary. "Monument Removals, 2015–2020." Google Maps. Last updated July 11, 2021. https://www.google.com/maps/d/u/o/viewer?fbclid=IwAR2DR-ULjxTtS9hoqZL-nkSsofae3 jIT6RrGykx400Rkc6mwtO5VNRfuiTo&mid=142t5-uHjv2fl293rKwx2R71IL-5kAJ80&ll=19. 271986802880892%2C-107.894722&z=3.

Hartley, Roger C. *Monumental Harm: Reckoning with Jim Crow Era Confederate Monuments*. Columbia: University of South Carolina Press, 2021.

Janney, Caroline E. *Burying the Dead But Not the Past: Ladies' Memorial Associations and the Lost Cause*. Chapel Hill: University of North Carolina Press, 2008.

Levin, Kevin M., ed. "Confederate Monuments Syllabus." Civil War Memory. Accessed July 14, 2021. http://cwmemory.com/civilwarmemorysyllabus/.

Mills, Cynthia, and Pamela H. Simpson. *Monuments to the Lost Cause: Women, Art, and the Landscapes of Southern Memory*. Knoxville: University of Tennessee Press, 2003.

Newson, Ryan Andrew. *Cut in Stone: Confederate Monuments and Theological Disruption*. Waco, TX: Baylor University Press, 2020.

Price, Evander. "The Silent Sam Syllabus: A Module for Teaching Confederate Monumentality." Monument Lab, February 5, 2019. https://monumentlab.com/bulletin/the-silent-sam -syllabus.

Southern Poverty Law Center. "Whose Heritage? Public Symbols of the Confederacy." Southern Poverty Law Center, February 1, 2019. https://www.splcenter.org/data-projects/ whose-heritage.

## CONTEMPORARY RACIAL VIOLENCE AND RACIAL JUSTICE ACTIVISM

Blain, Keisha N., ed. "#CharlestonSyllabus." African American Intellectual History Society. Accessed July 14, 2021. https://www.aaihs.org/resources/charlestonsyllabus/.

Davis, Angela Y. *Freedom Is a Constant Struggle: Ferguson, Palestine, and the Foundations of a Movement*. Chicago: Haymarket, 2016.

Kaba, Mariame. *We Do This 'Til We Free Us: Abolitionist Organizing and Transforming Justice*. Chicago: Haymarket, 2021.

Lebron, Christopher J. *The Making of Black Lives Matter: A Brief History of an Idea.* New York: Oxford University Press, 2017.

Ransby, Barbara. *Making All Black Lives Matter: Reimagining Freedom in the Twenty-First Century.* Berkeley: University of California Press, 2018.

Roberts, Frank Leon. "Black Lives Matter Syllabus." Black Lives Matter Syllabus. Last updated spring 2021. http://www.blacklivesmattersyllabus.com/.

Taylor, Keeanga-Yamhatta. *From #BlackLivesMatter to Black Liberation.* Chicago: Haymarket, 2016.

Uva Graduate Student Coalition for Liberation. "The Charlottesville Syllabus." *Medium*, August 11, 2017. https://medium.com/@UVAGSC/the-charlottesville-syllabus-9e01573419d0.

Vitale, Alex. *The End of Policing.* New York: Verso, 2018.

Williams, Chad, Kidada E. Williams, and Keisha N. Blain, eds. *Charleston Syllabus: Readings on Race, Racism, and Racial Violence.* Athens: University of Georgia Press, 2016.

## MEMORIALIZATION IN THE UNITED STATES

Doss, Erika. *Memorial Mania: Public Feeling in America.* Chicago: University of Chicago Press, 2010.

Savage, Kirk. *Monument Wars: Washington, D.C., the National Mall, and the Transformation of the Memorial Landscape.* Berkeley: University of California Press, 2009.

Savage, Kirk. *Standing Soldiers, Kneeling Slaves: Race, War, and Monument in Nineteenth-Century America.* Princeton, NJ: Princeton University Press, 1997.

Upton, Dell. *What Can and Can't Be Said: Race, Uplift, and Monument Building in the Contemporary South.* New Haven, CT: Yale University Press, 2015.

## RECONSTRUCTION AND JIM CROW LITERATURE AND CULTURE

Du Bois, W. E. B. *Black Reconstruction in America, 1860–1880.* 1935. New York: Free Press, 1999.

Foner, Eric. *Forever Free: The Story of Emancipation and Reconstruction.* New York: Vintage, 2006.

Foner, Eric. *Reconstruction: America's Unfinished Revolution, 1863–77.* Updated ed. New York: Harper Perennial, 2014.

Foner, Eric. *The Second Founding: How the Civil War and Reconstruction Remade the Constitution.* New York: Norton, 2019.

Gates, Henry Louis, Jr. *Stony the Road: Reconstruction, White Supremacy, and the Rise of Jim Crow.* New York: Penguin, 2019.

Goldsby, Jacqueline. *A Spectacular Secret: Lynching in American Life and Literature.* Chicago: University of Chicago Press, 2006.

Haley, Sarah. *No Mercy Here: Gender, Punishment, and the Making of Jim Crow Modernity.* Chapel Hill: University of North Carolina Press, 2016.

Hutner, Gordon, ed. "Reenvisioning Reconstruction." Special issue of *American Literary History* 30, no. 3 (Fall 2018): 403–651.

Thomas, Brook. *The Literature of Reconstruction: Not in Plain Black and White.* Baltimore: Johns Hopkins University Press, 2017.

Wood, Amy Louise. *Lynching and Spectacle: Witnessing Racial Violence in America, 1890–1940.* Chapel Hill: University of North Carolina Press, 2009.

# ABOUT THE CONTRIBUTORS

**Danielle Christmas** is assistant professor of English and Comparative Literature and Endowed Delta Delta Delta Fellow at the University of North Carolina at Chapel Hill. With affiliations in both Jewish Studies and American Studies, she publishes and teaches on a variety of topics including slavery and the Holocaust in American fiction and film, lynching in American literature and discourse, and white nationalist culture and politics. Her first book, *Plantation Predators and Nazi Monsters: Labor, Sex, and Madness in American Holocaust and Slavery Fiction*, is forthcoming from Rutgers University Press in 2022. She is currently working on her next monograph, *The Literature of Blood and Soil: White Nationalism and a New American Canon*. These projects have been supported by the Mellon Foundation, the American Council of Learned Societies, and the United States Holocaust Memorial Museum, as well as the University of North Carolina's Provost and Institute for the Arts and Humanities.

**Joanna Davis-McElligatt** is assistant professor of Black Literary and Cultural Studies at the University of North Texas. She is coeditor of *Narratives of Marginalized Identities in Higher Education: Inside and Outside the Academy* (Routledge, 2019) and *Narrating History, Home, and Nation: Critical Essays on Edwidge Danticat* (University Press of Mississippi, 2022). She is currently at work on her first monograph, *Black and Immigrant: Diaspora, Belonging, and Time in American Literature after 1965*, a critical exploration of representations of immigrants of African descent to the US from Afropolitans to Wakandan Americans.

**Garrett Bridger Gilmore** is instructor in the departments of English and Gender and Race Studies at the University of Alabama. His research interrogates the impact of the historical memory of slavery on twentieth-century political and literary formations, and his writing has appeared in *Mississippi Quarterly* and *North Carolina Literary Review*.

**Spencer R. Herrera** was born and raised in Houston, Texas, but has enjoyed living in Nuevo México for twenty years. He is coeditor of *Querencia: Reflections on the New Mexico Homeland* (University of New Mexico Press, 2020) and coauthor of *Sagrado: A Photopoetics across the Chicano Homeland* (University of New Mexico Press, 2013), winner of a Border Regional Library Association Southwest Book Award, a New Mexico-Arizona Book Award, and a Pima County Public Library Southwest Book of the Year Award. He is currently working on a book that examines monuments and memorials in Texas that intersect Anglo-Tejano histories. He completed his PhD in Spanish with a minor in film at the University of New Mexico. He is associate professor of Spanish at New Mexico State University in Las Cruces where he teaches Chicano/a Studies.

**Cassandra Jackson** is professor of English at the College of New Jersey where she teaches African American literature and visual culture. She holds a PhD in English from Emory University and BA from Spelman College. She is coauthor of *The Toni Morrison Book Club* (University of Wisconsin Press, 2020), a genre-bending group memoir, which received a starred review in *Publishers Weekly* and was selected as a Best Book of 2020 by *Library Journal*. She has also published two scholarly books on race in US literature and art, *Barriers Between Us: Interracial Sex in Nineteenth-Century American Literature* (Indiana University Press, 2004) and *Violence, Visual Culture, and the Black Male Body* (Routledge, 2011), as well as personal essays and op-eds in the *Huffington Post* and the *Washington Post*. Her memoir, *The Wreck*, which explores the relationship between her ancestors who died in the Colored ward of an Alabama hospital and her own experience as a Black woman navigating treatment for infertility, is forthcoming from Penguin Viking.

**Stacie McCormick** is associate professor of English, Comparative Race and Ethnic Studies, and Women and Gender Studies at Texas Christian University (TCU). She directs African American and Africana Studies at TCU and is author of *Staging Black Fugitivity* (Ohio State University Press, 2019), which examines how contemporary Black drama represents and engages with slavery. Her broader work also explores Black women's writing with respect to the land, postslavery subjectivities, adaptation, life writing, and the body. Currently, she is developing a manuscript that takes up Black women's critical engagement with obstetric racism and the medical-industrial complex. She is pursuing this work as a 2021–22 Mellon-ACLS Scholars and Society Fellow.

**Maria Seger** is assistant professor of English at the University of Louisiana at Lafayette, where she specializes in nineteenth-century US literature, Black and US ethnic literatures, and critical race and ethnic studies. She is currently at work on a book project, *At All Costs: Extralegal Violence and Liberal Democracy in US Culture*, which examines extralegal violence not as a lawless force that threatened US liberal-democratic governance but instead as emerging from and further entrenching the conditions it set. Her work appears in *Nineteenth-Century Literature, Callaloo,* and *Studies in American Naturalism.*

**Randi Lynn Tanglen** is an independent scholar based in Missoula, Montana. Previously, she was professor of English at Austin College in Sherman, Texas, where she taught American literature, American studies, gender studies, and writing. There, she also served as director of the Robert and Joyce Johnson Center for Faculty Development and Excellence in Teaching. Her writing has appeared in *Western American Literature, Southwestern American Literature, Legacy,* and various edited volumes. She is coeditor of *Teaching Western American Literature* (University of Nebraska Press, 2020).

**Brook Thomas** is Chancellor's Professor of English, Emeritus, at the University of California, Irvine. He is author of a number of books cross-examining US law and literature. The most recent is *The Literature of Reconstruction: Not in Plain Black and White* (Johns Hopkins University Press, 2017), winner of the C. Hugh Holman Prize. He has also published numerous essays on Reconstruction, most recently, "Reconstruction Matters in the Revival of Civil War Literature" in *American Literary Realism,* "The *Galaxy,* National Literature, and Reconstruction" in *Nineteenth-Century Literature,* and "The United States' Civic Myth of the Citizen-Soldier in the Era of the Civil War and Reconstruction" in *Amerikastudien/American Studies.* He is working on *The Ambassadors of Reconstruction,* a study of the neglected impact that understandings of Reconstruction had on US foreign policy.

**Michael C. Weisenburg** is reference and instruction librarian in the Irvin Department of Rare Books and Special Collections at the University of South Carolina and current editor of *Emerson Society Papers.* He has published on American literature in *The New England Quarterly, Rhetoric Society Quarterly,* and *Thoreau Beyond Borders* (University of Massachusetts Press, 2020), and he has a recent essay on Walt Whitman in *American Periodicals.*

**Lisa Woolfork** is associate professor of English at the University of Virginia, where she specializes in African American literature and culture. She is the author of *Embodying American Slavery in Contemporary Culture* (University of Illinois Press, 2008). In addition, her work concerns televisual representations, including an article on blood mixing in HBO's *True Blood* published in the *South Carolina Review* and a chapter on *All in the Family* and *The Jeffersons* in *Race-ing for Ratings: African Americans in Television* (Praeger, 2013).

In addition to courses on fictions of Black identity, Black women writers, and contemporary African American literature, she teaches a popular course on

George R. R. Martin's books and HBO's television series *Game of Thrones*, which garnered national recognition. She published an article about the rhetorical and social weight of Black women's names in *Rhetorics of Names and Naming* (Routledge, 2016), as well as an essay about the role of whiteness in *The Free State of Jones* for CNN. In 2016, she was named part of the inaugural class of the University of Virginia College Fellows, an ambitious two-year program for faculty to revise the undergraduate curriculum by crafting a new approach to undergraduate education. As part of that initiative, she created two new courses for first-year students that address a variety of systemic inequities including racism and white supremacy.

In the summer of 2017, she became a founding member of Black Lives Matter Charlottesville. This group protested against the white supremacist insurgency that had taken hold of the city during the "summer of hate." She was on the ground on August 11 and 12, 2017, in a variety of capacities including joining in nonviolent direct action, working with the bail fund, sewing for a creative arts team, and participating in a media collective. Her essay "'This Class of Persons': When UVA's White Supremacist Past Meets Its Future" was published in *Charlottesville 2017: The Legacy of Race and Inequity* (University of Virginia Press, 2018), a collection of essays about the terror events in Charlottesville. She also contributes op-eds to the *Huffington Post*, CNN, and the *Washington Post*. She is currently teaching a new course, "Sally Hemings University," which concentrates on what it would mean to center structures of study and knowledge production on a marginalized Black woman rather than the white man who held her captive. The course considers if liberation is possible within an institutional structure, particularly that of the university.

# INDEX

Page numbers in **bold** indicate figures.

abolitionists/abolitionism, 27, 122, 133–35, 147, 152, 256
absence, 170, 178, 195–97, 258
Academy Award, 159
Acoma Pueblo, 84–85, 91n8
Adams, Charles Francis, Jr., 32–33, 37
administration, 4, 120–21, 125
affectation, 87, 167, 169, 252–53
African American memorial (Columbia, SC), 66
African American Repertory Theatre (Dallas, TX), 181
Aitchison, Cara, 195
Alabama Supreme Court, 204
Albermarle County Hate-Free Schools Coalition, 216
Alberta (character), 177
Albuquerque, NM, 84–85
Alexander, Michelle, 181, 243
Alfred Mouton statue (Lafayette, LA), 3–5, 14
Alliance Theatre (Atlanta, GA), 170–72
alt-right, 102, 105–6, 161n9. *See also* white nationalism
*America Play, The* (Parks), 177–78
Angel of Peace, 198
Anglin, Andrew, 105, 107–8
anti-Blackness: as foundational, 253; institutional, 121, 252; persistence of, 5; profitability of, 11, 160; racism and, 226; violence and, 145, 147–48, 151–52, 214. *See also* white supremacy
anti-racism: assignments and, 234; as community defense, 125; as desired transformation of United States, 122, 225–27; equivocating between racism and, 127, 224; as motivating Confederate

monument removal, 5, 119, 121, 215–18, 230; texts and, 238–39. *See also* social justice
anti-Semitism, 223
"Anti-Slavery Men of the South" (Pollard), 26
Apel, Dora, 64
*Appeal to the Patriotic and Loyal Boys and Girls of Clarendon County*, **55**, 56
Appomattox, 100, 118
Arbery, Ahmaud, 243
Arcata, CA, 106
archive: accessed, 9, 118; Confederate monuments as, 252; critiques of, 12, 168–69; diversity of, 6; texts as, 127, 169, 237. *See also* repertoire
Arlington Confederate memorial (VA), 44
Armijo, Manuel, 80
*Army & Navy Journal*, 26
Arthur, Chester A., 123
appropriation: of civil rights logics, 129; Confederate monuments and, 45; of counter-monumentality, 252; political supporters and, 35; print culture and, 9; racial, 220–21; white nationalism and, 58
Atkinson, Ashlie, 142
Atlanta, GA: Confederate monuments in, 13, 198, 200–201; as setting of *Gone with the Wind*, 154; as staging site of *Native Guard*, 170–71, 173, 175
Atlanta Compromise, 199
Atlanta History Center (GA), 170–72, 199
*Atticus Finch: The Biography* (Crespino), 238
Augé, Marc, 65
Austin College (Sherman, TX), 235
Austin College Task Force on Diversity and Inclusion, 233

Baldwin, James, 241
Baltimore, MD, 13, 194, 196, 214

Barker, Deborah, 153
Barkley, Danielle, 153
Barnard, John Levi, 253
Barton, Clara, 31
Battle of Gettysburg (PA), 31
Battle of Glorieta Pass (NM), 81, 83
Battle of Shiloh (TN), 110
Battle of Thermopylae, 58
Baylor, John W., 81
Beauregard, P. G. T., 193
*Bedford, a World Vision* (Williams), 108
Beirich, Heidi, 108, 200
belonging, 6, 12, 180, 194, 201
Benjamin, Walter, 38
Bible, the, 256
Biden, Joseph, 258
Big Sam (character), 156
billboards, 13, 215–16, 218–19, 221, 223–24, 226
Birmingham, AL, 12–13, 194, 202, **203**, 204–5, 255
Birmingham Parks and Recreation Board (AL), 203
*Birth of a Nation, The* (Griffith): close reading of, 146–53, **149**; comparison to *Gone with the Wind*, 154–56, 158–60; as inspiring second Ku Klux Klan, 124; as Lost Cause film, 11, 36–37, 142–44
Black adaptation, 172
Black codes, 26
Black disenfranchisement: in *A Fool's Errand*, 123, 127, 132; Confederate monuments as symbolizing, 52; contemporary, 119, 166, 202; as discussed during Reconstruction, 23–26, 34; as part of Jim Crow, 86–87, 238, 240
Black equality: contemporary movements against, 11, 120, 178, 244; contemporary movements for, 46; law failing to achieve, 122–27, 239–40; Reconstruction failing to achieve, 22, 24, 26–27, 37
Black freedom: emancipation and, 29–30, 176–80, 196, 230; as incomplete, 166–67, 175, 180–82, 205–6; Jim Crow disassembling, 123, 230; liberalism and, 137; meaning of, 169; movement, 160; United States symbols as not representing, 256. *See also* emancipation

Black history: erasure of, 170, 174, 178, 183, 192, 200; making, 173, 176, 180; monumentality and, 66–67, 257–58; of present, 12, 167, 175, 182; teaching, 234, 237, 239, 244
*BlacKkKlansman* (Lee), 142–43
*Black Lightning*, 214
Black Lives Matter: 2020 uprisings and, 230, 255–56; activism, 13, 215–16; backlash against, 219–20; era of, 176; valuing Black life, 166–67
Black power movements, 142, 204
Black soldiers, 170, 173–74, 176–80, 182, 193
Black time, 169. *See also* temporality
Blanchard, Terence, 193
Blight, David W., 6, 22–23, 33, 37, 39n15
Blue Ribbon Commission for the Study of Race and Public Spaces, 216
*Bluest Eye, The* (Morrison), 241
Bong Joon-ho, 159
Booth, Susan, 170
Boston, MA, 214
Boyer, M. Christine, 65
Brady, Matthew, 27
*Bricks without Straw* (Tourgée), 37
Brock, Wendell, 171
Brown, Michael, 180
Brown, Sterling K., 180
Brown, Thomas J., 27–30, 34–35, 65
Brown, William Wells, 179, 231, 241
Bryan, William Jennings, 35
Bryant, Zyahna, 216
Bureau of Alcohol, Tobacco, Firearms, and Explosives, 110
Butler, Douglas J., 49
Butler, Rhett (character), 144, 154–55, **157**, 157–59

Caddo Indians, 258
Calhoun, John C., 29–31, 34–38, 256. *See also* John C. Calhoun statue (Charleston, SC)
Calpurnia (character), 239
Cameron, Ben (character), 147–50, 152
Cameron, Dr. (character), 150–51
Cameron, Flora (character), 143, 147–54, **149**
Camino Real de Tierra Adentro, 74–75, 79
Camp Lee, VA, 193
Carbone, Christopher, 103–5

Carlson, Tucker, 105, 107

Carr, Julian, 99–101, 118, 121–22, 129, 138

Carr, Mitch, 220, 222–24

Cato (character), 179

Chapel Hill, NC, 99, 101, 103–4, 118

Charles, Robert, riots, 241

Charleston, SC: as site of Confederate monument fundraising, 47; as site of John C. Calhoun monument, 8, 21, 27, 255; as site of Mother Emanuel church massacre, 5–6, 73, 167; as site of Rhett Butler's home in *Gone with the Wind*, 159

#Charlottesville, 214–15

Charlottesville, VA: in press because of Unite the Right rally, 102–4; as site of Confederate monuments, 12, 168, 214–16, 219, 222–23; as site of structural white supremacy, 13, 215, 225; as site of Unite the Right rally, 5, 171–72, 226, 230, 253; violence of Unite the Right rally and, 194, 203, 213

Charlottesville Free Press, 13, 219–20, 222

Chesnutt, Charles W., 14, 37, 195, 231–32, 241–43

Childs, L. D., 51–52, 58

chivalry, 236, 242

Christianity, 58–60, 85, 127, 222–23

Christmas, Danielle, 10, 252

Chrysostomos, John, 106, 113

Church, Francis P., 26

Church, William Conant, 26

Ciudad Juarez, Mexico, 75, 77, 85, 90

civility, 134, 221, 226

civil rights, 125–26, 129, 193

Civil Rights Act of 1875, 27

Civil Rights Act of 1964, 86–87, 90

civil rights movement: counter-monumentality and, 202, 204; as era of Confederate monument building, 6–7, 65, 86–87, 240; as threatening the Lost Cause, 35–36

Civil War: aftermath of, 122, 181, 241; battles, 81; causes of, 201; counter-histories of, 12, 167–70, 172–78, 180, 182–83; in film, 146–47, 154; fortunes resulting from, 82; history, 7, 60; invocations of, 110; memory, 5–6, 176; as ongoing, 21, 33, 46, 193; as part of United States history,

44; reenactors, 101; as secondary to Confederate monument building, 8, 22, 99, 230, 240; service, 25, 43, 76, 78, 80; southern redemption and, 144; the South's role in, 49, 58, 64–65, 236; as unifying for white people, 30–31, 126; as war, 90, 134, 171, 181, 236, 257; whiteness and, 129–30

Civil War Centennial, 86–87

Civil War uniforms, 21, 101, 177–82

*Clansman, The* (Dixon), 108, 123

Clarendon County, SC, 193

classicism, 9, 57–58, 60–61

Clay, Henry, 30

Clemson, Thomas Green, 35

Clemson University, 35

Cleveland, Grover, 27–28, 31–32

close reading: assignments, 14, 232–33, 242; of Confederate monument texts, 8, 10, 13, 28, 107; of counter-monumental texts, 11, 13, 217; as literary and cultural studies method, 5, 22, 145, 215

*Clotel* (Brown), 241

coexistence, 221–23

Colonel, the (character), 179

*Colonel's Dream, The*, 37

Colorado College, 142

Colorado Springs, CO, 142

colorblindness, 4, 125–26. *See also* white supremacy

Columbia, SC, 35

Columbian Exposition of 1893, 61

*Columbia Register* (SC), 57

Communist Party, 159

community: as academic mission, 231, 233, 236, 243; as affected by Confederate monuments, 4–5, 13, 67, 232–34; anti-racist organizing and, 119–20, 125, 213–17, 223, 225–26; belonging and, 12; conceptions of, 136; Confederate monument resistance in Black, 191–92, 194–97, 201–2, 205–6; creation through theater, 12, 167; expectations, 131; ideals, 126; narratives, 6; power, 130; print, 9, 45, 49, 51, 56, 64; racial history of, 54, 234, 237–39; sanctification of space by, 89–91

Confederate Army, 78, 81–83, 179, 198

Confederate Army Provisional, 110–11

Confederate flag: claims of "heritage not hate" and, 220, 223–24; as distinct from Confederate monuments, 22; as new Confederate monuments, 205; patriotism and, 235; as removed from states and state flags, 168, 257; sewn by Confederate women, 60; as symbol for indoctrinating children, 62, 230

Confederate flag wielding: by Confederate monument defenders, 21, 101–2; by Dylann Roof, 73, 167; by Strom Thurmond campaign, 36; by US Capitol attackers, 256–57; by white nationalist fiction, 109–12

Confederate ideology: John C. Calhoun as representative of, 27; postcards and, 62; teaching critiques of, 14, 231–32; in US cultural imaginary, 6; white women's role in, 11, 142–43, 148

Confederate Memorial Day, 28, 47, **48**, 54

Confederate memorialization, 5–8, 11, 43–67, 143–46

Confederate memory: in *A Fool's Errand*, 118–38; attached to US ideals, 60–61; counter-monuments and, 12–13; Lost Cause and, 21; reconciliation and, 44; sites of, 27, 51, 101, 238, 243; supporting white supremacy, 11, 108, 215, 223, 231; understanding, 5–10; in US culture, 14, 45, 49, 251

"Confederate Monument, Columbia, S.C." (Rotograph), **62**

Confederate monument (Florence, AL), **190**, 191, 206

Confederate monument building: advertising for, 9, 45, 47, 49, 51; causes of, 7, 54, 252–53; eras of, 8, 240; fundraising for, 52, **55**, 56; significance of, 7, 205

Confederate monument dedication: classicism in, 57–58; of John C. Calhoun statue, 22–23, 28, 31, 33–34, 37–38; materials analyzed from, 8–10, 46, 199–200; rededication and, 196, 236, 240; of Silent Sam statue, **98**, 99–100, 118, 121; teaching, 234–35, 238

Confederate monument removal: advertising for, 217; in Alabama, 202–3, 205; Black communities and, 192, 194, 196–98,

200–205; challenging Confederate ideology and, 14, 64, 252, 258; in Chapel Hill, NC, 100, 119–20, 138, 220; in Charleston, SC, 21–22, 33, 35, 38; in Charlottesville, VA, 13, 213–18, 225–26; in Grayson County, TX, 245n4; in Lafayette, LA, 3–5, 14; legal prohibitions against, 13, 67, 192, 196, 198, 200–203; movement, 5–6, 73, 159–60, 167–68, 171, 176, 255–58; in New Orleans, LA, 194; teaching and, 234; in Texas, 73, 85; white children threatened by, 106, 113; white nationalists threatened by, 10, 101, 105–6, 108–9, 111, 113

Confederate monuments: in contemporary Black communities, 192; in context, 33, 120, 160, 202, 233; debates over, 21–22, 73, 104–5, 253; engaging, 197, 204, 251; interpreting, 74, 197, 200, 204, 251–52; literary and cultural texts as, 10, 239–40; making meaning of, 5, 198, 203, 205, 232, 251–52; mutability of, 13, 192, 195, 197, 205, 218; news reporting on, 56, 58, 101; as pedagogy, 6, 13–14, 230–31; policing space, 13, 22, 72, 206; postcards of, 46; reading, 3, 5, 14; reception of, 5, 8, 232; as symbols of white nationalism, 107, 110; as symbols of white supremacy, 100, 167–68, 171, 194–95, 220, 224, 234, 238; teaching, 232, 252; as texts, 5–6, 8, 14, 232

Confederate Park (Memphis, TN), 196

Confederate soldier monument (Columbia, SC), 57, 59–62, **62**, 65, 109

Confederate soldiers and sailors monument (Birmingham, AL), 202–5, **203**

Confederate States of America, 78, 197, 224

*Confederate Veteran* (Nashville, TN), 49, **50**

Confederate women's monument (Columbia, SC), 59–62, **63**, 64–65

contact zone, 74–75, 88, 91

containment: of archives, 169; of Confederate monuments, 14, 197; in Lost Cause myths, 129; of white women, 11, 143, 147, 150–53

*Contending Forces* (Hopkins), 241

contextualization: attempts with Confederate monuments, 4, 13, 159–60, 198, 200–202; in counter-monumental texts, 168, 192, 219; historical, 33, 45–47, 58,

258; institutional, 124–25; logic of, 119–21, 129, 137–38; as method, 5–6, 8–11, 215; reading with, 251–52; recontextualization and, 14, 49, 60, 64; teaching, 233–39

Cortés de Moctezuma, Isabel de Tolosa, 83

counter-histories, 166–67, 170, 173, 182

counter-monuments: building Black monuments, **66**, 67, 206; channeling, 252–53; as cultural production, 10–12, 171–72, 174–75, 180, 182–83; definition of, 7, 167–68, 177, 251; living, 169; as pedagogy, 6; as statue, 13, 67; as text, 14, 124

Courtney, Susan, 147

COVID-19 pandemic, 255

Cox, Karen L.: *Dixie's Daughters*, 47, 54, 234; op-eds, 103; in southern studies, 6–7, 143, 146

Crespino, Joseph, 238, 240

critical pedagogy, 14, 232, 244

critical race theory, 182

Cromwell, Oliver, 32

cultural production, 8–12, 252

Cunningham, Sumner A., 49

Currey, David, 56

Curt Teich and Company, 63

Dailey, Jane, 86, 241

*Daily Stormer*, 10, 101, 104–7, 112–13

Dallas, TX, 181, 194, 243

Danto, Arthur, 73

Davis, Jefferson, 24–25, 27, 39n15, 80–82, 197, 202. *See also* Jefferson Davis memorial; Jefferson Davis Park (Memphis, TN); Stone Mountain Memorial Carving (GA)

Davis, Melvin, 181

Davis, Rebecca Harding, 26

Decatur, GA, 202

DeCeasare, Leah, 222

de Havilland, Olivia, 154

DeKalb County, GA, 200–202

DeKalb County Confederate monument (GA), 200–202, 205

Delaney, Martin, 34

democracy: Confederate monuments' appeals to, 61; knowledge and, 169; Lost Cause as undermining, 121; white supremacist appropriations of, 126–27, 130, 132, 138; will of the people and, 197

Denton, TX, 257

Denton Confederate soldier monument (TX), 257

Denton County Courthouse-on-the-Square (TX), 257

di Cavour, Camillo, 34

Dickinson, Jacob M., 43

disturbance of vision, 13, 195–98, 200–201, 203–4

diversity: celebrations of, 75, 88, 90, 233; Confederate monument defenders and, 220–21, 224; as institutional tolerance of ideas, 120–21

diversity regimes, 120–21, 125–26

"Dixie," 239

*Dixie's Daughters: The United Daughters of the Confederacy and the Preservation of Confederate Culture* (Cox), 234

Dixon, Thomas, Jr., 37, 108, 123–24, 127, 129

Domby, Adam H., 6, 118, 121, 130

Doss, Erika, 251

Douglass, Frederick, 233

*Down the Santa Fe Trail and into Mexico* (Magoffin), 92n23

Drake, William, 63

drama, 12, 167–73, 175–78, 180, 182, 252

*Dred Scott v. Sandford*, 206

Driver, Adam, 142

Du Bois, W. E. B., 199

Dubose, Mrs., 239

Dudley, David, 32

Duggan, Paul, 102–3

Dumas, Patrice, 142–43

Durham, NC, 214, 216

During, Simon, 238

Dwyer, Owen, 191–92

Earnest, Frank, 102–3, 107

East High Street (Charlottesville, VA), 215, 218

"Elegy for the Native Guards" (Trethewey), 174

elimination: of Confederate monuments, 107, 192; of white women in film, 11, 143, 146–48, 150, 153

Ellis Island (NY), 79, 86

El Paso, TX, 9, 72–75, 78–82, 84–85, 87, 89–91

El Paso del Rio del Norte, 75, 79

El Paso shooting, 72, 89–90
emancipation, 26–27, 123, 134, 152, 182. *See also* Black freedom
Emancipation Proclamation, 179–80
Enlightenment, 225
ephemerality: of Confederate monuments during removal, 197; of drama, 12, 167–68; as essential to counter-monumentality, 251–53; of print cultural materials, 9, 45, 47, 56, 64, 67, 217
Equal Justice Initiative, 239
Equestrian statue (El Paso, TX), 85
equivocation, 11, 121, 125–27, 129–30, 137, 201
*Escape: or, A Leap for Freedom, The* (Brown), 179
Española, NM, 85
Ewell, Mayella, 238
exclusion, 107, 120–21, 126, 253
extralegal violence: advanced by Lost Cause, 11, 123, 136; as backlash against Black freedom movement, 204; by Ku Klux Klan, 239; deployed to claim ownership of white women, 143–44, 154, 156; legitimized by state, 130, 138; subverting democracy, 127, 133

Facebook, 216–17
Fahs, Alice, 6
fascism, 103, 109, 214, 226, 256
*Father Comes Home from the Wars: Parts 1, 2, and 3* (Parks), 12, 167–68, 170, 176–78, 180–82
*Fathers, The* (Tate), 108
Faust, Drew Gilpin, 143
Federal Bureau of Investigation, 110
Ferguson, MO, 180
Field, Henry M., 32–33, 37
Field, Stephen, 32
Fifteenth Amendment, 25–26, 30
film, 7, 10–11, 123–24, 142–60, 173
Finch, Atticus (character), 238–40
Finch, Jean Louise "Scout" (character), 239–41
Finch, Jem (character), 239
1st Kansas Colored Infantry, 179
"First They Came for the Confederate Monuments . . ." (Chrysostomos), 106
Fish, Hamilton, 31

Fleming, Victor, 11
Florence, AL, 13, **190**
Florence City Council (AL), 209
Floyd, George, 202, 204, 230, 243, 255. *See also* George Floyd uprisings
Folt, Carol, 100
Foner, Eric, 6, 46
foolishness, 125, 127, 130–31
*Fool's Errand, A* (Tourgée), 11, 122–31, 133
Foote, Kenneth E., 89–90
Foreman, Edgar, 87
Forrest, Nathan Bedford, 197. *See also* Nathan Bedford Forrest Park (Memphis, TN)
Fort Bliss, TX, 81–82, 90
Fort Mill, SC, 52
*Fort Mill News* (SC), 58
Foster, Gaines M., 46
Foucault, Michel, 238
Fourteenth Amendment, 25, 30
Fourth Bluff Project, 197
Fox News, 103–5
"Fragile Statues of Whiteness," 103
futurity: Black freedom and, 169, 202, 205, 253; blank monuments and, 9, 74, 86–90, 94n52; Confederate monument debate and, 7–8, 105; counter-monuments and, 124, 178, 205–6; disturbance of vision and, 196–97; generational, 56, 106, 113, 236, 252; imagination and, 258; as intent of Confederate monuments, 10, 32, 54, 191–94, 241–42; of liberalism, 127; of teaching, 231, 244, 252; of United States, 178, 206, 258; white nationalist, 106–8; white supremacist, 192, 113; white women and, 60

Gable, Clark, 144, **157**
Gadsen, Christopher, 112
Gadsen flag, 112
*Galaxy*, 26
Gallagher, Gary W., 6–7, 21, 46
Garfield, James, 123
Garrett, Shawn-Marie, 177
Gathers, Don, 216
Gay, Roxane, 240
George Floyd uprisings, 3–5, 202, 204–5, 230, 255–57
Gettysburg Address (Lincoln), 43

Gettysburg monument (PA), 43
Gilman, Charlotte Perkins, 241
Gilmore, Garrett Bridger, 10, 252
Gish, Lillian, 143, **151**
Githens, Anna, 222
"Going to Meet the Man" (Baldwin), 241
Gone with the Wind (Fleming film), 11,
    142–44, 146, 153–56, 158–60, 173
Gone with the Wind (Mitchell novel), 221
"Gone with the Wind: A Complicated
    Legacy," 160
Gonzales, William E., 59
Gore, Frank, 109–13
Go Set a Watchman (Lee), 238, 240
Grant, Ulysses S., 21, 25, 27, 31, 34, 39n7
Grayson County, TX, 244
Grayson County Confederate monument
    (TX), 230–36, 238–39, 241–44
Grayson County Courthouse (TX), 233,
    235–39
"Greek Slave, The" (Powers), 27
Greeley, Horace, 27
Greener, Richard, 67. See also Richard
    Greener statue
Green Haven prison (NY), 181
Greensboro, NC, 122
Griffith, D. W., 11, 36, 124
Grist, Lewis M., 52
Guillory, Josh, 3–5
Gus (character), 147–50, **149**, 152

Hamburg, SC, 34
Hamilton (Miranda), 72
Hamilton, Melanie (character), 154–57
Hampton, Wade, 34–36. See also Wade
    Hampton statue (Charleston, SC)
Hannah-Jones, Nikole, 183, 258
Harnisch, Albert E., 28, 33–34, 37
Harper, Frances Ellen Watkins, 241
Harper's, 49
Harrier, Laura, 142
Harris, DeAndre, 194, 225
Harris, Joel Chandler, 28
Hart, Simeon, 74, 76, 78, 81–83, 86–87
Hartman, Saidiya, 166, 169
Hart's Mill (TX), 92n10
Hawthorne, Nathaniel, 231
healing, 8, 11, 22, 37–38, 90, 198

Health Sciences Park (Memphis, TN), 196
Henabery, Joseph, 147–48
Herald (Manning, SC), 47
heritage politics, 10, 101, 107–8, 111, 234
Hero (character), 176–80
Herrera, Spencer R., 9, **76**, 77, 235, 252
Heyer, Heather, 194, 213
Hicks, Kevin, 108
Highland, NY, 82
Highland County, VA, 193
Hill, Michael, 108–9
historical complexity, 37, 88–90, 120, 124, 202,
    251–52
historical erasure: Black, 12, 67, 169, 171–72,
    178, 183, 237; Confederate monument
    erection and, 5, 51, 253; Confederate
    monument removal and, 21–22, 100, 112,
    171, 192, 234; monumentality and, 72, 74;
    Oñate Crossing and, 85; in US literature,
    231
historical imagination, 36, 43, 56, 170, 177,
    179–80
historical mutability, 172, 177–78, 180
Hitler, Adolf, 22
Holden, William Woods, 139n36
Holloway, Kali, 215
Hollywood Writers' Congress, 159
Holocaust, 106
Homer (character), 176, 180
hooks, bell, 244
Hopi Indians, 85
Hopkins, Chandra O., 171, 173
Hopkins, Pauline, 241
Howard, Leslie, 154
Howell, Cameron, **66**
Hubbard, Thomas H., 43–44, 58
Hudspeth, Willie, 257
Huffington Post, 214, 222
Hughes, George, 237, 239, 243–44
Hurricane Camille, 174
Hurston, Zora Neale, 172
Hutner, Gordon, 7
Hyman, Nathan, 133–38

Iliad, 58
immigration, 9, 74, 79, 85, 88, 220
Imperceptible Mutabilities in the Third
    Kingdom (Parks), 177, 182

imperialism, 60–61, 235
inaction, 11, 121, 123, 128, 138
incarceration, 143, 166, 180–82, 258
inclusion, 120–22, 205, 224, 233
Indiana University, 222
injustice: Black, 33, 37–38, 183, 244; claims to white, 30, 110
institutions: advancing white supremacy, 11–12, 119–38, 240, 244, 252; archives as, 169; building and supporting Confederate monuments, 167–68, 214; challenged for structural racism, 167, 233, 243; educational, 173, 231–35, 243; failing at memorialization, 67, 89
"In the Sweet Bye and Bye," 235
*Invisible Empire, The* (Tourgée), 122
*Iola Leroy, or Shadows Uplifted* (Harper), 241
Islam, 222–23

Jackson, Andrew, 28, 30
Jackson, Cassandra, 13, 54, **190, 203**, 234, 252
Jackson, Stonewall, 43, 102, 202, 213. *See also* Stone Mountain Memorial Carving (GA); Stonewall Jackson statue (Charlottesville, VA)
Jacksonville, FL, 255
Jacobs, Harriet, 231
James, Henry, 26
Jamestown, VA, 225
Janney, Caroline E., 6
"Janney's Hall. For the Benefit of the Ladies' Memorial Association," **53**
Jean, Botham, 243
Jefferson, Thomas, 28, 213
Jefferson Davis memorial, 49
Jefferson Davis Park (Memphis, TN), 196
Jerusalem, Israel, 222
Jim Crow: as era of Confederate monument building, 6–8, 11, 101, 121, 123–24, 199, 216, 240; as era of formation of Lost Cause, 123–24, 153; justification for, 150; knowledge of, 121; labor, 54; laws, 86, 112, 238; legacies of, 242–44; segregation, 22; violence, 66; white victimization and, 153
John C. Calhoun statue (Charleston, SC), 8, 21, 23, 27–28, 32–33, 37
Johnson, Andrew, 24–25, 132

Johnson, Lyndon B., 87
Johnson, Mereda Davis, 202
Johnston, Joseph, 28
Johnston, Olin D., 36
Jones, Martha S., 196
Judaism, 222–23
Juneteenth, 182

Kantorowitz, Stephen, 35
Karcher, Carolyn L., 123
Kay, Gregory, 10, 101, 108–9, 111–13
Kearney, Stephen W., 80
Kelly Ingram Park (Birmingham, AL), 204
Kendrickson, Connie, 142–43
Kendrickson, Felix, 142
Kennedy, Frank, 154–57
Kennedy, John F., 28, 36
King, Martin Luther, Jr., 258
Krugman, Paul, 103
Ku Klux Klan: denunciations of, 26; as depicted in fiction, 109–10, 122, 124–25, 128–30, 137, 239; as depicted in film, 142, 147, 149–50, 152; federal reaction to, 32; members of, 196; state reaction to, 139n36; terrorism of, 213

labor: Black, 54; convict labor, 155, 181; free, 122, 124, 126, 137; indentured, 81; slavery and, 29, 34–35, 78; university, 121; white women's, 60
Ladies' Calhoun Monument Association, 28
*Ladies' Home Journal*, 49
Ladies' Memorial Association, 47, **48**, 51–52, **53**, 56, 59
Lafayette, LA, 3–5
Lamar, Howard R., 92n23
Lamar, Lucius Quintus Cincinnatus, 28–38
Lamar Company, 215
Landrieu, Mitch, 193
landscape: Black history as erased from, 170, 174; Confederate monuments as shaping, 47, 57, 171, 191–94, 243, 251; Confederate monuments' movement on, 64–65; Confederate monuments' visibility on, 6–7, 56, 166; contextualization failing to change, 200–201; counter-monuments reshaping, 172, 195–98, 202–6; memory and, 89, 202–3, 205–6

Lane, David, 105
Las Cruces, NM, 85
*Last Confederate Flag, The* (Lenard), 108
Lauderdale County courthouse (AL), 191, 206
League of the South, 108
Lee, A. C., 238, 240
Lee, Calinda, 199
Lee, Harper, 14, 238, 240
Lee, Robert E.: as Confederate officer, 23, 32–33, 36, 39n7, 43; in Confederate surrender, 24, 101; memorialized, 202, 214, 258. *See also* Denton, TX; Robert E. Lee statue (Charlottesville, VA); Stone Mountain Memorial Carving (GA)
Lee, Spike, 142
*Lee and His Lieutenants* (Pollard), 23
*Lee at Appomattox and Other Papers* (Adams), 32
Leigh, Vivien, 144, **157**
LeMahieu, Michael, 174
Lenard, Lloyd, 108
*Leopard's Spots, The* (Dixon), 123–24
Lewis, John, 202
liberalism, 61, 120, 125–27, 136–38
Lincoln, Abraham, 21, 29, 43, 147–48, 150
Linn Park (Birmingham, AL), **203**
"Literature and the Neo-Confederacy" (Hicks), 108
Little, Maya, 104
Loewen, James W., 192–93
Long, Corey, 225
Long, Walter, 147, **149**
*Los Angeles Times*, 160
loss: Black, 172; as component of the Lost Cause, 8, 33, 112, 146; Confederate land, 83; grieving, 51, 90, 150
*Lost Cause* (Louisville, KY), 49
Lost Cause: challenges to, 122–24; Confederate monuments as honoring, 21, 87; on contextual plaques, 199–201; definition of, 6–7, 235; differing versions of, 33–38; fiction, 108; films, 142–60, 252; historians, 109; history of, 7, 22–33, 39n15; as ideology, 43–49, 56–59; logic of, 121; national influence of, 63–67; as ongoing, 174, 221; sanitizing slavery, 102; storytelling, 10–11; white consensus

about, 8; white victimization and, 112; white violence and, 118–19, 129–30, 216
*Lost Cause: A New Southern History of the War of the Confederates, The* (Pollard), 23–25, 31
*Lost Cause Regained, The* (Pollard), 24
Lott, Eric, 54
Louisiana Native Guard, 167, 170, 174
Louisiana Purchase, 29
Louisville, KY, 255
Lowe, Lisa, 120
Lowell, James, 168
Lowell, Robert, 174
Lynch, Silas (character), 147–48, 150–52, **151**
lynching: of George Hughes, 236–39, 243; as inverted narrative in *Gone with the Wind*, 154–56, 159; in literature, 241, 243; monuments to victims, 202; postcards, 62–64; as narrative in *The Birth of a Nation*, 11, 143–46, 148, 150, 152

MacLeod, Nicola E., 195
MacTeer, Claudia, 241
Madison, James, 28
Magoffin, Dolores Valdés, 81
Magoffin, James W., 74, 76, 78, 80–83, 86–87
Magoffin, Joseph, 81
Magoffin, Susan Shelby, 92n23
Make It Right Project, 13, 215–21
manifest destiny, 78, 80, 82
Manso Indians, 84
*Marrow of Tradition, The*, 14, 195, 232, 237, 241, 244
Marsh, Mae, 143, **149**
Marshall, John, 28
Matamoros, Mexico, 80
Maycomb County (AL), 239
*McClure's*, 49
McCormick, Stacie, 11–12, 252
McCurry, Stephanie, 143
McKinley, William, 106
McPherson, Tara, 7, 143, 146, 158
"Memorial Day, May 10, 1875, at Memorial Cemetery, under the Auspices of the Ladies' Memorial Association, Charleston, S.C.," **48**
Memphis, TN, 13, 196–97
Memphis Park (TN), 196

methods, 5–6, 22–23, 101, 145–46, 215, 231–33
Mexican-American War, 8, 76, 78, 80, 82
Mexico City, Mexico, 79, 85, 91n8
Miles, Dudley H., 30
Miller, Dr., 242–43
Mills, Anson, 83
Mills, Charles, 125
Mills, Cynthia, 7, 54
Mills, W. W., 82–83
Milton, John, 25, 31, 38
Minneapolis, MN, 202
minstrelsy, 52, **53**, 54, 224
Miranda, Lin-Manuel, 72
miscegenation, 238
Mississippi River Park (Memphis, TN), 196
Mississippi state flag, 257
Mitchell, Margaret, 221
Mitchell, W. J. T., 65
Młodożeniec, Piotr, 221–22
Mobile, AL, 255
Monroe, James, 28
Montgomery, AL, 239
Monumental Bronze Company, 49, **50**
monumentality, 251–52, 255
monument(s): building new, 79; culture, 215, 251; dedication, 88; ethics of, 252; as honoring, 73, 79, 177; location, 87–89; memory and, 243; mutability of, 243, 253; syntax of, 255, 258. *See also* Confederate monument building; Confederate monument removal; Confederate monuments
"Monument" (Trethewey), 174–75
Monument Fund, 217, 223, 226
Moore, Robert, 225–26
*Moros y cristianos*, 93n32
Morrison, Toni, 65, 173, 231, 233, 241
Mother Emanuel church massacre, 5–6, 73, 167
Mouton, Alfred, 3. *See also* Alfred Mouton statue
Move the Mindset, 3
Museum of the Seam, 221

NAACP, 199
*Narrative of the Life of Frederick Douglass* (Douglass), 233

Nathan Bedford Forrest Park (Memphis, TN), 196
National Civil War Project, 170
National Collegiate Athletic Association, 93n45
nationalism, 30–31, 85
National Museum of African American History and Culture, 102
*Native Guard* (Trethewey), 11–12, 167–68, 170–76, 178, 180, 182
"Native Guard" (Trethewey), 173–74
nativism, 85, 91, 257
Nazis/Nazism, 22, 106
neo-Confederates: aesthetics, 57, 65; fiction, 101, 107–8, 113; ideology, 10, 14, 112, 143, 153; imaginary, 144; memory, 99; narratives, 252; people, 102–3, 120, 171–72, 223, 226
neo-Nazism, 223, 225–26, 256
New Deal, 35–36
New Historicism, 6, 10, 233
*New Jim Crow, The* (Alexander), 243
New Orleans, LA, 12–13, 80, 168, 193–94, 241
*News and Courier* (Charleston, SC), 47, 58–59
New York, NY, 180, 205
*New York Times*, 103, 237, 258
Niemöller, Martin, 106
Nixon, Richard, 256
Nolan, Alan T., 6
Norris, Samantha, 111
Northam, Pamela, 224
novel, 10–11, 101, 108–13, 122–38, 238–44
nullification, 29, 128
Nye, Carroll, 154

Oath Keepers, 256
Obama, Barack, 171
Ochiltree, Polly (character), 242
Odessa, TX, 181
Odyssey Dog (character), 180
O'Hara, Scarlett (character), 144, 154–59, **157**
Ohkay Owingeh Pueblo, 84
Old Man (character), 177
Oñate, Juan de, 74, 79–80, 83–86, 91
Oñate Crossing: as contemporary site, 83; in figures, **76**, **77**; historical erasure and, 85; as memorial site, 88–90, 93n45; as US

immigrant site, 75, 79, 86; as Simeon Hart
residence, 82
Oñate Crossing State Historical Sign at the
US–Mexico border, **76**
Orlando, FL, 72
Orlando nightclub shooting, 72
Osborne, James, 168
Osterweis, Rollin G., 46

Pääkkönen, Jasper, 142
paganism, 222
Page, Thomas Nelson, 124, 129
*Paradise Lost* (Milton), 31
*Paradise Regained* (Milton), 25
*Parasite* (Joon-ho), 159
pardoning, 81, 129–30, 139n36, 147, 150
Parks, Suzan-Lori, 12, 167–70, 173, 176–83
parody, 13, 218–24
past conditional temporality, 127
patriarchy, 161n5, 252
patriotism: Black soldiers', 178; Confederates',
43, 63–65, 235–36; John C. Calhoun's,
29–31, 36–38; Lost Cause, **55**, 56, 242–43;
white nationalists', 111–12
pedagogy, 6–8, 230–34, 240, 252. *See also*
critical pedagogy
Penny (character), 177, 179–80
performances of fugitivity, 180
permanence: counter-monuments
disrupting, 168, 204; monuments' appeal
to, 10, 65, 191–92, 200–201, 251–53; of
nation, 31
Phillip II (king), 83
*Phoenix* (Columbia, SC), 47, 52
Piedmont Park (Atlanta, GA), 198–99
Piedmont Peace monument (Atlanta, GA),
198–99
plantation culture, 28, 46
*Playing in the Dark: Whiteness and the
Literary Imagination* (Morrison), 231, 233
Plessy, Homer, 37
*Plessy v. Ferguson*, 32
Poe, Edgar Allan, 231
poetry, 10–12, 72, 167–72, 174, 218, 255
police: advancing white supremacy, 214, 225;
connection to slavery and Jim Crow,
243; expansion, 119–21; violence, 166–67,

180–82, 202–5, 256; in white nationalist
fiction, 109–11
Polk, James K., 80
Pollard, Edward A., 23–27, 31, 33, 37
Portal to Texas History, 237
postcards, 46, 61–64, **62**, **63**
Powers, Hiram, 27
Pratt, Mary Louise, 75
Prejean, Fred, 3
Preston, John S., 57
Price, Evander, 193
pride, civic, 64; in Black uprisings, 255; in
Confederate monuments, 193; regional,
45, 52, 101, 107
print culture, 8–9, 12, 43–67
*Profiles in Courage* (Kennedy), 28
Project Say Something, 209n40
property: Black people's relation to, 195,
198, 205–6, 253, 257–58; concern for
protecting, 109, 119; Confederate loss of,
81–82; destruction during uprisings, 256;
indigenous dispossession of, 258; white
women's relation to, 11, 143–59
*Protocols of the Elders of Zion*, 106
Proud Boys, 256
public space: challenges to Confederate
monuments in, 182, 191, 195–97, 216;
as civic space, 237–38; Confederate
monuments dominating, 8, 12–14, 21,
196, 200–201; Confederate monuments'
removal from, 175–76, 205–6;
Confederate monuments' teaching
children in, 230; harm of Confederate
monuments in, 223–24, 226; limited, 22;
neo-Confederate efforts to claim, 101;
reorientation in, 257–58; visibility of, 251
Public Theatre (New York, NY), 180
Pueblo Indians, 84–85
Pugh, Catherine, 194
Pulitzer Prize, 240
Purifoy, Danielle, 120

*Race and Reunion: The Civil War in
American Memory* (Blight), 22
racial capitalism, 252. *See also* labor;
property; redlining
racial contract, 133–34

Raleigh, NC, 255
Ramsay, Lenox, 181
Rayner, Alice, 178
reading: ambiguity, 217–18, 258; how to read monuments, 4–6, 251–53; monuments as texts, 8–9, 13, 236; texts as monuments, 10–14, 101, 137, 143–45, 238–44; why to read monuments, 14, 253
reception studies, 5–6, 8, 13–14, 23, 130, 232–33
reconciliation: Confederate memorialization and, 6–8, 22–38, 39n15, 198–200; Lost Cause and, 159; racial, 196; white supremacy and, 44, 130, 200
Reconstruction: as era of Black freedom, 86–87, 230; failure of, 121–38, 221, 241; fiction of, 7, 10–11, 252; monument building, 10–11, 57, 65; monument controversy, 43–47; representation in Lost Cause narratives, 148, 153–55; retreat from, 8, 22–38
redemption: of history, 31; of South, 11, 27–28, 143–52; of white women, 153–59
redlining, 194
Reed, Kasim, 198
Rehabilitation through the Arts, 181
repertoire, 169–70
Rhind, J. Massey, 34
Richard Greener statue, 66, 67
Richmond, VA, 205, 224, 255
Ridley, John, 160
Rio Bravo, 80. See also Rio Grande
Rio Grande, 75, 78–80, 84–85
Robert E. Lee statue (Charlottesville, VA): advertising for and against removal of, 13, 215, 217–19, 221, 223; erection of, 213; neo-Confederate support for, 103
Robert E. Lee statue (New Orleans, LA), 168
Robinson, Tom, 238–39
Rogin, Michael, 150
romance, 11, 111, 143–46, 152–53, 156, 158–59
"Romance of the Negro, The" (Pollard), 26
Romero, Levi, 89
Roof, Dylann, 167, 172
Roosevelt, Franklin D., 36
Rose, Richard, 199–200
Rotograph Company, 62

Route 250 bypass (Charlottesville, VA), 215, 218
Ruckstuhl, F. Wellington, 59–60
Rumors of War (Wiley monument), 205
"Rumors of War" (Wiley paintings), 13, 205
Runaways, The (characters), 180

Sagrado: A Photopoetics across the Chicano Homeland (Romero), 89
San Antonio, TX, 76, 78, 81
sanctification, 89–90
San Jacinto Day, 235
Santa Fe, NM, 79–80, 84
Savage, Kirk: Monument Wars, 5–6, 192; Standing Soldiers, Kneeling Slaves, 7, 54, 66, 243, 251
Savage, Tom, 137
Schedler, George, 87
Scott, Dred, 206
Scott, Harriet, 206
Scribner's, 49
"Sculptor Interprets the Memorial" (Ruckstuhl), 59
secession: neo-Confederates and, 103, 109, 113; of Texas, 80–83; of the South, 23–29, 35–36, 220
Seger, Maria, 11, 234, 252
segregation: as advanced by Lost Cause, 36, 201; at Confederate monument events, 52, 54; as consequence of reconciliation, 22; desegregation and, 225; enforced by Confederate monuments, 257; in Lafayette, LA, 4–5; as part of Jim Crow, 22, 86–87, 194; supporters of, 26, 32, 192
Selma, AL, 194
sentimentality, 107–9, 111, 113, 161n5
Servosse, Comfort (character), 122, 125–28, 130–37
Servosse, Metta (character), 133
settler colonialism, 8–9, 75, 252, 258
1776 Commission, 258
sexual violence, 11, 143–45, 150–54, 157–59, 238, 240
"Shall Cromwell Have a Statue?" (Adams), 32
"Shall White Minorities Rule?" (Tourgée), 127–28
Shank, Barry, 61
Sharpe, Christina, 175

Shaw, Stephen J., 195

Sheley, Erin, 153

Sherman, TX, 12, 230–31, 233–39, 241–43

Sherman, William, 28

Ship Island, MS, 170, 174

Showing Up for Racial Justice, 215

Sibley, Henry H., 81, 83

Silber, Nina, 6, 103

Siegmann, George, 147, **151**

Silent Sam statue, 10–11, **98**, 99–103, 108, 118–21

Simpson, Pamela H., 7

"Sins of the Fathers" (Duggan), 102

site-specific performance, 171, 175, 180

*1619 Project, The* (Hannah-Jones), 183, 258

16th Street Baptist Church (Birmingham, AL), 204

slavery: afterlives of, 166, 169, 174–75, 180–82, 243, 258; Black Civil War soldiers and, 177–79; as central to US founding, 75, 252, 256; as Confederate cause, 8, 201, 230; counter-histories of, 166–67; as endorsed by Confederate monument building, 44, 54, 78, 191, 216; erasure of, 191–92; history of, 121–28, 176, 181, 183; legacies of, 5, 9, 231, 238, 242–44; Lost Cause Unionism and, 21–31, 38; reckoning with histories of, 65–67, 126, 174; as sanitized by Lost Cause, 102, 134–36, 154, 160, 173, 236; support for in El Paso, TX, 80–81, 83; in US literature, 239

Smith (character), 176, 179

Smith, Ellison, 36

Snyder, Robert, 64

social justice: Confederate monuments' impact on, 6, 12, 73, 196, 255; as educational mission, 231–33, 238–41; healing and, 8, 11, 22–23, 33, 37–38; ideals of, 122, 125–27

Sons of Confederate Veterans, 5, 101–2

Sontag, Susan, 63

Sorkin, Aaron, 238

South Carolina Heritage Act, 67, 105

South Carolina state flag, 168

South Carolina State House, 46, 57, 64–65, 109

"Southern History" (Trethewey), 173

Southern Marble and Granite Company, 51–52

Southern Poverty Law Center: on contextualization plaques, 200; research on hate groups, 108; "Whose Heritage," 5, 86, 232, 234, 240

Southwest, 9, 72–91, 235

Spur 1966 (El Paso, TX), 77, 93n45

Stallworth, Ron, 142

"Stand Your Ground" laws, 166

Star of David, 222–23

*State, The* (Columbia, SC), 59

states' rights, 21, 24, 201, 220, 224, 235–36

Statue of Liberty (NY), 79

Staunton, VA, 214

Stephens, Alexander, 236

St. John's Episcopal Church (Washington, DC), 256

St. Louis, MO, 80, 82, 180

Stoneman, Elsie (character), 143, 147–48, 150–54, **151**, 156

Stone Mountain, GA, 175

Stone Mountain Memorial Carving (GA), 171, 202

Stonewall Jackson statue (Charlottesville, VA), 213, 215, 217–19, 221, 223

Story, Joseph, 28

Story, William Wetmore, 28

"Story of a Hero, The" (Pollard), 26

storytelling, 101, 176, 197

Stowe, Harriet Beecher, 231, 241

Strom Thurmond statue (Charleston, SC), 46, 65

Stuart, J. E. B. statue (Richmond, VA), 205

Sumner, Charles, 28, 256

Superior Court of DeKalb County (GA), 202

Sykes, Reverend (character), 239

Taft, William Howard, 44

Take 'Em Down 901, 197

Take 'Em Down NOLA, 168

Tanglen, Randi Lynn, 14, 252

Taoism, 222

Taos, NM, 79

Tara plantation, 154–55, 159

Tate, Allen, 108, 168

Taylor, Breonna, 243

Taylor, Diana, 169

teaching, 12–14, 182–83, 226, 230–44, 252

temporality: Confederate monuments and, 9–10, 192, 196–97, 200–201, 218, 236–37; counter-monuments and, 12–13, 169, 172, 204–5; reorientation of, 257; white supremacy and, 224, 241, 244. *See also* past conditional temporality
Tennessee General Assembly, 198
Tennessee River, 192
Texas Department of Transportation, 89, 93n45
Texas Historical Commission, 79
Texas Rangers, 237
Texas Revolution of 1836, 93n24
"Textbook Racism" (Yacovone), 233
*Third Revolution, The* (Kay), 10, 101, 108–9, 112
Thirteenth Amendment, 25, 30
Thomas, Brook, 7–8, 46, 129, 131, 234, 252
Thomas, James, 120
Thomas, Rhondda Robinson, 35
"Thomas Jefferson Is the R. Kelly of the American Enlightenment" (Woolfork), 242
Thomas Jefferson statue (Charlottesville, VA), 213
Three Percenters, 256
Thurmond, Strom, 36–37, 46. *See also* Strom Thurmond statue (Charleston, SC)
Tillman, Ben, 34–35; statue (Charleston, SC), 35
Times Square (New York, NY), 205
*To Kill a Mockingbird* (Lee), 14, 232, 237–40
*Topdog/Underdog* (Parks), 177
Tourgée, Albion, 11, 37, 118, 122–34, 136–38
tourism, 4, 45, 62
Trachtenberg, Alan, 178
Treaty of Guadalupe Hidalgo, 92n24
Trethewey, Natasha, 11–12, 167–68, 170–75, 178, 180, 182–83
Trouillot, Michel-Rolph, 169
Truman, Harry S., 36
Trumbo, Dalton, 159
Trump, Donald, 107, 159–60, 172, 239, 256, 258
Tubman, Harriet, 196
Tulsa, OK, 243
Tulsa race massacre, 243
Turner, Frederick Jackson, 28
Twain, Mark, 26

*12 Years a Slave*, 160
Twitter, 255–56

Ulysses (character), 176–77, 180. *See also* Hero (character)
Uncle Jerry (character), 131
*Uncle Tom's Cabin* (Stowe), 241
Union Army, 167, 176, 180
Unionism, 29, 31–33, 36, 38
United Confederate Veterans, 49, 99, 102, 235
United Daughters of the Confederacy: Arlington Confederate memorial and, 44; Dixie Chapter Number 35 (Sherman, TX), 235; as emblems of southern sentimentality, 107; as fundraisers for Confederate monuments, 118, 174, 201, 257; as influenced by print culture, 47, 49, 51–52, 56; Lafayette, LA chapter, 3–4; as neo-Confederates, 101, 104; role in white supremacy, 146, 236
Unite the Right rally: associating Confederate monuments with white nationalism, 5, 213, 223; causing further Confederate monument activism, 230; causing further Confederate monument removals, 203; disavowed by neo-Confederates, 102–3; Donald Trump's endorsement of, 239; hashtag activism and, 13; violence of, 194, 213, 215, 223, 225–26, 253
universities, 12, 120–21, 125, 231–33, 235
University of Missouri Confederate rock, 22
University of North Carolina at Chapel Hill: anti-racist activism and, 230; Nikole Hannah-Jones and, 183; Silent Sam statue and, 10, **98**, 99–100, 104, 118–21, 168, 216
University of North Carolina Board of Governors, 119
University of South Carolina: archives, 9; building renaming at, 69n41, 69n42; as integrated institution, 35; monuments at, 46, 67
University of Texas at Austin, 168
University of Texas at El Paso, 75, 78, 89, 93n45
University of Virginia, 13, 213, 225, 230
University of Virginia Citizens Justice Initiative, 213

"Unsure about Confederate Statues?
   Ask Yourself If You Support White
   Supremacy," 103
"[Unveiling of the Confederate Monument,
   June 2, 1913]," **98**
Upton, Dell, 7
US Bureau of Reclamation, 89
US Capitol, 255–57
US Capitol attack, 255–57
US Congress, 256
US Department of Homeland Security, 89,
   110
US exceptionalism, 153
US literary history, 6, 14, 168, 230–44
US National Guard, 256
US Supreme Court, 27–28, 32, 206
US v. Cruikshank, 32

Valdez de Beremende, Maria Gertrudes,
   92n23
Vance, Charles, 52
victimization: South's claims of, 221; white
   men's claims of, 11, 143, 150–53, 159; white
   nationalists' claims of, 106, 109; white
   supremacists' claims of, 129–30, 136;
   white women's claims of, 104, 143, 150–53
Victoria (queen), 61
Virginia General Assembly, 227n3
Virginia state police, 225
Virginia Supreme Court, 227n3
Voting Rights Act of 1965, 112

Wade Hampton statue (Charleston, SC), 35,
   62
Wagner, Bryan, 195
wake work, 175
Wallace, George, 192
Walters, John, 131
Walthall, Henry B., 147
War of 1812, 29
Warren, Calvin, 169
Washington, Booker T., 199
Washington, DC, 255
Washington, George, 28
Washington, John David, 142
Washington Post, 103–4
Washington Post magazine, 102
Watchmen, 181

Waugh, Joan, 6
Webster, Daniel, 28–30
Weisenburg, Michael C., 9, 252
Wellington, NC, 242
"What to the Slave Is the Fourth of July?"
   (Douglass), 233
White, Samuel, 52
white children: fundraising for Confederate
   monuments, **55**, 56; participating in
   dedication of Confederate monuments,
   62, 118, 213, 235; taught by Confederate
   monuments, 6, 54, 230; white nationalists'
   securing the future for, 105–6, 113
White Citizens' Council, 238
white flight, 13, 192, 194
white fragility, 103, 143, 146
White House, 147, 256, 258
white nationalism: appropriating classicism,
   58; increasing influence of, 14, 213, 244;
   media espousing, 10, 101–2, 104–9, 112–13;
   symbols of, 257; in Unite the Right rally,
   226; violence of, 256. See also alt-right
white supremacy: addressed by Confederate
   monument resistance, 199, 201; anti-
   Black violence of, 87, 194, 242–43, 253, 258;
   anticipating counternarratives, 129; as
   backlash against civil rights, 87, 90; Black
   intimidation and, 230, 257; Confederate
   monuments as embodying, 78, 86,
   118–20, 159, 168, 203; Confederate support
   as advancing, 81; cultural supremacy
   and, 238, 241; culture of, 213, 242–43;
   discussed on Fox News, 105; extralegal
   violence of, 123, 130, 149–50; futurity of,
   193; history of, 202, 225; as ideology, 125,
   200, 219, 234, 241, 257; imagery of, 221;
   imaginary of, 147; insurrection of, 255–57;
   landscape and, 205; law and, 158, 205;
   literary themes of, 233, 240; logic of, 134,
   137–38, 252; naturalizing, 226; persistence
   of, 142, 145, 214–15, 224; politics and,
   237; resistance to Reconstruction, 128,
   133, 148, 152; as revised after the Civil
   War, 45, 64–65, 126; secession and, 220;
   shaping literary canon, 123; shaping
   space, 195; structural, 121–23, 131–32, 182,
   225, 252–53; subtext of, 232, 239–40, 244;
   taught to children through Confederate

monuments, 230; terrorism and, 213, 216–17, 223, 230, 244; white women's role in, 143, 236

"White Supremacy Is Still Welcomed in Charlottesville" (Woolfork), 214

white women: in Lost Cause literature, 146; perceived innocence of, 142, 146, 148; as property, 145, 147, 153–56, 159; requiring protection, 143–46, 149, 151–52, 157, 236, 242–43; role in Confederate ideology, 11, 54, 59–60, 142–43, 235; warned to be passive, 150, 152, 158

Whitman, Walt, 26

"Whole Point of Confederate Monuments Is to Celebrate White Supremacy, The" (Cox), 103

"Whose Heritage? Public Symbols of the Confederacy" (Southern Poverty Law Center), 234

"Why Those Coexist Bumper Stickers Bug Me" (DeCeasare), 222

"Why We Did Our Billboard Parody" (Carr), 220

Wicca, 222

Wichita Indians, 258

Wiegman, Robyn, 129

*Wikimedia Commons*, **149, 151, 157**

Wiley, Kehinde, 13, 205–6

Wilkes, Ashley, 154–59

Williams, Caroline Randall, 230, 242

Williams, Ellen, 108

Williams, Rhaisa, 172

Willis, Deborah, 178

Wilmington, NC, 241

Wilmington race riot, 241, 243

Wilson, Charles Reagan, 46

Wilson, Woodrow, 31, 147

Wilson Dam (AL), 192

Winberry, John J., 57, 87–88

Wise Man (character), 128

Wolters, Wendy, 64

"Women's Monument, Columbia, S.C." (Teich), **63**

Wood, Amy Louise, 147

Woodruff Arts Center, 171

Woodward, C. Vann, 46

Woolfork, Lisa, 13, 214, 242, 252

"Worshipping the Confederacy Is about White Supremacy—Even the Nazis Thought So" (Silber), 103

WVIR NBC29, 216

*X-Files, The*, 214

Yacovone, Donald, 231, 233

"Yellow Wallpaper, The" (Gilman), 241

*Yorkville Enquirer* (SC), 47, 52

*Yorkville Enterprise* (SC), 52

Young, Kevin, 168, 174

"You Want a Confederate Monument? My Body Is a Confederate Monument" (Williams), 230, 242

Zaldívar, Juan, 84

Zaldívar, Vicente, 84

Zeebo (character), 239

Zimmerman, Flip, 142

Zuni Pueblo, 84

CPSIA information can be obtained
at www.ICGtesting.com
Printed in the USA
BVHW071944230722
642812BV00005B/9